Where to Watch Birds in

EAST ANGLIA

Including
Norfolk, Suffolk, Essex and Cambridgeshire
SECOND EDITION
Peter and Margaret Clarke

Foreword by Lord Peter Melchett

Christopher Helm

A & C Black · London

© 1987 Peter and Margaret Clarke
Reprinted 1987, 1988
Second Edition © 1991

Photographs by Peter Clarke
Line drawings by Alan Wood
Maps by David Henderson

Christopher Helm (Publishers) Ltd,
a subsidiary of A & C Black (Publishers) Ltd,
35 Bedford Row, London WC1R 4JH

ISBN 0–7136–8097–0

A CIP catalogue record for this book
is available from the British Library

This book is dedicated to the memory of R.A.R.

Printed and bound in Great Britain by
Biddles Ltd, Guildford and King's Lynn

CONTENTS

FOREWORD

This is a book that will appeal to the many expert bird watchers already familiar with East Anglia and its birds, as well as the ever increasing number of newcomers to the region and its spectacular wildlife. For the experts, the detailed calendars, with lists of species to be found at different locations at different times of the year, will provide convenient and detailed information, along, no doubt, with plenty to argue about! For the newcomer to either East Anglia or bird watching, the detailed descriptions of where and when to go to the best places to see birds will be invaluable.

For the experts, I hope this book will encourage them to visit places which they haven't been to before, or which only get irregular watching. There seems little doubt that we still have a great deal to learn about the birds of East Anglia, particularly away from the most famous reserves.

For newcomers to bird watching, I have no doubt that Peter's and Margaret's infectious enthusiasm will encourage them to see more for themselves.

This book makes clear that East Anglia still possesses wildlife habitats of great richness, where a huge profusion of wild birds can be seen at many different times of the year. However, two other messages, one optimistic and one profoundly depressing, come ringing through its pages. The optimistic note is that many areas, now rich in birds, have become so in recent years because conservation organisations have bought land and managed it with sensitivity and expertise, greatly increasing the number and variety of birds and other wildlife the areas support.

The profoundly depressing message is that so much of East Anglia is now a barren desert as far as bird watchers are concerned. Peter and Margaret note areas lost to birds, and mourn our lost hedgerows, woodlands, ponds and other features. These once made the whole of the countryside a place which birds and people could share, rather than the pesticide-laden food factory producing surpluses for the EEC to dispose of, that so much of it has become.

This terrible destruction has taken place because of Government policy, through Government incentives, prices and grants. There is nothing natural about this process. Just as it was done by our Government in our names, we can insist that the policies which caused the destruction should be changed, so that this terrible process is not only stopped, but we start to make good the damage.

So while you enjoy East Anglia's birds, take this book's advice and join at least one conservation organisation. Do all you can to insist that a future book on where to watch birds in East Anglia will have to be at least ten times as long, because we will have started to restore the countryside to the balance of interests, local residents and workers, visitors and wildlife, to which it rightly belongs.

Lord Peter Melchett

ACKNOWLEDGEMENTS

We would like to record our thanks and appreciation to all the following people who have helped so readily in many ways: P. Allard, Miss V. Beckett, T. Bennett, R. Berry, Mr and Mrs G. Buxton, Mrs A. Cryer, R. Darrah, V. Eve, M. Fiszer (and the Paston Group), H. Ginn, P. M. Griggs, R. Hobbs, J. Howard, R. Harold, R. Jones, R. Kelly, C. Kirtland, P. Lawson, Lord Peter Melchett, J. Minneyhane, N. Mood, J. Morley, J. O'Sullivan, A. R. J. Paine, J. Pemberton, A.Rivett, R. Scott, Miss A. Starling, Mr and Mrs Seaton, M. Stott, J. Sorensen, G. Smith, C. Hanson Smith, Miss M. Warland, G. White and P. White. We would also like to record our thanks to all staff at Christopher Helm Ltd for their professional guidance and expertise throughout the 'birth' of this book.

In particular we would like to mention our personal appreciation of the help given by: Derek Moore of the Suffolk Trust for Nature Conservation who gave such a 'flying' start to Peter Clarke's 100 mile (160 km) walk through Suffolk and Essex; to Mr D. Baksa of Opticron Limited for supplying the superb 10×40 Alpin binoculars which certainly did not add much to the weight of the rucksack; to Martin Coates (and his family) for a marvellous whistle-stop tour of the Peterborough area (the A1 'racetrack' never forgotten!); to Peter Gotham and Lesley for their generous hospitality at Old Hall Marshes (such a superb vegetarian dinner never before, nor since); to Mr and Mrs Colin Todd, and their friend Richard of the Southend Ornithological Group, who so freely made a perfect stranger welcome in their home and helped tremendously with a tour of that most interesting area; to Alan Wood for supplying the wealth of drawings which grace the pages of this book; to Mr and Mrs M. Cox of Holme for helping Peter Clarke renew acquaintance with east Norfolk and the Swallowtail butterfly; to Malcolm (Chalkey) White and Eileen for many very pleasant hours spent in the field exploring reserves that were little known to us; to Miss P. A. Clarke for undertaking the initial drafts for the maps in this book; to Cliff Waller for a delightful morning at Walberswick; to Miss Vivien M. Leather, M.B.E. and Peter Etheridge for their terrific hospitality and help in the Minsmere area; and last but not least to Arthur and Pauline Allerton of Lowestoft for their prompt offer of hospitality and very great help in that area.

We would also like to thank the following people who have helped with the revision of the County Lists to the end of 1989: Peter Allard of the Norfolk and Norwich Naturalists' Society; John Clarke and Martin Coates for Birds of Huntingdonshire and Peterborough; Colin Kirtland of the Cambridge Bird Club; John Miller of the Essex Birdwatching Society, and Steve Piotrowski of the Suffolk Ornithologists' Group.

INTRODUCTION

In writing this book we have included a much wider area than is usually regarded as 'East Anglia' – which term we use in its broadest sense. Geographically, the four counties of Norfolk, Suffolk, Essex and Cambridgeshire comprise a fairly neat manageable region, although we have drawn the line at including in East Anglia some of the undoubtedly good birdwatching sites to be found in the Greater London area of Essex.

Our task has been made much easier by virtue of the enormous amount of literature which has already been published, and is still being published, on these four counties. There must be few other areas in Britain so well documented. The reason, of course, is that East Anglia has long been famous for the richness of its birdlife and for its largely unspoiled habitats and also because it is served by such a wealth of dedicated conservation bodies. In post-war years, where else in Britain could one see Bearded Tits except on the Norfolk Broads; or where else Avocets except at Havergate off the Suffolk coast; while the Ouse Washes in Cambridgeshire offer breeding Black-tailed Godwits; and in Essex a wealth of wildfowl along the remote Dengie Marshes or Nightingales in leafy lanes.

In the last 40 years traumatic changes have taken place in the English countryside. On the debit side, such changes make for grim reading. In East Anglia, the brunt of fast advancing developments in farming, the holiday trade and other commercial ventures has largely been borne by Essex, Cambridgeshire and Suffolk; while Norfolk has seen great changes in agriculture and forestry. In Essex many of the old 'unimproved' grasslands, have been drained and ploughed for grain crops; and, we are told, that 90 per cent of the county is now either 'bricks and mortar' or under cultivation. Cambridgeshire has seen the destruction of its hedgerows to make way for vast prairie-like fields. In Suffolk the situation is little better with severe reductions of the uncultivated gorse and heather covered sandy tracts known as the Sandlings; ever-more prairie-like fields; and the increasing demands of the holiday trade. Norfolk, although perhaps less affected, has lost miles of hedgerows and great areas of The Brecks have been planted with dense conifer forests; and the Norfolk Broads are gravely under threat from pollution and pressures related to farming and the multi-million pound holiday industry.

As a result of these 'developments' with their various insidious spin-offs (especially pesticides), many birds have disappeared from their haunts, while other species, such as owls and hawks, have become very scarce. Red-backed Shrikes, Nightingales, Nightjars, and Stone Curlews have all decreased (though they can still be found in many of their safeguarded habitats). On the previously little-used beaches increasing pressures have banished the Little Terns and Ringed Plovers except where stretches have been set aside by conservation bodies.

On the credit side, the delightful Bearded Tit can now be found in all four counties and it has colonised all the main reed-beds of Suffolk and Essex where these precious habitats have been saved by conservation bodies. It has also spread along the north Norfolk coast and even into land-locked Cambridgeshire. Another colonist has been the Marsh Harrier; and perhaps both these treasured marshland birds have over-flowed from prime habitats in the Netherlands. The Avocet too, has extended its East Anglian range considerably, nesting wherever its unique habitat of brackish pools is found on coastal marshes.

Ospreys are now regular passage migrants to the region; and this obviously reflects the successful protection afforded on their northern breeding grounds. The Essex coastline, now largely protected, attracts vast numbers of waders and wildfowl as does that part of the coast of Norfolk along the Wash. These intertidal mudflats and saltings help provide winter sanctuary for a significantly high proportion of European populations, thus making them of international importance.

The debt that we all owe to the East Anglian conservation bodies cannot be measured in monetary terms, but the authors do hope and urge that everyone who lives in East Anglia, or visits it from time to time, will endeavour to support one or more of them. Many superb habitats have been saved in the 'nick of time' by these dedicated charitable organisations but sadly many others were lost. Conservation is still trailing far behind commercial developments, which threaten to trans-form established sanctuaries into isolated oases wherein wildlife is expected to be contained much in the manner of the fabled and foolish villagers who sought to keep the Cuckoo (and so the summer) with them all the year round by building an encircling fence round the bird! It is hoped, too, that readers will not neglect considering the worthy efforts of the World Wide Fund for Nature, the Friends of the Earth and Green-peace; all organisations concerned in trying to make the world a better and safer place for both humans and animals.

We have, therefore, drawn extensively on the literature available and information so freely given to us. Norfolk, of course, is our 'home' county and we have watched wildlife here since the early 1940s. However, we could not, and would not, dare to claim that we know every nook and cranny of the county; and there are many areas which we have never visited. Both of us have periodically visited the beautiful Suffolk coastline while a 'refresher' tour (by Peter Clarke) on foot in the summer of 1985 has hopefully brought our information up to date and filled several gaps in our knowledge. Essex we knew not at all (if one discounts childhood visits to Southend and Epping Forest), but again a walking tour revealed unexpectedly good birdwatching habitats. The Ouse Washes of Cambridgeshire had long been known to us, but research decreed that we should explore those areas more intimately. Several of the prestigious reserves of Cambridgeshire have in fact become completely isolated in a vast praire-like farmland, but one artefact (Grafham Water) has become a very valuable bird sanctuary and one hopes that this will long continue. Also, it was a pleasant surprise to see the development of a Country Park (Ferry Meadows near Peter-borough) in which wildlife conservation receives high priority.

Unfailingly in our research efforts, we were met with courtesy at every approach, with many friends offering useful advice and guidance. We do not claim that we personally know thoroughly all the East Anglian birdwatching sites. Such knowledge would require the experience of several lifetimes. Rather, we have used our reasonably wide experience of Norfolk, and rather less knowledge of the other counties, to combine this with research into the county bird books and reports. That there are omissions and mistakes we have no doubt, but we hope that these are minimal. We would be pleased to receive any additional information (or corrections) which might be incorporated in future editions.

Much of the factual information in this book is available to anyone who cares to join all the various county organisations, but we venture to suggest that this is the first time for many years that such a wealth of information has been compiled into one volume and we sincerely hope that bird watchers will find it a ready source of reference and pleasure.

Peter and Margaret Clarke
Holme-next-Sea

USING THIS BOOK

In defining geographical areas and sub-dividing them for explanation there will inevitably be some overlapping and some inconsistency. Birds too, of course, acknowledge no man-made definitions or boundaries so we have tried in this book to reconcile these variations whilst making them as clear as is possible for the birdwatcher setting out to visit East Anglia for the first time.

Firstly, we have divided East Anglia into Norfolk, Suffolk, Essex and Cambridgeshire. Each area is supported with maps and then divided again into those areas of information that most people will want to know initially – habitat, species, timing, access, calendar.

Secondly (and as it is not easy for any naturalist to attempt an artificial division of a habitat which may cover several different reserves each of which may be important for their own particular species) we have tried to describe a large similar habitat under one heading, but with sub-divisions as regards what is to be found in the various reserves therein. These sub-divisions are not uniform throughout the book, because in several cases it simplifies the presentation of the habitats and species in a more natural manner.

In the *Habitat* section we have in some cases outlined their history and threats, because it is very easy to forget that a habitat is always under change whether it is from natural or man-triggered causes; marshy meadows dry out, grassy fields may become scrub-covered, while woodlands will deteriorate without proper management.

The *Species* section is more straightforward, but we have included many references to semi-rarities and rarities. There may not be much chance that readers will come across these rarer vagrants; but they must, from time to time, cross *someone's* path – and that surely is one of the added thrills of birdwatching, in that you never know when you may come across some exotic species from a distant land. The commonest species are not mentioned, except where large numbers may be seen on migration or in large flocks in winter quarters, on the grounds that you can watch most of these in your own garden anyway.

Timing, apart from the season, is not really critical, but we have indicated the best tides and times of day where these are important.

The *Access* details have largely been taken from up-to-date nature and wildlife reserves' literature, but it is always as well to obtain further details from the organisation concerned in advance of any planned trip. Many of the reserves are well signposted and there are usually detailed maps of the reserve paths and hides available at their centres so we have felt it unnecessary to include this information, but instead have pin-pointed a route to the reserve or birdwatching spot from the nearest major road or town.

The *Calendar* section indicates the best months for seeing the birds mentioned in each birdwatching zone, but any attempt to fit the vagaries of bird movements into a man-made calendar cannot be wholly successful.

NORFOLK

THE WASH COAST
THE NORTH COAST
SHERINGHAM AND CROMER
THE EAST COAST
THE BROADS AND BREYDON WATER
THE INTERIOR

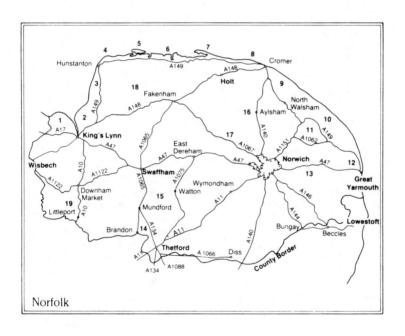

Norfolk

Key to Symbols		
Major roads	Deciduous woodland	
Minor roads	Coniferous woodland	
Rivers	Marshland	
Track	Parking	P
Railway Track	Picnic site	⊗
Embankment	Lighthouse	
Lakes	Sea	

Habitat

The Wash coast from the Norfolk border at Terrington Marsh to the small seaside town of Hunstanton includes some of the most desolate and inaccessible coastline in the county. A major river, the Great Ouse, flows into the Wash via the port and town of King's Lynn. The coast either side of the mouth of the Ouse has largely been reclaimed from the sea for agricultural purposes, but there is now a moratorium on further development of this nature. High seawalls intersect the arable fields, but to the seaward side a short saltmarsh gives way to a limitless expanse of oozing mud which is crossed by innumerable salt water drains. The countryside west of King's Lynn and the immediate coastal area are unsinspiring being mainly flat agricultural land, well drained via the Great Ouse. North of King's Lynn vast prairie-like fields offer scant shelter from the elements and there are few public trackways.

This hostile area though, adjoins the vast mudflats of the Wash which are one of the most important winter wader habitats in Britain. At Snettisham, north-east of King's Lynn, the Royal Society for the Protection of Birds (RSPB) have leased some 3,000 acres (1,600 ha) of tidal mudflats from the Crown Commissioners; and, to the south of the beach road, they have taken over a series of old gravel workings adjacent to the coastline. Northwards from these gravel pits a development of caravans and holiday chalets is off-putting, but the area is of great interest to the birdwatcher.

The botanist too, will enjoy this region where clumps of yellow-horned poppies, white sea campion, cushions of pink sea-thrift and carpets of yellow bird's-foot trefoil brightly clothe the shingle ridges and rough grassy fields. Clumps of sea holly and sea kale can also be found here. North of the Snettisham beach road agriculture is still dominant, but smaller fields, meadows and woodlands on the private Ken Hill Estate enhance the scenery thanks to good conservation over many years. Over 130 acres (52 ha) of Ken Hill Estate have been leased to the local authority as a Coastal Park, comprising rough grassland, drains, sedge and reed clumps adjacent to the shore. Colonies of common blue butterflies exist here and the day-flying six-spot burnet moth can be seen. There are two marked guided walks and an observation hide.

Further northwards towards Heacham and Hunstanton there is another hotch-potch collection of caravans and chalets with a promenade running between the two places. Here, the shore becomes more sandy or shingly with countless groynes to lessen the ravages of the winter gales. The seas of the Wash are very shallow with extremely low tides exposing miles of mud or sand. Hunstanton itself boasts of a short range of cliffs which stand like a bastion on the corner of the Wash coast, which curves gently here to form the beginning of the west-east running north coast of Norfolk. Because of their unique structure these cliffs have been designated a site of special scientific interest (SSSI). Their brown carrstone (quarried locally and much used in buildings) base is topped with a thin layer of red fossiliferous limestone and white chalk above. Offshore, the ebbing tide exposes large mussel scalps, while below the cliffs there are a few rock strewn pools which are quite rare on the Norfolk coast.

Away from the coast, inland between King's Lynn and Hunstanton the countryside changes dramatically. Well-wooded estates on a green sand scarp provide for most visitors an unexpected sharp contrast to the flat farmlands and marshes. From its source about 7 miles (11 km) inland the River Babingly winds tortuously to the coast; to the north Sandringham Warren and Wolferton Wood are intersected by quiet minor roads. The whole of the Sandringham Estate is a beautiful area of mixed deciduous and conifer woodlands, heathlands, bracken-covered slopes and great shrubberies of rhododendrons which are ablaze with colour from late May. As a seat of the Royal Family, and for obvious reasons of security, much of the area is private and well-keepered, but it is accessible to the general public during the summer months, when a Country Park with picnic sites and a forest walk are open. Red squirrels used to be seen quite frequently in all the wooded areas of the region, but they have largely been replaced by the grey squirrel which has also colonised agricultural land.

Between Snettisham village and the coast the well-wooded rising grounds of the private Ken Hill Estate provide another haven for many summer birds in an area so dominated by open farming lands. There is much of interest to be seen from the minor roadways and public footpaths and the area is good for botanists and entomologists. A unique valley left by glacial melt waters can be explored at Ringstead Downs just inland from the seaside town of Hunstanton. The steep grassy sides of this dry valley in the middle chalk are a delight for botanists. Typical chalkland flowers – squinancywort, rock rose, ploughman's spikenard, wild strawberry, mignonette, stemless thistle, thyme and many other plants – can be found here. Entomologists too, will find the area rewarding with common blue, small heath and several other species of butterflies. Sadly, an ancient colony of chalk-hill blue butterflies has become extinct. Scrub from the adjoining woodlands has greatly encroached on the grassy slopes, but the 26 acres (10.5 ha) of chalk grassland remaining is still the largest example of its kind in the county. Ringstead Downs are managed by the Norfolk Naturalists' Trust, but are part of the larger and private L'Estrange Estate which comprises well-wooded and keepered parkland.

TERRINGTON MARSH TO SNETTISHAM
Maps 1 and 2
Species

Inhospitable as the Wash coast can be, especially during the winter months, it is one of Britain's major wintering habitats for a variety of waders. Peak counts have estimated 74,000 Knot, 52,000 Dunlin, 18,000 Oyster-catcher, 8,300 Bar-tailed Godwit, between 6,000 and 7,000 Curlew and Redshank, 3,000 Grey Plover, nearly 1,500 Sanderling, 900 Turnstone and 500 Ringed Plover while some 14,000 Shelduck over-winter here. Limited access roads or pathways to the coast traverse vast arable regions which at times can be singularly birdless. Low tide reveals miles of mudflats which are inaccessible and dangerous, even with local knowledge. The shores on either side of King's Lynn do not

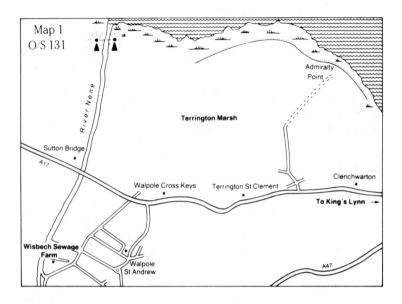

Map 1
O/S 131

River Nene

Admiralty Point

Terrington Marsh

Sutton Bridge
A17

Walpole Cross Keys   Terrington St Clement

Clenchwarton

To King's Lynn →

Wisbech Sewage Farm

Walpole St Andrew

A47

seem to be favoured with any seabird passage although birdwatchers have probably neglected these shores in favour of better known and more easily accessible points along the north coast.

The Terrington marsh region, west of King's Lynn, will sometimes reward the watcher with a passage of skuas, Kittiwakes and wildfowl in autumn. Large roosts of waders may be seen on fields adjacent to the coast when flood tides drive the birds off the mudflats. These autumn roosts are often composed of Knot, Redshank, Dunlin, Ringed Plover, Bar-tailed Godwit, Grey Plover, Oyster-catcher, Turnstone and Curlew. Pink-footed Geese and wild swans can sometimes be seen on the arable fields which passing Marsh Harriers hunt over during the summer months. In winter, roving Hen Harriers, Short-eared Owls and Merlins frequent the area. After autumn gales or in hard winter weather seabirds can quite often be seen in the River Ouse in King's Lynn itself and past years have yielded Bewick's and Whooper Swans, Glaucous Gulls, Smew, Red-necked Grebes, Gannets, Kittiwakes, Cormorants, Shags, Red-breasted Mergansers and Little Gulls. Black Terns have been seen on spring and autumn passage; Black Redstarts have been heard singing on old buildings in the town and may have nested or attempted to nest.

However, because of the easier access and footpaths, the majority of birdwatchers head for the coastline around Snettisham northwards to Hunstanton. Amongst the very few strictly resident species, Kestrels can be seen hovering over the open fields on most days throughout the year. Skylarks are present all year with local numbers augmented in late autumn by thousands of their brethren from the Continent. Herons frequent the many dykes or winter flood meadows and there are a couple of small heronries in the region. A few pairs of Stock Doves can also be found. Both partridges frequent the region, but the Red-legged is far commoner than the ever-decreasing Grey. A few pairs of Tawny Owls inhabit the landward fringe of the marshes, while the Barn Owl is now a very scarce resident everywhere. Little Owls have never recovered from the pollution, originating in farm chemicals, which decimated them in the 1950s. However, for this species there have been signs of a comeback in several areas recently. Although the Short-eared Owls can be seen in any month of the year, only the odd pair have been known to stay and breed. Numbers fluctuate greatly from year to year with, no doubt, the strength of the local vole population being a controlling factor. Usually more of these beautiful owls can be found during the winter months and without doubt migrant birds arrive from the Continent to find an easy living; they quarter the open fields or glide along the steep seawalls hoping to surprise a rodent or small bird feasting on the fallen seeds from summer plants.

Even though wholly resident species are so few, there is a great variety of winter visitors, summer breeding birds and spring and autumn passage migrants using the area. Birdwatchers should not be put off by the holiday development areas which are at their busiest for only a short while in July and August. For most months of the year the caravans and

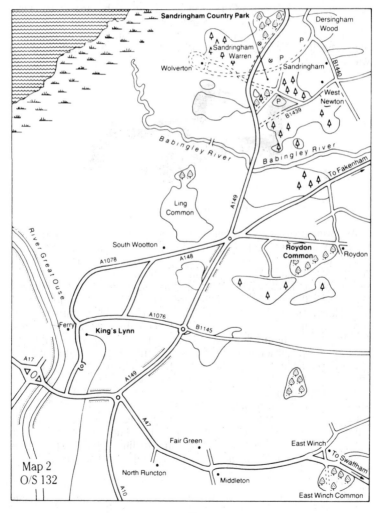

chalets are deserted. In late winter Pink-footed Geese resort increasingly to the water-logged meadows where the new growth of grass will sustain them until they leave for the north in March. The best places to see them are the beautiful grazing meadows behind the Snettisham Coastal Park. With the backdrop of small arable fields and wooded estates this is a scene typical of a Peter Scott painting. Curlews too, frequent these fields prior to their departure and flocks can total 200 to 300 birds. Bewick's Swans occasionally drop in when they leave their winter haven on the Ouse Washes en-route for the Netherlands on the first stage of their long flight to Arctic Siberia.

At this time Meadow Pipits begin to make their return, to take up territories along the seawalls or on rough grasslands. Lapwings indulge in courtship displays and many pairs make their shallow nesting scrapes on the grass or arable fields. Flocks of Shelduck which frequent the winter mudflats now begin to form pairs dotted about the fields. Many pairs nest in the region and some will do so up to several miles inland, although the Shelduck is primarily confined to the sea coast. Pairs nesting on the warrens of the Sandringham Estate escort their newly hatched ducklings on a long march to the coast, through woodlands, across heather slopes and a busy main road to reach the shallow coastal waters.

A·R·W·

Pair of Shelduck with young

As spring progresses a variety of summer birds pass through the area. Garganey are often seen; and occasionally a pair nest in the area. The grassy meadows – especially where there are cattle grazing – attract numbers of migrant Yellow Wagtails and frequently the beautiful Blue-headed Wagtail. A few White Wagtails, too, usually frequent the pastures, but as with all migrant species they are 'here today and gone tomorrow!' The Marsh Harrier, the largest and most buzzard-like harrier of all, arrives at this time and can often be seen throughout the summer hunting across the fields on typically raised wings in gliding flight. The wintering Hen Harrier, too, often passes through as late as April. It is not usually seen again until October. Even though fully protected all the year round these large raptors are not welcomed on well-keepered estates.

The Ring Ouzel is a regular passage migrant to Norfolk and in the spring months of April and May it can often be met with either on the rough grass adjacent to the coast or from the high seawalls. With a light wind from the south or east in April and May almost anything can turn up. Hoopoes have been noted from time to time while Dotterel have frequented the grassy shingle ridges for several days. Passing Montagu's Harriers are sometimes seen, but this is another nationally declining species.

Hobbys make increasing appearances, but they are more usual in late summer or early autumn. Then, flocks of young martins and swallows provide prey for this swift-flying falcon but it rarely nests in Norfolk, although it is a regular passage migrant.

Reed-beds or areas of sedge are strictly limited in this region, but where they do occur Reed and Sedge Warblers breed. Occasionally the reeling song of a Grasshopper Warbler can be heard and Bearded Tits have been noted in summer. Strange as it may seem both Whinchats and Stonechats are extremely rare breeding birds in Norfolk, but they are regular enough as passage migrants to this and many other coastal areas. Odd Stonechats may be seen in very early spring up to May; but the first Whinchats do not pass through until late April. The first Wheat-ears arrive mid- to late-March and generally a pair or two stay to nest. Wheaters continue passing until early May when the larger Greenland race makes its appearance.

Offshore, the main arrival of Common and Little Terns takes place from late April and both these species plus Sandwich Terns (who can come as early as late March) can be seen fishing the shallow waters of the Wash during the summer months. The disused gravel pits to the south of Snettisham Beach have been purchased and wardened by the RSPB. Great improvements have now been made to the pits with many new shingle islands and strategically placed observation hides. Common Terns breed here, as do Oyster-catchers and Ringed Plovers. A few spring waders such as Common Sandpipers, Ruff, Black-tailed Godwits, Spotted Redshanks and Greenshanks or Avocets may drop in.

After the peak of the breeding season in June, wader passage increases steadily throughout the summer and autumn. This is when the gravel pits and adjoining coastline offer the perennial 'wader spectacular'. Arctic breeding waders from the European and Asian continents frequent the vast mudflats of the Wash in their tens of thousands. Most can hardly be seen even with the aid of a telescope when the tide is at its lowest ebb. Occasionally a flock of waders may break the far horizon and a few Bar-tailed Godwits or Oyster-catchers may be seen near the shore. As the tide begins to flow, however, the scene changes with more and more waders being obliged to move ever nearer to the shingle-ridged beach. Grey packs of Knot flock in cheek by jowl with browner backed Red-shanks and pied Oyster-catchers, Sanderlings, Turnstones, Bar-tailed Godwits, Dunlins and Ringed Plovers occur in their hundreds. During the higher spring tides every last patch of mud is covered by the sea and many waders seek a roosting place on the shingle ridges and on the islands in the pits. Thousands more flight on to the adjoining arable fields and along the coastline northwards past Hunstanton to roost on higher ground in the vicinity of Scolt Head Island. Other waders to be seen on or around the gravel pits include Green, Common and Wood Sandpipers, Little Stints, Curlew Sandpipers, Greenshanks, Spotted Redshanks, Ruff and Purple Sandpipers. All through the winter months vast numbers of Knot and Oyster-catchers frequent the mudflats together with hundreds of Grey Plovers, Bar-tailed Godwits, Dunlins, Sanderlings and Redshanks, but with the short winter days the highest tides frequently occur in darkness, which makes watching impossible. In any season the high tides which occur in the middle of the day are neap tides which means that the sea does not come in or go out very far, and waders can then remain undisturbed on the flats, quite far distant.

From late October, Pink-footed Geese return to seek out and forage on old root crop fields which have not yet been ploughed. Large flocks frequent some of the vast arable fields between Snettisham and the Wootton Marshes, but as food supplies diminish they will range several miles inland from the coast in search of suitable fields. Usually though, they return to the coastal mudflats for the night. The gravel pits and other small brackish pools near the shore are always worth a visit during the winter months especially after a gale at sea, when wildfowl may seek sanctuary on calmer waters. Any of the three species of divers may turn up, but the Red-throated is much the most frequent visitor. All five species of grebe have been seen at various times, but the Black-necked is much the rarest. The pits are noted for Goldeneye which can usually be seen in courtship display in early spring. Red-breasted Mergansers, too, frequent these coastal pools and in hard weather conditions, the odd Smew may be seen. Tufted Duck are usually present all year and groups of non-breeding Eider Duck have been noted in nearly every month either on the pools or on the sea. Other diving duck using the pools during winter are Pochard, Scaup, Long-tailed and Wigeon.

Winter passerines include small flocks of Snow Bunting which might be found anywhere along the shingle ridges where they can find a rich harvest of seeds from yellow-horned poppies, sea campion and other saltmarsh plants. Shorelarks are seldom seen along these shores. Neither is the Lapland Bunting although it may well be overlooked on the arable fields. Roving small bands of Linnet, Reed Bunting and Yellow Bunting may be encountered. The vast coastal area to the south of Snettisham is also the winter stronghold of Twite.

Autumn sea passage does occur off Snettisham with on-shore winds, often of gale-force, driving skuas, Gannets and Kittiwakes close inshore. But sea watching enthusiasts will find better places at Hunstanton and elsewhere in north Norfolk. Autumn passerine movements can also be observed with parties of hirundines steadily following the coastline southwards. In late October many of the large diurnal thrush movements along the north Norfolk coast turn south at Hunstanton to continue following the coast past Snettisham to eventually spread out across the Fens and the Midland Shires. In general though, there are very few 'falls' of passerines, as occur on the north coast. Perhaps the lack of coastal cover is one reason. Some species which are usually regarded as purely winter visitors may spend all or part of the summer on the Wash mudflats and these may include parties of non-breeding Sanderling and Knot; quite recently, large skeins of Brent Geese have been noted as late as May or June. Shelduck, too, seem to be favouring the shallow waters of the Wash as a place to carry out their post-nesting moult in late summer and autumn. Many hundreds though, still flight eastwards in July to their more traditional moulting waters off the Heligoland Bight. Although the Wash coast is an open, bleak region with temperatures even in summer a few degrees below other nearby areas, it is well worth visiting in practically any month of the year.

SNETTISHAM TO HUNSTANTON CLIFFS

Map 3

Moving northwards from the Snettisham Coastal Park, the coastline becomes much more commercialised between Heacham and Hunstanton but, even so, outside the peak holiday season the area is usually productive. Black Redstarts on migration can often be found amongst the beach huts in March and April and at least one bird has wintered there. Another favourite area for this species is immediately north of Hunstanton – again amongst the seaside beach huts along the edge of the golf-course. The innumerable weed-covered groynes between Heacham and Hunstanton regularly attract up to two dozen wintering Purple Sandpipers; they can also be found on the rocky shore or mussel scalps below the Hunstanton cliffs. Adjacent to the shoreline a few grazing meadows and small lagoons often attract nice birds, such as

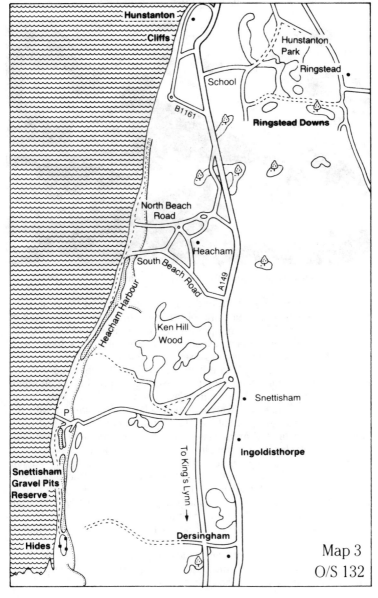

Map 3
O/S 132

Pink-feet in early spring or a Garganey in late March or April. Short-eared Owls also hunt this area and Yellow Wagtails frequent the water meadows on migration. Offshore there are often quite large flocks of wintering sea duck. Rafts of several hundred Common Scoter are frequent with Velvet Scoter often up to 100 strong. A Surf Scoter stayed for over two months one spring. Eider, too, can be seen in most months, but peak is usually in February and March with rafts of several hundred birds; though they do not nest on the Norfolk coast, the adult birds have summered which may indicate future colonisation. In hard weather large numbers of Scaup may also appear close inshore.

Purple Sandpiper. Winter visitor to the coastal regions

The sea between Heacham and Hunstanton is one of the best areas for watching winter sea duck and observing autumn seabird passage in rough seas. The cliffs are unique on the mainly low-lying Wash coast and, from their tops, many excellent sea watching days have been recorded over the years. Like most sea watching though, there is always a large element of luck. A 'good' sea can be empty while, conversely, calm waters might produce something exciting. A morning watch might be very productive, but later in the day observers may see little. Some years ago a fortunate birdwatcher on holiday at Hunstanton with his family discovered an adult Sabine's Gull on the shore one August Bank Holiday! This delightful Arctic visitor stayed in the area until November; but, initially, birders had to 'mix it' with hordes of holiday-makers!

Another never failing source of pleasure is the colony of Fulmar Petrels on the cliffs. Although a couple of hundred birds may be present in early spring, probably no more than 30 to 40 pairs nest or attempt to nest, with two or three dozen young being raised annually. The adult Fulmars desert their fully grown youngsters on the nesting ledges in August to spend a few months at sea before returning to the cliffs in December.

Strong to gale force north-west winds in autumn seem to be the 'best' for rough weather watching from the cliffs or promenade. Several public shelters offer some protection from the elements; one October, a lucky observer shared one with a Yellow-browed Warbler which flew in to seek insects against the glass windows! A typical movement on an October day with a north-west wind would include large flocks of Kittiwakes swirling along the breakers every so often; and small parties of Gannets gliding against the wind. Arctic Skuas, too, would be fairly frequent with, perhaps, one or two engaging late Sandwich Terns to rob them of their last meal. Great Skuas too, would be passing – hugging the wave tops – their bulky bodies and white wing flashes distinctive even at long range. Pomarine Skuas are often seen on such days as this, but it takes practice to distinguish the immature birds who lack the

A. R. Wood.

Great skua

distinctive 'twisted' tails of the adults. The Long-tailed Skua is much rarer, but it has been noted from the cliff tops on a number of occasions; but usually a little earlier in the autumn.

In an October 'blow' numbers of divers of three species may be seen with the Red-throated being the most frequent. Fulmars, too, in their hundreds; and the first Wigeon moving along the coast. Great-crested Grebes may be flying against the wind if only to regain their favourite feeding spots, while a Slavonian or Red-necked Grebe will sometimes appear close inshore. The Black-necked Grebe is also quite often observed from these cliffs, but more usually much later on in winter. If the winds have been blowing strongly for several hours some species of shearwaters could be identified, although the Norfolk coast does not usually enjoy such numbers as does the south-west of England. Still, the Manx Shearwater is usually seen in rough seas, while both Sooty and Cory's Shearwaters are regularly noted in very small numbers between August and December. Petrels are even rarer, but both Leach's Petrel and Storm Petrels have occurred at times.

Other winter wildfowl which appear in these October storms are the first returning Brent Geese and a few Bewick's Swans. Increasing numbers of Teal, Mallard, Pintail, Shelduck, Scoter and Eider will amost certainly be passing by, while the first Red-breasted Mergansers and Goldeneye are usually noted. Long-tailed Duck and Velvet Scoter may be seen, and there could be a few Cormorants or Shags passing. A variety of auks may also speed past making identification a problem if they are at long range – Razorbills and Guillemots are extremely rare off the Norfolk coast, but with severe gales from the northern North Sea areas scores of Little Auks may sometimes become 'wrecked' along the coast. The larger Black-backed Gulls lie in wait for any such unfortunates and quickly seize and swallow whole any in a weakened condition. Many gulls can also become storm driven with Glaucous Gulls being seen not infrequently from the cliffs. The much rarer Iceland Gull is also noted from time to time. Little Gulls often appear in late autumn 'blows', but also often in clam sea conditions when other sea birds are not moving. The most prized gull of all though is the Sabine's and several have been recorded during onshore gales. Plenty of the commoner gulls may be passing, but the rarish Mediterranean Gull does not often appear in rough weather movements, though it has been seen in almost all months of the year and in all weather conditions.

Mixed up with this ceaseless pageantry of seabirds passing over the tumultuous seas will be flocks of waders seeking a sheltered sand bank from the strong wind. These may include Knot, Grey Plover, Bar-tailed Godwit, Dunlin, Sanderling, Turnstone, Ringed Plover and Redshank. If Lapwings migrating from the Continent have been caught up in the gales, they too will be doggedly beating westwards, barely lifting their wings above the breaking surf.

Hunstanton cliffs are, therefore, well worth a visit in every month of the year. The least productive month is June, but even then, there should be hundreds of fishing terns passing; while in July, the first Arctic Skuas arrive to harry them.

With the turn of the year numbers of offshore wildfowl generally increase and off the cliffs is a regular spot for Long-tailed Duck which can number anything from a dozen to over 100 birds. Some of them may stay through March and into April when the drakes may be seen displaying. Many species spend the winter on the shallow seas and can be seen from the cliffs whatever the wind or weather. Calm seas, though, make for easier identification! Between December and March there are usually a few divers close inshore, with single numbers of Red-throated and Black-throated Divers. One or two Great Northern Divers are also often present.

Single numbers of Slavonian and Red-necked Grebes will often spend some days fishing off the cliffs. The Black-necked Grebe is much the rarest of the family and only irregular single birds are seen in February as a rule. Great-crested Grebes are the commonest with gatherings of 40 to 50 birds in hard weather in January. The Red-breasted Merganser is the commonest of the sawbills with peaks of 50 birds in some years.

A·R·W·

Long-tailed Ducks (winter plumage)

The Goosander is much rarer with only single numbers at the turn of the year. Smew are rarer still and most likely to occur in very hard weather. As always, the splendid white Smew drakes (known as the 'White Nun' by the old Norfolk wildfowlers) are outnumbered by the drab females (redheads). Another 'hard weather' duck is the Scaup – irregular in its appearances, but sometimes totalling over 100 birds. The most frequent wintering fowl is the Common Scoter and often there are rafts of one or two thousand birds. Velvet Scoter are more irregular, but usually up to a score of birds are present and exceptionally 'peak counts' of 100 birds. Eider, too, are fairly common winter residents with usually between 30 and 70 birds present from December to March and sometimes through the summer months as well. Peak counts of nearly 500 birds have been made. Some Goldeneye can always be found from late winter to early spring with usually between 20 and 50 birds present. (Nearly 200 have been recorded in some years.) Amongst the thousands of shore scavenging gulls, one or two Glaucous Gulls are usually noted in the opening months of the year. Both the 'weak tea coloured' immatures and the ghostly white adults have been seen. If not disturbed there are usually 100 or so Brent Geese to be seen feeding on the weed-covered boulders below the cliffs. Rarities seen from the cliffs include a few sightings of Peregrine Falcons with slightly increasing records from the Norfolk coast in recent years suggesting that this species is making a comeback. Before being decimated by poisoned prey in the 1950s, it used to be a regular winter visitor to the coast. Strangely enough, the Grey Phalarope has only been noted on a few occasions from the sea pools below the cliffs.

SANDRINGHAM TO KEN HILL AND RINGSTEAD

Map 3

The striking changes in habitat once the coastal marshes are left behind offer an equal contrast in the numbers and variety of bird species, with few of the marshland and sea coast birds being seen. Winter flocks of Pink-footed Geese are nomadic seeking out the old root crop fields in a vast area to the west and north-west of Sandringham. Many nesting pairs of Shelduck frequent the more open slopes, while the odd pair of Oyster-catchers often choose to nest on stony arable fields several miles from the coast. Flocks of 100 to 200 Golden Plover may also be met with frequenting winter cornfields anywhere in the area.

Resident Woodland tits include the Great, Blue, Coal and Marsh in good numbers. The Willow Tit is frequently found; and it has a preference for damp habitats not essentially in woodlands. Parties of Long-tailed Tits roam the woodlands in winter and several pairs nest on the bushy or gorse covered slopes.

All three woodpeckers can also be found, but the Green commonly frequents open arable country and sand dunes, especially in winter. The Lesser Spotted Woodpecker is the rarest of the three, but it does occur both in the wooded areas and in quite small copses and large gardens here and there. Nuthatches and Treecreepers can be found throughout the year in nearly every woodland. In the Sandringham picnic area some woodland birds have become extremely tame especially during the winter months. Suitable offerings will quickly attract the usual complement of tits, frequently Nuthatches and occasionally a Great

Spotted Woodpecker; or even the normally shy Jay if the donor remains concealed.

Goldcrests can usually be found either in company with mixed bands of tits and finches in the winter months or in scattered breeding pairs in or near larch trees. Crossbills undoubtedly breed in this area, as birds have been noted in every month of the year. Resident numbers may be augmented by irruptions from the Continent, while the rare Two-barred Crossbill has been noted. The best place to see Crossbills is in the immediate area of the main Sandringham car park; and if there are any roadside puddles, this is a good spot to keep watch. Crossbills also occur at Ringstead Downs and in Ken Hill Woods. In spring many pairs of Redpolls return to the area and are likely to be seen wherever there are suitable young plantations. The status of the Hawfinch is always difficult to determine, due to its shy and retiring habits; but a family party has been noted at Ringstead Downs. Birds of prey are not very frequent in these large rigorously-keepered estates, but in winter Hen Harriers may occasionally be seen over arable fields, while in summer Marsh Harriers may occur. The occasional Sparrow Hawk is seen and the odd pair of nesting Long-eared Owls have been recorded. Several pairs of Woodcock inhabit the old deciduous or mixed woodlands and their unique roding can be watched on early spring evenings.

Crossbills

From mid-April several species of summer passerines filter into the greening woodlands. The Willow Warbler is the commonest of these, frequenting the woodland edge, rides or clearings. Chiff-chaffs and Blackcaps are frequent, while Garden Warblers can be found wherever there is suitable undergrowth and scrub. Lesser Whitethroats are found in the more open habitats of taller hedgerows or bramble thickets. Both the Redstart and Wood Warbler are rare breeding birds in Norfolk, but the odd pair of each may be discovered in these woodland areas. Very small numbers of Nightingales can still be located, but this species is, perhaps, still in a range withdrawal. The best place for Nightingales is Snettisham Common, but the new by-pass may hasten its end. Spotted Flycatchers are fairly generally distributed in the area preferring the outskirts of woodlands or large gardens. Pairs of Tree Pipits can be found where woodland adjoins open common or heathland, but habitats tend to change character frequently after tree felling and re-afforestation. Mature pine woods are cleared; and when re-planted, become suitable habitats for Tree Pipits, Yellow Buntings, Willow Warblers and occasionally Nightjars. The latter species still occurs, but both the bird and its habitat are extremely vulnerable, so birders should exercise the greatest care and restraint when in likely habitats by keeping strictly to minor roads or pathways. This is another species which is declining, not only in Norfolk but generally in Britain, so those haunts which are known come under increasing pressures.

Although migrants can turn up in any of the woodland areas, anything out of the ordinary is usually from chance encounter. Passing Common Buzzards are occasionally seen over the Ken Hill Estate; and a Red Kite once frequented the Sandringham area. Great Grey Shrikes have occurred on open bushy commons, but they are not regular. In the Ringstead Downs area some of the less common migrants have been noted from time to time with Ring Ouzels being fairly regular and (not infrequently) Wrynecks are seen. Bramblings sometimes frequent the Downs in late autumn when hordes of Redwings, Blackbirds, Song Thrushes and Fieldfares invade the area for the wild fruits. After a 'fall' of coastal migrants a few Redstarts and Pied Flycatchers may make their appearance in the sheltered valley. The whole region is very popular with holiday-makers and day trippers. There are upwards of half a million visitors annually to the Sandringham Country Park alone. Therefore, it is wise to avoid Bank Holiday times, and when members of the Royal Family are in residence at Sandringham House. In particular, telescopes should not be used too blatantly in this area. They might even induce a security check! The Country Park is officially closed during the winter months, but there are many quiet minor roads in the area which are always worth exploring in all seasons.

Timing

The best time to vist the Wash coast is about two hours before high water and two to three days before and after the new and full moons when tides are usually at their highest and lowest. During the neap tides between the moons, the tide does not come in or go out very far with the result that a neap tide may leave a vast area of mudflats continually uncovered with birds always far distant. Another factor is that the full and new moon tides usually occur quite early in the day so that during a short winter day a high tide can occur under cover of darkness in the morning – say at 6.00 a.m. and again in the evening at about 6.40 p.m. Wader watching apart, though, any time of day is suitable for exploring the coastal region.

Wildfowling does occur in the area, but it is useful to remember that there is no shooting on Sundays in Norfolk. After gales at sea, the Snettisham coastal pools may be rewarding. North or easterly winds in autumn may bring drift migrants to the coastal areas. In spring, visible passage movements of finches and hirundines usually take place in light south-westerlies while a southerly airflow can bring 'overshooting' migrants from southern Europe. The Wash coast at Terrington Marsh faces mainly northwards; but from King's Lynn to Hunstanton it becomes a west-facing coastline. Therefore mudflat watching is difficult in the afternoon and evening, but on the other hand, there is a good light for watching the inland fields, pools and marshes from the shoreline.

The same tide rules apply to Heacham and Hunstanton especially when seeking Purple Sandpipers which are often pushed on to the groynes or even the promenade by a high tide. From Hunstanton cliffs though, sea watching can be good at any state of the tide, but a telescope is essential. A high tide may usefully bring sea duck closer in to the shelter of the cliffs especially if there is a strong east wind blowing. Here again, identification is made more difficult with a westerly setting sun; and morning, therefore, is usually the best time. Gales or strong winds between north-west and east are best for watching autumn sea passage. Hard weather in the New Year is best for numbers and variety of seafowl. Time of day – apart from setting sun – does not matter although there is less distrubance on the beaches in early morning. The peak holiday season months of July and August are perhaps best avoided (but remember our earlier story of the Sabine's Gull!). Low tide is good for large numbers of gulls, Bar-tailed Godwits, Redshanks, Grey Plovers, Sanderlings, Oyster-catchers and Turnstones in winter.

For the wooded areas of Sandringham, Ken Hill and Ringstead Downs almost any time of the year or day is propitious, but again, holiday pressures are greatest in July and August. A spring woodland chorus is always best at dawn, while dusk is best for the Woodcock, Nightjar and Long-eared Owls. After the end of the breeding season most woodlands seem very quiet and deserted, especially if the weather is hot. Equally, a cold wet day, at the peak of the spring season, can stifle the most ardent songsters.

Access

The whole area can be explored from King's Lynn which is served by the A17, A47, A10 and A148. For Terrington Marsh, west of King's Lynn, leave the A17 east of Terrington St Clements and follow a minor road to Ongar Hill. Proceed left on foot to Admiralty Point; or right, to explore the mouth of the Ouse as far up river as West Lynn.

The west facing coast of the Wash between King's Lynn and Hunstanton is served by the A149. The two towns are about 15 miles (24 km) apart and many of the minor roads off the A149 are well worth exploring. There is very little public access to the vast North Wootton marshes, but a public footpath which is not easily found, does run along the east bank of the River Ouse from King's Lynn.

Sandringham Country Park is well sign-posted from the A149 and is open during the summer months. For access to the RSPB reserve at Snettisham Gravel pits, turn left off the A149 as signposted, if approaching from King's Lynn. En-route to the pits it is worth stopping about ¼ mile (0.4 km) along the beach road where an adjoining common is favoured by Nightingales. A footpath skirts the edge of the common and Ken Hill Wood and goes across fields to join the coastal footpath.

After exploring the common proceed along the road to the beach and car park on the right at Snettisham Coastal Park. From here cross the road and proceed on foot southwards past a caravan site and many chalets to the gravel pits reserve where there are four excellent observation hides. This reserve is open at all times throughout the year.

From the Snettisham Coastal Park car park, a footpath can be followed northwards through the Park area to Heacham and Hunstanton. The coast can also be reached from the large sprawling village of Heacham by following the north or south beach roads. The most favoured stretch for observing wintering duck and Purple Sandpipers is that between the north beach road and Hunstanton. Alternatively, there are several well sign-posted sea-front car parks at Hunstanton where the promenade can be followed southwards to Heacham. The Hunstanton cliffs, which lie to the north of the town, are edged by a long green and gardens which can be reached easily from any car park in the town.

For Ringstead Downs leave the A149 at Heacham and follow a minor road towards Ringstead turning left down a rather concealed track entrance just before reaching the village. Alternatively, coming from King's Lynn on the A149 look out for a 'modern' glass high school on the right just on the outskirts of Hunstanton. Turn right along a minor road beside the school; then turn right at the bottom where the road becomes an unmade track. Hunstanton Park is open to visitors on Thursdays only, throughout the year and its entrance gates are just past Old Hunstanton Church off the A149.

Calendar

Resident Grey Heron, Canada Goose, Egyptian Goose, Sparrow Hawk (a very scarce resident, but also passage migrant), Kestrel, Red-legged Partridge, Grey Partridge (declining), Woodcock, Stock Dove, Barn Owl (scarce), Tawny Owl, Long-eared Owl, Little Owl (both latter two species scarce), Green, Great and Lesser Spotted Woodpeckers, Goldcrest, Long-tailed Tit, Marsh Tit, Willow Tit, Coal Tit, Nuthatch, Treecreeper, Crossbill (plus irruption birds) and Hawfinch (very scarce).

December–February Red-throated Diver, Black-throated Diver, Great Northern Diver (in small numbers), Great-crested Grebe, Red-necked Grebe, Slavonian Grebe (usually present in small numbers), Fulmar Petrel (return to the cliffs in December with many pairs prospecting in February), Bewick's Swan, Whooper Swan (these two wild swans are usually just passing, but occasionally staying in area), Pink-footed Goose (flighting variable), White-fronted Goose (much rarer), Brent Goose, Shelduck, Wigeon, Teal, Pochard, Tufted Duck, Scaup, Eider, Long-tailed Duck (more usually off Hunstanton cliffs), Common Scoter, Velvet Scoter, Goldeneye, Smew (scarce hard-weather fowl), Red-breasted Merganser, Goosander (scarce), Hen Harrier, Merlin, Peregrine (scarce, but increasing), Oyster-catcher, Knot, Sanderling, Purple Sandpiper (Heacham to Hunstanton), Dunlin, Snipe, Bar-tailed Godwit, Curlew, Redshank, Turnstone, Mediterranean Gull (occasionally), Little Gull, Sabine's Gull, Iceland Gull (latter two species rare), Glaucous Gull (more regular), Kittiwakes (in gales), Guillemot, Razorbill (auks in small numbers), Puffin (very scarce), Short-eared Owl (annual, but numbers irregular), Rock Pipit, Twite and Snow Bunting.

March–May Some of the divers, grebes, auks and duck often linger into March or early April when some assume breeding plumage. Fulmar Petrel, Pink-footed Goose, Brent Goose (latter two species also in March), Shelduck, Garganey (scarce on coastal pools), Shoveler, Tufted Duck, Eider (non-breeding, but has summered), Marsh Harrier, Hen Harrier (up to March – early April), Montagu's Harrier (very scarce, but passage migrants in summer months), Oyster-catcher (breeds), Avocet (scarce, but regular on passage), Ringed Plover, Grey Plover, Lapwing, Knot (some birds summer), Sanderling (also summers), Snipe, Black-tailed Godwit (passage), Dotterel (rare passage migrant), Whimbrel (on passage), Sandwich Tern, Common Tern (breeds), Little Tern, Nightjar (some breed on heaths), Hoopoe, Wryneck (latter two species scarce passage migrants), Tree Pipit, Yellow Wagtail, Nightingale, Black Redstart (passage), Redstart, Whinchat, Stonechat, Wheatear, Ring Ouzel (passage), Grasshopper Warbler, Sedge Warbler, Reed Warbler, Lesser Whitethroat, Garden Warbler, Blackcap, Wood Warbler, Spotted Flycatcher and Redpoll.

June–July Fulmar Petrel, Eider, Common Scoter (sometimes summering), Marsh Harrier, Oyster-catcher, Ringed Plover, Knot, Sanderling, Arctic Skua (first in July), Sandwich Tern, Common Tern, Little Tern, Nightjar and Wheatear. Many of the smaller passerines will, of course, still be present in the woodland areas, but this is not the best time to see them.

August–November Divers, grebes, auks and sea duck possible in gales from September. Also Manx Shearwater, Sooty Shearwater, Cory's Shearwater (latter two species quite rare), Storm Petrel, Leach's Petrel (latter two species quite rare in September–November), Gannet, Bewick's Swan, Whooper Swan (latter two species from late October), Pink-footed Goose (from late October), Brent Goose (from mid-October), Shelduck, Wigeon, Teal, Eider, Common Scoter, Velvet Scoter, Long-tailed Duck, Goldeneye (latter two species from October), Red-breasted Merganser, Marsh Harrier (up to September), Hen Harrier (from September), Merlin (from October), Peregrine, Oyster-catcher, Ringed Plover, Grey Plover, Knot, Sanderling, Purple Sandpiper (not often before October), Dunlin, Black-tailed Godwit, Bar-tailed Godwit, Whimbrel (not after October), Curlew, Redshank, Greenshank, Green, Wood and Common Sandpipers, Turnstone, Pomarine Skua, Arctic Skua, Long-tailed Skua (from August but very scarce), Great Skua, Little Gull, Sabine's Gull (scarce), Kittiwake (in gales), Sandwich Tern (in October), Common/Arctic Terns (to October), Short-eared Owl (from October), Black Redstart, Redstart, Pied Flycatcher, Whinchat, Wheatear, Ring Ouzel (latter five species mainly in 'falls'), Twite and Snow Bunting (latter two species from October).

HOLME TO KELLING

Habitat

The north coast for nearly 25 miles (40 km) from Holme-next-Sea to Kelling is of great scenic beauty comprising sandy beaches, mudflats, shingle-ridges, marram grass dunes, winding saltwater creeks, sheltering pine-afforested dunes and fresh grazing marshes. This coast has been included in an Area of Outstanding Natural Beauty (AONB) and is now designated a Heritage Coast. Apart from a few minor gaps, this whole coastline is further protected by a chain of nature reserves which includes, at Holkham, the largest national nature reserve (NNR) in England.

This wild and still largely unspoilt coastline has long been the haunt of naturalists, artists, poets, wildfowlers and fishermen. The diverse scenery and ease of access now makes it a very popular holiday coast receiving over half a million visitors annually. The coastline is largely the result of natural physical changes which have taken place over the centuries. The action of the sea and the wind have created dunes from the shifting sand flats which are stabilised in their early stages by marram grass. Once established the sand dunes in turn help create the formation of salt-marshes on their landward side. These slow processes are still evolving and several small, once busy, ports such as Cley and Blakeney are now silted up and cannot be navigated except by the lightest craft. At Holme-next-Sea remains of old seawalls can be seen nearly a mile away from the present shoreline while saltwater drains can easily be traced on what are now reclaimed fresh grazing marshes. Between Holme and Brancaster the remains of an ancient forest can be seen at several places along the shore – evidence that in a past era the coastline extended much farther seawards.

From Holme to Stiffkey the inter-tidal zone is composed of extensive sandy beaches, mudflats, saltwater creeks, and saltmarshes which are periodically flooded on the highest tides. On the lowest tides the shallow seas recede for considerable distances, but on the flood tides can come in at an alarming rate to cover the sands. From Blakeney Point eastwards the shingly beaches shelve away steeply so that the deeper water close inshore often provides good views of seabirds.

Several caravan sites exist, with some more obtrusive than others. There are strict controls on any future developments of this nature and, on the whole, development by man has, up to now, added to the attractions of this coastline. This is nowhere more obvious than at Holkham where reclamation of the saltmarshes was carried out from the seventeenth to the nineteenth century. To stabilise the outer dunes and afford protection to the newly reclaimed farmlands, Corsican pine trees were planted by the Coke family from about 1850. This whole area is now a mecca for birders throughout the year. Thousands of migrant birds find food and shelter amongst the 3 miles (4.8 km) of afforested sand dunes and the Speckled Wood butterfly can be found here as well as the Brown Argus.

The grazing meadows and arable fields to the landward side of

Holkham attract many wintering geese and other wildfowl. Holkham Park – the seat of the Coke family – is to the south of the A149. Encircled by its high brick wall it is one of the finest estates in Norfolk with a large lake and well timbered grounds which are well worth a visit in any season. A large herd of Fallow Deer are kept in the Park as well as a large flock of Canada Geese.

Periodically, the sea seeks to reclaim its own with devastating surges breaking through the fragile dune system to flood acres of farmland. An early attempt was made by the Holkham Estate to enclose the vast area of Lodge Marsh to the east of Wells, but the scheme proved to be a losing battle with the sea and it was abandoned. Lodge Marsh and The Binks sands remain an unspoilt area of vast mudflats, sands and saltmarshes under the watchful protection of the Nature Conservancy Council as part of the Holkham National Nature Reserve.

In the most recent surge of 1953 the sea broke through the defences at several places on the north Norfolk coast. Reclaimed agricultural land adjacent to the coast at Titchwell was devastated by a breach in the seawall allowing the sea to flood the land after nearly 200 years of cultivation. The farmland was abandoned and quickly reverted to a natural saltmarsh where ridges of an old potato field could be seen for some years after. In 1973 this marsh was purchased by the RSPB who proceeded to develop it as a reserve to such good effect that it now rivals Minsmere (Suffolk) as a prime sanctuary.

Other reclamations and developments by man include the coastal golf-courses of Old Hunstanton and Brancaster and these are always attractive to many different species of migrants from scrub haunting warblers to open ground chats and plovers. Many small villages along the route of the A149 belong to a bygone age of labour intensive farming and the inshore fishing industry. Between Hunstanton in the west and Sheringham in the east only the small town of Wells-next-Sea still retains its port where small cargo ships can still dock by the quayside on the highest tides. Some small fishing boats still use the channels at Thornham and Brancaster. Most of the villages survive because of the tourist trade and the demand for second holiday homes.

While the main coast road and the marshlands to the north of it rarely rise more than 25 ft (7.5 m) above sea level, the gently rising land to the south is predominantly agricultural, but wooded estates and vales provide an interesting backdrop to the coastal scene. Superb natural sanctuaries for wildlife exist at Scolt Head Island and Blakeney Point, both long established as nature reserves and famous for their large colonies of Sandwich and Common Terns. Scolt Head though, only becomes recognisable as an island when high tides fill its jig-saw network of creeks to completely separate it from the mainland. It boasts one of the highest sand dune systems in Norfolk while the ever-changing dunes and complex fragile eco-system have long claimed the attentions of students and scientists.

On the east side of Scolt Head and between the Holkham Dunes (or Meals) the River Burn finds an outlet to the sea after beginning life about 6 miles (9.5 km) inland near the village of South Creake. It winds down to the sea through the small villages of North Creake, Burnham Thorpe and past Burnham Overy mill on the A149.

Blakeney Point, further eastwards, is a unique peninsula extending parallel to the coast for over 3 miles (4.8 km) from its mainland connection at Cley-next-Sea. It is clothed intermittently for much of its length by the semi-evergreen shrubby sea-blite bush (usually referred to as sueda), a Mediterranean species reaching its most northerly limit on the Norfolk coast. The Point is also renowned historically for the numbers and variety of migrant birds which make a landfall there to seek food and shelter amongst the sea-blite bushes. Usually colonies of common seals can be seen on the far point as well as a few grey seals at times. The vast areas of mudflats and saltmarshes between the Point and the villages of Blakeney and Morston are an important wintering habitat for Brent Geese, waders and other wildfowl.

Two small rivers flow into this huge marine basin from Cley and Stiffkey. The source of the River Stiffkey is some 7 miles (11 km) inland near Swanton Novers, but it takes a very winding course across country before turning seawards at East Barsham and then on through the attractive villages of Little Walsingham, Wighton, Warham and Stiffkey where it then flows into the harbour via Freshes Creek.

The River Glaven flowing into the harbour through Cley Channel originates by Selbrigg Pond near High Kelling only 3 miles (4.8 km) from the coast. Its inland journey is through countryside of great interest to the naturalist; from its source the small stream flows through Holt Lowes, which is a unique wet heath and valley mire given SSSI status. Some 96 acres (38.04 ha) of the adjacent area have been designated a Country Park by the North Norfolk District Council. Holt Country Park offers a car park, visitor centre and waymarked paths with free public access. On the Lowes a nationally rare club moss can be found. The Glaven turns seawards at Hunworth and then on through the villages of Letheringsett, Glandford and Cley to the sea.

Two beautiful heaths exist at Salthouse and Kelling where they reach the relatively lofty height of 200 ft (60 m) less than 1 mile (1.6 km) from the sea. They have become subject to much disturbance in recent years and periodically fires destroy the heather, bracken and gorse. These heaths were the last major stronghold in Norfolk of the Red-backed Shrike but are still good birdwatching country with a few pairs of Nightingales, the odd pair of Nightjars, Tree Pipits and occasionally a wintering Great Grey Shrike. An alien plant from New Zealand – the pirri pirri bur – has established itself here.

Further west at the back of Brancaster, Barrow Common rises steeply from the main coast road. This is another attractive heathland site adjoining a private wooded vale. From Cley to Kelling extensive fresh marshes lie between the coast road and the stony ramparts of the shoreline which are a critical part of the sea defences. These marshes have long been famous as the resort of wildfowl and waders with the Cley Marsh Nature Reserve being established in 1926.

HOLME AND THORNHAM

Map 4

Species

Since the authors established the Holme Bird Observatory Reserve in 1962, it has become internationally renowned for the variety and abundance of migrating birds which may, in the right weather conditions, make a landfall or traverse the coastline. Geographically, Holme is ideally suited to study the various streams of migrants which traditionally follow the north-facing Norfolk coastline westwards until reaching the shores of the Wash off Gore Point. At this point migrants must alter course if they are to continue following the coastline which gradually assumes a south-westerly course. Other migrants make a landfall in the marram sandhills or in the scrub and pine-covered observatory reserve where they may stay for several days before resuming their journey. Although Holme does not have the same holding power as an island observatory, birds are encouraged to stay by the varied nature of the habitat – bounded by the sea on one side and vast fresh grazing marshes on the other. The belt of Corsican pine trees and high sand dunes offer some protection from on-shore winds in which conditions falls of migrants may occur. Up to the end of 1989, over 300 species have been recorded in the area and this includes 21 species of warblers.

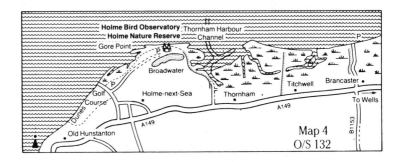

Map 4
O/S 132

Although the emphasis is on migration, (with not many breeding birds), there are usually interesting species to be seen throughout the year. The mixture of habitats each provide characteristic birds in the appropriate seasons. Thus, the fresh grazing marshes are good for wildfowl in the winter months, the bushes and trees for small migrants in spring and autumn, the fresh water pools for waders from mid-summer; and the saltings for winter finches, larks, pipits and buntings. Even in the off-peak periods such as the latter half of June and July, the area is well worth a visit. Apart from the chance of seeing the odd Spoonbill, a passing Osprey or harrier, the sand dune flora is good with miniature stork's bill, forget-me-not, corn salad and many other species on the short rabbit-grazed turf. In the dunes, hound's tongue, prickly lettuce and sea bindweed can be found. Along the upper shoreline purple sea rocket and saltwort flourish until the first frosts, while the saltmarshes are purple with sea lavender in July. The dual attractions of an exciting migration point and a superb safe, sandy beach is enjoyed by many birders with young families.

Spring is usually slow to arrive on these coastal marshes especially if a cold easterly airflow covers the country. By mid-March Brent Goose flocks begin to depart from the grazing marshes while the resident flocks of Canada Geese begin to split up into noisy courting pairs. Early Wheatears have been seen in the first week of March, but it is more often the third week before these birds arrive. At this time a migrant Black Redstart or an early Ring Ouzel may appear. Wintering visitors from elsewhere begin to appear and these include a few Stonechats and Pied Wagtails. Redwings, Fieldfares and Blackbirds too, begin to congregate in coastal meadows prior to their departure northwards. Given a fine

Snow buntings. Winter visitors to the coastal regions

calm evening this month, these winter visitors can often be seen flying off high to the north-east on a course which will take them back to their Scandinavian homelands. A few Hooded Crows and Hen Harriers may appear before they also move north. Any over-wintering Snow Buntings, Shorelarks or Lapland Buntings on the saltings will now decrease in numbers, but single birds of all three species may linger on into April. The end of March and early April is a good time to look out for migrant Firecrests which regularly appear in single numbers at this time. Sparrow Hawks are also regular passage migrants in very small numbers; and a bird ringed here one spring was found dead later entangled in a clump of barbed wire in Kent.

Other first returning migrants may include Marsh Harriers and Avocets, although both these species have occasionally spent the whole winter on the Norfolk coast in recent years. From the second to the third week of April the first returning Swallows, Sand Martins, Willow Warblers, Chiff-chaffs, Sedge Warblers, Yellow Wagtails and Blackcaps may arrive. Diurnal passage may include parties of Linnets and Meadow Pipits flying westwards – more often than not flying into the face of a stiff south-westerly breeze. A cold easterly airflow with leaden skies at this time brings migration to a standstill and quite often many outgoing winter visitors are grounded to await more favourable conditions. These birds may include numbers of Goldcrests and Robins en-route for Scandinavia. A Robin caught one spring had been ringed at Falsterbo, Sweden in a previous year, while another bird caught and ringed at that time was found in Germany a few days later. During one spring a fierce east wind held up scores of Fieldfares on the grazing marshes until early May.

Very little seabird passage is noted in the spring, but the sea can prove quite interesting at times with an increase in the numbers of Red-breasted Mergansers, Goldeneye, Great-crested Grebe, Eider, Common Scoter and Long-tailed Duck. Single numbers of Velvet Scoter, Red-throated, Black-throated and Great Northern Diver may be seen in April as well as odd Red-necked and Slavonian Grebes. Sandwich Terns are usually the first to arrive in late March or early April from which date onwards all can be seen in varying numbers along the shore. The fishing grounds off the Wash are good and a steady stream of terns can be seen carrying fish back to their mates sitting on eggs or tending chicks on Scolt Head Island.

Given south-westerly winds in late April and early May passerine passage continues unabated with Swallows pouring westwards along the coast in company with House Martins and some Sand Martins. Parties of Linnets, Goldfinches and Redpolls also moving west are a feature of May mornings while Turtle Doves will often pass in their hundreds. In a late spring, passage may continue until early June with Swallows still proceeding westwards. Swifts arrive in early May and local Reed Warblers begin to sing from the reed-fringed pools. A spell of easterly winds in May can produce almost anything. More Ring Ouzels may drop in to forage on the open dunes or grazing marshes for a few days. The Hoopoe is almost an annual visitor and it too, prefers the short grassland. The larger, brighter Greenland race of the Wheatear often appears in some numbers at this time, together with a few Whinchats.

A 'fall' of small birds may include single numbers of Redstarts and Pied Flycatchers with the cock birds in their resplendent spring plumage. Scores of Willow Warblers may appear amongst the now greening sea buckthorn bushes with the odd Garden Warbler, Lesser Whitethroat and Spotted Flycatcher. Semi-rarities which often appear at this time may include Wryneck, Red-backed Shrike, Nightingale and Wood Warbler. Other rarities which may turn up include Rough-legged Buzzard, Red-footed Falcon, Red-spotted Bluethroat, Serin, Ortolan Bunting and Golden Oriole.

Species of much rarer occurrence include: Little Bittern, White Stork, Honey Buzzard, Tawny Pipit, Red-rumped Swallow, Thrush Nightingale, Black-eared Wheatear, Fan-tailed Warbler, Bonelli's Warbler, Collared Flycatcher, Icterine Warbler, Marsh Warbler, Alpine Swift, Red-breasted Flycatcher, Lesser Grey Shrike, Woodchat Shrike and Common Rosefinch.

Visitors are often surprised to observe Cuckoos frequenting this coastal reserve and calling from quite open fence posts. The spring wader passage is but a shadow of the great autumn flights. Very small numbers of Dunlin, Common Sandpipers, Greenshank, Spotted Redshank and Black-tailed Godwit may stay a short time on the fresh water wader pools. Some Bar-tailed Godwit, Sanderling, Turnstone and Grey Plover can usually be found on the shore, while the occasional Whimbrel announces its overhead passage with seven quickly repeated clear whistles. A feature in April is the appearance of 100 or so Golden Plover on the adjacent grazing marshes. With many birds acquiring full breeding plumage it is easy to see that some (and probably all) are of the northern race which has a more contrasting black and white plumage.

By June migration has usually finished, but nevertheless several nice birds often appear. Ospreys are now annual visitors to the Norfolk coast and this reflects the breeding success of pairs guarded by the RSPB in Scotland. Immature birds have been known to spend a week or so in the area, fishing in the shallow seas or saltwater creeks. A Hobby often makes an appearance to put the local hirundines in a frenzy. Marsh Harriers can be seen almost daily hunting over the rough grazing while Avocets have become a regular feature in recent years. Family parties of Crossbills may irrupt at this time to stay in the Corsican pines for a few days. Pairs of handsome Shelduck frequent the sand dunes which have by now changed their bleak brown winter hues for subtle spring tones of green and grey.

It seems that soon after the last migrants have gone through, the first autumn passage migrants start to arrive. Post-nesting dispersal is evident as early as June when flocks of Lapwings begin to arrive from the Continent to fly on a westerly course heading for Ireland where they can avoid mid-summer heat and dehydration of damp marshes. It is usually mid-July though, before the freshwater waders arrive to frequent muddy pools on the adjoining marshlands until September. The first species to come are Green Sandpipers, Common Sandpipers, Little Ringed Plover, Ringed Plover and Ruff. By the end of July wader passage is in full swing with Dunlin, Spotted Redshank, Greenshank, Little Stint, Redshank and Snipe frequenting the pools. Wood and Curlew Sandpipers are fairly regular, but fluctuate in numbers from one season to the next. Temminck's Stint occasionally occurs and there is always a chance to see Pectoral and White-rumped Sandpiper. A Wilson's Phalarope once stayed a few days and there have been two records of Marsh Sandpipers – rare vagrants from eastern Europe.

A complex of small wader pools has been created by the NNT and the observation hides are unique because they give excellent short-range viewing of waders. A few Black-tailed or Bar-tailed Godwit also frequent the larger pools at this time, but generally after mid-September all the pools become very quiet apart from the odd Redshank, Dunlin and Snipe. The pools have also yielded good views of Jack Snipe (which is almost an annual visitor), Water Rails, Bearded Tits, Spoonbill and Bittern. Sadly, the largest area of brackish water known as Broad Water, has been kept flooded by the NNT for many years and this has banished the throngs of small waders which used to appear there in the autumn.

Waders passing in July and August include good parties of Curlew, Whimbrel and some Bar-tailed Godwit and Golden Plover. In August the shore waders begin to reach peak numbers and, on the highest tides at the times of the new and full moons, the tidal flights are one of the most spectacular sights in birdwatching. Tens of thousands of Knot swirl past the sand dunes, pale wing linings flashing silver in the sun one moment, then grey, as countless birds quickly turn in perfect unison. Black and white Oyster-catchers stream sedately past often overtaken by flocks of swift flying Bar-tailed Godwit and Grey Plover. About two hours before high tide is the best time to take up a vantage point on the dunes. These flights continue throughout the autumn, but as the days shorten the flights take place more under cover of darkness.

In July the first Arctic Skuas arrive offshore to harass the hordes of fishing terns, now dispersing from their colonies on Scolt Head and Blakeney Point. Most Shelduck have by now left the area to gather in large parties on sea areas in the Wash and off the Heligoland Bight, where they undergo a complete moult. August sees the start of the passerine migration but, in reverse of spring conditions, migrants mainly arrive in light variable winds or in a good 'blow' from the east or north-east. If strong south-west or west winds prevail visible migration is a non-event! It seems most likely that 'drift migration' provides the main supply of migrants arriving at Holme in the autumn months. Migrants setting off southwards from Scandinavia in calm, clear anti-cyclonic weather may be forced to land when meeting unexpected bad weather conditions such as sea fog or low cloud. An east wind increasing in strength may also cause lateral drift especially when birds are unable to navigate if the solar system becomes obscured. With the hump of the Norfolk coast jutting out into the North Sea it is thus ideally situated to receive disorientated southward moving migrants.

Therefore, with the first east winds in August everyone is on the look-out for the first Pied Flycatchers. Even at this early date in the autumn all the cock birds have moulted out their black and white spring plumage and resemble the females or young. Redstarts also arrive, disappearing into the sea buckthorn bushes with a flirt of their rufous red tails. Almost annually a few semi-rarities such as Barred Warbler, Icterine Warbler and Wryneck are seen. With patience most can be observed from good watching points on either side of the long belt of Corsican Pine trees intermixed with elder, bramble and willow trees. At the Holme Bird Observatory Reserve the central area of cover is clearly marked 'Reserved for the Birds'. Birders keep on the outside with the welcome result that birds are not disturbed and may stay several days before resuming their journeys.

Wryneck. Passage migrant mainly to the coastal regions

A typical August 'fall' might, then, include a couple of dozen Pied Flycatchers, ten Redstarts, a score of Garden Warblers, a few White-throats, Chiff-chaffs and Willow Warblers with a Wryneck, Barred or Icterine Warbler to add excitement to interest. Other species often concerned in these early falls are Wood Warbler, Tree Pipit and some-times a juvenile Red-backed Shrike. Autumn falls may occur at any time of the day but seldom in the early morning. More usually birds start to arrive in mid-morning while even in late afternoon falls are not unknown. Quite often birds arriving one day have gone by early the next morning.

Summer passerines can continue to arrive in September up to the third week. However, by mid-September the peak time for Wrynecks and Icterine Warblers is past, but Barred Warbler, Red-breasted Fly-catcher, Black Redstart and Firecrest may turn up at any time until early November. The rare Greenish and Arctic Warblers have been noted on several occasions between August and October. Yellow-browed

Warblers from Northern Siberia are almost annual if there are light south to south-east winds in September and October.

The main departure of hirundines takes place in September – sooner or later, according to the weather conditions. Their passage is still mainly westerly so a turn southwards probably occurs in the Fen country. Most local Swifts have disappeared by early September, but a few late birds hang on until early October. Large numbers of Whinchats and Wheatears often pass through, frequenting marshland fencing. From late September Goldcrests and Robins may arrive from the Continent on an easterly wind. In October the bushes may be swarming with these two species who will usually move on within a few days. Quite often the bold Great Grey Shrike appears at the same time to prey upon his fellow travellers. Holme has become especially noted for Pallas's Warblers and they have been noted several times in October generally after an easterly airstream has been blowing for a day or so.

Pallas's Warbler

At this time the first thrushes begin to arrive with Redwings crossing the coast non-stop to fly on strongly inland. In the third week vast numbers of Redwings may cross the coastline while many Blackbirds prefer to seek the shelter of the bushes to rest and feed before going on to wintering places all over west and south-west Britain. Blackbirds can be seen from the sand dunes flying in across the North Sea in small parties, thankful to make landfall after setting out some hours previously from the Scandinavian or Dutch coast. Lines of Herring and Black-backed Gulls on the shore keep a sharp look out for any stragglers or tired birds who are quickly intercepted within a few hundred yards of the shore and forced down into the sea where they are promptly seized and swallowed whole! Ring Ouzels may appear again at this time, but now they prefer to frequent the bushes to feast upon the autumn fruits. Flocks of finches also arrive and these are mainly composed of Chaffinches and Bramblings. Irruptions of resident breeding birds also takes place. On calm mornings parties of Bearded Tits can be seen pitching into the reeds or flying on westwards like long tailed darts. Woodland species often move through in fair numbers, but these irruptions invariably proceed eastwards. Long-tailed, Willow, Blue, Great and Coal Tits, Great and Lesser Spotted Woodpeckers and Nuthatches are the chief participants, but Greenfinches, Yellow Buntings and Tree Sparrows are often associated travellers.

The Waxwing, another irruption species from northern Europe, used to be an annual visitor in varying numbers, but few appeared anywhere in the country until a large influx in the autumn of 1988 which may herald another cycle of abundance.

The individual Hen Harrier and Merlin begin to appear about now, hunting over the grazing marshes. More irregularly, a Rough-legged Buzzard or two may put in a welcome appearance during this month. Long-eared Owls and Woodcock are regular migrants in very small numbers. Sharp eyes are needed to spot a tired Long-eared Owl asleep in the bushes; but Woodcock are more usually flushed from sand dune bramble patches. Sparrow Hawks, Peregrines (and once, a Red Kite) have all been noted in late October.

A ringed Long-eared Owl. Resident and winter visitor to the region

From August to late October sea watching can be good whenever there is a strong onshore wind between north-west and north-east. Small numbers of Manx and sometimes Sooty and Cory's Shearwaters are seen in August and September. Gannets are frequent in all these months with some birds often fishing close inshore. After the first few Arctic Skuas in July there is an increase in numbers during the next two months. Long-tailed Skuas are sometimes seen in August and September, while the peak month for Great and Pomarine Skuas is usually October. Hundreds of Common and Sandwich Terns frequent the shallow seas of The Wash throughout August and September with not a few lingering on into October when Arctic Terns are regularly noted. October gales can also bring Guillemots, Razorbills and Little Auks close inshore, while numbers of Brent Geese, Wigeon, Scoter and Eider may be passing. Kittiwakes are usually associated with rough sea conditions, but Little Gulls more often occur offshore in calm seas. Red-throated, Black-throated and Great Northern Divers are frequently noted. After the breeding season on inland waterways the Great-crested Grebe soon returns to these shallow shores and they can be seen all autumn and winter, often in company with the Red-necked and the Slavonian Grebe. Rarer seabirds which might occur in gales are Leach's and Storm Petrels, Sabine's Gulls and Grey Phalaropes.

With their leaf drop in November the sea buckthorn bushes reveal the full glory of their thickly clustered orange berries. Soon after the first frosts, Fieldfares begin to return from the depleted inland hedgerow harvest to swarm upon these berries which are rather acid and less nutritious. The crop may last until the New Year when the birds move on once again to forage on inland root-crop fields.

On the rough grazing marshes, now free of cattle, wildfowl congregate in numbers. Up to 1,600 Brent Geese and 1,100 Wigeon have been recorded. Sometimes, with the turn of the year, a few Pink-feet may take up residence on the marsh while hunting Hen Harriers and Short-eared Owls may be seen in all winter months. The saltings adjoining the Holme side of the Thornham Harbour channel usually support numbers of Twite, Linnet, Skylark, Snow Bunting and sometimes Shorelarks. Lapland Buntings are often present in autumn and early winter. A few Rock Pipits frequent the edges of the saltwater drains. By Christmas many Shelduck have returned to people the bleak shore in company with Bar-tailed Godwits, Grey Plovers and Sanderlings. On the sea there are usually rafts of Common Scoter (with a few Velvets amongst them) and Eiders; while Red-breasted Mergansers and Goldeneye can often be seen.

Another good watching area is by the Hunstanton golf-course which extends well into the Parish of Holme. It is best to explore the seaward dune edge of the links by starting from the Holme Parish Council Car Park. (No one should trespass on the greens or fairways.) There are patches of sea buckthorn scrub where Barred Warblers and Wrynecks are often seen in autumn. Dotterel on passage in the spring have often been reported from this area.

Holme Marsh Bird Reserve managed by the Norfolk Ornithologists' Association (NOA) in co-operation with an enlightened farmer, Lord Peter Melchett, offers a quiet corner with observation hides at pools. Many of the species recorded elsewhere in Holme can also be seen here with the added attractions of regular wintering Kingfishers and Water Rails. Marsh Harriers, Hen Harriers and Short-eared Owls are regularly seen from the hides, but it is not a reserve for those in a hurry!

Timing

Most of the best areas at Holme are under the control of either the Norfolk Ornithologists' Association or the Norfolk Naturalists' Trust. The reserves are open daily throughout the year to non-members and advance bookings are only required for parties of ten or more. Visiting outside opening hours is discouraged in order to keep the area quiet and to enable management work to be done. In any case there is little advantage in early morning watching on this site. Records prove that very few birds have occurred in the early morning that have not been seen later in the day and very often a visitor in the morning only misses good birds in the afternoon (and vice-versa!).

Weather wise it does not matter when you visit. A strong west wind in autumn will mean few passerine migrants, but waders should be good.

As elsewhere on the north Norfolk coast, sea watching may be best from two hours before high tide time. Be careful about going out of sight of the sand dunes in foggy weather as the tide recedes vast distances and flows in again at an alarming rate. Adjoining marshes beyond Broad Water are private and shot over during the shooting season between 1 September and 31 January. A Saturday is often choosen for a shoot, but never a Sunday when shooting is banned in Norfolk. Least productive weeks are probably mid-June to mid-July and between mid-February and mid-March unless cold weather delays spring dispersal of winter wildfowl. Holme can be an exciting or a frustrating place. Visitors in the morning may see everything while newcomers in the afternoon may see very little; or the reverse situation may occur! Visitors are welcomed, but don't expect any reserve warden to be over enthusiastic if you arrive a few minutes before closing time!

Access

The Holme Bird Observatory Reserve and the Holme Dunes Nature Reserve can be approached from two directions by car or on foot.

By road turn off the A149 down the beach road signposted 'NOA Watchpoint' on the Hunstanton side of Holme village. Take the second turning on the right (the first will take you into the village where there is a pub, a telephone box and a small general shop) which is a very rough private road (owners' right of way along this road); this improves after about ½ mile (0.8 km) and leads to the reserves which are about 1½ miles (2.4 km) along, and well off, the beaten track. Note that after about ½ mile (0.8 km) there is a car park on the left after some bungalows are passed and this is primarily for the use of holiday-makers and beach users. There is a road toll payable in summer to use this car park, but note that this is not a permit fee to the reserves. Any road toll paid will be offset against the reserve permit obtainable from the reserve centres which are another mile (1.6 km) along the track. Two car parks are provided at the end of this road, and permits should be obtained.

The reserves, which adjoin one another, are open daily to non-members from 10.00 a.m. to 4.00 p.m. and the Holme Bird Observatory Reserve is fully wardened daily and managed by the Norfolk Ornithologists' Association. The Holme Dunes Nature Reserve is managed by the Norfolk Naturalists' Trust. The joint permit system successfully in operation for many years has been unilaterally abolished by the NNT which often results in confusing our many visitors. As the NNT are 'first in line' on the approach road their permits are sold often without any indication that these are not valid for our Bird Observatory Reserve. Intending visitors to our Bird Observatory Reserve should be aware that they are not *obliged* to pay for a permit to the Nature Reserve as well. The Observatory has always maintained a daily log and highlights are displayed in its centre about 200 yds (180m) east of the car parks and at the end of the pine belt.

The alternative route, on foot, is to leave the A149 at Thornham. Go down Staithe Lane on the left as you approach the village from the west. Beware of leaving your car on the Staithe which is regularly flooded and well under water at the highest tides! Always *check tide times locally.* Walk alon; the high seawall from the Staithe, which is a public footpath to Holme, about 4 miles (6.4 km). Much of this path has been boarded to stop erosion, while yellow trail markers help guide the way. This is a section of the Norfolk Long Distance Coastal Footpath. After just over

1 mile (1.6 km) turn off left as signposted to reach the Observatory's centre where there is a display on various natural history subjects. Young families in particular are welcomed; and the attractive sandy beaches are a useful ploy to introduce conservation at an early age!

On the west side of the Holme reserves yet another car park can be found at the end of the beach road. Instead of turning right down the private road, continue for a few more yards and turn right as signposted into the Parish Council Car Park (for which there is a charge in summer; a refreshment stall may be manned there on fine weekends). At the back of the car park the coastal footpath can be picked up, skirting the edge of the golf-course eastwards and then along a seawall past some very attractive bushy paddocks where horses are often grazed. Many rare migrants have been spotted in this area. The path then goes on to a boarded stretch to follow the highest ridge of the sand dunes round past the Holme reserves to Thornham village.

Another footpath opposite the end bungalow on the private road to the reserves crosses a footbridge over the River Hun and skirts the boundary of Redwell Marsh, a wetland pasture acquired by the Norfolk Ornithologists' Association. It leads into the village centre. To explore the Holme Marsh Bird Reserve, follow the village road past the church and turn left down a lane on a sharp right hand bend of road back to the A149. Park on the right where indicated after a few yards and follow directions to the two hides at pools. If you intend to use this reserve please join the NOA.

To explore the perimeter of the golf-course, park in the Holme Parish Council car park and pick up the path along the coastal dunes to the west and follow this along the seaward edge of the links to near the golf-club house. A left-hand turn here will pick up another path back to the Holme beach road and this skirts the River Hun and the south edge of the course. This is about a 2½ mile (4 km) round trip.

Calendar

Resident Grey Heron (breeds in the area), Grey-lag Goose (from feral stock), Canada Goose, Mallard, Sparrowhawk, Red-legged Partridge, Grey Partridge, Snipe (and winter visitor), Redshank, Stock Dove, Barn Owl, Tawny Owl, Little Owl (breeds in adjoining parishes), Green Woodpecker, Lesser Spotted Woodpecker, Skylark (also winter visitor), Nuthatch and Corn Bunting.

December–February Red-throated Diver, Great Northern Diver, Great-crested Grebe, Red-necked Grebe, Slavonian Grebe, Cormorant, Pink-footed Goose, Brent Goose, Shelduck, Wigeon, Shoveler, Scaup, Eider, Long-tailed Duck, Common Scoter, Velvet Scoter, Goldeneye, Smew (in hard weather), Red-breasted Merganser, Hen Harrier, Merlin, Peregrine (sightings on increase), Water Rail, Oyster-catcher, Ringed Plover, Golden Plover, Grey Plover, Lapwing, Knot, Sanderling, Dunlin, Bar-tailed Godwit, Curlew, Turnstone, Glaucous Gull, Guillemot, Razorbill, Kingfisher, Shorelark, Rock Pipit, Stonechat, Twite, Lapland Bunting and Snow Bunting.

March–May Red-throated Diver, Great Northern Diver, Great-crested Grebe, Red-necked Grebe, Slavonian Grebe, Shelduck, Gadwall, Teal, Shoveler, Tufted Duck, Eider, Long-tailed Duck, Common Scoter, Velvet Scoter, Goldeneye, Red-breasted Merganser, Marsh Harrier, Hen Harrier (seldom after March), Sparrow Hawk, Rough-legged Buzzard, Osprey, Oyster-catcher, Avocet, Ringed Plover, Golden Plover, Grey Plover, Lapwing, Knot (a big decrease in March), Sanderling, Dunlin, Black-tailed Godwit, Bar-tailed Godwit, Whimbrel, Curlew, Spotted Redshank, Greenshank, Green Sandpiper, Wood Sandpiper, Common Sandpiper, Turnstone, Mediterranean Gull, Glaucous Gull (not after March-April), Sandwich Tern, Common Tern, Little Tern, Cuckoo, Hoopoe, Wryneck, Tree Pipit, Yellow Wagtail, Nightingale, Bluethroat, Black Redstart, Whinchat, Stonechat, Wheatear, Ring Ouzel, Fieldfare, Redwing (latter two species not after April as a rule), Grasshopper Warbler, Sedge Warbler, Reed Warbler, Lesser Whitethroat, Wood Warbler, Firecrest, Spotted Flycatcher, Pied Flycatcher, Golden Oriole, Serin, Redpoll and Common Rosefinch (rare).

June–July Spoonbill, Gadwall, Teal, Shoveler, Tufted Duck, Eider, Common Scoter, Marsh Harrier, Montagu's Harrier (rare passage migrant), Osprey, Red-footed Falcon (rare), Oyster-catcher, Avocet, Little Ringed Plover, Ringed Plover, Grey Plover, Lapwing, Sanderling. Little Stint, Dunlin, Ruff, Black-tailed Godwit, Bar-tailed Godwit, Whimbrel, Curlew, Spotted Redshank, Greenshank, Green Sandpiper, Common Sandpiper, Arctic Skua, Mediterranean Gull, Sandwich Tern, Common Tern, Little Tern, Sedge Warbler, Reed Warbler, Lesser White-throat and Crossbill.

August–November Red-throated Diver, Black-throated Diver, Great Northern Diver, Great-crested Grebe, Red-necked Grebe, Slavonian Grebe, Cory's Shearwater, Sooty Shearwater, Manx Shearwater, Storm Petrel, Leach's Petrel, Gannet, Cormorant, Shag (all previous species more usually in, or after, on-shore gales), Bittern, Bewick's Swan, Whooper Swan (wild swans end October–November), Pink-footed Goose, Brent Goose, Wigeon, Eider, Long-tailed Duck, Common Scoter, Velvet Scoter, Goldeneye, Red-breasted Merganser, Hen Harrier (first in October), Sparrow Hawk, Rough-legged Buzzard (from October), Merlin, Hobby (not often after August), Peregrine, Water Rail (from September), Oyster-catcher, Avocet (not after September), Little Ringed Plover, Ringed Plover, Golden Plover, Grey Plover, Lapwing, Knot, Sanderling, Little Stint, Temminick's Stint, White-rumped Sandpiper, Pectoral Sandpiper, Curlew Sandpiper, Dunlin, Ruff, Jack Snipe, Woodcock (not before late October), Black-tailed Godwit (not often after October), Bar-tailed Godwit, Whimbrel (not often after October), Curlew, Spotted Redshank, Greenshank, Green Sandpiper, Wood Sand-piper, Common Sandpiper, Turnstone, Pomarine Skua, Arctic Skua, Long-tailed Skua, Great Skua, Mediterranean Gull, Little Gull, Sabine's Gull, Glaucous Gull, Kittiwake, Sandwich Tern, Common Tern (latter two terns, scarce after September), Little Tern (scarce after August), Arctic Tern, Black Tern, Guillemot, Razorbill, Little Auk (after gales at sea), Long-eared Owl (late autumn migrant), Short-eared Owl, King-fisher, Wryneck, Shorelark (from mid-October), Tree Pipit, Rock Pipit (from October), Yellow Wagtail, Waxwing (now a very rare irruption species, but best times were last week in October and first week in November), Black Redstart, Redstart, Whinchat, Stonechat, Wheatear, Ring Ouzel, Fieldfare, Redwing, Sedge Warbler, Reed Warbler, Icterine Warbler (not after mid-September), Barred Warbler, Lesser Whitethroat,

Whitethroat, Garden Warbler, Blackcap, Greenish Warbler, Arctic Warbler, Pallas's Warbler (not usually before mid-October), Yellow-browed Warbler (from mid-September), Wood Warbler (not after mid-September), Goldcrest (main influx late October), Firecrest, Spotted Flycatcher, Red-breasted Flycatcher, Pied Flycatcher, Bearded Tit, Red-backed Shrike (not after mid-October), Great Grey Shrike (not before mid-September), Brambling (from October), Siskin, Twite (from October), Redpoll, Crossbill, Lapland Bunting (from October), Snow Bunting (from mid-September, more usually October), and Ortolan Bunting (not as a rule after September).

(In the above listings it should be noted that the following commoner freshwater waders are usually in single numbers after mid-September and very few in October: Little Ringed Plover, Little Stint, Curlew Sandpiper, Ruff, Spotted Redshank, Greenshank, Green Sandpiper, Wood Sandpiper, Common Sandpiper.)

TITCHWELL

Map 4

Species

In 1973 the RSPB purchased over 400 acres (160 ha) of derelict farmland at Titchwell which had been abandoned since 1953 when rough seas burst through the seawalls. Successive tides regularly flooded the land which quickly reverted to its natural saltmarsh state. Since then expert management has created a variety of attractive habitats such as salt-marsh, tidal reed, fresh reed, brackish marsh, fresh marsh, willow copse and plantation, sand, shingle and sand dunes. While there are some local birders who have nostalgic memories of this wild marsh as it was in the 1960s, no one can deny the impressive bird colonisation that

Marsh Harrier

speedily took place with the creation of suitable habitats. Bittern, Marsh Harriers and Bearded Tits soon established themselves, while Avocets have founded a flourishing colony.

A feature of the winter months from December to March is the roost of Hen Harriers which congregate in the drier reed beds in the late afternoon. Up to 5 birds have been recorded daily, but a record count of 22 birds in March 1982 included 7 beautiful grey cock birds. Although the harriers mostly disperse over a wide area during the day, there are usually one or two birds hunting in the immediate area of the reserve. Other birds of prey which might be encountered at this time are the Merlin and the Short-eared Owl; the former intent on zooming into a flock of Twite on the saltmarsh while the owl flaps and glides diligently over the ground in search of voles. In addition to several hundred Twite there are about two or three dozen Snow Buntings to be seen on the shore or saltings. Shorelarks are infrequent but have been recorded. Plenty of Brent Geese frequent the area coming in to drink and bathe on the reserve pools.

Other wildfowl to be found on Titchwell Marsh during winter are two or three hundred Teal, a hundred Wigeon and lesser numbers of Pochard, Gadwall, Tufted Duck and Shoveler. Off the beach there are usually modest numbers of Goldeneye, Long-tailed Duck, Common Scoter, Eider and Red-breasted Mergansers on the sea. Even during the summer months numbers of moulting immature Eider and Common Scoter frequent the sea area between Titchwell and Scolt Head, Purple Sandpipers can often be seen off the end of the Titchwell bank, feeding amongst the peaty remains of the old forest bed exposed at low tide or at high tide scurrying round the large heap of bricks and concrete (the remains of a wartime blockhouse) at the edge of the shore. Red-throated Divers can be seen offshore and there is always a chance of seeing a Black-throated or Great Northern Diver. Grebes, too, are usually present with Great-crested being the most common, and only single numbers of Red-necked and Slavonian.

Walking along the main bank there is a chance of seeing one of the resident Bitterns make a brief flight from one reed bed to the next while a Barn Owl may be seen hunting along the southern edge of the reserve especially towards dusk. Water Rails – more often heard than seen –

Spoonbill. Annual summer visitor to the coastal reserves

are resident, with undoubtedly an increase in winter from migrant birds. From mid-March in mild weather Bitterns begin to boom from the reed beds. Their extraordinary call has been likened to a distant foghorn or lowing cow. An audible intake of breath is followed by a deep penetrating boom which can be heard from some distance away. While on duty at the Holme Bird Observatory Reserve on a calm day the authors have frequently heard the Bittern call from the Titchwell reed beds over 2 miles (3.2 km) away!

Springtime brings the first returning Marsh Harriers and Avocets while Bearded Tits pair off in the reed beds. The whole marsh teems with the excitement of courtship displays from noisy head winding Shelduck, piping Ringed Plovers, Redshanks, clamourous Black-headed Gulls and aggressive Avocets who yelp after anything that dares to encroach upon their territory. The Garganey has declined in many areas, but in recent years one or two birds seem to be dropping in during the spring. In May and June the reed beds are alive with Sedge and Reed Warblers while nearly every year a Grasshopper Warbler is heard in song. Spoonbills which may arrive at this time have been known to stay for several weeks and it is hoped that one day they may nest which would be the first time in Britain for many centuries.

In autumn, wader passage is good, with plenty of the smaller sandpipers frequenting the brackish marsh from July. Wood, Common, and Green Sandpipers are annual and so are Little Stints and Little Ringed Plovers. Curlew Sandpipers are regular, but fluctuate in numbers, plentiful in some years and scarce in others. Some larger species, such as Ruff and Black-tailed Godwit, have shown a spectacular increase due to the creation of special habitats for them; Spotted Redshank, Greenshank, Dunlin, Bar-tailed Godwit, Grey Plover and Redshank are all frequent visitors to the reserve. Rare waders noted in recent years include Black-winged Stilt, Baird's Sandpiper, Wilson's Phalarope and White-rumped Sandpiper.

Titchwell March is also in the process of acquiring a reputation for some of the rarer passerine migrants as the developing area of trees and bushes by the main car park proves more and more attractive; it is well worth a watch at migration times. Of the semi-rarities none, as yet, have established annual status but will no doubt do so in future years. Species already recorded a few times include Firecrest, Red-breasted Flycatcher, Red-backed and Great Grey Shrikes, Crossbill, Barred and Icterine Warblers, Black Redstart, Red-spotted Bluethroat, Wryneck, Hoopoe, Golden Oriole and Cetti's Warbler. Before the RSPB established the reserve there were records of Arctic and Yellow-browed Warblers from a nearby area, and both these species could easily turn up again. Some of the rarer reed and swamp haunting warblers will obviously be attracted, but are not easily seen. A Great Reed Warbler was seen to frequent a reedy ditch and sallow carr for a few hours in May 1984. In September 1982 a Booted Warbler frequented an area of low vegetation on the main seawall and was the first accepted record for the county. Most birders though will have fond memories of a superb adult Ross's Gull which arrived in May 1984 in full breeding plumage.

In mid-summer there are usually a few non-breeding Little Gulls to be seen swooping over the lagoons to feed off the surface of the water much after the manner of marsh terns. Both adult and immature Little Gulls may occur at any time between mid-April and July. Similarly Black Terns often appear, especially if the wind is from an easterly quarter in early May. On the shore both Little and Common Terns can be watched going about their breeding activities from a unique hide which is sunk into the side of a sand dune to give unusual eye level views of the birds. In 1980 a Gull-billed Tern was seen from this hide for nearly three weeks in July. Its popularity with birders was not shared by 'protectionists' because this rare tern was seen to pick up and eat the eggs of Little Terns, a species already under threat because of public pressures on its habitats. The RSPB has leased many acres of foreshore land from the Crown Commissioners and have wired off a small section of the beach to safeguard the nesting terns.

Timing

Any time of the year is a good time, depending on what species you wish to see. The best time of the day is probably morning, but there are problems in high summer with the morning sun to the east of the seawall, but private marshes to the west of the wall (which can be viewed through binoculars) can be quite interesting. There are superb lighting conditions all afternoon and in the evenings. Weak winter sunlight is less troublesome in the mornings. High tide times are not really crucial, although a good tide may bring more waders on to the reserve, and numbers of seabirds closer inshore. To observe the winter harrier roost, go in mid-afternoon and be prepared to wait until dusk; weekends are very much busier than weekdays. Wildfowling does take place on the adjoining areas, but not on the RSPB reserve.

Access

From the A149 the RSPB reserve entrance is roughly mid-way between the villages of Titchwell and Thornham and signposted 'Titchwell Marsh'. The turn off is on the marsh side of the main road and only a few yards further along is the car park which is free to RSPB members, but no overnight parking is permitted. Toilets are nearby and the gates are locked at 8.00 p.m. Intending coach parties should book at least one month in advance.

The nature reserve centre also only a few yards away is open during the summer months at times indicated outside the centre. Leaflets and reports can be obtained here and there are displays on the ecology of the reserve. There is no charge.

A seawall, muddy in wet weather, runs alongside the western boundary of the reserve to the beach; from the seawall, which is about 1 mile (1.6 km) long, there are lead-offs to some observation hides with facilities for wheelchair users. The hides are open during daylight hours throughout the year except for the Beach Tern hide which is only open from April to July inclusive. Although most species can be seen well from the observation hides with binoculars a telescope is useful for examining parties of waders on the far side of the brackish marsh.

Calendar

Resident Grebe, Heron, Bittern (booming mid-March to late June), Gadwall, Shoveler, Tufted Duck, Canada Goose, Grey-lag Goose (feral – and can be seen in any month), Kestrel, Red-legged Partridge, Grey Partridge, Water Rail (also increase in winter), Oyster-catcher, Lapwing, Ringed Plover, Redshank, Barn Owl, Tawny Owl, Skylark, Bearded Tit (increase in winter), Redpoll and Tree Sparrow.

December–February Red-throated Diver, Great-crested Grebe, Red-necked Grebe, Slavonian Grebe, Brent Goose, Shelduck, Wigeon, Teal, Pintail, Eider, Common Scoter, Goldeneye, Red-breasted Merganser, Hen Harrier, Merlin, Grey Plover, Knot, Sanderling, Purple Sandpiper, Dunlin, Jack Snipe, Snipe, Bar-tailed Godwit, Curlew, Redshank, Turnstone, Short-eared Owl, Rock Pipit, Twite and Snow Bunting.

March–May Spoonbill (April onwards), Shelduck, Garganey (very scarce irregular), Pochard (non-breeding), Marsh Harrier, Montagu's Harrier (always a chance of this decreasing and rare passage raptor), Sparrow Hawk, Avocet, Ringed Plover, Grey Plover, Sanderling, Dunlin, Snipe, Black-tailed Godwit (a few on spring passage), Bar-tailed Godwit, Whimbrel, Curlew, Turnstone, Little Gull, Black-headed Gull (a large breeding colony), Sandwich Tern, Common Tern, Little Tern, Black Tern (from late April), Yellow Wagtail, Stonechat (not after March), Wheatear (non-breeding), Grasshopper Warbler, Sedge Warbler, Reed Warbler, Blackcap, Lesser Whitethroat, Willow Warbler and Reed Bunting.

June–July Spoonbill, Pochard, Eider, Common Scoter (latter two species often moulting parties on sea), Marsh Harrier, Osprey (always a good chance of passage bird), Hobby (scarce non-breeding summer visitor), Oyster-catcher, Ringed Plover, Avocet, Lapwing, Snipe, Little Gull, Sandwich Tern, Common Tern, Little Tern, Yellow Wagtail, Grasshopper Warbler, Sedge Warbler, Reed Warbler, Lesser White-throat, Blackcap and Willow Warbler.

August–November Red-throated Diver, Great-crested Grebe, Red-necked Grebe (from October), Brent Goose (from October), Wigeon, Teal, Eider, Common Scoter, Goldeneye (from October), Red-breasted Merganser, Marsh Harrier (decrease after August, but single birds have wintered), Hen Harrier from October), Sparrow Hawk, Merlin (from October), Oyster-catcher, Avocet (not usually after early September but odd birds have wintered on coast), Little Ringed Plover, Ringed Plover, Grey Plover, Lapwing, Knot, Sanderling, Little Stint, Temminck's Stint (scarce), Curlew Sandpiper (annual, but fluctuates), Purple Sandpiper, Dunlin, Ruff, Jack Snipe, Snipe, Black-tailed Godwit, Bar-tailed Godwit, Whimbrel (not after October), Curlew, Spotted Redshank, Redshank, Greenshank, Green Sandpiper, Wood Sandpiper, Common Sandpiper, and Turnstone. (Smaller waders may appear in July and between then and October there is always a chance of an American vagrant turning up.) Arctic Skua, Great Skua, Pomarine Skua (occasionally), Little Gull, Sandwich Tern, Common Tern, Little Tern (not after August), Black Tern (possible on the reserve and the sea), Short-eared Owl, Rock Pipit (from October), Twite (from October) and Snow Bunting (from September).

Scolt Head Island and Brancaster area

Map 5

Species

In 1923 Scolt Head Island was one of the earliest nature reserves to be established on the Norfolk coast. It was immortalised by the first volunteer watcher Miss E. L. Turner who wrote a graphic description of the island in her book *Bird Watching on Scolt Head* which was published in 1928. The island is now partly owned by the National Trust and the Norfolk Naturalists' Trust, and was leased to the Nature Conservancy Council in 1953 to be declared a national nature reserve in the following year. For the birdwatcher the main attraction on this island of 1,820 acres (728 ha) is the large colonies of nesting terns and plovers in May and June. Access on the island is restricted near the main breeding colonies of course, but there is plenty to see with up to 3,000 pairs of Sandwich Terns and up to 300 pairs of Common Terns in peak years. Breeding waders include Redshank, Oyster-catcher and Ringed Plover. Turnstone, Dunlin and Bar-tailed Godwit can be found along the salt-water creeks or on the shore. There are many pairs of Shelduck, and some Little Terns also nest. Breeding passerines are few, but include Linnet, Meadow Pipit and Reed Bunting. With some of the highest sand dunes on the Norfolk coast there are unrivalled views over the mainland separated by Brancaster Harbour and Norton Creek.

Sandwich Tern. Breeding colonies on the Norfolk and Suffolk coasts

A maze of saltmarsh creeks were aptly dubbed the jig-saw marsh by Miss Turner and no attempt should be made to explore these potentially dangerous water-ways. For the all-round naturalist, Scolt Head offers many hours of exciting discoveries. Plant succession in the formation of saltmarshes and sand dunes is particularly fascinating. A barren shingle-ridge may initially be colonised by sand couch grass which exists on nutrients provided by the tideline deposits. Rain or dew on the stone surfaces provide moisture while the extensive root systems provide stability in this harsh environment. As the shingle-ridges build up, other plants such as saltwort and sea rocket may gain a foothold in the sand accumulations. When the ridge is above tidal inundations, marram grass becomes established and is very soon the dominant plant, thriving just as long as wind blown sand continues to be deposited. Once the mobility of a dune lessens and new dunes shield it from the blowing sand, other plants such as sand-sedge, sea bindweed and various grasses begin to take over. An older dune may be further colonised by ragwort, hounds tongue, bramble, wild privet, elder, mosses and lichens.

In the spring, patches of pink sea-thrift brighten the edge of the dunes while from July the saltings become a haze of purple sea lavender. The sea holly attracts a host of insects to its steely blue blossoms, while later in the season, the sea aster offers nectar to late butterflies such as Small Tortoiseshells or the immigrant Painted Lady and Red Admiral.

During the autumn months Scolt Head undoubtedly plays host to vast numbers of migrant passerines. Miss Turner, writing in 1924, records sightings of Black Redstarts, Bluethroats, and Red-backed Shrikes. However, Scolt Head remains pretty inaccessible outside the summer tourist season when a daily boat service is operated. Visitors should never attempt to negotiate the creeks and mudflats to get out to, or from, the island at low tide. Dangerous, swiftly flowing tides can, without

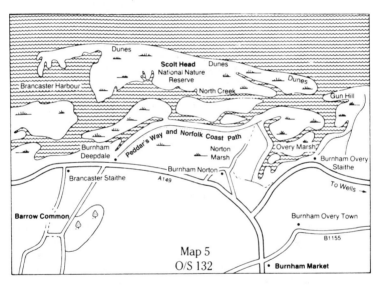

Map 5
O/S 132

warning, seal off the deeper creeks. On the whole it is better to enjoy a summer trip to the island and explore more easily accessible coastal points for autumn migrants.

Norton Marsh On the landward side of Scolt Head a seawall runs from Burnham Deepdale with creeks on one side and cultivated fields on the other. The wall goes round to Burnham Norton. This is an extremely interesting area during the winter months when roving flocks of finches and buntings might be encountered on the, as yet, unspoilt grazing pastures of Norton Marsh. The adjoining creeks, too, are worth a look for various diving duck and grebe occur there on the high tides. However, the Norton Marshes have become a focal point for birders wishing to meet up with the elusive and nondescript Lapland Bunting which particularly favours this area during the winter months from late October to early March. Numbers fluctuate from year to year, but over 100 birds have wintered there, often in near company with hundreds of Yellow, Corn and Reed Buntings.

Barrow Common At the top of a steep hillside just inland from Brancaster, Barrow Common is very attractive to the naturalist. Birdlife is varied in summer with Linnets, Redpolls, Yellow Buntings, Whitethroats and Lesser Whitethroats, Garden Warblers, Blackcaps and occasionally Nightingales to be seen. Red-backed Shrikes used to nest and passage birds may still turn up. Stray Common Buzzards turn up from time to time, but it is unlikely that they will ever establish a foothold in Norfolk while gamekeeping thrives. Adjoining minor public roadways at the back of the common. There are private woodlands which harbour woodpeckers, Nuthatches, Treecreepers and Long-eared Owls. A Golden Oriole was once heard in song there. The winter months can be birdless on the common, but Hen Harriers do hunt the area and Great Grey Shrikes have wintered for several weeks.

Equally uninspiring in winter is the large area of farmland behind Brancaster, but in a radius of about 8 miles (12.8 km) inland large numbers of Pink-footed Geese can often be found between November and March. There is no 'usual spot' as these geese like to forage during the day on unploughed fields where sugar beet, carrots or potatoes have been grown. At dusk they flight out to roost on coastal sand banks and return early the next morning. Again, there are no routine flight lines due to so many controlling factors. (Farming activities may put them off one area for a while.) Wind or weather can alter feeding areas and wildfowlers on the coast may persuade them to change routes. There is no more wild sound in birdlife than the gabble of a thousand Pink-footed Geese as they cross the coastal marshes at dusk in 'V' formation. In foggy weather they become bemused and often fly around in circles overhead until the skies clear and they can see that it is safe to land.

SCOLT HEAD ISLAND

Timing

There are regular boat services from Brancaster Staithe from about April until early September. Best time for visiting the tern colonies is May and June. Boats usually leave about two or three hours before high tide. If the boat service is still available it is worth exploring in August for passerine migrants which are most likely to occur in east or north-east winds. Birders should *never* attempt to cross to and from the island over the mudflats and creeks.

Norton Marshes No particular time of day, but the mornings are probably best if one is searching for Lapland Buntings on a short winter's day. Look out for Hen Harriers and Short-eared Owls at this time. Wildfowling occurs in the area so do remember that no shooting takes place on Sundays and marshes are, therefore, that much quieter.

Barrow Common Early morning is best for spring bird song. Weekends usually bring more people and plenty of dogs. In winter any time of the day is suitable, though Hen Harriers and Short-eared Owls may be more active in the late afternoon. For exploring surrounding agricultural lands for Pink-footed Geese the middle of the day is best, but many fields are surprisingly hidden by contours; it could therefore be worth taking up a vantage point at dawn or dusk to discover the routes to those fields being frequented.

Scolt Head Island

Access

By boat from Brancaster Staithe up to two or three hours before high tide between April and September. Make enquiries at the quay. It is sign-posted off the A149 in the centre of the village. Scolt Head Island has a full-time warden (in summer, assistants as well) and there is restricted access in the breeding season and no dogs allowed. Please read the reserve signs.

Norton Marshes Leave the A149 at either of two small villages, Burnham Deepdale or Burnham Norton. They are about 2½ miles (4 km) apart and east of Brancaster Staithe. Park, where possible, off the minor road on the marsh side of the A149 and join the Long Distance Coastal Footpath which eventually links the two villages after winding out and round the marshes.

Barrow Common Leave the A149 at Brancaster Staithe by the Jolly Sailors pub. Barrow Common is on either side of the road about ¾ mile (1.2 km) inland. Explore the narrow unclassified roads in the area for winter geese.

Scolt Head Island

Calendar

April–August Shelduck, Eider, Common Scoter, Oyster-catcher, Ringed Plover, Grey Plover, Sanderling, Bar-tailed Godwit, Redshank, Turnstone, Arctic Skua, Sandwich Tern, Common Tern, Little Tern. Could be a chance of unusual drift migrant in April and August.

Norton Marshes
December–February Brent Geese, Shelduck, Wigeon, Red-breasted Merganser, Goldeneye (last two species possibly in creeks), Hen Harrier, Golden Plover, Short-eared Owl, Twite, Lapland Bunting, Snow Bunting, Yellow Bunting, Reed Bunting and Corn Bunting. Always a general selection of commoner birds outside this season, but not noted for anything in particular.

Barrow Common

Calendar

Resident Stock Dove, Tawny Owl, Long-eared Owl, Green Woodpecker, Great Spotted Woodpecker, Goldcrest, Marsh Tit, Coal Tit, Long-tailed Tit, Nuthatch and Treecreeper.

December–February Pink-footed Geese, Hen Harrier, Golden Plover, Woodcock and Great Grey Shrike.

March–May Tree Pipit, Nightingale (not regular), Lesser Whitethroat, Whitethroat, Garden Warbler, Blackcap, Chiff-chaff, Willow Warbler, Spotted Flycatcher, Redpoll.

June–July Usually very quiet at this time, but chance of Common Buzzard.

August–October As for June-July.

HOLKHAM AND WELLS
Map 6
Species

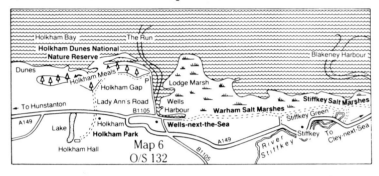

Amazingly, up to the late 1960s the Holkham to Wells area was virtually unknown except to a handful of botanists, entomologists and a few local birdwatchers who mainly visited the area in hard winter weather when interesting grebes and ducks could be seen. Crossbills were known to frequent the pine woods, but few birders ever explored the extraordinary 3 mile (4.8 km) stretch of pine trees extending westwards from the Wells beach road. Perhaps the better known and long established attractions of Blakeney Point and Cley always received undivided attention during the autumn months.

However, in the autumn of 1968 three extremely rare Asiatic birds were discovered in the Holkham–Wells area, the Arctic Warbler, Dusky Warbler and Radde's Warbler; and from that time onwards, the area was firmly on the ornithological map, with ever increasing numbers of bird-watchers coming to this unique area.

From 1971 a long list of rare migrants included Rose-coloured Starling, Serin, Woodchat Shrike, Bonelli's Warbler, Rustic Bunting, yet more Radde's and Dusky Warblers, Roller and Pallas's Warbler. In 1975 the fame of the pine woods was permanently sealed with the appearance of Olive-backed Pipit, Rosefinch, Black-throated Thrush and still more records of Dusky, Radde's and Pallas's Warbler. In 1989 the first American Red-breasted Nuthatch for Britain occurred. Few birders neglect these woods nowadays! Perhaps, as a result, there is less interest and pressure on Blakeney Point?

In 1967 the Nature Conservancy Council established the Holkham National Nature Reserve comprising a vast area of over 4,000 acres (1,600 ha) of coastal marsh and dune owned by the Holkham Estate and 5,400 acres (2,160 ha) of inter-tidal sand and mudflats between Overy Staithe and Blakeney which were leased from the Crown Commissioners. It is a unique area safeguarded for wildlife through the generosity of the Earl of Leicester whose ancestors progressively drained and reclaimed natural saltmarshes to the west of Wells to create marshland pastures. On the seaward side of this newly reclaimed land Corsican Pines were planted from 1850 onwards to afford protection from blowing sand and tidal surges. Similar reclamation schemes were attempted (some pine trees still remain) to the east of Wells, but were abandoned long ago to leave one of the largest natural saltmarshes in England.

National attention focused on the Parrot Crossbill which bred for the first recorded time in Britain in 1984 (and again in 1985) at the Wells end of the pine trees. The Common Crossbill (which also breeds here), attracts most birders from February onwards. The Wells end of the pinewoods is a very popular spot even on weekends throughout the winter months. At the end of the mile-long beach road from Wells Quay there is a large car park, toilets and a well-kept caravan site and an ice cream stall – an environment which did not unduly disturb the nesting Parrot Crossbills! (In this most unromantic of settings one of the authors has sat snugly in a car, licking an ice-cream and watching these rare birds drink at a puddle in the gravel roadway!)

In spite of holiday attractions Holkham and Wells is a fascinating area all year round with perhaps June and July being the least rewarding months for birders. In the first two months of the year the flocks of wild geese reach their highest numbers of the winter when several hundred Pink-footed and White-fronted Geese may be present as well as one or two thousand Brent Geese. Best viewing points are not so much from the pine woods, but from the A149 main coast road at Holkham looking northwards across the farmlands (parking not now allowed beside the A149). At times Barnacle Geese flocks arrive in the New Year if the weather becomes hard on the Continent, or in north-west Scotland. The rare Lesser-whitefronted Goose has been seen while a Red-breasted Goose stayed in the area for several weeks one winter. After the end of the shooting season (31 January) Brent Geese become very tame and can be seen at close range from Wells Quay where the odd Shag may also winter. It is interesting to note that in this area, for almost 100 years prior to the last war, up to 8,000 Pink-footed Geese wintered here, but their numbers rapidly declined during and after it. Only in recent years have numbers here and in West Norfolk started to rise again.

In hard weather Goosanders also may arrive. They head for the lake in Holkham Park which is not part of the Holkham Nature Reserve although considerate and careful birdwatchers are sometimes allowed to visit both park and lake if permission is requested beforehand. There is a large flock of Canada Geese and usually a few Great-crested Grebes to be seen on the lake and in recent years numbers of Cormorants have made a winter roost there. A small feral population of Egyptian Geese breed in the area and Kingfishers are seen quite often.

Other winter attractions of the shore and marshlands are flocks of roaming Snow Buntings, one or two Short-eared Owls and the Hen Harrier; while there is always a possibility of seeing a Peregrine. Goose numbers diminish quickly during March, but the first Chiff-chaffs arrive and a splendid drake Garganey may put in an appearance on the Holkham Park Lake. At this time, in recent years, a few Hawfinches have been observed in the tops of hornbeam trees at the main entrance to Holkham Park and in pine trees at the end of the private roadway to Holkham Gap. As usual at the end of winter outgoing visitors or north-ward travelling migrants may make a brief appearance and this area often produces a Rough-legged Buzzard or Common Buzzard. One or two magnificent Cranes, too, have been sighted; and once, a White Stork frequented the farmlands. On another occasion a Red Kite spent some time near inland woods.

In April the smaller winter migrants departing may congregate in their hundreds amongst the pine trees and these may include Siskins, Bramblings and Redpolls. Other spring migrants to occur at this time include Firecrests, Ring Ouzels, Redstarts, Tree Pipits, Blackcaps, Grasshopper Warblers, Pied Flycatchers and Whinchats. Along the shore, the first Common Terns and a few waders such as Greenshank and Whimbrel may be seen. From the end of April to May there is a chance to observe much rarer migrants. Firecrests and Ring Ouzels may still be present while a Wryneck may be watched searching for insects on the bare sand dunes. Wood Warblers often occur on passage, but they do not stay to nest. A rare Red-breasted Flycatcher has turned up on more than one occasion and this is unusual in the spring as it is more regular as an autumn drift migrant. Passing Montagu's Harriers have been recorded in May and in this month in 1984 there was a sad, but incredible record of a White-tailed Sea Eagle being found dying of gun-shot wounds. It had been ringed as a nestling on 5 June 1983 at Warder See, Schleswig-Holstein in West Germany. It was a tragic end for a magnificent bird which, surprisingly enough, had only been seen by one or two birders before it was shot.

Red-breasted Flycatcher

June and July are usually quiet months in birdwatching activity, but a naturalist will find plenty of interest in the plant and animal life while there is still always the chance of seeing Crossbills.

The migration scene progresses apace from August when the first Pied Flycatchers and Redstarts may arrive on the first east wind. Icterine Warblers, Barred Warblers, Wrynecks and Red-backed Shrikes are fairly regular migrants in single numbers at this time. Offshore the first Arctic Skuas and sometimes Manx Shearwaters are seen with strong on-shore wind in this month and the next. Red-breasted Flycatchers often appear in September when large falls of Redstarts, Flycatchers and leaf warblers may still occur. From mid-month, the most beautiful Yellow-browed Warbler can almost be guaranteed, provided the weather is fine with a light south or south-easterly wind. At any time in September an early Snow Bunting may appear, but it is usually October before numbers of other winter visitors such as Redwings and Fieldfares begin to appear. On east wind days swarms of Goldcrests may arrive to add to the difficulty of picking out rarities. Inevitably, a Great Grey Shrike also appears and one or two Honey Buzzards have been noted. (They have usually given good displays to observers. There was one classic sighting of a Honey Buzzard which was watched at a range of a few yards as it was completely engrossed in digging out a wasps' nest.)

Offshore in Holkham Bay during suitable weather conditions there may be Guillemots, Razorbills, Red-necked Grebes, Slavonian Grebes, Black-throated Divers, and Goldeneye present in very small numbers. However, in this area diminutive waifs wind-drifted from Siberia provide the ultimate birdwatching thrill so the bushes are carefully watched after a blow from the north or east. Both Radde's and Dusky Warblers have now occurred several times and there can be no other mainland spot in Britain where these rare skulking vagrants can be watched. Add for good measure a tiny Pallas's Warbler glowing like a jewel with yellow rump patch as it hovers at the end of a branch much in the manner of a Goldcrest. The Pallas's Warbler has 'everything'. In addition to the rump patch, it has conspicuous double yellowish wing-bars, a long super-ciliary, a yellow crown stripe, rarity status, and the distinction of being the smallest leaf warbler of the Palearctic region. Add to that the mind-bending feat of it even appearing in this country thousands of miles from its nearest breeding territory in southern Siberia and its wintering quarters in south-east Asia and you have an avian super star!

At this time Bramblings, Siskins and Redpolls re-appear amongst the pines although greater numbers of Siskins at least usually appear in the spring. November gales from the sea may bring a further assort-ment of wildfowl and some Long-tailed Duck or Great Northern Divers, in addition to increases in the numbers of Red-necked and Slavonian Grebes, Goldeneye and Brent Geese. Between now and December goose numbers increase with many more Pink-feet and some White-fronts arriving, while Holkham Bay still shelters numbers of grebes, divers and auks. Quite often a few Hawfinches begin to gather in small parties in the Park hornbeams where they may stay until the spring.

Lodge Marsh to the east of Wells Harbour channel is dangerously attractive to the naturalist. Several lives have been lost in the area over the years and anyone contemplating visiting the area should arm them-selves with sound local knowledge beforehand and contact one of the summer wardens who guard the remote terneries on the far sands. The deep saltwater creeks look easy enough to cross when empty, but glutinous mud can trap the unwary as the creeks insidiously fill on the rising tide. Remnants of pine afforestation on Lodge Marsh undoubtedly receive a good sprinkling of migrants; and once, a Roller spent some time there. Numbers of Common, Sandwich and Little Terns nest on the distant shingle banks in company with Oyster-catchers and Ringed Plovers. It is more prudent perhaps to follow the Long Distance Footpath

Ringed Plover at nest

on the south side of the marsh which runs for nearly 4 miles (6.4 km) from Wells to Stiffkey and then continues for about another 6 miles (9.6 km) to Cley and Blakeney.

Timing

Any time of the day really, but in the early morning it is better to walk westwards through the woods, and vice-versa in the evening. The region is of interest all the year round, but there is less avian interest in June and July. Migration is best observed with, or after, an east or north wind in late April, May, August, September and October, though once a good fall of migrants has occurred, there may be many birds in the area irrespective of wind conditions. Autumn thrush and finch movements are not dependent on east winds however, and often take place in light to moderate westerly winds. This is a popular holiday area so there are likely to be plenty of folk around at Bank Holidays and any weekend. High tide is best for watching Holkham Bay.

Access

The two main access points for Holkham-Wells are from Wells itself and from the A149 at Holkham.

From Wells take the 1 mile (1.6 km) beach road which terminates in a car park (fee payable), toilets, public information centre and caravan site. Look at the Quayside in Wells for Brent Geese or Shags, and the harbour channel for grebes, divers and auks. Explore any of the woodland paths (unless marked private). An area known to bird watchers as The Dell is an excellent spot for watching, with most of the rare warblers being seen in the clumps of birch trees there. From the car park walk past the boating lake and then through a swing gate. Further along westwards a small woodland pool often attracts Crossbills and many migrants. The shoreline is attractive with wintering Snow Buntings, while Holkham Bay is worth watching for divers, auks and grebes.

From the A149 at Holkham, on the marsh side of the road, turn down the private Lady Ann's Road and seek permission to birdwatch from the Gatehouse by the large iron gates. For winter goose watching use Lady Ann's Road and examine the fields on either side. Parking is now prohibited beside the A149 between Holkham village and the point where the B1155 joins the A149. The western end of Holkham Reserve can also be explored from Burnham Overy Staithe village where a seawall runs for 1 mile (1.6 km) alongside Overy Creek towards Gun Hill. The creek is worth watching for winter grebes while the sand dunes and adjoining marshes are good for harriers and Short-eared Owls. For the marshes of the Holkham Reserve east of Wells take the Long Distance Footpath on the east side of Wells Quay. (Parking allowed by Wells Quay, but there is a fee.) The minor roads round the walled perimeter of Holkham Park are worth exploring for woodland birds during the spring and winter months; while the woodlands in the Park are private many birds can be seen and heard from the adjoining roads.

Calendar

Resident Little Grebe, Great-crested Grebe (on the lake), Grey Heron (a small heronry in the Park), Greylag Goose, Canada Goose, Egyptian Goose (in the Park and on adjoining marshes), Tufted Duck, Kestrel, Red-legged Partridge, Grey Partridge, Lapwing, Snipe, Woodcock (also winter visitor), Redshank, Stock Dove, Barn Owl, Tawny Owl, Kingfisher, Green Woodpecker, Great Spotted Woodpecker, Lesser Spotted Woodpecker, Skylark, Goldcrest (also an influx in October), Marsh Tit, Coal Tit, Nuthatch, Treecreeper, Tree Sparrow, Redpoll, Common Crossbill, Parrot Crossbill bred in 1984 and 1985 and may well do so again.

December–February Red-throated Diver, Black-throated Diver, Great Northern Diver, Great-crested Grebe (winter visitor on sea), Red-necked Grebe, Slavonian Grebe, Black-necked Grebe (odd birds are still seen offshore or in the harbour channel), Cormorant, Shag, Bean Goose, Pink-footed Goose, White-fronted Goose, Brent Goose, Shelduck, Wigeon, Gadwall, Teal, Shoveler, Pochard, Long-tailed Duck, Goldeneye, Red-breasted Merganser, Goosander (in hard weather on sea or lake), Hen Harrier, Merlin, Peregrine, Oyster-catcher, Grey Plover, Dunlin, Bar-tailed Godwit, Curlew, Turnstone, Glaucous Gull, Guillemot, Razorbill, Black Guillemot (very scarce, but has wintered in sea area), Puffin (also very scarce), Short-eared Owl, Rock Pipit, Lapland Bunting and Snow Bunting.

March–May Some seabirds, geese and duck are still left in March depending on the mildness of the season. Shelduck, Garganey (the lake is the best site), Marsh Harrier, Rough-legged Buzzard, Oyster-catcher, Ringed Plover, Grey Plover, Dunlin, Bar-tailed Godwit, Whimbrel, Curlew, Greenshank, Green Sandpiper, Common Sandpiper, Turnstone, Sandwich Tern, Common Tern, Little Tern, Black Tern (not before the end of April), Hoopoe (very occasionally in the dunes), Tree Pipit, Yellow Wagtail, Redstart, Whinchat, Wheatear (latter two species passage migrants), Ring Ouzel, Grasshopper Warbler, Sedge Warbler, Reed Warbler, Lesser Whitethroat, Whitethroat, Garden Warbler, Blackcap, Wood Warbler (passage migrant), Chiff-chaff, Willow Warbler, Firecrest, Spotted Flycatcher, Pied Flycatcher, Brambling and Siskin.

June–July Marsh Harrier, Oyster-catcher, Ringed Plover, Sandwich Tern, Common Tern, Little Tern, Sedge Warbler, Reed Warbler, Lesser Whitethroat, Garden Warbler, Blackcap, Willow Warbler, Chiff-chaff and Spotted Flycatcher. Rather a quiet period.

August–November Red-throated Diver, Black-throated Diver, Great Northern Diver, Great-crested Grebe, Red-necked Grebe, Slavonian Grebe, Manx Shearwater (in storm conditions), Gannet, Bewick's Swan, Whooper Swan (passage birds of the last two species end in October to early November), Brent Goose, Wigeon, Teal, Long-tailed Duck, Goldeneye, Red-breasted Merganser, Honey Buzzard (scarce visitor in early autumn), Hen Harrier, Rough-legged Buzzard, Merlin, Peregrine (winter divers, grebes, geese, duck, hawks not usually before October), Oyster-catcher, Ringed Plover, Grey Plover, Sanderling, Dunlin, Bar-tailed Godwit, Whimbrel, Curlew, Greenshank, Green Sandpiper, Common Sandpiper, Turnstone, Pomarine Skua, Arctic Skua, Great Skua, Little Gull, Sandwich Tern, Common Tern, Black Tern, Guillemot, Razorbill, Little Auk (in October gales), Puffin (very scarce), Short-eared Owl, Wryneck, Tree Pipit, Black Redstart, Redstart, Whinchat, Wheatear, Ring Ouzel, Icterine Warbler, Barred Warbler, Lesser Whitethroat,

Whitethroat, Garden Warbler, Blackcap, Arctic Warbler, Yellow-browed Warbler, Pallas's Warbler, Dusky Warbler, Bonelli's Warbler (all last four named warblers are extremely rare), Wood Warbler, Firecrest, Spotted Flycatcher, Red-breasted Flycatcher (rare, but fairly regular), Pied Flycatcher, Red-backed Shrike, Great Grey Shrike (usually October), Brambling, Siskin, Lapland Bunting and Snow Bunting.

Stiffkey and Morston Marshes

Maps 6 and 7

Species

The villages of Stiffkey and Morston lie about 2 miles (3.2 km) apart and the old undisturbed saltmarshes to the north of the A149 can be explored from either village with access to the Long Distance Footpath. This area has, perhaps, been rather neglected by birders in favour of the better known attractions at Wells to the west and Blakeney Point and Cley to the east. However, it is a most valuable area for wintering wildfowl, nesting species and has an excellent saltmarsh flora. In addition some very good migrants have been seen here with the most notable being the Little Bunting; one autumn a single Little Bunting stayed for several days.

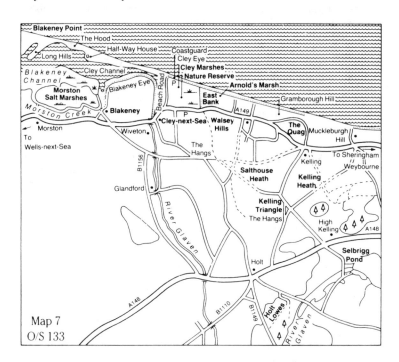

Eastwards from Stiffkey a narrow belt of trees (private) skirts the footpath and these are worth looking at in the autumn months when good numbers of migrants are likely to occur including Wrynecks, Icterine and Barred Warblers, which have been observed from the footpath. On passage Wheatears and Whinchats are plentiful along the track which runs at the landward edge of vast saltmarshes along to Morston Quay. This path is well worth exploring at any time of the year, for wildfowl, raptors and passerine migrants. During the winter months there are good numbers of Redshank (also breeding pairs in summer), Wigeon, Teal and Brent Geese. Hen Harriers and Short-eared Owls may be seen quartering the marshes. The Morston marshes used to be a stronghold of the Lapland Bunting and some birds can still be found there during the winter months, frequenting areas of saltmarsh where there is a succession to sea grass; or on the nearby arable fields which can be observed from the footpath. One or two tracks nearer to Morston lead out to the edge of the saltmarsh and overlook the channel behind the spit of Blakeney Point. As always when following marshland tracks ensure that your retreat is not going to be cut off by the incoming tide. A seemingly dry creek at low tide can fill very quickly as the tide turns. It can also fill from an inland direction creeping round in circuitous channels. From the edge of the channel large numbers of Brent Geese and Wigeon can be observed.

Brent Geese. They are changing their winter habitat from intertidal zones to fresh grazing marshes

In the spring, follow the Long Distance Footpath westwards from Morston keeping a lookout for open ground birds such as Black Redstarts, Whinchats, Wheatears and Ring Ouzels. Hoopoes have occasionally been seen. From Morston Quay another good section of the Footpath can be followed to Blakeney Quay along the landward side of the marshes and the deep Morston Creek. Blakeney Quay can often provide one or two interesting birds, but it is a very popular spot during the holiday season, and on most weekends. Black Redstarts have been seen by the Quay and, in winter, a diver or grebe may appear on the tide. However, it is more rewarding in autumn and winter to explore the pastures, fields and marshes of Blakeney Eye by following a footpath on the seawall from the east side of Blakeney Quay. This runs out to the edge of Cley Channel and from there it curves round to link up with the Cley West Bank. Again it is a region that has not been too well watched, but there can be few birders in Britain who do not know the path now, after the appearance of the famous Little Whimbrel there in August 1985. The discovery of this great rarity came after watchers were fanning out from Cley in search of the equally rare Greater Sand Plover which had been seen at several different spots in the area.

In the reed-fringed pool immediately east of Blakeney Quay Water Rails are regular winter visitors and a Spotted Crake has been noted in autumn. The fields on the right hand side of the path from Blakeney Quay are good for Curlew and Golden Plover in winter. Wheatears come through on passage and Whinchats occur frequently. On the left of the bank by the north-east corner of the path, Cley Channel can be watched without any danger of being cut off by the rising tide. Flocks of waders are often pushed across the mudflats by the tide to congregate not far off the bank; and there is always a good chance of seeing a diver or grebe in the channel especially during late autumn.

Timing

The whole area is worth a visit at any time of the year though bear in mind the popularity of Blakeney in the tourist season and a strong local wildfowling element during the winter months. The middle of the day may be the best time, but high tide, or just before, is best for watching the creeks and channels.

Access

Turn off the west edge of Stiffkey village down the road called Greenway to a campsite and car park at the end. Pick up the Long Distance Footpath, running eastwards for 2½ miles (4 km) to Morston Quay where there is a park and toilets. Alternatively, turn off in Morston village to quay and car park and explore along the path westwards. In a field on your left there is a 'historic mound' where, in 1888, between 80 and 85 Pallas's Sandgrouse were congregating during the spectacular invasion of these strangers from the Russian Steppes.

From the Morston Car park the Long Distance Footpath can be picked up again on the east side of the quay and this runs for about 1½ miles (2.4 km) to Blakeney Quay where there is another car park (fee payable) and toilets. From Blakeney Quay the footpath runs along the seawall, out around Blakeney Eye to link up with the Cley West bank making a walk of about 3 miles (4.8 km). Stout footwear and warm clothing are essential in winter as all these footpaths are liable to flooding and likely to be very muddy at times. On the highest tides make sure that your vehicle is well above the high tide mark as high tides have been known to spill well over the Blakeney Quay! The area, including the Stiffkey and Morston Marshes, has been safeguarded by the National Trust and their bye-laws should be read and observed.

Calendar

Resident Kestrel, Red-legged Partridge, Grey Partridge, Oyster-catcher, Ringed Plover, Lapwing, Redshank and Skylark.

December–February Brent Goose, Shelduck, Wigeon, Teal, Red-breasted Merganser, Eider, Scoter, Goldeneye (last four species sometimes seen in the channels), Hen Harrier, Merlin, Peregrine (a very regular wintering area 25 years ago and this species is now re-appearing at many of its old winter haunts), Water Rail (by fresh or brackish pools), Ringed Plover, Golden Plover, Grey Plover, Dunlin, Snipe, Bar-tailed Godwit, Curlew, Turnstone, Barn Owl, Short-eared Owl, Rock Pipit, Stonechat and Lapland Bunting.

March–May Shelduck, Marsh Harrier (passage migrants), Grey Plover, Bar-tailed Godwit, Whimbrel, Curlew, Turnstone (note that wintering waders often remain until April-May), Sandwich Tern, Common Tern, Little Tern, Short-eared Owl (has bred in the area), Yellow Wagtail, Black Redstart, Whinchat, Wheatear and Ring Ouzel.

June–July Plenty of gulls and terns and nesting waders, but otherwise quiet.

August–November Red-throated Diver, Great-crested Grebe, Slavonian Grebe, Red-necked Grebe (possible in deeper channels), Brent Goose (from late October), Wigeon, Teal, Eider, Common Scoter, Red-breasted Merganser, Hen Harrier, Merlin, Peregrine, Water Rail, Spotted Crake, Ringed Plover, Golden Plover, Grey Plover, Dunlin, Snipe, Bar-tailed Godwit, Whimbrel, Curlew, Short-eared Owl, Wryneck, Rock Pipit, Black Redstart, Redstart, Whinchat, Stonechat, Wheatear, Ring Ouzel, Icterine Warbler, Barred Warbler, Great Grey Shrike, Brambling, Lapland Bunting and Little Bunting (on two occasions only).

BLAKENEY POINT

Map 7

Species

This peninsula of shingle and sand which extends westwards for over 3 miles (4.8 km) from Cley beach comprises some 1,300 acres (520 ha) which were acquired by the National Trust in 1912 which made it one of the first nature reserves to be safeguarded in Britain. It remains a most fascinating place and is unashamedly romantic on a high summer's day with the tide flowing swiftly and silently into the creeks edged with the grey-green sea purslane and bordered by saltings soon to be purple with sea lavender. There is the constant cry of terns, gulls and piping plovers mixed with the excited chattering of groups of school children on an educational visit to see this most famous of tern sanctuaries; yachts with blue and orange sails are at one with the green sea and the wide blue skies; holiday visitors – bare-foot-bikinied – disembark from the small motor boats that ply back and forth from Morston Quay; sandy 'blow outs' in the dunes reflecting a desert heat – with the white sands too hot for the unclad foot; all this is the 'smiling face' of Blakeney.

By contrast, an inclement day in late autumn can be dramatically grim, with scant shelter from the wind driven rain; everywhere silent and deserted with lowering grey skies merging with the foam capped waters as the tide races and hisses over the shingle-ridges and up the creeks. Blakeney in all its moods has something to offer the birdwatcher at almost any time.

The Point has a long and auspicious ornithological history, albeit a bloody one, for 40 or 50 years before it was purchased by the National Trust. This was the favourite resort of Victorian bird collectors, with many professional people travelling to Cley and Blakeney at the end of August for the traditional start of the autumn migration that, given the right weather conditions, would see thousands of migrants frequenting the area. Much as we may now decry the actions of the Victorians, it was the accepted thing then to shoot birds and mount them in glass cases. There were none of the modern aids available to them, such as prismatic binoculars, telescopes and pocket guides. Their maxim was: 'What's hit is history' and 'What's missed is mystery'! At any rate their records helped establish the fame of Blakeney Point. Two species added for the first time to the British List were Pallas's Warbler and the Yellow-breasted Bunting.

Blakeney Point is really the end of a great stony shingle-ridge which begins at Weybourne about 6 or 7 miles (10 km) to the east and runs along the edge of ornithologically rich marshlands until nearing the end of the Cley beach road. Here the peninsula begins, segregated on one side by the sea and the other by the Cley Channel and Blakeney Harbour. Because of its isolation and its almost complete separation from the mainland, Blakeney Point continues to receive and hold masses of wind-drifted small passerines whenever the autumn winds blow from the east or north. There is only one traditional way to search its length for birds and that is from the end of the Cley beach road. The approximate 3½ miles (5.6 km) to the far point can be one of the toughest bird walks in England. It is very easy to walk 15 miles (24 km) or more in one day if one adds up all the mileage involved in exploring creeks and dunes, to say nothing of the long stretches of deep shingle in which it seems, every stride forward goes back at least half! Add up the time, too, which is required to walk out exploring every likely spot and watching the sea every so often, or waiting for some interesting small bird to show itself from a dense patch of cover and it becomes obvious that a full day is needed to 'do' Blakeney properly. It offers a unique combination of sea watching and searching for migrant passerines perhaps not equalled anywhere else in Britain. Curiously enough, the old collectors almost always ignored the Vernal migration; and it must be admitted that even now spring passerine migrants can be pretty scarce, comprising not a fraction of 'the hordes' that can occur in autumn.

Nevertheless, Cley Bird Observatory which was in operation between 1949 and 1963 had Heligoland-type bird ringing traps sited on Cley beach and on the Point. These accounted for the first two spring and first autumn records of Sub-alpine Warblers for the county. A beautiful cock Red-spotted Bluethroat was caught and ringed in June 1954. Another curious phenomenon is that the Victorian collector would visit Blakeney in September or October in the almost certain hope of securing a Bluethroat for his cabinet. That pattern has changed with the different weather systems in the past 20 years and now Bluethroats are regular to the coastline in spring, but a very great rarity in the autumn months. Oddly, the Point does not seem to be a favoured spot for these resplendent spring Bluethroats, but is it perhaps because present-day bird watchers neglect this difficult to observe habitat?

Another change that has taken place with the shift in weather systems is that drift migration often occurs much earlier in the first few days of August if there is an east wind. Nearly everything depends on the winds and weather as the old gunners knew full well. There were many blank years recorded even in those days, when west winds blew strongly throughout the autumn and only waders appeared in any numbers. However, with an east wind which has been blowing for a couple of days in mid-September a pilgrimage out to Blakeney Point could be very rewarding.

Start off from the Cley car park as early as possible in the morning (most local hotels, guest houses, and bed-and-breakfast establishments in the area are well aware of and sympathetic to birders' habits!). Take your choice of walking on the left or right hand side of the shingle-spit. On the sea side the sea watching may be quite good, but you will miss all the 'bushes' and Cley Channel which are on the left side. Unless you are a confirmed sea watcher the bushes will exert their magnetic possibilities. Probably alternating passage from side to side of the shingle-ridge is a good compromise. If the tide is out there may be some quite firm short stretches of sand to walk upon. Because of the deeply shelving shoreline all the way from Weybourne the tide can only rise and fall against the steep shingle embankment. At the far Point the shore becomes shallower with a greater expanse of sand uncovered at low tide. The sea all along this deep water coastline can provide some extremely good watching with seabirds often close in or even over the beaches. Lines of Kittiwakes may be passing and in mid-September there will still be plenty of Sandwich and Common Terns which must all be examined. Sabine's Gull with its buoyant tern-like flight occurs regularly in very small numbers. All four skuas occur with the Long-tailed being the rarest. Gannets may be passing or fishing offshore, while the odd diver, grebe or auk will need to be examined with a telescope. This is a good coast for passing shearwaters at this time of year with Manx and Sooty being regularly noted. Other seabirds which can frequently be seen include Little, Mediterranean and Glaucous Gulls. Black Terns too, often appear, feeding as they pass, by dipping down to the surface of the sea.

A·R·W·

Arctic Skua chasing Common Tern

About half-way along the Point a stone house stands four-square to all the elements. It is not permanently occupied and the bushes in the vicinity of 'Half-way House' (as it is popularly known) often prove good. The bushes clothe the point for much of its length and are much the most important vegetation for migrant birds. As elsewhere along the Norfolk coast, the semi-evergreen shrubby sea-blite bushes flourish at the edge of the saltmarsh to provide sanctuary to many invertebrates and birds seeking shelter and food. Walk slowly along the outside edges watching every bird that flies. Binoculars must always be at the ready for often there is no more than a few seconds' glimpse of a bird as it flies ahead for a few yards, lands, and then dives quickly into cover again. Redstarts are common and their russet red tails provide easy identification. Wheatears may be plentiful and less shy, keeping more on open ground or along rabbit trackways. Often a Black Redstart is conspicuous too, on or nearby Half-way House. Hippolais, Phylloscopus and Sylvia warblers are less obliging and a patient wait may be required if you suspect that an Icterine or Barred Warbler has flipped into the sueda bushes a few yards ahead.

If there has been a large fall of small migrants you may have difficulty in deciding whether to push on to the end of the Point or not, but there are plenty of other good spots all the way to the old Lifeboat House which has long been converted to house an informative display, warden's quarters, and a small shop which sells guide books, postcards, confectionary, souvenirs and soft drinks during the summer months. It may be closed in late autumn so it is wise to carry your own provisions in that season.

Onwards from Half-way House a bulge of sand dunes on the estuary side of the Point is known as The Hood and this is where the old Cley Bird Observatory had a wooden ringing hut and Heligoland-type ringing traps. Keep a look out as you go for Wrynecks and Red-backed Shrikes which are both regular migrants in small numbers. In bad weather conditions both species can skulk in the sueda bushes. The majority of the shrikes that occur are the brown juveniles, but a splendid cock bird is sometimes seen. Amongst the sand dunes there may be the odd Ring Ouzel and Tree Pipit with several Whinchats perching on the fading stems of ragwort. Bluethroats were more usually in the densest clumps of sueda and were always one of the most difficult birds to flush – in complete contrast to the confiding behaviour of present day spring Bluethroats who often hop out into the open like tame Robins! There may be Willow Warblers, Chiff-chaffs, Whitethroats, Lesser Whitethroats, Garden Warblers, and Blackcaps all lurking amongst the bushes in addition to many Pied Flycatchers who are not quite so skulking unless the weather is really foul. Spotted Flycatchers occur quite commonly and there is always a good chance of meeting up with a Red-breasted Flycatcher. This tiny flycatcher is rather like a mini Garden Warbler with pure white panels at the base of its tail which it flirts conspicuously and it too, can be a very skulking bird. The end of the Point is a good area for them especially in old bush-lupin plants round the Tea House and in the 'Plantation' (a small clump of white poplar). More Black Redstarts may be found in this area frequenting bare dunes and in the area where there are some old seaside huts.

Later on in October the whole Point may be swarming with Goldcrests and Robins wind-drifted in from the Continent. During an unprecedented fall of Robins in October 1951 members of the Cley Bird Observatory caught and ringed over 100 birds in a few hours; every small bush held two or three dozen Robins 'ticking'. Later recoveries from these ringed birds indicated that their destination that autumn was really the shores of the Mediterranean. Great Grey Shrikes seldom fail to arrive with the falls of migratory birds and, more usually, they are seen on the farthest half of the Point. Small numbers of Firecrests may arrive in any month from August to October, but in an avalanche of small birds they are difficult to locate. October can also see multitudes of Blackbirds, Song Thrushes, Redwings and Fieldfares arriving while Woodcock can be flushed from the sand dunes. Long-eared Owls are regular in late October and there is always the chance of one of the Asiatic warblers such as Pallas's, Yellow-browed, Arctic or Greenish. If you have any energy left after reaching the far Point and the Tea House, there are always the adjoining mudflats to scan for waders and wildfowl!

From autumn and all through the winter Grey Plover, Bar-tailed Godwit, Dunlin, Turnstone, Curlew and Redshank are present. From October large numbers of Brent Geese in company with Wigeon frequent the harbour following the ebbing and flowing tides. Most birders make the trip out to Blakeney Point in the hope of seeing some of the rarer migrants for which it is justly famous. In addition to the more regular 'semi-rare' migrants there have been other remarkable and extremely rare vagrants recorded over the years: Little Shearwater, White-tailed Sea Eagle, Gyrfalcon, Lesser-crested Tern, Sooty Tern, Pallas's Sandgrouse (in the 1880s), Scops Owl, Desert Wheatear, Sub-alpine Warbler, Greenish Warbler, Arctic Warbler, Pallas's Warbler, Yellow-browed Warbler (although much more regular in recent years), Radde's Warbler, Dusky Warbler, Woodchat Shrike, Rose-coloured Starling, Two-barred Crossbill, Rosefinch, Rustic Bunting, Little Bunting and Yellow-breasted Bunting.

A trip out to see the Blakeney Point tern colony in summer is almost as traditional as the autumn migration pilgrimage. It is best to forget the long walk from Cley and enjoy the pleasures of a boat trip from Morston Quay (or Blakeney). You can return in comfort on the same tide or, if you wish to stay longer than the tide allows, you can wear old plimsolls to splodge back across the gluey mud on a well worn track. Boats are always waiting at the quayside about two hours before high water. It is about a 20 minute trip across to the Point although the boatman might make a slight deviation to 'show off' a party of common seals that may be resting on one of the sand-bars in the harbour. From the Quay, Morston Creek winds across saltings where on mud spits as yet uncovered by the tide there may be several Shelduck or Grey Plover. Common and Little Terns are intent on their fishing, plunging headlong into the creek after a rapid hover above their prey of shrimp or stickle-back. The creek soon gives way to the broad expanse of Blakeney Harbour with the long peninsula of the Point etched sharply in the morning sun and the old Lifeboat House a conspicuous landmark at its western extremity. Many more fishing terns now make their appearance with pied Oyster-catchers loudly 'kleep-kleeping' across the waters.

Oyster-catcher with young

The landing stage is at Pinchen's Creek named after Bob Pinchen – the first 'watcher' in 1901. From here you are requested to watch your step in following the path to the Lifeboat House which is a short distance away. Nest-scrapes, eggs and small chicks are so well camouflaged that it is easy to tread on them unless a careful watch is kept. Ringed Plovers pipe anxiously while Oyster-catchers add their clamour. The warden and his assistants are always ready to help you and answer questions. Any instructions they give should be respected – to help the National Trust protect this unique area of birds and plants. During the breeding season the main nesting areas are roped off and visitors are requested not to enter them. From the Lifeboat House there are paths leading to the observation hides which are all well sited for watching the terns going about their nesting affairs. Tern numbers have fluctuated over the years. The Sandwich Terns first bred in 1920 and have reached a maximum of 3,800 pairs in the last ten years. Common Terns were first recorded nesting in 1830. From a peak of over 2,000 pairs in the 1950s numbers have been declining in recent years and now number only between 200 and 300 pairs. Little Terns too, have declined with currently around 100 pairs. The Arctic Tern finds the southern limit of its British range in Norfolk with only a few sporadic pairs nesting. In recent years up to six pairs have nested on the Point.

Of the gull family the Black-headed is a common nesting bird with the babel from several hundred pairs adding to the general clamour. Other species to nest sporadically include a few pairs of Herring Gull, Common Gull and Lesser Black-backed Gull – all well outside their normal breeding range.

Timing

To see migrant passerines visit the Point from early August until early November when an east or north-east wind is blowing. Migrants can appear simultaneously with an east wind, but more often after a lapse of 24 hours. From Cley, better to start as early in the day as possible as there is so much ground to cover. Although not notable the spring migration may produce something in April and May when the wind is between the north and the south-east. The north-east wind in May 1985 that battered the Norfolk coast brought in unprecedented numbers of rare migrants including many Bluethroats to Blakeney Point. In fact, all along the coast it was more like an autumn fall. Bank holiday weekends in spring and autumn are always busier, especially with boat trips to the Point.

Access

From the Cley-next-Sea beach road car park it is an almost 4 miles (6.4 km) trudge out to the far Point. It is still the best way of searching the Point for passerine migrants, but the going is mainly loose shingle for much of the walk. Less tiring and time consuming is the boat trip from Morston Quay, about 2½ miles (4 km) from Cley, but there are serious disadvantages. In order to return by boat on the same tide there is, at most, three hours on the Point. In addition after the close of the holiday season in early September the boat service may not be so frequent or it may not run at all. It is, therefore, better to walk the Point from Cley from September onwards and use the boat service in summer to see the tern colonies, and in August if a migration is taking place. Even on a hot summer's day bear the fickle east coast in mind. Weather conditions can change so quickly. It may be shorts and shirts when you leave Morston, but sweaters and boots may be needed if sea mist suddenly rolls in. Because of the currents and deep gullies the National Trust advise that bathing is dangerous. There are toilets by the Lifeboat House and a 400 ft (210 m) walkway from here to the main observation hide. There are special facilities for disabled people, but they should contact the warden before a visit is made.

Calendar

Resident There are very few wholly resident birds. They are the Red-legged Partridge, Oyster-catcher, Redshank, Black-headed Gull and Skylark. The latter four species also increase as winter visitors.

December–February Brent Geese, Shelduck, Wigeon, Scaup, Eider, Common Scoter, Goldeneye, Red-breasted Merganser, Hen Harrier, Grey Plover, Dunlin, Bar-tailed Godwit, Curlew, Turnstone, Glaucous Gull, Shorelark, Rock Pipit, Hooded Crow and Snow Bunting. Most of these species may be seen into March.

April–June Shelduck, Ringed Plover, Common Gull, Lesser Black-backed Gull, Herring Gull (the latter three species of gulls breed, single numbers infrequently; otherwise passage migrants and winter visitors), Sandwich Tern, Common Tern, Little Tern, Arctic Tern, Meadow Pipit, Linnet and Reed Bunting.

July Many of the nesting waders and terns are still present, but will be dispersing with their young.

August–November Red-throated Diver, Black-throated Diver, Great Northern Diver, Great-crested Grebe, Red-necked Grebe, Slavonian Grebe (the last six species may occur in small numbers on the sea with larger numbers in on-shore gales), Cory's Shearwater, Sooty Shearwater, Manx Shearwater (some of the latter three species in gales from August to September), Storm Petrel, Leach's Petrel (both possible in late autumn gales), Gannet, Brent Goose, Wigeon, Scaup, Eider, Common Scoter, Goldeneye, Red-breasted Merganser, Hen Harrier, Merlin (the last two species from September), Peregrine, Grey Plover, Purple Sandpiper, Dunlin, Bar-tailed Godwit, Curlew, Turnstone, Pomarine Skua, Arctic Skua, Long-tailed Skua, Great Skua, Mediterranean Gull, Little Gull, Sabine's Gull (a good area for this delightful visitor from the north), Glaucous Gull, Kittiwake, Sandwich Tern, Common Tern, Arctic Tern, Black Tern, Guillemot, Razorbill, Little Auk (in October gales), Puffin (scarce), Short-eared Owl, Long-eared Owl, Hoopoe, Wryneck, Shorelark (from October it may winter), Tree Pipit, Rock Pipit (from October), Wren, Dunnock, Robin (these common birds are included because they do occur in the bushes with other less common migrants and it is always a thrill to see large numbers of migrating birds whether rare or common), Bluethroat, Black Redstart, Redstart, Whinchat, Wheatear, Ring Ouzel, Blackbird, Fieldfare, Song Thrush, Redwing (the last four species are common migrants arriving in October–November), Grasshopper Warbler, Sedge Warbler, Reed Warbler, Aquatic Warbler (rare) (Locustella and Acrocephalus warblers do occur as migrants amongst the bushes but in very small numbers), Icterine Warbler, Barred Warbler, Arctic Warbler, Pallas's Warbler, Yellow-browed Warbler, Radde's Warbler, Dusky Warbler, Bonelli's Warbler, Greenish Warbler (the last seven Phylloscopus Warblers are extremely rare), Chiffchaff, Willow Warbler, Goldcrest, Firecrest (rare, but regular), Spotted Flycatcher, Pied Flycatcher, Red-breasted Flycatcher, Red-backed Shrike, Great Grey Shrike, Hooded Crow, Chaffinch, Brambling, Crossbill, Rosefinch (rare), Lapland Bunting and Snow Bunting (may winter).

Cley-next-Sea
Map 7
Species

Cley marshes were acquired as a nature reserve in 1926 by the Norfolk Naturalists' Trust and, like Blakeney Point, they had a bloodthirsty history before coming into the conservation fold. The Cley and Salthouse marshes were regularly 'worked' by the same old Victorian bird collectors who went to Blakeney. Indeed, such was the interest in stuffed birds that a local man set up and ran his own taxidermist's shop in Cley village. He became famous for his skilled work and to this day the old shop is still known as 'Pashley's shop' by local people – although it is no longer a shop. The Cley area was also famed for its wildfowling, not only for local men shooting for their living, but also for many rich sportsmen. The few local hotels at Cley and Blakeney probably found a useful extension in their season by catering for them. Even as late as the 1950s the winter shooting was let on the Cley Reserve in order to obtain funds and the authors can well remember seeing one Royal Duke enjoying his pursuit.

However, apart from shooting on a few restricted areas (not on the reserve) and on some of the extensive privately owned Salthouse marshes, most of the region has now become a birdwatchers' paradise. More rare waders have been seen at Cley than anywhere else in Britain and a check list of the area (which includes Blakeney Point) records 325 species. The whole region now caters extensively for birdwatchers and tourists. Not only local hotels, but scores of other establishments such as furnished holiday homes and bed-and-breakfast houses have sprung up to meet the demand. Cley is usually pretty full in the autumn months and the appearance of a great rarity generally creates traffic problems for the local police while there may be queues to get into some of the hides! All this sounds a bit off-putting and not really quiet birdwatching, but in practice there is generally plenty of room and many nearby quiet areas which can be visited. Although the spring and autumn months are the best times, winter is pretty good with plenty of wildfowl and waders and not so many human visitors.

White-rumped Sandpiper and Pectoral Sandpiper

The aims of the Norfolk Naturalists' Trust are: 1) To encourage the breeding of marsh and reed birds. 2) To provide feeding and roosting habitats for passage migrants and overwintering species. 3) To provide bird watching facilities.

There can be no doubt of the continuing success of these policies.

The Avocet first returned to establish a breeding colony in Norfolk at Cley in 1977 and it is now well established. Bearded Tits have bred annually since the early 1950s and Black-tailed Godwits have made several attempts to found a colony. Bitterns are present and usually breed. A series of well planned observation hides on the marsh are well worth the permit fee and should not be missed at any time. First of all though the 'new' visitor may prefer to explore the rewarding periphery of the reserve where many good birds can be seen as well as offering a good general idea of the whole area.

Setting off from Cley village it is best to take the beach road from the A149 down to the shingle beach where there is a car park, coastguard look-out and seasonal tea-kiosk. Head eastwards along the seawall to join up with the East Bank – a high grassy seawall which is also the eastern boundary of the Cley Marshes Nature Reserve. This is probably one of the best known bird walks in Britain and it joins the A149 again east of Cley village and almost opposite another small reserve at Walsey Hills owned by the Norfolk Ornithologists' Association. The East Bank gives good general views over Cley Marsh on one side and over Arnold's Marsh on the other. The latter is also a small reserve of 29 acres (11.6 ha) and is owned by the National Trust, though managed by the Norfolk Naturalists' Trust. It was left to the nation by E. C. Arnold, an old sportsman and bird collector and has attracted a succession of rarities over the years. The first British record of a Semi-palmated Sandpiper occurred there in 1953, and so did the Ross's Gull which was a new county record there in 1984. Almost all the handful of Caspian Tern records have come from Arnold's Marsh. In winter, Smew, Long-tailed Duck and Goldeneye may occur; but generally the marsh has been allowed to deteriorate.

No permits are required for the East Bank footpath which is a public one. Very many birdwatchers have commenced their hobby from this bank by trying to identify the various species of waders which can be seen in all their confusing plumages. No essay on the birds of Cley could be complete without reference to one of Britain's top ornithologists and a leading bird artist, the late and still much lamented Richard Richardson (1922–77) who informally and spontaneously 'presided' over groups of birdwatchers watching for waders, passing migrants or sea watching during storms. It was a self-appointed unpaid task, which few people at that time could fill with such easy expertise and with the ability to pass on his encyclopaedic knowledge of birds. Young or old, duke or dustman, were all treated alike. If 'R.A.R.' was holding 'court' on the East Bank that was the place to be! His keen eye missed nothing and he was rarely unable to make certain identification. During his time as Honorary Warden of the Cley Bird Observatory (which he established) from 1949 to its close in 1963 he was responsible for the post-war rekindling of interest in birdwatching and not a few senior ornithologists of today were influenced and helped by his expertise and personality.

A drain which flows through the sluice gate near the seaward end of the East Bank marks the boundary of Arnold's Marsh and to the south side of this there are extensive private marshes. Good views over these can be enjoyed from the bank and many a good wader has been seen on a muddy drain known as The Serpentine. Where the East Bank joins the road again, it is always worthwhile walking a few yards eastwards to call in at Walsey Hills Watch Point where an old Royal Observer Corps Post on top of a gorse covered hill has been converted into an information centre by the Norfolk Ornithologists' Association. It is well patronised with a good exchange of bird news through the permanent warden on duty there. If you want to find out where the Snow Buntings are or when the Pectoral Sandpiper was last seen this is the place to go. Within its limitations it is also a very good spot for birds. Its comparatively lofty eminence gives a grand-stand view over the vast Cley and Salthouse Marshes. Migrant raptors such as Osprey, Marsh Harrier, Hen Harrier, Hobby and Sparrow Hawk are regularly seen. Several warblers and finches breed in the thicket of blackthorn, elder and bramble. Walsey Hills used to be the headquarters of the old Cley Bird Observatory and Heligoland traps and a ringing hut were sited there. This was the site where one of the only two Melodious Warbler records for the county was caught and ringed in 1957. It is still a very good spot for attracting the commoner and rarer passerine migrants. From Walsey Hills it is nearly 1 mile (1.6 km) back to the centre of Cley village with the coast road skirting the marshes owned by the Norfolk Naturalists' Trust. On the left of the road is their reserve centre where permits can be obtained for visiting the marsh. There are also public observation hides here.

Osprey

Although the Cley area has such an outstanding list of rare birds including seabirds, geese, duck, hawks and passerines it reigns supreme for the abundance and variety of its waders, which can be seen from the hides on the reserve. From the end of Marsh to the end of October there is plenty to see with the peak months being May, June, July, August and September. In the spring Avocets can be seen courting, making their nest scrapes and defending their territory against all comers. If a passing Marsh Harrier dares to invade their air space it is immediately mobbed by a host of angry Avocets, as well as Lapwings, Shelducks and Black-headed Gulls. Spoonbills often arrive in late spring to while away the summer months on the reserve. Bitterns can usually be heard booming and very occasionally this skulking resident may appear in front of one of the hides or it may be seen flying low from one clump of reeds to another. A nestling Bittern ringed at Cley in 1950 was found in Cheshire the following year. This species has greatly declined in Norfolk during the last 30 years and it may be absent from its known haunts in some years.

Bearded Tits breed annually in varying numbers and may be seen in the reed-beds from paths through the reserve or from the East Bank. Having three or four broods in a season this most beautiful of British birds is usually pretty active except in strong winds when they prefer to skulk in the shelter of the reeds. On calm bright mornings in late September or early October their remarkable irruption flights can be witnessed. After much musical chatter a dozen or twenty birds may spring out of the reed beds to gain height before setting off in swift arrow-like flight calling with characteristic 'pinging' notes. This irruption flight, often westwards, may take them for up to 30 miles (48 km) before they find a patch of reeds to drop into the rest awhile. If no reed beds are available, they will come down into the most uncharacteristic cover such as trees, bushes, and once, short vegetation on a cliff top! Ringing has shown that birds retrapped in Norfolk during the autumn and winter originated from Suffolk and Holland; while newly ringed birds have been found in Yorkshire. Another juvenile bird ringed in Kent was controlled at Salthouse and later at King's Lynn thus showing the traditional urge of young birds to wander.

Ruff are usually present in spring on the Cley marshes in varying numbers, frequently 50 or more birds. Breeding has been suspected, but never proved; which is not surprising, as only the inconspicuous brown female broods and raises the young. The promiscuous males don spring plumage of great diversity leading to the claim that no two spring Ruffs are alike! There can be almost any combination of buff, black, brown and white, with bars and streaks. The 'ruff' is usually of a different colour to the 'ear tuffs'. Identification is easy enough when the cocks are displaying or fighting amongst themselves, but many a birdwatching beginner has been 'stumped' by finding an oddly marked Ruff. Even larger numbers of Ruff may assemble on Cley Marsh in the autumn months when all their spring finery is lost.

The Black-tailed Godwit is another beautiful wader which is an annual spring visitor to Cley in small numbers. Breeding has been attempted on several occasions and, once, young were raised almost to the flying stage. This is another of the lost breeding species trying to make a comeback at several localities in East Anglia. The rich glowing chestnut red breast is only assumed during the spring and is usually lost by early autumn when numbers of birds present may increase. Other ever present waders include numbers of Redshank, Lapwing and Snipe who all nest in varying numbers, and use the marsh all the year round.

Waders on spring passage regularly include Common Sandpipers, Greenshanks, Spotted Redshanks (often in their jet black breeding plumage), Little Stints, Curlew Sandpipers, Dunlin, Green and Wood Sandpipers. Either here or on the more saline Arnold's Marsh, Bar-tailed Godwits, Turnstones, and Grey Plovers may put in a brief appearance before leaving for the north. The more regular rarer passage waders can include Kentish Plover, Temminck's Stint, Little Ringed Plover and Red-necked Phalarope. Golden Plover too, can usually be found in the area. If not on the drier parts of the marsh they are often on the upland arable fields nearby. These fields or the shingle beaches often produce a spring Dotterel or two.

Several Marsh Harriers are usually noted on spring passage while late Hen Harriers are sometimes still present in April. In late May or June a Montagu's Harrier may put in a brief appearance, but it seems to be ever-decreasing. Sparrow Hawks sometimes breed in the area while a migrant Hobby may occur at any time from late April. Arnold's Marsh is a

Dotterel

good place to see Sandwich, Common and Little Terns. Sandwich Terns nested here in large numbers up to about 40 years ago, but they then deserted the site. Almost always though, there are still large gatherings of birds here in the early spring before they adjourn to the colonies on Blakeney Point or Scolt Head Island. Little and Common Terns nest or attempt to nest while Ringed Plovers and Oyster-catchers frequent the areas of shingle. Black Terns regularly appear on spring passage in May, but in varying numbers from a few birds to several score. Exceptionally this dainty marsh tern may arrive in hundreds on an east wind blowing direct from the Dutch Polders. When this happens every marshland pool will have myriads of gyrating Black Terns dropping down to feed off the surface of the waters.

In recent years Little Gulls have become a feature from mid-summer with between 6 and 24 birds spending several weeks on the marsh. The majority are first summer birds 'tatty' of head and still showing the black diagonal wing bars of immaturity. A good passage of wagtails usually occurs on the marshlands with Yellow Wagtails plentiful (a few stay to breed) and the superb Blue-headed Wagtail not infrequent. White Wagtails too, are an annual migrant while the odd pairs of Pied Wagtails also nest in the area. Traditionally the Garganey used to be one of the first spring migrants to arrive, but numbers have decreased to only one or two breeding pairs.

On nearby Walsey Hills the thickets may shelter a tiny Firecrest resplendent in glowing bronze green plumage, set off by a starkly white superciliary stripe. Little Grebes usually nest on the adjoining pond while Reed and Sedge Warblers and Reed Buntings can be found in some numbers in the whole area. If any spring drift migration takes place Walsey Hills may produce an odd Redstart, Pied Flycatcher, or Ring Ouzel. Hoopoes quite frequently turn up on passage, but more usually on open ground habitats. On passage, Wheatears and Whinchats may abound in fields and fence-lines and Black Redstarts occur annually from mid-March in small numbers.

Another more recent regular feature has been the almost annual appearance of Red-spotted Bluethroats in small single numbers during May. They can turn up almost anywhere – on the marsh, along the East Bank or by Walsey Hills. In mid-summer the marsh is still a hum of activity and quite early in July the first returning waders begin to put in an appearance. From now until October several species of American waders may turn up especially if strong westerly winds have been blowing across Britain. Almost annual visitors in recent years include Pectoral and White-rumped Sandpipers. Even rarer sightings have

Red-spotted Bluethroat

included Baird's Sandpiper and Buff-breasted Sandpipers from the New World; while from eastern and north-east Europe have come Terek, Broad-billed and Marsh Sandpipers.

Most of the regular spring passage waders will now appear in larger numbers and there is still a good chance of seeing Dotterel, Red-necked Phalarope, Temminick's Stint and Little Ringed Plover. Late autumn waders frequently include Jack Snipe and occasionally a Grey Phalarope after storms at sea. The elusive Spotted Crake now appears almost annually on the marsh, but many hours can be spent watching for this swamp dweller to show itself briefly. Walsey Hills in autumn can be more rewarding with, possibly Barred Warbler, Firecrest, Red-breasted Flycatcher and Yellow-browed Warbler amongst larger numbers of the commoner passerine migrants. In early September the first Lapland Bunting may be heard passing over or, with luck, found in grassy patches. Shorelarks may arrive from October. These shingly beaches used to be their winter stronghold but, for some unknown reason, their numbers have declined in recent years, yet there are often some birds still to be found wintering in the region. The coastal area sporadically receives a few Rough-legged Buzzards from October, while Hen Harriers are regular annual visitors.

There are increasing numbers of Brent Geese and large flocks of Wigeon. Many other wildfowl find a sanctuary on the marsh. Herds of Bewick Swans and a few Whoopers can be seen passing westwards in late October and early November, but they do not often stay in the area. Because of the deeper water and scant recession of the tides, sea watching is good at any time during the autumn, but especially during or after onshore gales. There is little protection from the elements, so protective clothing is essential. Watch from the end of the East Bank or from the area of the coastguard station where some shelter may be available.

Red-throated Divers are usually present in small numbers while several hundred may occur in bad weather. Black-throated and Great Northern Divers occur in small numbers. Great-crested, Red-necked and Slavonian Grebes may also be present in small numbers. Some grebes and divers may be present throughout the winter months and modest numbers of Manx Shearwaters and small numbers of Sooty Shearwaters are seen in autumn gales. Leach's and Storm Petrels may be spotted, but always in very small numbers with the latter species much the rarer of the two. Gannets can be plentiful in some autumns, but not often seen after October. As elsewhere along the coast the Long-tailed is the rarest of the skuas, but a few are seen annually up to October. Pomarine Skuas are much more plentiful and can occur at any time from August to October, with a greater proportion in late October when Great and Arctic Skuas may still be passing. Great Skuas more usually occur during on-shore gales when they fly past non-stop with heavy body and white wing patches distinctive at quite long distances. Arctic Skuas are the commonest often staying in the sea areas when there are plenty of fishing terns still around in August and September.

Another much prized species is the Sabine's Gull with the Cley sea area being particularly favoured. Small numbers have occurred in northerly gales. The Cley beaches are also good for Glaucous and Iceland Gulls, both visitors from the Arctic regions in single numbers with the latter species being the rarest of the two. Little Gulls can appear offshore in any weather conditions while Mediterranean Gulls have been noted increasingly in every month of the year; summer and early autumn seeming to be the most favoured period. While a few Razorbills and Guillemots can be seen in most months the greatest numbers occur from September to November. The Black Guillemot is extremely rare off the Norfolk coast, but one or two birds may spend the winter offshore in the Cley area. Little Auks usually occur in varying numbers during northerly gales in late autumn. Only a few Puffins are noted in autumn and winter. Common Scoters and Eiders may be seen offshore in any month, and there are small flocks present all winter.

A·R·W·   Little Auks

Eastwards from the East Bank and Arnold's Marsh there are almost 2 miles (3.2 km) of extremely interesting grazing marshes, freshwater pools and reed beds, most of which are privately owned and managed primarily for wildfowling. Some 68 acres (27.2 ha) at the eastern end are owned by the National Trust and leased to the Norfolk Naturalists' Trust while 14 acres (5.6 ha) are owned and managed by the Norfolk Ornithologists' Association. Access to most of this marsh is therefore restricted, but it can be observed from the main coast road from Walsey Hills to Salthouse; from the shingle beach; from the beach road at Salthouse; or from an old public trackway which intersects the marshes mid-way between Walsey Hills and Salthouse. This track is popularly known to birdwatchers as 'the iron road' because it was clad with steel scaffold pipes during wartime. Most of the species which occur on Cley marsh must also occur on these marshes which physically are part of the whole coastal system. They are certainly worth looking at, at any time; and Baird's and White-rumped Sandpipers have been noted from the public trackways. The eastern end of the marsh seems to have some special attraction for pipits with Richard's, Tawny and Red-throated recorded there from time to time. The area on either side of the Salthouse beach road has long been favoured by Shorelarks. Another public trackway (bumpy and muddy in wet weather) skirts the landward side of the marshes east of Salthouse village.

Timing

There is something of interest all year round with perhaps the end of June to early July being the least rewarding time for passage waders, but there are plenty of resident birds present. Late winter into early spring can also be quiet unless the weather is extra hard. Many birdwatchers avow that early rising is essential, but this is a highly debatable point. Certainly, there is so much to see and many areas to cover that time available must not be wasted! As with all habitats, migrant birds may be present one minute and gone the next. If you venture down the East Bank first thing in the morning or in the late evening you will have the sun in your eyes on one side or the other. The middle of the day is probably a good compromise. High tide time in the morning is usually best for sea watching. Wind directions are important between March and November. Light to moderate south-westerlies in early spring are best for incoming migrants. An east wind in late spring can produce exciting rarities and passage migrants. West winds in autumn will probably mean plenty of waders, but few passerine migrants. Usually, there is a spell of easterlies at some time in the autumn. On-shore gales in autumn may bring numbers of seabirds close inshore. Hard weather during the winter will increase numbers of wildfowl and bring in Smew, Scaup and perhaps Barnacle Geese. Wildfowling does take place in the area, but never on Sundays. It is always busier with birders at weekends with the peak season May and September to October. Cley and Salt-house beachers are also very popular with sea anglers especially in the autumn and winter months.

Access

The picturesque village of Cley-next-Sea lies on the A149 between Wells and Sheringham. Public transport is generally poor. In the summer season one bus daily traverses the coast road. The nearest railway is at Sheringham 8 miles (12.8 km) away. The narrow winding village street of Cley is not suitable for parking.

If visiting the Cley Marshes Nature Reserve there is a (NNT) car park on the south side of the A149 east of Cley village. Just at the back of the car park is the (NNT) centre where permits for the reserve are obtainble between 10.00 a.m. and 5.00 p.m. There is also some very limited parking space at the (NOA) Watch Point nearly 1 mile (1.6 km) east of the village. Alternatively, there is another car park at the end of the Beach Road immediately on the east side of the village.

From the beach road car park it is a ¾ mile (1.2 km) walk to the end of the East Bank. About half-way along, a path leads off right to the two (NNT) North Hides, but permits are required. From the end of the East Bank it is generally worth a look further along the shingle-ridge for a few hundred yards, but be careful not to disturb the nesting terns and Ringed Plovers on the north-east side of Arnold's Marsh and putting to flight any duck which may be on the pools in winter. Return to the East Bank where the watching is good from either side all the way to where the bank joins the A149 again nearly opposite Walsey Hills. A conifer wood opposite (could be due for felling in the near future) is always worth a look from the outside (it is private) and a freshwater lagoon adjacent to it holds breeding Little Grebes and Tufted Duck. At the (NOA) Watch Point on Walsey Hills the Information Centre there is manned daily Tuesdays to Sundays inclusive, as well as on Bank Holidays from mid-March to mid-November. It is also manned at weekends throughout the winter months. If the warden is not on duty there is a notebook with recent sightings on the door. From this centre there is a telephone link with other reserves and the warden usually has worthwhile information about the whole of the Norfolk coast.

Walsey Hills thicket is worth exploring (with the warden's permission) and in spring there is usually a Firecrest and some drift migrants in May. Autumn can produce anything if an east wind is blowing. From the top of the hill there are marvellous views over the coastal marshes and the distant peninsula of Blakeney Point. When proceeding on foot back along the main road towards Cley which is about 1 mile (1.6 km) away, keep a lookout on the adjoining marshes of the reserve. Good views can often be obtained of waders and wildfowl. On the left of the road there is a free public hide which is useful, especially in wet weather. The perimeter of the Salthouse Marshes can be explored either from Walsey Hills or from the Salthouse beach road car park. From Walsey Hills take the A149 eastwards watching the marshes on your left and the line of bushes on right. There is no roadside footpath so great care must be taken. 'The iron road' which is about ½ mile (0.8 km) along leads to the shingle beach and is well worth doing in order to look over the private marshes on either side. From the Salthouse beach road car park explore on either side for Shorelarks and Snow Buntings. Muddy pools in late summer and autumn may attract good waders. A walk eastwards towards Gramborough Hill (a mound on the edge of the beach) may produce Wheatears and a Ring Ouzel in the spring or autumn. The shingle beach can be followed to the very eastern end of the coastal marshes where the Norfolk Ornithologists' Association has purchased 14 acres (5.6 ha) for a small reserve, but no hides are sited. The going on the loose shingle is very strenuous, but a Long Distance Footpath is routed at the edge of the marsh along the base of the shingle-ridge. Alternatively, there is a bridleway diverting from the A149 about ⅓ mile (0.5 km) east of Salthouse village.

Snow Buntings

There is plenty of accommodation in Cley village, but it is wise to book if intending to visit at peak periods. Alternatively, accommodation can be found at Blakeney (but this is also a popular yachting centre) and at the quiet market town of Holt 4 miles (6.4 km) inland from Cley on the A148. The B1156 links Blakeney and Holt. There are also minor roads between Cley and Holt which are very interesting.

Calendar

Resident Little Grebe, Bittern, Grey Heron, Mute Swan, Greylag Goose, Canada Goose, Gadwall, Sparrow Hawk (and passage migrant), Kestrel, Red-legged Partridge, Grey Partridge, Water Rail (also winter visitor), Lapwing (numbers increased by passage migrants and winter visitors), Snipe, Redshank, Black-headed Gull (the numbers of the last three species are increased by winter visitors), Stock Dove, Barn Owl, Tawny Owl, Long-eared Owl (also autumn passage migrant), Kingfisher, Green Woodpecker, Great Spotted Woodpecker, Lesser Spotted Woodpecker, Meadow Pipit (a decline in winter), Pied Wagtail, Stonechat (also passage migrant), Goldcrest (also common October migrant), Bearded Tit (also irruptive migrant), Long-tailed Tit, Marsh Tit, Willow Tit, Coal Tit, Nuthatch, Treecreeper, Tree Sparrow (plus winter visitor), Redpoll (also passage migrant), Hawfinch (quite rare, but has bred in the area), and Corn Bunting.

December–February (and usually into March) Red-throated Diver, Black-throated Diver, Great Northern Diver (only a few records of divers in this period), Great-crested Grebe, Red-necked Grebe, Slavonian Grebe, Black-necked Grebe (only a few grebes seen in this period with latter species the rarest), Cormorant, Shag (only single numbers), Bewick's Swan, Whooper Swan (occasionally a few stay for winter), Bean Goose, Pink-footed Goose (both latter species only occasional), White-fronted Goose (small numbers fairly regularly), Barnacle Goose (irregular in small numbers), Brent Goose, Shelduck, Wigeon, Teal, Pintail, Shoveler, Pochard, Tufted Duck, Scaup, Eider, Long-tailed Duck (usually only single birds), Common Scoter, Velvet Scoter (irregular and scarce in this period), Goldeneye, Smew (only single birds in hard weather), Red-breasted Merganser, Goosander (very small numbers more often in hard weather), White-tailed Sea Eagle (always an extremely rare visitor and even more so in last 20 years, but may return as signs of an increase in part of breeding range), Hen Harrier, Common Buzzard (very scarce), Rough-legged Buzzard (an irregular visitor), Merlin, Peregrine, Golden Plover, Knot (more frequent on mudflats to west of Cley), Sanderling (again more frequent on sandy shores to west), Dunlin, Jack Snipe (only single numbers), Woodcock (may resort to coastal marshes in hard weather), Bar-tailed Godwit, Curlew, Spotted Redshank (very rare as winter visitor), Greenshank (odd birds over-winter), Turnstone, Iceland Gull (rare), Glaucous Gull (fairly regular in small numbers), Guillemot, Razorbill, Black Guillemot, Little Auk, Puffin (all the auks are in very small numbers at this time and latter three species much the rarest), Short-eared Owl, Shorelark (becoming scarcer on shingle banks between Cley and Salthouse), Rock Pipit, Hooded Crow (now very irregular), Twite, Lapland Bunting (small numbers), and Snow Bunting.

March–May (but most species after March) Fulmar (from nearby breeding colonies), Purple Heron (a rare vagrant, but May is the best month), Spoonbill, Shelduck, Garganey, Shoveler, Tufted Duck, Eider, Common Scoter (non-breeding parties of the latter two species on the sea), Honey Buzzard (rare, but a few May records), Black Kite (extremely rare vagrant, but three April–May records), Red Kite (a rare and irregular visitor), Marsh Harrier, Hen Harrier (not usually after

April), Montagu's Harrier (scarce and decreasing passage migrant, not usually before May), Common Buzzard (very occasionally in March and April), Rough-legged Buzzard (irregular), Osprey (single birds almost annual in April and May), Hobby (one or two in May), Spotted Crake (has been seen in April–May, but autumn better), Corncrake (a very rare vagrant, end of May), Crane (a rare vagrant, but slightly increasing), Avocet, Little Ringed Plover (small numbers on passage), Kentish Plover (single birds April–May with best place being Arnold's Marsh. Much harried by Ringed Plovers), Dotterel, Golden Plover, Grey Plover, Little Stint (usually May), Temminck's Stint (not before May), Pectoral Sandpiper (has occurred in May, but more regular in autumn), Curlew Sandpiper, Dunlin, Broad-billed Sandpiper (a very rare vagrant, but a couple of late May records and two in early June), Buff-breasted Sandpiper (a rare vagrant with three May records), Ruff (best months are April–May when lekking males may be seen in most years), Black-tailed Godwit (usually small numbers present from mid-March), Whimbrel, Curlew (last two species mainly passage birds), Spotted Redshank (generally small numbers from April), Greenshank (usually a few birds April–May), Green Sandpiper (small numbers), Wood Sandpiper (a few most years, but not often before end April), Terek Sandpiper (only three records in late May and early July), Common Sandpiper, Spotted Sandpiper (only two records late May–early June), Turnstone, Red-necked Phalarope (one or two birds sometimes seen in May), Lesser Black-backed Gull (non-breeding passage bird), Sandwich Tern (usually in the area pre-nesting), Common Tern (from mid-April), Arctic Tern (scarce offshore passage migrant), Little Tern (from mid-April), Black Tern (not usually before latter half April with May best month), Alpine Swift (a very rare vagrant, but a handful of records in May–June), Hoopoe (an irregular passage migrant from mid-April), Tawny Pipit (a very rare vagrant with one or two records in May and June), Red-throated Pipit (a very rare vagrant with a few records May–June), Water Pipit (occasionally in early spring), Yellow Wagtail, Blue-headed Wagtail (mainly from late April), White Wagtail (passage migrant), Red-spotted Bluethroat (usually one or two mid-April to May after easterly winds), Black Redstart (small numbers up to end April), Redstart (odd birds after east wind), Whinchat, Stonechat (small numbers in early spring), Wheatear (good numbers on passage and a few pairs have bred), Ring Ouzel (small numbers), Grasshopper Warbler (a few pairs breed end April on), Savi's Warbler (a rare vagrant April–May), Sedge Warbler, Reed Warbler, Sub-alpine Warbler (only two records in May and June), Lesser Whitethroat, Whitethroat, Blackcap, Pied Flycatcher (odd birds with east wind), Great Grey Shrike (sometimes a passage migrant March–April), Ortolan (one or two May records, but more frequent autumn).

June–July Fulmar, Little Egret (several records of this rare vagrant in June and occasionally late May), Spoonbill, Shelduck, Garganey, Shoveler, Tufted Duck, Eider, Common Scoter (latter two species non-breeding parties offshore), Marsh Harrier, Hobby, Quail (birds are heard almost annually), Avocet, Little Ringed Plover, Pectoral Sandpiper (single birds from July), Curlew Sandpiper (a few from July), Dunlin, Broad-billed Sandpiper (two June and one July records), Black-tailed Godwit, Bar-tailed Godwit (from July), Whimbrel, Curlew (latter two species passing flocks from July), Green Sandpiper, Wood Sandpiper, Common Sandpiper (the last three species from July), Mediterranean

Gull (records in every month, but July favoured), Little Gull (small numbers of mainly immature birds), Caspian Tern (rare vagrant with three records in period), Sandwich Tern, Common Tern, Little Tern, White-winged Black Tern (a rare vagrant with four records), Yellow Wagtail, Grasshopper Warbler, Sedge Warbler, Reed Warbler, Lesser Whitethroat, Whitethroat and Blackcap.

August–November Red-throated Diver, Black-throated Diver, Great Northern Diver (latter two species in less numbers than Red-throated and more usually later in autumn), Great-crested Grebe, Red-necked Grebe, Slavonian Grebe (not in August), Cory's Shearwater (a handful in records), Great Shearwater (a great rarity in onshore gales with seven records in period), Sooty Shearwater (a few noted most years), Manx Shearwater (not usually after September), Storm Petrel, Leach's Petrel (both petrels may occur in late autumn gales), Gannet, Cormorant, Shag (small numbers), Little Bittern (only four records in this period), Bewick's Swan, Whooper Swan (both wild swans passing late October but Whoopers scarce), Brent Goose (first in October), Wigeon, Teal, Pintail, Shoveler, Pochard, Tufted Duck, Scaup, Eider, Long-tailed Duck (a few, but not often before November), Common Scoter, Velvet Scoter (small numbers from late October), Goldeneye, Red-breasted Merganser, Honey Buzzard (only a handful of records), Hen Harrier (not before October), Common Buzzard (occasional visitor from October), Rough-legged Buzzard (irregular winter visitor from October), Osprey (one or two almost annually but not after September), Merlin, Hobby (not after September), Peregrine (only single birds, but increasing), Spotted Crake (one or two almost annually), Avocet (most depart September), Dotterel (mostly odd birds in August–September), Golden Plover, Grey Plover, Knot, Sanderling, Little Stint, Temminck's Stint (not often after September), White-rumped Sandpiper (six records July–October), Baird's Sandpiper (only three records), Pectoral Sandpiper (almost annual in single numbers), Curlew Sandpiper, Purple Sandpiper, Dunlin, Buff-breasted Sandpiper (six records in this period), Ruff (decline after September), Jack Snipe (very small numbers from October), Woodcock (immigrant from October), Black-tailed Godwit, Bar-tailed Godwit, Whimbrel, Curlew, Spotted Redshank, Greenshank, Green Sandpiper, Wood Sandpiper, Common Sandpiper (the last nine species decrease in October and most have left by the end of the month), Turnstone, Red-necked Phalarope (one or two most autumns), Grey Phalarope (one or two most years in or after gales, but not before October), Pomarine Skua, Arctic Skua, Long-tailed Skua, Great Skua (Long-tailed rarest in the first half of the period; Arctic may decline in latter half whereas more Pomarines may be seen. Great Skua in any month, but peaks in October. Most skuas tend to appear close inshore during northerly gales), Mediterranean Gull, Little Gull (more usually offshore at this time), Sabine's Gull (single birds in northerly gales, but still a rarity), Iceland Gull, Glaucous Gull (former much rarest and not before late October as a rule while Glaucous is usually in small single numbers), Kittiwake, Sandwich Tern, Common Tern (not many of latter two species after September), Arctic Tern, Black Tern (not after mid-October and usually offshore), White-winged Black Tern (only three records in recent years), Guillemot, Razorbill, Black Guillemot, Little Auk, Puffin (very small numbers for the latter three species, from late September, but quite large wrecks especially of Little Auks may occur after severe gales), Short-eared Owl, Wryneck (not after mid-September), Shorelark (not before October), Richard's Pipit (not before mid-September), Tawny Pipit (only a handful of records), Rock Pipit, Yellow Wagtail (few after September), Waxwing (now a very scarce irruption visitor, but late October–early November was the best time), Bluethroat (was regular in September–October after an east wind, but now rarely appears in autumn), Black Redstart, Redstart, Whinchat (the latter two not after October), Wheatear, Ring Ouzel, Aquatic Warbler (only a rare vagrant in August and September), Icterine Warbler (scarce migrant and not after mid-September), Barred Warbler (usually one or two after a north or east wind), Lesser Whitethroat, Garden Warbler, Blackcap (the last three species may occur in drift migration up to September), Yellow-browed Warbler (one or two records from Walsey Hills, but not August), Red-breasted Flycatcher (one or two records from Walsey Hills), Pied Flycatcher (as a drift migrant after an east wind), Great Grey Shrike (single birds may appear from mid-September), Twite (from October), Lapland Bunting (not usually before September), Snow Bunting (first from early September, but more usually later in month), and Ortolan Bunting (almost annual in ones and twos, but not after September).

SALTHOUSE AND KELLING HEATHS AND HOLT LOWES

Map 7

Species

The area lying roughly between the small town of Holt and the villages of Cley-next-Sea and Weybourne is of great interest to birders and naturalists all the year round. Despite the strong attractions of the nearby Cley reserve, this region provides an almost welcome relief from the flat coastal marshes with, of course, a much greater variety of wood and heathland species many of which are not found along the marshes. Much of this richly wooded area is private, but there is plenty of open heathland to which the public have access and many minor roads from which it is easy to watch woodland species.

Salthouse and Kelling Heaths, little more than 1 mile (1.6 km) apart, are separated only by agricultural fields. Over 20 years ago the birdlife of these two heaths was similar, but due to increasing general disturbance and frequent fires, both these heaths have seen a reduction in the numbers of birds breeding there. This is especially so in the case of Kelling, but this heath is still attractive for the various winter birds which also continue to frequent Salthouse Heath.

Immediately inland from Salthouse village, Salthouse Heath is one of the major attractions for birdwatchers because on its unfenced tracts of scrubby, bracken-covered heathland a few diminishing pairs of Nightjars cling to their historical site. Birdwatchers venturing on to the heath should set an example to others by exercising the greatest care and restraint in parking vehicles beside the metalled road and only using existing trackways to explore on foot. Nightjars are very vulnerable to disturbance and a sitting bird flushed from its eggs or young in a bare scrape amongst the bracken might well desert, or be prevented from returning to, her brood. This mainly crepuscular bird does not really become active or vocal until about half an hour before sunset, when its weird churring song may be heard. It is a remarkable experience to stand on the edge of some trackway on the heath as the mist vapours begin to rise at sunset when, suddenly, the eerie rapid churring intrudes on the silent dusk long after most other birds have retired for the night. The far carrying call may continue for long periods with a rapid change of pitch from time to time. If you are fortunate one may appear in silent erratic flight before the light fades. Loud 'wing clapping' is frequently heard during the breeding season as well as a soft 'co-ic' or 'cuic' alarm note. Never attempt to leave a trackway as you may do untold damage or disturb other roosting birds.

That other famous nocturnal singer, the Nightingale, can also be found nesting round the perimeter of Salthouse Heath where it nests in the tangled base of roadside thickets. There are still several pairs to be found here, and on the roadside slopes of Muckleborough Hill which is on the A149 coast road west of Weybourne. Although a Nightingale sings at any time of day it often merges with other birdsong. Only at night can the richness and power of its song be fully savoured. Nightingales begin to sing almost as soon as they arrive on their territories from mid- to third week of April. Song continues fully until the young hatch in late May or early June when it greatly diminishes.

Another well known spring 'pilgrimage' for most birdwatchers is a short trip to the area of 'The Hangs' woods which lie between Kelling and Holt, but are also approachable from either Kelling or Salthouse Heaths. Three minor roads form a triangle in the middle of this most beautiful private woodland and from beside the roads a good variety of woodland species can be observed. 'Kelling Triangle', as it has become known to most birdwatchers, is one of the few regular sites in Norfolk where Wood Warblers can be seen and heard from beside the road. There should not be any intrusion into the bird's territory, which in any case is fenced, private and keepered. Old oaks support Nuthatches and Treecreepers, with Great Spotted, Lesser Spotted and Green Wood-peckers to be found in the area. Crossbills have occasionally been seen, and have probably nested on several occasions. Hawfinches too, are sighted from time to time; and there could be several pairs of this shy species breeding in these old woodlands.

In early spring during the evenings Woodcock may be found in roding flight through the clearings in the woods here or on the edge of Salt-house Heath. A dusk or night-time visit is required if one is to stand any chance of hearing a Long-eared Owl. The odd pair still manage to breed in the Salthouse Heath area and you may be lucky enough to hear the ghostly moaning call or even the 'rusty hinge' squeak of hungry young-sters. Lost breeding species include the Stone Curlew which only mustered the odd pair or two on rabbit grazed stony heath or nearby arable fields. Single birds do still appear at times. The Kelling and Salthouse Heaths used to be the breeding stronghold of the Red-backed Shrike in north Norfolk with up to a dozen pairs breeding annually. Sadly, it has gone as a breeding species, probably due to climatic changes and a range withdrawal. Odd birds though, still turn up from time to time. Curiously enough, autumn records of wind-drifted migrants from Scandinavia seem to be on the increase, but they are more usually seen along the coastal region.

Historically, Salthouse Heath was always the winter home for a splendid Great Grey Shrike, and this bold predator still occurs in late autumn if not always staying throughout the winter. It used to stay until quite late in the spring when prey might include Blue Tit, Linnet and

A ringed Great Grey Shrike. A winter visitor to the region

Dunnock. One auspicious day in May members of the old Cley Bird Observatory caught and ringed a very late Great Grey Shrike as well as a superb male, Woodchat Shrike which had newly arrived as an 'overshooting' migrant from southern Europe. The winter heathlands can be pretty bleak and birdless, but often a Hen Harrier hunts the open habitat, or perhaps a Merlin dashes past, in pursuit of some luckless passerine. Quite often in mid-winter there are large gatherings of mixed finches going to roost in the nearby private rhododendron woods. Brambling, Greenfinches, Chaffinches and Linnets find these large clumps of leafy evergreen shrubs very snug roosting quarters in hard weather. Both Long-eared and Tawny Owls have been observed 'taking' birds (as they go into roost) and 'wing bashing' the bushes later in the night in order to flush a victim.

It seems amazing nowadays that the Montagu's Harrier used to nest on Salthouse Heath up to the end of the last century, but no doubt the area of heathland was more extensive and remote than it is today. This most elegant of all the harriers still appears on spring passage very occasionally. Apart from Kestrels and the odd Sparrow Hawk most other raptors are rare. There have been single records of Red Kites and Goshawks on the heaths. Once a magnificent Honey Buzzard, busily engaged in digging out a wasp's nest, was shot in mistake for a crow! It seems difficult to look forward to the return of any large raptors when they are shown so little mercy by those safeguarding the interests of game preservation. The Hen Harrier, along with the Rough-legged Buzzard are perhaps the most regular of the rarer raptors to visit the heaths during the winter. Woodlarks too, have vanished as a breeding species from Salthouse Heath; and this follows the general declining trend of this species in East Anglia. It is now an extremely rare visitor and more likely to be seen as a lone migrant on the coast.

Tree Pipits, Yellow Wagtails, a few pairs of Shelduck and the occasional pair of Stonechats continue to breed on Salthouse and Kelling Heath, but in competition, as they are, with humans' increasing leisure time, dog walking, scrambling and model aircraft flying they may decline to extinction.

Other nesting species to be found include Long-tailed Tits and Redpolls in the gorse or birch-covered scrub. Summer warblers include Whitethroats and Lesser Whitethroats in the tangle of roadside scrub, while at the woodlands' edge there are Blackcaps, Garden Warblers, Chiff-chaffs and Willow Warblers, Spotted Flycatchers too, are not uncommon.

The adjoining arable fields around the perimeter of the heathlands should never be neglected and they can usually be looked over from a convenient roadside verge. Golden Plover frequent these cultivated fields during the winter months, and in the early spring. In late May or early June listen for the unmistakable call of a Quail coming from the growing crops. It seems to be heard almost annually and breeding has been proved. The call of the Corncrake has also been heard on one or two occasions.

Nearly 2 miles (3.2 km) from the 'Kelling Triangle' is Selbrigg Pond, the very attractive source of the River Glaven which winds from here through afforested heathland. Selbrigg is not one of the better known birdwatching sites and no doubt it would repay more regular watching. Ospreys have dropped in here from time to time and Kingfishers have been seen.

From Selbrigg Pond, the tiny Glaven brook takes a cool rippling south-westerly course to the south of Holt where Holt Lowes provide a splendid example of a wet valley mire. Woodland and heathland species are plentiful and 96 acres (38.4 ha) have been established as a Country Park and managed by the North Norfolk District Council. One section of the Park is heath and common land with views over the Glaven Valley while the other part comprises mainly Scotch and Corsican Pines with a car park in the woodland; and a picnic site beside a pond on the edge of the wood. There are waymarked trails and a nature trail. Obviously the area will be more popular at weekends and holiday times, but it is rich in birdlife. The birdwatcher can easily avoid busy times by visiting weekdays or in the early morning. There is an adjacent example (SSSI) of lowland heath and of valley mire (not part of the Country Park) where the botanist and entomologist can find much of interest. Sparrow Hawk, Woodcock, Marsh and Long-tailed Tits are resident while summer birds include Tree Pipit and Garden Warbler plus all the more common visitors. Kingfishers, Siskins, Redpolls and Cross-bills are seen from time to time.

The Glaven valley is worth exploring in its lower reaches between Glandford and Cley-next-Sea. The water meadows usually hold Snipe and Yellow Wagtails while sometimes a pair of Grasshopper Warblers breed. The hedgerows alongside the minor roads on either side of the river invariably used to attract Waxwings in the hey-day of their irruptions, and will do so again when another phase begins. An especially attractive spot for them is the small private garden beside the hump-backed bridge over the River Glaven by Wiveton Church. Ospreys on spring passage have hunted along the Glaven valley upstream as far as Bayfield Hall (private) and Letheringsett.

Timing

In spring the morning is obviously the best time to visit woodland areas. Very early morning is advisable in May and June when a passing Golden Oriole may sing briefly. If possible it is best to avoid summer weekends on Kelling and Salthouse Heaths. Wind direction is not important although in strong winds and rain birdsong may not be good. With east winds there is always a chance of a rarity. Norfolk's only Rock Thrush was seen one May on Salthouse Heath! An evening visit is essential in order to listen for Nightjars, and Long-eared Owls; or to see roding Woodcock and winter roosts of finches going into the rhododendrons.

Access

The area can easily be worked by car from Cley-next-Sea on the A149 or from Holt on the A148 and the two places are about 4½ miles (7.2 km) apart on the B1156. The roads across and round the heaths are mostly minor ones. There is public access to Salthouse and Kelling Heaths. There are no car parks as such, but as the roads over the heaths are unfenced it is possible to pull just off the road in several places. Many trackways traverse the heaths and these should always be explored on foot – never in a vehicle. Public footpaths are few. One runs from the (NOA) Watch Point at Walsey Hills to the edge of Salthouse Heath, but it is not popular with most birdwatchers. Another more interesting path comes to a dead end! It leads from opposite the large rhododendron wood on Salthouse Heath and skirts arable fields on one side and conifer plantations and open heathland on the other for about ¾ mile (1.2 km). This is a good track to follow for the possible sound of a Long-eared Owl.

The 'Kelling Triangle' is in the middle of fenced private woodlands, but there are roadside verges where it is possible to park. A walk round the triangle of roads should produce plenty of woodland birds. From the Triangle take the road to join the A148 at High Kelling (not to be confused with Kelling) 1 mile (1.6 km) away. Almost opposite, another minor road leads for ½ mile (0.8 km) to Selbrigg Pond. Holt Country Park and Lowes are best explored from the town of Holt by taking the B1149 for about 1 mile (1.6 km) and then turning left into a car park which is open all year. There is a visitor centre, information boards, waymarked trails, a nature trail and a picnic area beside a pond on the edge of the wood. The Park is managed by the North Norfolk District Council.

Another good public footpath runs for 2 miles (3.2 km) from the west side of Muckleborough Hill near Kelling on the A149. This runs across Kelling Heath and over the unfenced road where it soon diverges into two paths which terminate on the Weybourne–Bodham road. One comes out at the Station Halt belonging to the North Norfolk Railway who run steam trains during the summer season from Sheringham. Alternatively, a minor road opposite Weybourne Church leads across Kelling Heath to the 'Kelling Triangle'.

For the Glaven valley take the Holt road from Cley on a sharp corner of the A149 and then take the first turning on the right along a minor road which first branches right to cross the Wiveton hump-backed bridge, while further along there is a left hand turn inland at Glandford Ford. It is advisable not to try and negotiate the Ford, but it is an attractive spot to linger awhile. Glandford is ½ mile (0.8 km) from Cley.

Calendar

Resident Sparrow Hawk, Red-legged Partridge, Grey Partridge, Snipe, Woodcock, Stock Dove, Turtle Dove, Barn Owl, Tawny Owl, Long-eared Owl, Kingfisher, Green Woodpecker, Great Spotted Woodpecker, Lesser Spotted Woodpecker, Long-tailed Tit, Marsh Tit, Willow Tit, Coal Tit, Nuthatch, Treecreeper, Tree Sparrow, Redpoll, Crossbill, Hawfinch and Corn Bunting.

December–February Hen Harrier, Common Buzzard, Rough-legged Buzzard (the last two species very scarce and irregular), Merlin, Golden Plover (on arable), Short-eared Owl (more usually on coastal marshes, but does wander on to heaths), Stonechat, Great Grey Shrike, Brambling and Siskin. Winter visitors may be seen up to end of March–early April, but summer visitors not usually before mid-April.

March to April–May Shelduck, Garganey (does occur on some inland ponds), Tufted Duck, Black Kite (one recorded on Salthouse Heath), Red Kite (one recorded on Kelling Heath), Montagu's Harrier (irregular and scarce), Goshawk (only one on Salthouse Heath), Osprey (does occur in Glaven valley), Hobby (very casual), Quail (calling late May–June, but rare), Corncrake (extremely rare), Stone Curlew (probably only irregular birds), Dotterel (end April–May), Turtle Dove, Nightjar (not often before mid-May), Hoopoe (very occasionally end April–early May), Woodlark (now very rare), Tree Pipit, Yellow Wagtail, Nightingale, Stonechat, Wheatear (mainly as passage migrant), Ring Ouzel (a passage migrant to open fields), Grasshopper Warbler, Lesser White-throat, Whitethroat, Garden Warbler, Blackcap, Wood Warbler (only the odd pair or two), Spotted Flycatcher (early May), and Woodchat Shrike (a rare vagrant).

June–July Usually only resident and summer breeding birds, but possibility of Quail calling.

August–November Most summer birds dispersed and difficult to find after July while winter visitors not usually before October. Hen Harrier, Common Buzzard, Merlin, Golden Plover, Waxwing (late October–early November are the best times), Great Grey Shrike (not often before mid-September), Brambling (October onwards) and Siskin.

SHERINGHAM AND CROMER MAP 8

Habitat

The small, popular and heavily developed seaside towns of Cromer and Sheringham about 4 miles (6.4 km) apart on the A149 might seem improbable birdwatching localities, but there are many attractions in the immediate areas and either town would make a good centre from which to explore the whole of the north and east coastline of Norfolk. Inland from the two towns a range of beautifully wooded hills with interesting valleys contradict the widely held belief that Norfolk is flat. The highest point in Norfolk is reckoned to be here, at the Roman Camp, a National Trust property of 71 acres (28.4 ha) where the hills rise over 300 ft (90 m).

The range of cliffs extending for about 20 miles (32 km) between Weybourne and Happisburgh reach their highest point of some 250 ft (75 m) in the vicinity of Cromer. These cliffs, which are of soft glacial material, are of major geological importance with a complete sequence of Pleistocene deposits. Occasionally land springs undermine the soil bringing down huge masses of cliff top. The cliffs therefore vary from being a sheer drop, to overhung, or sloping face. Nevertheless along these 20 miles (32 km) the Fulmar Petrel has established and maintained its largest southernmost breeding colony on the east coast of Britain. Here and there along the cliffs a deep ravine connects to the beach. The upper beach from Weybourne to Sheringham is mainly composed of large flints smoothly rounded by the action of the sea over many years. Large stretches of sand are revealed at low tide while to the east of Sheringham there is an extensive bed of flints, chalk and seaweed-covered primitive rocks where delightful pools are exposed by the ebbing tides. This type of sea bed extends for up to 2 miles (3.2 km) offshore for a 15 mile (24 km) stretch between Sheringham and Mundesley. It provides a remarkably rich lobster and crab fishing area for the local fishing industry centred at Cromer and Sheringham. Fine cliff-top golf-courses exist to the west of Sheringham and to the east of Cromer which also boasts a pier and a working lighthouse.

To the east of Sheringham, on the very outskirts of the town, Beeston Bog has long been a small paradise. For many years it has been sadly mis-used and neglected, but a management plan was drawn up in 1984 with a small band of local volunteers (under the auspices of the local councils and the Nature Conservancy Council) carrying out conservation work on the 62 acres (25 ha) of Beeston Regis Common, as it is now called. This work has dramatically enhanced the rich flora and fauna that were in danger of disappearing.

Map 8

Species

The area provides good opportunities for watching woodland birds while seabird passage can be interesting in autumn gales and passerine migrants can be met with along the cliff tops. By Upper Sheringham, which is an old agricultural village, the Sheringham Hall and Park were

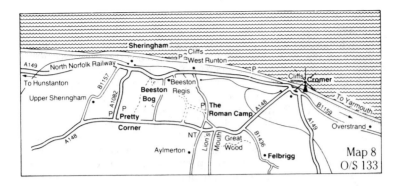

privately owned, but the Park has now been acquired by the National Trust. Early in the nineteenth century this estate was purchased by the Upcher family who commissioned Humphrey Repton, the greatest landscape gardener of the time, to lay out the park and build a new hall. The woodlands have been extended by successive generations of the Upcher family who specialised in the planting of rhododendrons which give a magnificent display in May and June. All the typical woodland birds such as Nuthatches, Treecreepers, woodpeckers and tits occur. In summer Blackcaps, Garden Warblers, Whitethroats, Spotted Flycatchers, Redpolls and the odd pair of Nightingales can be heard or seen in the Park and adjoining areas. Woodcock nest here and, once, Goshawks were recorded in the region.

Despite some commercialisation 'Pretty Corner' about 1 mile (1.6 km) inland from Sheringham is well worth a visit in the spring. There are several public footpaths through the woodlands and valleys where woodpeckers, tits, Nuthatches, Treecreepers and summer warblers can also be found. In winter the woods are rather more silent, but offer good sightings of the resident species amongst the leafless trees. Two foot-paths wind down towards sea level to traverse Beeston Bog which is adjacent to the A149. This used to be a wildlife paradise with Yellow Wagtail, Red-backed Shrike, Nightjar, Grasshopper Warbler and Snipe breeding there. Alas, all have gone, but recent attempts at conserving the area may well induce the return of some of these species. Yellow Wagtails can still be seen on passage. Snipe, Long-tailed Tit, Blackcap and Whitethroats can be found, in addition to many bog plants.

Behind West Runton on the A149 a minor road climbs steeply to the well wooded areas of the Roman Camp, Beacon Hill, The Lion's Mouth and Felbrigg Hall. There are several interesting footpaths across the National Trust properties of the Roman Camp and Beeston Regis Heath comprising over 100 acres (40 ha) of woodland and open heathland which are well worth exploring for all the typical woodland birds. The mature woodlands of the region extend across the A148 to Felbrigg Hall and Woods which is another fine estate owned by the National Trust. All these high wooded areas are extremely good for finding a few pairs of breeding Wood Warblers, best located by listening for the males' long quivering trill from early May.

The Redstart is another species usually scarce in Norfolk as a breeding species, but plentiful enough in autumn east wind drift conditions. Up to a dozen pairs of Redstarts have nested in these mature woodlands on the Cromer Ridge which must be regarded as their Norfolk stronghold.

The area is rather neglected by birdwatchers in favour of the coastal attractions and it deserves more attention. In 1978 a pair of Pied Flycatchers successfully bred in the area for the first time in Norfolk. An interesting theory was advanced that this pair were probably wind-drifted migrants originally bound for Scandinavia, but brought to the Norfolk coast by persistent east winds in that particular spring which also produced above average numbers of other Scandinavian bound travellers such as Wrynecks and Red-backed Shrikes.

A cliff-top walk westwards from Sheringham will produce Wheatears and Whinchats in the spring while the adjoining links may attract an 'overshooting' Hoopoe probing the short turf with its long downcurved bill. Fulmar Petrels return to their nesting stations there by December, but peak activity continues in April and May. Fulmars first began prospecting these cliffs in 1940 and breeding was proved in 1947. A few pairs of Sand Martins and the odd pair of Kestrels also breed in these soft cliffs. Apart from the golf-course, the inland region is mainly agricultural land.

Hoopoe with spider. A rare visitor to the region

Although not regular the Richard's Pipit has been seen here in late autumn as has the rarer Tawny Pipit. Incredibly, these cliffs have been the brief autumn haunt of two Pied Wheatears in 1983 and 1985 which are extremely rare vagrants from eastern Europe. An even greater rarity turned up here in 1978 when an Alpine Accentor was seen, caught and ringed. What brought this rare stranger from its home on the high mountain slopes of central and southern Europe to a low, mud cliff on the Norfolk coast we shall never know. Odd Lapland and Snow Buntings are sometimes seen on the arable fields and even a few Shorelarks may turn up from time to time. It is interesting to note that the first recorded Shorelark for Britain was shot on the beach at Sheringham in 1830.

To the west of the town the cliffs rise in a huge mound known as 'Beeston Hump'. Apart from Fulmars there is not usually a great deal to be seen here, but an Alpine Swift and a Great Grey Shrike have been seen in recent years. Immediately in front of the town, a sewer outfall is always worth looking at. In 1952, what was then only the third county record of Mediterranean Gull, was seen here annually until 1957. Since then, of course, this species is seen annually in every month of the year somewhere along the coast. The outfall though, has provided little Gulls, Black Terns and Sabine's Gulls in more recent years. Sea watching can be quite good during on-shore gales, but usually sea birds are much farther out than they are in similar conditions a few miles along the coast at Cley. Unless you are lucky though, sea watching only rewards the persistent and dedicated watcher in *all* weathers. Good passages of divers, auks and skuas may be seen in autumn months. Winter sea duck though, are minimal perhaps because of the deeper waters and rocky bottom offshore. Few waders frequent the shoreline, but the rocky shore between Sheringham and West Runton will often hold small parties of Turnstones, an odd Redshank or two, and, with luck, one or two Purple Sandpipers.

These beaches usually produce one or two of the rarer gulls from the Arctic. A Glaucous Gull usually puts in an appearance most winters, but the rarer Iceland Gull only occurs irregularly now, although it used to be more frequent. Cromer has become ornithologically historic because the first Collared Doves to arrive in Britain bred on the outskirts of the town in 1955! However, the main attraction for the birdwatcher will be the delightful pathway on the east side of the town which goes past the lighthouse and then along the cliff tops to Overstrand with an alternative divergence across the east end of the links. Spring migrants may include Wheatears, Black Redstarts and Ring Ouzels, while Hoopoes also turn up from time to time. An Alpine Swift has also been recorded on more than one occasion.

Timing

The only consideration to bear in mind is that the area is a heavily developed holiday zone and therefore there are greater pressures on Bank Holidays and during July and August. The Woodlands are best anyway in the spring and winter months. Wind direction is best on-shore for autumn sea watching, otherwise there is no great advantage. Migrants in spring may arrive in moderate south-westerlies, rarities from late April in east or south-east winds. Autumn migrants usually arrive in north or east winds.

Access

The two seaside towns of Sheringham and Cromer are about 4 miles (6.4 km) apart on the main coast road, the A149. They are served by the A148 from King's Lynn or the A140 from Norwich. Either town would be a good centre from which to explore either the north Norfolk coast or the Norfolk Broads area; although public transport from the towns is very limited especially to the north coast. British Rail have a single branch line from Norwich with a fairly regular service.

Follow the cliff-top footpath at Sheringham westwards from one of the sea-front car parks for about 4 miles (6.4 km) and return by the same route, watching out for migrant passerines, Fulmars or passing seabirds. The entrance to Sheringham Park is signposted off the A148 Cromer to Holt road by the junction with the Upper Sheringham road. The Park is open throughout the year from dawn to dusk. Sheringham Hall itself is privately occupied. From Upper Sheringham Church take the minor road to the top of the hill and Pretty Corner, where there are two car parks on either side of the A1082 which goes back to Sheringham 1 mile (1.6 km) away. Nearly ½ mile (0.8 km) from the Pretty Corner car park a footpath on the north side of the A148 leads down for about 1 mile (1.6 km) through woods to Beeston Bog and the A149. There is also a loop path across the other side of the Bog.

The Roman Camp woods can be explored via West Runton (a village midway between Cromer and Sheringham) by taking a minor road on the south side of the road in the village centre. At the top of the hill turn off right to the car park. (There are nearby tea rooms.) From here there are several interesting paths for walkers giving superb views over the coastline. A footpath from the car park can be followed to one such viewpoint set up by the National Trust on Beeston Regis Heath. South of the A148 the road traverses some beautiful woodlands with the 500 acre (200 ha) Great Wood of Felbrigg Hall on the south side of the road. Where possible it is worth pulling off the road to stop and listen for woodland birds. The Lion's Mouth, which is a grove of old beeches and other trees, is worth looking at and Wood Warblers have occurred there. To visit Felbrigg Hall (NT) and grounds take the B1436 (from the A148) and turn off right as indicated before reaching Felbrigg village. There is an admission charge to the Hall and Gardens. It is open from the end of March to the end of October every day, except all day Tuesdays and Friday mornings. There is a restaurant and you are free to walk in the mature woodlands.

For late autumn and winter shore waders with a chance of Purple Sandpipers, explore the rocky shore east of Sheringham. Park by the sea-front and follow the promenade to its end and then along the beach. Low tide is best and beware of the incoming tide which can reach the base of the cliffs and cut off your return! For the Cromer cliffs, park along the minor roads on the east side of the town and follow a cliff path past the Lighthouse. Watch the adjoining golf-course for passerine migrants. Ring Ouzels are sometimes seen on the bracken-covered slopes, while Hoopoes have occurred on the short turf of the links.

Calendar

Resident Sparrow Hawk, Woodcock, Stock Dove, Barn Owl, Tawny Owl, Long-eared Owl, Green Woodpecker, Great Spotted Woodpecker, Lesser Spotted Woodpecker, Woodlark (used to breed, but now rare casual), Goldcrest, Long-tailed Tit, Marsh Tit, Willow Tit, Coal Tit, Nuthatch, Treecreeper, Crossbill and Hawfinch (latter two species occasionally reported but may be overlooked).

December–February There may be the odd diver, grebe, duck or auk offshore, but not noted for wintering seafowl. Fulmar, Cormorant, Shag (rare), Purple Sandpiper (usually one or two), Dunlin, Redshank, Turnstone, Mediterranean Gull, Iceland Gull (now very irregular), Glaucous Gull (one or two almost annual), Shorelark (not regular, but worth a look at the west end of Sheringham cliffs when not at more regular haunts), Lapland Bunting, Snow Bunting (the latter two species are also irregular and in any case can usually be found more easily elsewhere), and Corn Bunting.

March to April–May Fulmar, Mediterranean Gull, Stonechat, Whinchat, Wheatear, Ring Ouzel, Hoopoe, Yellow Wagtail, Tree Pipit, Nightjar (from early May, but rare), Nightingale, Black Redstart, Redstart, Grasshopper Warbler, Lesser Whitethroat, Whitethroat, Garden Warbler, Blackcap, Wood Warbler (only a few pairs, but Cromer Ridge main stronghold in Norfolk), Willow Warbler, Chiff-chaff, Spotted Flycatcher, Pied Flycatcher (only odd migrant birds, but has bred once).

June–July Woodland birds usually silent and skulking at this time.

August–November A seabird passage does occur from September in on-shore gales and these may include: Red-throated Diver, Great-crested Grebe, Red-necked Grebe, Fulmar, Manx Shearwater, Gannet, Cormorant, Brent Goose, Shelduck, Wigeon (the latter three species from October), Eider, Common Scoter, Arctic Skua, Great Skua, Kittiwake, Little Gull, Razorbill and Guillemot. Autumn passerines and winter visitors may include Wheatear, Whinchat, Black Redstart, Tawny Pipit, Richard's Pipit (both the latter two species are extremely rare and not regular, but the cliffs west of Sheringham are the best spot), Shore-lark, Lapland Bunting, Snow Bunting (the latter three species are also irregular) and Corn Bunting.

Happisburgh to Winterton
Habitat

The coastline between Cromer and Happisburgh is perhaps the least interesting section of the Norfolk coastline. The B1159 winds between the coastal holiday villages with the range of cliffs almost continuous to Happisburgh (it is pronounced Hazeburgh!). There are no shore nesting birds, but Fulmars have colonised the higher cliffs at Happisburgh where the red and white lighthouse is visible from afar in the nearby flat Broadland region. Few visiting birdwatchers bother to explore the region. Certainly most birdwatchers would steer clear of an area where a Gas Terminal Complex has been established. Nevertheless, an enthusiastic band of local ornithologists have highlighted the Paston area with their constant watching over several years. Migration *does* occur along this coast with vast numbers of seabirds moving offshore, while staggering numbers of migrating finches have been recorded in spring and autumn. With such regular watching the usual quota of rarities have also been discovered.

Beyond Happisburgh the Norfolk coastline becomes much more interesting with the cliffs giving way to marram covered sand hills. There is still holiday development and the coastline is very popular in summer. The best stretch of coastline for birdwatchers is between Sea Palling and Winterton. Here and there stunted copses of sycamore and other scrub provide a perfect attraction for coastal passerines while the beautiful Horsey Estate (NT) has a splendid history of wildlife conservation for uncommon breeding species and migrants. A vast dune system extends southwards from Horsey to Winterton. The Winterton Dunes National Nature Reserve has been established here by the Nature Conservancy Council to extend northwards from Winterton for nearly 2 miles (3.2 km) and covers an area of 259 acres (104.6 ha). It is the largest mainland dune system on the East Anglian coast. These dunes are the result of wind and sea currents over many years and have become established in front of an old coastline a cliff section of which can still be seen to the south of the beach road at Winterton Great Valley. The dune slacks are of special interest because they have been colonised by plants more characteristic of acid soils. The cross-leaved heath and royal fern can be found here and there is a colony of natterjack toads. Adders are commonplace and the grayling butterfly and green forester moth also occur here. Extending along the landward edge of the dunes there is an extensive area of scrub and short trees including silver birch and alder. This is another area well away from the more popular birding sites, but it has become renowned for the variety and numbers of raptors which may occur on migration or as winter visitors. In recent years, due to the attentions of local birdwatchers, some very nice passerine migrants have also been noted.

The mature wooded grounds of Horsey Hall stand out in splendid isolation offering sanctuary to migrant passerines and summer visitors. Long before it was widely known that Golden Orioles were annual visitors to Norfolk, the beautiful mellow fluty notes of passing orioles were heard almost annually by the late Major A. Buxton in the 1940s. Reed-fringed Horsey Mere is some 500 acres (200 ha) and being one of the Broadland waterways nearest to the sea coast, regularly attracts good numbers of winter wildfowl.

Between Winterton and Great Yarmouth the coastline holiday development of chalets and caravan sites offer little of interest to the birdwatcher. It is interesting to recall though, that the sand dunes once extended all the way to Yarmouth. Yarmouth Denes to the north of the town used to be the resort of the 'olden-days' bird catcher; and it was here that the only record of Citril Finch for Britain was that of a bird caught alive there in January 1904.

Although much of the coastal region is predominantly agricultural the region encompassed by the B1150 from Bacton to North Walsham; the A149 from North Walsham to Stalham (both small market towns) and the B1151 from Stalham to Happisburgh is well worth exploring. A unique wetland common can be found at East Ruston near Stalham. Bacton Woods, Witton Heath and Crostwight Heath are other attractive areas.

Maps 9 and 10
Species (all areas)

In discussing the species which might be seen on the coast or offshore between Mundesley and Happisburgh it should be remembered that this is a very much neglected area as far as most birdwatchers are concerned. Most of the information here has come from the notes made by a pioneering band of local enthusiasts who have spent many long hours sea watching often with little result. Although their unique notes have highlighted the Paston–Bacton area, there seems to be no reason why other sections of this coast should not be just as productive if given attention regularly by birders. Also, it should be remembered that many of the notes refer to passing birds – for example, large numbers of sea birds may be passing offshore in strong winds, while spring and autumn passerine flights are also controlled by wind and weather conditions. Therefore, a casual day trip may well prove unrewarding, even when conditions seem favourable.

Red-throated Diver

During December and the early part of the year about half a dozen Purple Sandpipers frequent the groynes and some have stayed into April. Peak numbers of Red-throated Divers occur early in the year with up to 300 birds passing or present. Single numbers of Black-throated Divers may be seen through the winter up to March, with the odd record also of Great Northern Diver. Grebes are rather scarce, but Great-crested, Red-necked and Slavonian have all been noted in small numbers. Quite often one or two Shags are reported in the area. Wildfowl moving at sea may include: Goldeneye, Scaup, Common Scoter, Red-breasted Merganser and Shelduck. Small numbers of Velvet Scoter, Eider, Wigeon and Brent Geese have been noted. Auks are usually very scarce at this time, but single Puffins have been seen in the first three months of the year.

In February and March, huge gull movements have been noted with many species flying east en-route for the Continent. A few Little Gulls and Kittiwakes have been seen. At this time in a mild season passerines may be noted also proceeding eastwards back to their Continental breeding grounds in flocks totalling several thousands. The commonest outgoing migrant is the Starling closely followed by Chaffinches, Skylarks, Bramblings, Siskins, Rooks and Fieldfares. A few herds of Bewick's Swans may pass eastwards, honking musically as they leave their winter home. The shoreline here is much favoured by Glaucous Gulls with single birds being noted in the last and first five months of the year. The Iceland Gull is much rarer, with a few single records in the early spring. A few Snow Buntings usually winter in the area, either on the beaches or on arable fields, but they too depart by the end of March. Incoming spring migrants may include a few Wheatears, a Black Redstart or two and an early Ring Ouzel in March.

During April and May incoming parties of finches may be impressive and several thousand Linnets, Goldfinches and some Greenfinches return from their winter foraging on European farmlands. Linnets and Goldfinches ringed in Norfolk have been recovered in France, Spain and Portugal, Meadow Pipits too, will be returning on a westerly course and a few terns offshore will be heading for their sanctuaries on the North

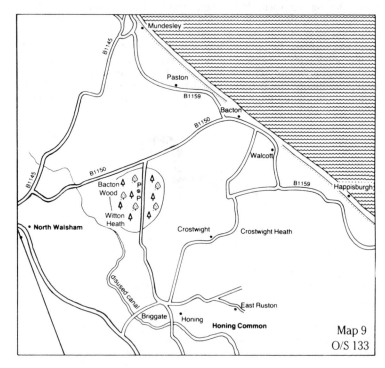

Map 9
O/S 133

Coast. Other migrants which have been noted at this time include Lesser Black-backed Gulls, Hen Harrier, Sparrow Hawks, Stonechats, Hooded Crows, Merlins, Ospreys and Firecrests.

May and June records have included a few sightings of Hobby, Rough-legged Buzzards and one Goshawk. A Red-footed Falcon stayed for two weeks in May while an adult Sabine's Gull delighted observers as it flew west one May day. Shortly after this, a fine cock Red-spotted Bluethroat arrived. Single Mediterranean Gulls have occurred between March and October. Other spring rarities include one record each of Serin and Ortolan in May.

In June and July it is usually very quiet, but the sea has produced odd Mergansers, Scoter, Arctic and Great Skuas, Manx Shearwaters and Gannets. During August a few more seabirds may arrive, together with a few waders such as Dunlin, Curlew and Whimbrel flying past. The first drift passerines can appear on an easterly wind with single numbers of Pied Flycatchers, Redstarts or even a Wryneck and Red-backed Shrike. Small numbers of Great Skuas, Arctic and Pomarine Skuas can be seen in any month from now up to November with the greatest numbers usually during on-shore gales, when many storm-driven Little Auks have been seen. The numbers of Gannets, Kittiwakes and auks equal if not surpass the numbers seen farther along the coast at Cley. Rarities seen at this time include Sabine's Gull, Black Guillemot and Leach's Petrel. Sea duck which may occur include Long-tailed, Goldeneye, Eider, Velvet Scoter and Scaup. Brent Geese are seen passing on their return to their north coast haunts together with large numbers of Teal and Wigeon. Generally a few herds of Bewick's and some Whooper Swans head west en-route for the Welney Washes. Both Sooty and Manx Shearwaters occur fairly regularly in September and October. Late autumn raptors may include sightings of Merlin, Hen Harrier and Rough-legged Buzzard. Lapland Buntings are noted on passage and the first Snow Buntings return. A Richard's Pipit and Long-tailed Skua have been recorded in November. One or two Black Redstarts move through and Long-eared Owls have been seen arriving across the sea.

Anyone could be forgiven for thinking that this species account has been compiled in error from a north coast site; and it proved beyond doubt that there are plenty of 'unknown' localities waiting to be discovered in this well watched county. This part of the coast though, offers little suitable habitat for waders, so imagine the delight and surprise of an observer who noted three Avocets flying westwards one May morning. A sight that would hardly raise an eyebrow on the north coast! One of the authors has old wartime records of Black Redstart, Glaucous Gull and Snow Buntings on the coast in the nearby Bacton area, and these three species are still occurring regularly. Moreover, a private ringer working from a small cliff-top garden at Happisburgh has trapped and ringed no less than three Pallas's Warblers plus Dusky Warbler, Yellow-browed Warbler, Firecrest and Red-breasted Flycatcher!

The interior region between Bacton – North Walsham – Stalham and Happisburgh holds no known specialities, but good numbers of summer warblers breed on the various commons and along the edge of woodlands. Woodland species such as tits, woodpeckers, Nuthatches and Treecreepers can be found in winter and roving bands of Siskins frequent alder trees. East Ruston Common is attractive in summer with Snipe and Grasshopper Warbler breeding in the area. Uncommon birds regularly seen include Common Buzzard, Firecrest, Osprey and Marsh

Harrier while Woodchat Shrike and Red Kite have been noted.

The vast sand dunes at Horsey extending southwards to Winterton provide the best raptor watching area in Norfolk. No less than 17 species of birds of prey have been recorded in the region with at least 10 of these fairly regular. Only the White-tailed Sea Eagle has not appeared for decades, but as the decline of this magnificent bird seems to have been halted with a slight upwards trend in Scandinavian pairs, wandering immature birds may well re-appear in their old haunts. Traditional raptors of the region are, of course, harriers who have hunted and nested there since time immemorial. In the last two or three decades all have declined until only the occasional pair of Marsh and Montagu's Harriers nest in closely guarded secret localities. These two species though, still pass through the coastal area in small numbers annually. A Marsh Harrier quartering the reed beds with half raised wings is still a not uncommon sight in Broadland. The more slender winged Montagu's Harrier is now one of Britain's rarest breeding birds, but there is always a good chance of seeing one of these graceful birds on migration in the Winterton area. Hen Harriers are more regular, arriving in October and usually departing by early April. Late birds though, may overlap with early Montagu's to provide an identification exercise!

Hardly a spring goes by without an Osprey appearing, attracted no doubt by the extensive waterways nearby. The Rough-legged Buzzard is irregular, although a dozen or more have been noted in the spring and autumn. Common Buzzards are fairly regular with eight being seen in one day. Other not infrequent visitors include Goshawk, Merlin and Hobby. Sparrow Hawks occur annually on migration with records of 8 and 10 birds in the air together. Kestrels, of course, breed and are present all the year round with migrant birds also passing through. The rarest of the rare have included sightings of Red Kite, Black Kite, Red-footed Falcon, Honey Buzzard and Peregrine.

The Waxham–Horsey–Winterton area also receives a good scattering of rarer passerine migrants. Great Grey Shrike sometimes arrive in late autumn and have stayed in the scrub-edged duneland area to prey upon their smaller neighbours. Once, one of these bold predators was seen eating a cock Bearded Tit! It obviously had no respect for one of our treasured breeding birds. Meat is meat! In addition to the usual Pied Flycatchers and Redstarts, Wrynecks, Red-backed Shrikes, Barred Warblers and Firecrests are fairly regularly seen. The dune area is a noted place for Richard's Pipits if these long distance migrants should reach Britain in late autumn. The Tawny Pipit, too, has been noted several times, but more usually in May and June. Two extreme rarities found here were Isabelline Shrike and Pied Wheatear while a Sardinian Warbler near Waxham in 1973 was the first for the county. Other rare or semi-rare migrants seen from time to time include Bluethroats, Yellow-browed and Pallas's Warblers, Greenish Warblers, Ortolan Buntings, Aquatic Warblers, Icterine Warblers, Golden Orioles and Radde's Warbler.

The area still attracts a few wintering Hooded Crows, but this species seems to be ever-decreasing from the days when it was a common enough winter sight. One reads in old manuals that 'lines of Hooded Crows were seen passing continuously hour by hour'! Great-crested Grebes too, have declined as a breeding species, but there are usually a few pairs on Horsey Mere and Martham Broad.

Horsey Mere offers sanctuary to hundreds of Wigeon in winter along with Teal, Tufted Duck, Shoveler, Pochard, Gadwall and Goldeneye. There are often a few Bewick's and Whooper Swans on the nearby marshlands. Little Gulls appear in winter and Bitterns may be seen at any time, although this species is also declining as a breeding species. Bearded Tit numbers fluctuate with their populations high after an irruption from elsewhere, or very low after a severe winter. Black Terns regularly appear over many of the waterways in spring and this species used to nest in the Norfolk Broads area very many years ago.

The coastal dunes are one of the best places in Norfolk to see Stonechats either as breeding pairs, passage migrants or winter visitors. Other breeding summer migrants include Yellow Wagtails and Grasshopper Warblers on the marshes and Little Terns on the shore. Two rare breeding passerines are Savi's Warbler and Cetti's Warbler. Savi's Warbler is a summer visitor that became extinct as a breeding bird about the middle of the nineteenth century and now it seems to be making a slow return to its old haunts. The sedentary Cetti's Warbler is newly colonising south and east England, but is subject to severe decreases during bad winter weather. The Ruddy Duck too, seems to be a potential colonist, for they have been seen on Horsey Mere and on many of the other Broads since 1977.

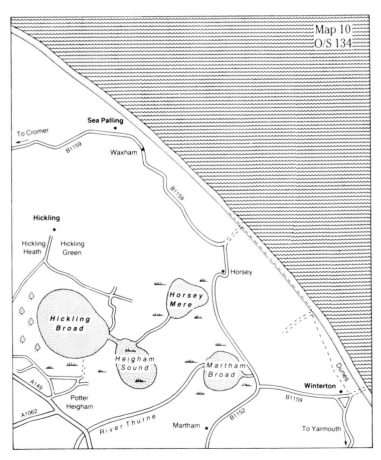

Timing

For the coastal regions the usual criteria applies as regards north or easterly winds for migrants in late spring or autumn, and avoidance of peak holiday periods. Best times for visiting wood and heath habitats are in the first half of the day with the least productive season being late summer and autumn.

Access

The most scenic route is from Cromer on the B1159 which serves all the coastal villages to Winterton, a journey of about 27 miles (43.2 km). Shortly beyond Winterton the B1159 joins the A149 to continue to Great Yarmouth or goes back to Cromer via Potter Heigham, Stalham and North Walsham. Between Cromer and Great Yarmouth, which are 35 miles (56 km) apart, there are four other roads which connect to the A149 from the coastal B1159. They are the B1145, B1150, B1151 and B1152 with the last three roads being more useful routes than the first.

At Bacton 8 miles (12.8 km) and Paston 10 miles (16 km) from Cromer access to the coast is limited, but a footpath runs from the apex of the minor loop road on the north side of the B1159 at Paston. Alternatively, access points to the shore are at Bacton Green which, though an uninspiring area, has a wealth of migrant passerines and passing sea-birds in the right conditions.

For Bacton Wood and Witton Heath take the B1150 from Bacton, 4½ miles (7.2 km) to North Walsham. After nearly 2 miles (3.2 km) turn left down a minor road to the car park and picnic site on the right. Explore Bacton Wood and Witton Heath by the footpaths which are indicated by Forestry Commission signs.

The best approach to Honing and East Ruston Common, two villages about 1 mile (1.6 km) apart, is to continue for about 2¼ miles (3.6 km) on the minor road from Bacton Wood car park. Do not cross the River Ant, which lies to the south of Honing village, but take the road sign-posted East Ruston. Just before reaching this village stop beside an unfenced section of road and watch over Mown Fen on the right and East Ruston allotment (not a vegetable allotment) on the left. About 300 yds (270 m) south of East Ruston Chapel the Long Distance Footpath skirts Honing Common. This path established by the Norfolk County Council runs from Cromer to Great Yarmouth and some sections are of great interest to birdwatchers. It is known here as the Weaver's Way because of the area's past links with the weaving industry which was important between the twelfth and eighteenth centuries.

Another interesting route is from Honing. Take the minor road past the Church on your left and after just over 1 mile (1.6 km) turn right at the first minor crossroads. Stop after another ¾ mile (1.2 km) to look over Crostwight Heath. From here, it is possible to follow minor roads for 3¼ miles (5.2 km) to Bacton.

For Horsey follow the B1159 for 23 miles (36.8 km) from Cromer to Horsey Windmill which is just to the south of the village. The Mill and Horsey Mere are National Trust property. The Mill is open from the end of April to the end of September and admission is free, except to the balcony which is only open from July to September. Although too distant for serious birdwatching there are superb views over Horsey Mere and the surrounding marshlands. It is best to seek permission on the spot to walk along the path for a short distance from the car park near the Mill to a place where much of the Mere can easily be seen. Horsey Hall and grounds are private, but the wooded grounds adjoin part of the B1159. Walk north from the Horsey Windmill car park to look and listen for spring migrants around the small village. As everywhere in Broadland most of the marshes are private and access is always difficult or restricted.

The Waxham marram hills can best be explored by parking near the Church at Waxham nearly 3 miles (4.8 km) north of Horsey on the B1159, and following the marram hills southwards or northwards. Weather-stunted deciduous trees (mainly sycamore) are on the land side of the dunes and are well worth examining for autumn migrants. Martham Broad (NNT) is best looked at from West Somerton 2 miles (3.2 km) south of Horsey. Take the public footpath from near the post office. This leads to the south edge of the Broad but is not clearly signposted though it follows the tow path for a short distance before veering left.

For the Winterton Dunes National Nature Reserve of 259 acres (103.6 ha) there is a car park at Winterton beach. From there a footpath can be followed for 5½ miles (8.8 km) to Waxham. The Winterton Ness about 1½ miles (2.4 km) north from the car park is a good area from which to watch for migrant raptors. The area of scrub on the landward side of the path should be watched for autumn migrants. This reserve is managed by the Nature Conservancy Council by agreement with the owner of the Burnley Hall Estate and with the co-operation of the Winterton Parish Council.

Calendar

Resident Great-crested Grebe, Bittern, Heron, Tufted Duck, Sparrow Hawk, Redshank, Water Rail, Barn Owl, Tawny Owl, Kingfisher, Green Woodpecker, Great Spotted Woodpecker, Lesser Spotted Woodpecker, Stonechat (and winter visitor), Cetti's Warbler (only odd pairs), Goldcrest, Firecrest (no proof of breeding; mainly passage migrant), Bearded Tit, Marsh Tit, Willow Tit, Coal Tit, Nuthatch, Treecreeper, Redpoll and Corn Bunting.

December–February (winter birds often into March) Red-throated Diver, Black-throated Diver, Great Northern Diver, Little Grebe (on fresh water), Red-necked Grebe, Slavonian Grebe, Fulmar, Cormorant, Shag, Bewick's Swan, Whooper Swan, Brent Goose, Sheluck, Wigeon, Gadwall, Teal, Shoveler, Pochard, Scaup, Eider, Common Scoter, Velvet Scoter, Goldeneye, Red-breasted Merganser, Ruddy Duck, Hen Harrier, Merlin, Water Rail, Golden Plover, Purple Sandpiper, Curlew, Glaucous Gull, Puffin (scarce), Stonechat, Great Grey Shrike, Siskin, Redpoll and Snow Bunting.

March–May (summer migrants not usually before April) Fulmar, Sheluck, Ruddy Duck, Marsh Harrier, Montagu's Harrier, Goshawk, Sparrow Hawk, Buzzard, Rough-legged Buzzard, Osprey, Hobby (May–June), Peregrine, Mediterranean Gull, Lesser Black-backed Gull (regular passage migrant), Iceland Gull (rare), Sandwich Tern, Common Tern, Little Tern (all the terns are passage migrants, but Little Terns nest), Black Tern, Hoopoe, Wryneck, Tree Pipit, Yellow Wagtail, Nightingale (only the odd pair or two may be found), Black Redstart, Whinchat (passage migrant), Wheatear, Ring Ouzel, Grasshopper Warbler, Savi's Warbler (only single birds, but increase may occur), Lesser Whitethroat,

Garden Warbler, Blackcap, Spotted Flycatcher, Golden Oriole, Red-backed Shrike (usually odd passage birds), Brambling, Siskin and Ortolan Bunting (May).

June–July Although most summer birds still present, passerines less obvious. Only odd birds on sea.

August–November (summer birds not often after October, winter birds not before September) Red-throated Diver, Black-throated Diver, Great Northern Diver, Great-crested Grebe, Red-necked Grebe, Slavonian Grebe, Fulmar, Sooty Shearwater, Manx Shearwater, Storm Petrel, Leach's Petrel, Gannet, Cormorant, Shag, Brent Goose, Wigeon, Gadwall, Teal, Shoveler, Pochard, Scaup, Eider, Common Scoter, Velvet Scoter, Goldeneye, Red-breasted Merganser, Ruddy Duck, Honey Buzzard, Marsh Harrier, Hen Harrier, Goshawk, Sparrow Hawk, Common Buzzard, Rough-legged Buzzard, Merlin, Peregrine, Golden Plover, Purple Sandpiper, Woodcock, Pomarine Skua, Arctic Skua, Great Skua, Mediterranean Gull, Little Gull, Sabine's Gull, Glaucous Gull, Kittiwake, Sandwich Tern, Common Tern, Arctic Tern, Black Tern (usually along the sea in autumn), Guillemot, Razorbill, Black Guillemot, Little Auk, Long-eared Owl, Wryneck, Richard's Pipit, Bluethroat, Black Redstart, Wheatear, Ring Ouzel, Icterine Warbler, Barred Warbler, Greenish Warbler, Pallas's Warbler, Yellow-browed Warbler, Dusky Warbler, Radde's Warbler, Red-breasted Flycatcher, Pied Flycatcher, Red-backed Shrike, Great Grey Shrike, Brambling, Siskin and Snow Bunting.

THE BROADS AND
BREYDON WATER

Habitat

A line drawn on a map from Lowestoft (Suffolk) to Norwich and Mundesley would encompass the region wherein all the famous waterways can be found which constitute the Norfolk Broads. There are three major rivers, the Bure, Yare and Waveney which drain the region to sluggishly wind across flat marshlands to enter the vast tidal basin of Breydon Water before all find a common outlet into the North Sea at Great Yarmouth. This area has long claimed the attention of many famous naturalists because of the unspoilt and richly varied flora and fauna to be found along the lower reaches of the rivers.

The River Bure starts life about 6 miles (9.6 km) south of Holt in north Norfolk and winds south-eastwards through the towns of Aylsham and Wroxham. At Wroxham it enters a major Broads complex before skirting the desolate Halvergate Marshes to flow into Breydon Water by the Yarmouth A47 river bridge. Two other important tributaries, the River Ant and the River Thurne, flow into the Bure from the coastal marshes to the north.

The source of the River Yare is about 15 miles (24 km) west of Norwich and it flows through agricultural land to skirt the city before winding south-eastwards to enter Breydon near Burgh Castle. The River Wensum from its source near Fakenham joins the Yare immediately south-east of Norwich.

The River Waveney for most of its length from its distant source at Redgrave Fen 5 miles (8 km) west of Diss forms the county border with Suffolk before eventually flowing northwards about 3 miles (4.8 km) inland from Lowestoft to enter Breydon near Burgh Castle.

All three rivers are affected by the sea coast tides in their middle and lower reaches. The River Yare at Norwich which is 29 miles (46.4 m) from its outlet at Yarmouth rises and falls by 1.6 ft (0.4 m) during each tide cycle. Although the Broadland rivers are not saline, they are brackish especially in their lower reaches which favours saltmarsh type vegetation instead of the more typical reed swamps along the margins. Breydon Water is a tidal estuary with vast expanses of mudflats and adjoining saltings.

All the more important of the Norfolk Broads lie along the course of the Ant and the Thurne, the lower reaches of the Bure from Wroxham, the Yare from Norwich. The word 'Broad' suggests the opening out of a river and comes from the Anglo-Saxon word 'braedan' – to broaden. But, apart from the great tidal basin of Breydon Water (which is also derived from the Anglo-Saxon) – which is not really a 'Broad' in the accepted sense of the word – many of the Broads are situated at a comfortable distance from the main rivers as if to emphasise their separate identity. Yet in spite of their seeming physical isolation from the rivers they are still near enough for all the historians to have assumed a causal relationship and to have been convinced of their natural origins.

Most of the Broads which lie in shallow basins hold less than 10 ft

(3 m) of water although 15 ft (4.5 m) has been recorded at Rollesby and Fritton while as little as 5 ft (1.5 m) has been measured at Hickling and Horsey. Their artificial origin as ancient peat workings is now all but proven; and the signs of this once widespread activity are there for all to see : the presence of clear cut islands of peat; and vertical sides to the basins instead of natural sloping margins. Interestingly, as long ago as 1834 a Mr Samuel Woodward, upon noting the clearly defined edges of Barton Broad suggested that its origin was 'most probably artificial', although he did not even hint that the other Broads were not natural.

However, in parts of Salhouse and Martham Broads, Ormesby-Rollesby-Filby Broads and Fritton Lake, a sandy or gravelly bottom is found on the landward sides of these waters, which momentarily suggests natural origins, but if we move away from the gravel margins, the bottoms are identical with other Broads; that is to say, mud and undisturbed peat, and steep peat workings just beneath the surface of the waters.

Apart from the foregoing physical features, which point to artificial 'turf pits', it is impossible to imagine any ecological upheaval which could have produced in the flat alluvial plains such vast sheets of water. Even so, one may ask, how did man with primitive tools manage to excavate pits of such depth before they rapidly filled with water? To that question, one can only answer that in Saxo-Norman times, the mean sea level lay more than 10 ft (3 m) below its present value and that much diminished tidal effects in the river valleys might well have eliminated all risks of flooding. Tidal water probably only reached the 'compression peat', which in itself allowed only very slow seepage of water into the actual workings. As far as rainwater is concerned, when it found its way into the pits it was probably baled out by very primitive methods such as the ladle and the gantry (*still* used on the Somerset Levels).

So how old are The Broads? In the absence of maps it is difficult to say. One can only refer to 300-year old records, while the rest is part guesswork. Christopher Saxton showed Fritton Lake and Ormesby-Rollesby-Filby Broads on his map of 1574. But in order to have created 2,600 acres (1,040 ha) of waterways, the digging for turf must have continued over a long period of time. The demand for peat too, must have been great at the time of the Doomsday Survey as Norfolk (*and* Suffolk) were then the most densely populated counties of England; while Norwich and Great Yarmouth were among the largest towns in the country. It is on record that Norwich Cathedral Priory used 'as many as 400,000 turves in a single year' while at South Walsham in the latter half of the fourteenth century '200,000 turves a year produced an annual income of £7'.

Ironically, in view of the low sea levels and negligible tidal influence on the peat workings it was probably the sea itself which put an end to the excavations which were then destined to become a naturalists' paradise and a holiday area of national importance. In 1287 serious flooding affected Yarmouth and Hickling and turf production declined at South Walsham. More sea flooding occurred in the ten years after 1300 and again in 1340; and who knows to what extent sea floods disrupted the livelihood of the turf diggers? Thus, we owe the unique Broadland environment to our commercially minded ancestors; a modern parallel can be found in the numerous gravel pits which have been created by the demand for shingle and sand.

However, it seems that the Norfolk Broads may have passed their prime as a wildlife sanctuary and unless a multi-million pound scheme is forthcoming very soon, further rapid deterioration in all the various habitats can be expected. Even in 1930 an eminent ornithologist, Dr B.B. Riviere, writing in *The Birds of Norfolk* touched upon one of the threats to Broadland: 'Owing to the decreasing demand for litter, many marshes have recently reverted to rough tangles and this is the primary reason why the Yellow Wagtails and Lapwings have decreased in numbers as breeding species'. Marsh litter was used in stock keeping while reed and sedge beds were harvested for many centuries for thatching. Alder wood was used for brush making and turnery. The exploitation of these natural resources all helped to hold natural succession in check which, in the case of Broadland, is from open water through fen to scrub and alder woodlands (carr).

Harvesting of these crops began to diminish from the time of the First World War. Since then natural succession has continued largely unchecked with the result that many hundreds of acres of previously open fenland have now become dense alder carrs. Reed and some sedge is still in commercial demand and this has been responsible for keeping some fen in an open condition. The mechanical cutters though, which now have to be employed, are too efficient from a conservation viewpoint. The old skilled marshmen who used a traditional hand scythe have almost gone and a mechanical cutter leaves no untidy clumps (which were not worth the bother to cut by hand) and can now reach boggy areas formerly denied to manual labourers. Traditionally, the fen crops were transported by boat, so many dykes were kept cleared or created to facilitate transport by shallow bottomed boats. With the disappearance of an intensive labour force many of these dykes have now silted up and grown over.

Farming is playing an increasing role in the decline of Broadland. Over the centuries more and more land has been brought into agricultural use through embankment of the rivers and from drainage. Original windmill driven pumps were gradually replaced by steam engines, diesel driven pumps and, nowadays, electrically driven ones provide even more efficient drainage. Traditionally the reclaimed marshes were mainly used for cattle grazing, but some arable crops were grown. With the greater efficiency of the drainage system it was realised that productivity of the crops was much improved if the water table was dropped. The increasing acreage of arable fields has now reached such serious proportions that the government have now been prodded into paying 'compensation' to farmers who do not plough; moreover, leached farm fertilisers have contributed to over-enrichment of the waterways which in turn, has led to the massive proliferation of minute algae. This has had the effect of preventing weed growth and destroying all dependent animals. One particular algae which occurs in brackish waters is responsible for releasing toxins into the water which have created disastrous 'fish-kills' almost annually in recent years. The continuous fall-out of dead algae is adding to the sediment with a centimetre or more of mud being deposited annually in many broads. A bacterium which also occurs in these deep deposits proliferates during hot weather to such an extent that another toxin is released which has brought about the deaths of several thousand waterfowl. This enrichment is also thought to cause the loss of marginal reed swamp which again in turn leads to bank erosion with yet more mud deposition.

Another major source of enrichment is treated effluent from sewage works; but an experimental phosphate removal plant has been installed at Stalham. Other sources of nutrients come from intensive livestock units, natural processes and a large gull roost in the case of Hickling Broad. Added to all these problems upwards of 500,000 people visit the Broads annually for holidays 'afloat', sightseeing water tours and to use privately owned boats. A staggering 2,000 craft are available for weekly hire on the 125 miles (200 km) of navigable waterways. In addition to these craft there are over 7,500 privately owned boats licensed to use the waterways.

The Norfolk Broads are now a multi-million pound industry and it seems likely that such powerful vested interests will only be reconciled to the urgent needs of nature conservation with great difficulty. Perhaps they can be convinced that it is the Conservation Goose that lays the golden egg?

Yet in spite of all the enormous problems and pressures, Nature Conservation bodies such as the Royal Society for the Protection of Birds, the Nature Conservancy Council, the Norfolk Naturalists' Trust and the National Trust have established a number of nature reserves. Ways have been developed to remove mud from long neglected dykes; trees and scrub invading fens have been cleared; and a waterborne nature trail has been opened to foster public interest and education. On Ranworth Broad a Broadland Conservation Centre has been established. The Norfolk County Council has been concerned in organising dedicated bands of volunteers who give their time freely to help dig out encroaching scrub and clear ditches.

We have dwelt at length on the past and present habitat and the problems that are occurring because the Norfolk Broads are unique in Britain. Nowhere else in the country do so many different types of wetland habitats occur together offering such a varied flora and fauna. The Broads were created by man and unless there are massive injections of cash and effective conservation control by a single body it is grimly obvious that much of the area will be an historic memory to birdwatchers in the next century! Ironically, the thousands of holidaymakers probably know the Norfolk Broads better than most birdwatchers, because access from the land has always been difficult and restricted. There are so many private marshes, moorings and towpaths that it would seem the only way to explore the Broads is by boat. However, for most birdwatchers this may be impractical and inconvenient. Certainly, one of the well-organised water trails such as that from Hickling, and from Wroxham, in the summer season would be a very rewarding experience, giving a good insight into the Broadland habitats, but with no certainty that any birds will be seen!

However, there are at least ten Broads, or Broadland reserves, which can be visited by birdwatchers in addition to the far-famed Breydon Water. Of these ten, Horsey Mere has already been discussed in the previous coastal section. The other major Broad of this region, and perhaps of the whole complex, is Hickling Broad. These 1,355 acres (542 ha) are owned by the Norfolk Naturalists' Trust, and were established as a National Nature Reserve by the Nature Conservancy Council. It is a large, shallow Broad surrounded by extensive reed swamp, sedge beds, oak wood and alluvial marshland which has a rich flora and fauna and especially good numbers of moths and dragonflies. Nevertheless, the chief interest is the birdlife. The reed swamp is the stronghold of the Bearded Tit, Bittern and Marsh Harrier, although the latter two species have declined as breeding species. Artificial wader pools have been created and the open waters of the Broad attract vast numbers of wildfowl during the winter months. This is too, the home of the swallow-tail butterfly which may be seen on sunny days flying over the sedge fens from mid-May. With any luck, closer views may be obtained when this beautiful insect visits some of the marshland flowers which grow in profusion. The black and yellowish green cross-banded caterpillar lives on the leaves of milk parsley, fennel and other umbellifers.

Pair of Bearded Tits

Another major complex of Broads lie to the south-east of Hickling and comprise Filby, Rollesby and Ormesby all adjacent to one another. The latter has well wooded shores, but all are private and well used for fishing and yachting. Both the A149 and A1060 roads cross through these Broads where some viewing during the winter months may be rewarding. In the valley of the River Ant the 365 acres (146 ha) of Barton Broad are also owned by the Norfolk Naturalists' Trust, but access is difficult and limited. The adjacent areas include extensive growth of alder-carr with some birch and oak. Due to the high eutrophic content of the water, aquatic vegetation and dragonflies have declined.

Down river from Barton Broad the superb How Hill Estate is managed by the How Hill Trust as an environmental centre. The 360 acres (144 ha) comprise reed beds, sedge, marsh, meadow and woodland, broad and pools. How Hill was established as a private estate in 1904. The owner was a prosperous local architect, Edward Boardman, who created a Broadland Estate in miniature, including a couple of windmills. The estate is now frequented by swallow-tail butterflies, harriers and Bearded Tits. On its slight eminence, How Hill commands a sweeping vista across the valley of the River Ant.

Several interesting Broads can be found in the Bure valley, but most can only be visited by boat. Wroxham Broad, where many regattas are held, is best avoided, but from Wroxham itself the Bure can be explored by hired boat or by a guided tour. Downstream from Wroxham, Hoveton Great Broad is managed by the Nature Conservancy Council and is part of the Bure Marshes National Nature Reserve complex which includes

Ranworth and Cockshoot Broads. In 150 years the area of open water on Hoveton Great Broad has decreased by nearly half to about 70 acres (28 ha). There are extensive areas of adjoining swamp fen over which ½ mile (0.8 km) of sleepered trail has been established. This is the only pathway through the reserve to the edge of the Broad and it gives a unique insight into the formation and complex natural succession which all the Broads are facing. The swamp fen is a dangerous area and no one should attempt to step off the sleepers. The typical habitat of alder carr, sedge fen, open Broad and a small example of a turf pond can all be seen. Turf ponds were created by shallow excavations, rarely more than about 4 ft (1.2 m) deep, for peat after the deeper pits became flooded. The peat secured though, was of inferior quality and the practice died out early this century.

Ranworth Broad is also owned by the Norfolk Naturalists' Trust and comprises 144 acres (57.6 ha). It is connected to the River Bure by a channel known as Ranworth Dam. The surrounding area is mainly fen and alder carr. Much of the aquatic vegetation has gone, but some of the sedge fen is still commercially used with plenty of interesting plants such as yellow loosestrife, marsh pea, milk parsley and royal fern to be seen. The floating Broadland Conservation Centre here explains the problems of the Broads and is open every day except Monday, from April to October between 10.30 a.m. and 5.30 p.m., but only from 2.00 p.m. to 5.30 p.m. on Saturdays.

Farther along the Bure valley the small village of Upton lends its name to a small broad and fen which is also well away from the main river and only connected to it by dykes. Upton Fen (NNT) reserve is very important because it is fed by relatively clean spring water. Much of the site is covered by alder carr or young oak woodland. Habitat management includes scrub clearance from the open fen and clearance of the dyke system. Several rare species of orchids and sedge can be found, in addition to a strong population of swallow-tails and other butterflies, dragonflies, and grass snakes. White admiral butterflies can also be found here. The reserve is extremely boggy and visitors should keep to the paths.

The River Yare winds its way from Norwich seawards through agricultural grazing marshes. The most interesting habitats can be found between Brundall and Reedham.

A short distance downriver is Strumpshaw Fen, another very attractive area. It is rather more accessible and has been managed by the RSPB since 1975. The 600 acres (240 ha) of Strumpshaw Fen Reserve straddle either side of the River Yare with a frontage to the privately-owned Rockland Broad on the south side of the river. Within the reserve is the complete range of Broadland habitats: open water, fen, sallow and alder carr, woodland, grazing marshes and dykes. The usual pollution problems have led to over-enrichment with a poor flora and fauna in those waterways which are still connected to the River Yare. Embankments have been made to seal the fen off from the polluted Yare with the result that aquatic vegetation is returning. The areas which were never connected to the river are rich in plants, birds and invertebrates. Much management work is still being carried out (it never ceases on any reserve!) including scrub clearance from the fen and clearing out the old dyke systems. The RSPB manages an area of very rich grazing marshes which is important because most of this type of marsh elsewhere has been too well drained, ploughed or sprayed with weedkiller or fertiliser to be attractive to wildlife. About 400 species of plants have been recorded on the reserve many of which were once widespread in Broadland before pollution eliminated them. Notable plants include: water soldier, bur-reed, sweet flag, sweet grass, flowering rush, marsh sowthistle, great spearwort, marsh pea, yellow and purple loosestrifes, great water dock, meadow sweet and milk parsley. Amphibians are increasing with toads, frogs, smooth and great-crested newts seen regularly. The naturalised European green terrapin is a somewhat odd inhabitant; while the Chinese water deer may be encountered. The reserve is rich in invertebrates with good numbers of butterflies (including small numbers of swallow-tails) and dragonflies.

Also on the south side of the River Yare, about two miles (3.2 km) to the north of Rockland St Mary, the RSPB acquired Surlingham Church Marsh in 1984 to link up with their Rockland Marsh. This reserve of 230 acres (93 ha) lies all along the banks of the River Yare and is a complex mosaic of reed and sedge beds, open water and meadow fen. Breeding birds include Water Rail, Snipe, Pochard and Cetti's Warbler. In winter Hen Harrier, Water Rails, Water Pipits, Bearded Tits and Jack Snipe are often present.

South of Strumpshaw Fen Reserve wide grazing marshes comprise the Yare Valley with the pastures at Buckenham especially noted for winter wildfowl. The River Chet flows into the south side of the Yare by Norton Staithe about 1½ miles (2.4 km) from Reedham. About 1½ miles (2.4 km) upstream from where it joins the Yare there is another very important wetland site known as Hardley Flood. This is not one of the old peat pits, but a spillway on the north side of the River Chet which has breached the wall in two places. The site is permanently flooded by the tidal water which moves freely between the river and the marsh. There is some fringing mud which attracts waders and also a large area of reeds and some observation hides provided by the Norfolk Naturalists' Trust.

At Reedham the valleys of the River Yare and River Waveney meet. To the north the great valley of the River Bure unites with the Halvergate Marshes to make one vast basin of some 50,000 acres (20,000 ha) of damp, low-lying grasslands. An intricate network of drainage dykes, created over 200 years ago, preclude all but the most experienced marshmen from exploring the area. Nevertheless, a section of the Weaver's Way footpath crosses the controversial Halvergate Marshes between the village of Halvergate and Great Yarmouth. Until the 1970s the pattern of land use had changed very little over the years, being mainly summer grazing of beef cattle and a few sheep. Most of the land lies at a lower level than the embanked rivers which are strongly tidal. Drainage takes place through the network of dykes and drains to pumping stations. Due to poor cattle prices and high subsidies on wheat during the late 1970s arable farming escalated; associated lowering of water tables to improve crop production followed. This great alluvial basin is a major national breeding haunt of Shoveler, Lapwing, Snipe, Redshank and Yellow Wagtails and there are important winter concentrations of wildfowl, waders and raptors. Until the trend towards drainage and arable farming is halted, the Yare basin faces the serious threat of degradation.

In 1985 and 1986 the RSPB acquired 365 acres (148 ha) of the Berney Marshes comprising part of the Halvergate Marshes. This development is an important 'conservation wedge' which may lead to the protection of a greater area.

Breydon Water has a bloody history for this was a resort of the old punt gunners in the latter half of the nineteenth century and up to the early part of this century. More rare birds were shot on Breydon than anywhere else in Britain. Many hardy local men got their living from wildfowling and fishing throughout the year. Amongst them was a true naturalist, Arthur Patterson, who gave up the gun to produce an historic and astounding series of books on the wildlife and the lives of the marshmen who lived in the region.

Breydon Water is now a local nature reserve comprising over 1,100 acres (440 ha) under the joint management of the Great Yarmouth District Council and the Norfolk County Council. The seaside town of Great Yarmouth would seem an unlikely place for birdwatchers but the outlet of the three rivers to the south of the town is worth watching for gulls, while the outfall by the power station about ½ mile (0.8 km) to the north is also attractive to these species. Moreover, Black Redstarts regularly breed in the town and in the vicinity of the power station.

Maps 10, 11, 12 and 13

Species

Not all that many years ago the Norfolk Broads were almost the exclusive haunt of Bitterns, harriers and Bearded Tits which meant that the birdwatcher wishing to see these specialities usually paid a visit to Hickling or Horsey. In more recent years the north Norfolk coast and other regions of East Anglia can now offer the same attractions so the Broads have, perhaps, become slightly neglected by birdwatchers, especially as Bitterns have declined to around eight booming males and Marsh Harriers have failed to nest for several years.

Brood of Marsh Harriers at Hickling in the mid-1950s

However, the Broads – in spite of pollution problems – are still a unique habitat with plenty of birds to see at most times of the year. Moreover, two new species – the Savi's and Cetti's Warblers are beginning to colonise the Broadland valleys. The Savi's Warbler used to nest in small numbers prior to the mid-nineteenth century but became extinct soon after this. In recent years up to six pairs of this summer migrant have nested at Hickling and birds have been noted at Hardley Flood and Strumpshaw Fen. The sedentary Cetti's Warbler is an explosive colonist with 63 singing males now recorded in the valleys of the Rivers Bure, Yare and Waveney, although numbers are reduced in a hard winter. In the last few years the American Ruddy Duck look like being another colonist soon – from its original beginning as a feral bird which first bred in Somerset in 1960. It is such a spreading and successful colonist that it was admitted to the list of British Birds in 1971. Birds have been noted at Hickling, Strumpshaw Fen, Filby, Ormesby and Hardley Flood.

Great-crested Grebe with young

There are still good numbers of Great-crested Grebe to be found with up to 40 pairs occurring on Hoveton Great Broad. Marsh Harriers passing through on migration can still be seen in most springs, while the rarer Montagu's Harrier has also been noted on passage with one pair breeding at a secret location in recent years. Hen Harriers regularly winter in the region with up to six birds in the Hickling area. Another exciting possibility is that Black Terns may one day begin to colonise the Broads. Up to the early-nineteenth century this species used to breed 'in myriads' in many of the fens. Black Terns still regularly pass through on spring migration, when scores of birds may be seen feeding over the waterways dipping down in flight to snatch some fly or aquatic insect off the surface. Some pairs spent the summer on one Broad, but did not breed. They can appear on easterly or south-easterly winds at any time from late April, and can be seen over any of the Broads or drains. Hickling, Rockland and Horsey though, seem to be favoured by this delightful marsh tern.

Other terns from the coast are moving into the Broads where facilities are provided for them. For many years Common Terns have nested on man-made rafts at Ranworth Broad, Hardley Flood and Breydon Water. Over 50 pairs have nested on Hardley Flood rafts, while other pairs have more recently nested at Hickling. More surprisingly, Little Terns have begun to nest at Hickling some 3 miles (4.8 km) from the *coast* (to which habitat this species is usually restricted in Britain). The Ruff is another long lost species, but large numbers still appear almost annually on migration especially at Hickling. Unusually, up to 70 birds have recently taken to wintering in the whole region of the Broads. Another passage wader which may stay to nest one day is the Black-tailed Godwit which can usually be seen at Hickling in the spring. From time immemorial the Spoonbill has visited Breydon Water and Hickling Broad. This graceful crested bird with a long spoon-shaped bill has not nested in Norfolk for over 300 years, but it may well do so again one day.

The Crane is an extremely rare vagrant to Britain and is declining as a breeding species in Europe. It is, therefore, quite astounding that one or two birds have been seen regularly in Broadland all year round since 1979.

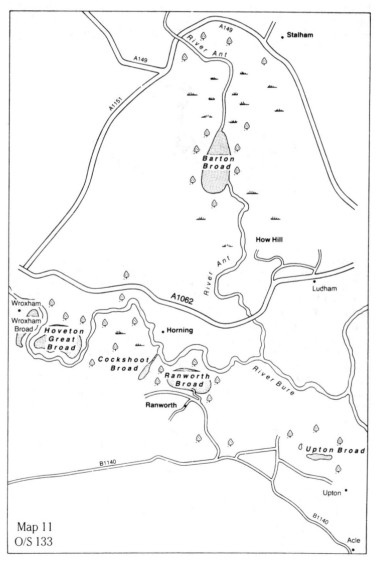

Map 11
O/S 133

Not unexpectedly, with the pollution of the waterways, there has been a major decline in herons with possibly less than 60 pairs from a high of over 200 pairs in the early 1960s. The Purple Heron has been sighted a few times at Hickling where a Night Heron and a Great White Egret have also been recorded. The Osprey is a regular visitor to some of the larger Broads during the spring months and usually attracts the furious attentions of nesting Lapwings and Common Terns. Another speciality is the Water Pipit which arrives in small numbers from late autumn to spend the winter months in the Hickling and Cantley areas. This migrant from the mountain districts of central Europe often stays until April frequenting damp pastures or the muddy edges of shallow waterways.

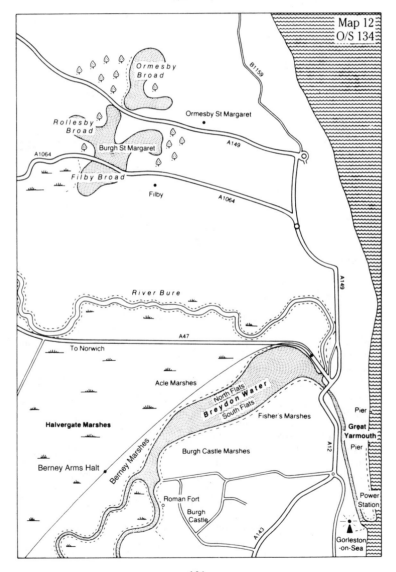

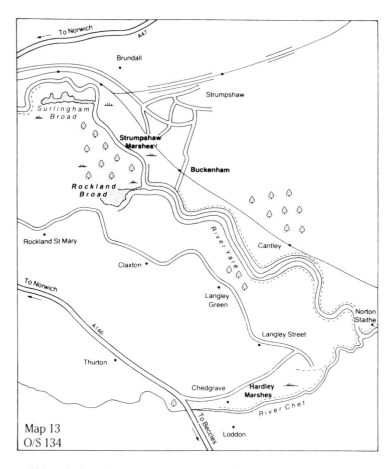

Map 13
O/S 134

Although there is nothing special about Cormorants, mention must be made of a large roost of these birds at Ranworth Broad where some 350 birds flight in from their daytime fishing on the sea or other Broads. Previously they used to roost on Scroby Sands which was an island offshore from Great Yarmouth, but which disappeared beneath the waves in 1977.

There is little doubt that Hickling Broad Reserve provides one of the best birdwatching sites in the region. It is the main Broadland haunt of the Bearded Tit with up to 100 pairs breeding. This is one of the most beautiful of British birds and is the only small reed-bed bird with a long tail and rich tawny-brown plumage. To hear their vibrant 'ping-ping' calls emanating from a stand of brown reeds on a still winter's day is delight enough; but spot a pair near their nest in late spring, expertly straddling the reed stems, their yellow bills stuffed with black St Marks flies and you have a long famous Fenland sight. The cock bird really *does* have a beard. The black mark running from the eye downwards is actually an appendage (or beard) of long black feathers and not just a stripe. The incubation and fledging periods are remarkably short with the young fledged only three weeks after the eggs are laid. Two broods are regular and three quite often so that by the end of a good summer the reed beds may be swarming with Bearded Tits; and at this time, irruption flights often occur.

Hickling is good for waders; and scrapes have been created by the Norfolk Naturalists' Trust. The Temminck's Stint drops in almost annually and up to ten birds have been seen in a season. Avocets are fairly regular (and breeding has been attempted), while a few pairs of Garganey nest almost annually somewhere in the area. Other passage waders which regularly make use of the reserve area are Greenshanks, Dunlins, Wood, Green and Common Sandpipers, Ruff, Little Stints, Turnstones, Spotted Redshanks and Black-tailed Godwits. More casual species include Red-necked Phalarope and Pectoral Sandpipers.

Rare waders have included a couple of Black-winged Stilts and a Wilson's Phalarope in full breeding plumage. Little Gulls appear annually and nesting has been attempted. Rough-legged Buzzards, wandering from their route along the nearby coastal dunes, are quite often seen in autumn and a Great Grey Shrike not infrequently appears along a sparse marshside hedgerow. Much less obvious are a few migrant Spotted Crakes which may appear in the open briefly from the shelter of the dense reeds.

One or two Long-eared Owls have nested in the wooded areas, but this species is more likely to be heard than seen! The damp pastures around the reserve often attract migrant Yellow Wagtails and several of the rarer forms have been noted including the 'Grey-headed'. During the winter months the great expanse of Hickling Broad becomes a sanctuary for up to 2,000 duck including large numbers of Wigeon and Pochard with quite a few Shoveler, Gadwall and Goldeneye. In severe weather single numbers of Smew and Red-breasted Mergansers may arrive. Up to 1,000 Coot help swell the winter wildfowl numbers. Odd birds, more usually associated with the sea, may turn up and these have included Red-throated Diver and Slavonian Grebe.

The most important reserve in the Yare Valley for visiting birdwatchers is Strumpshaw Fen where over 80 species breed regularly including Marsh Harrier, Cetti's Warbler, Long-eared Owl and Bearded Tit. Savi's Warbler has bred and may soon be a regular colonist. Grasshopper Warblers usually hold about 20 territories on the reserve. Thanks to the improved waterways and attempts at sealing off pollution, Kingfishers are regular and increasing. So too, are other water birds such as Shoveler, Pochard, Gadwall, Tufted Duck, Little Grebe and Great-crested Grebes. Occasional Garganey now nest and Water Rails are increasing. Although some of the commoner sandpipers occur on passage there is a scarcity of suitable habitat for waders. The woodlands include all the local tit species, three species of woodpeckers, Nuthatches, Treecreepers, Goldcrests, Tawny Owl and Woodcock. In summer Garden Warblers and Spotted Flycatchers can be found. The grazing marshes attract nesting Yellow Wagtails, Snipe, Redshank and Lapwings. Large numbers of hirundines feed over the area in summer attracted by the swarms of wetland flies while in autumn Swallows congregate in their thousands. On Rockland Broad, across the river, Black Terns are regularly seen on passage and in severe weather Smew may arrive.

In winter numbers of wildfowl increase and include Teal, Shoveler, Mallard and Gadwall. Hen Harriers have taken to feeding over and roosting in the reed fen. The Great Grey Shrike is a regular winter visitor. On the adjoining Buckenham Marshes protection has resulted in a good increase in the numbers of Bean Geese wintering there and this is their only regular wintering site in Britain. Over 300 birds frequent the damp marshes in company with up to 7,000 Wigeon and sometimes White-fronted Geese. Lower down the Yare Valley on the River Chet, Hardley Flood, a permanently flooded reserve is an important sanctuary for winter wildfowl and waders, which include Teal, Shoveler and Jack Snipe. Marsh and Hen Harriers regularly occur. Breeding birds include Bittern, Pochard, Gadwall and Common Terns. Rarities seen here include White-winged Black Tern, Great Snipe, Ferruginous Duck, Blue-winged Teal and Ruddy Duck.

Two Bean Geese and one Pink-footed Goose

The How Hill Estate supports; Marsh Harriers, Bearded Tits, Sparrow Hawks and Cetti's Warblers while in winter Hen Harriers are often recorded. This wonderful reserve – easy of access – has long been neglected by birdwatchers, but it is unlikely to be in future; in December 1985 the first ever American passerine reached Norfolk, a Black- and White-Warbler, was found there by a startled birdwatcher. Subsequently, literally thousands of watchers descended on How Hill hoping to glimpse this beautiful bird.

The limitless expanse of Breydon Water seems at first sight a daunting place for birdwatchers. It is 3 miles (4.8 km) in length and about 1 mile (1.6 km) wide in places. When the tide is out birds can be very far distant, and the use of a telescope is essential at all times. The north-eastern corner of the mudflats is one of the best spots as it is the last to be covered by the rising tide. Two public observation hides are sited here, but they are usually kept locked and, although they are very useful in wet weather, watching can just as easily be carried out from the seawall.

In historic times Breydon had an unenviable reputation for the numbers of birds that were annually shot. These included many rare and beautiful species such as Avocets and Spoonbills and it is a wonder that the latter two species still visit annually; and there are usually plenty of other passage waders on these flats in spring and autumn. Tern rafts have brought in nesting Common Terns and plenty of non-breeding gulls. The Mediterranean Gull is seen nearly every month of the year, either on Breydon or by the river mouth in Yarmouth itself, and has occurred in all plumages from the brown juvenile to the pearly grey and white adult with its black hood. Breydon is also acquiring a reputation for the rare Broad-billed Sandpiper, which have, in recent years, been recorded almost annually at the end of May or in early June.

The main channel taking the waters of the Yare and Waveney flows rather nearer to the southern shore so that a pathway along this gives better views of any diving duck or grebes that might be feeding in the deeper waters of the channel. The rough marshlands to the south of Breydon Water are still attractive to wintering Twite, Snow Buntings, Lapland Buntings, Hen Harriers, Short-eared Owls and Bewick's Swans. Other winter birds on Breydon might include Shelduck, Pintail, Wigeon, Brent Geese, Goldeneye, Scaup, Grey Plover, Knot and Bar-tailed Godwits.

In spring, passage waders include Ruff, Spotted Redshanks, Whimbrel, Curlew and Black-tailed Godwit. On autumn passage greater numbers pass through over a longer period of time. The Halvergate Marshes, immediately to the north-east of Breydon Water, used to be the wintering stronghold of White-fronted Geese with up to 5,000 frequenting the area in the 1940s. But after only two decades of modern drainage, numbers declined rapidly until, today, they hardly amount to three figures. Lapwings and Redshank still occur in large winter flocks but both have declined as breeding species. Short-eared Owls hunt over the desolate fields during the winter months fluctuating in numbers according to the vole populations. Over 100 were seen in the 1964/65 winter.

However, since the acquisition of the 365 acres (148 ha) by the RSPB, artificial flooding has attracted wintering flocks of Wigeon, Teal, Pintail, Mallard and Shelduck, as well as Brent and White-fronted Geese and Bewick's Swans occasionally. Snipe, Yellow Wagtail and Redshank nest on the marshes, which have been visited by Ruff, Avocet and Spoonbill.

Black Redstarts have bred in the town of Great Yarmouth for many years and one or two can usually be heard or seen near the power station to the south of the town. A sewage outfall nearby usually attracts a swarm of gulls which might include Mediterranean, Little and Glaucous Gulls.

Timing

Time of day is not too critical and in any case very much depends on opening times of the various reserves. Wind direction is not really important either, although an easterly wind may bring in Black Terns from the Continent in spring. Late June and July tend to be the worst times for birds, but very good for marshland vegetation and insects. Best months in spring are April, May and early June. In autumn, any month from August to November; while winter wildfowl may dramatically increase in severe weather during December and January. Obviously, in such a popular holiday area the surrounding villages may well be very busy during July and August.

The tide is important at Breydon and it is best to be in position by the north-east corner about 1½ hours before high tide time to watch waders being washed off the main mudflats to this last area to be covered by the rising waters. Although paths run along the northern and southern shores of Breydon, the southern path offers better lighting conditions and nearer viewing of the main channel.

Access

For the Hickling Broad National Nature Reserve take the minor road on the south side of the B1159, ½ mile (0.8 km) on the Stalham side of Sea Palling. Follow this for about 2 miles (3.2 km) to Hickling which is still 2 miles (3.2 km) away from the reserve. Hickling Green adjoins Hickling and from the Greyhound Inn here take Stubb Road. Ignore 'No access to Broad' signs (this is true) and take the third turning right at a minor crossways.

The reserve is open daily, except Tuesdays, from April to October inclusive between 9.30 a.m. and 6.00 p.m. Permits are required and advance applications are advisable for tours and trails. The waterborne trail only operates on Tuesdays, Wednesdays and Thursdays from the end of May to mid-September. During the winter months the reserve can only be visited by special arrangement with the warden. Alternative and unrestricted access to a small part of the reserve can be had by following minor roads from Hickling Green to Hickling Heath and Catfield Common; then make for the church at Potter Heigham just over 3 miles (4.8 km) away. Park by the church and take the road to the west for about 150 yds (135 m) to a corner where the road bends left. Follow the public footpath to the right, then left where it becomes a wide track across an arable field. At the edge of the wood there is a (NNT) sign about the Hickling reserve. Cross the style and walk through the woodland to reach the Weaver's Way. This footpath can now be followed in either direction for about 1 mile (1.6 km), or for longer if you wish, with a good chance of seeing a swallow-tail butterfly or hearing a Savi's Warbler. Bearded Tits frequent the adjoining reed and sedge fen and there is also a good chance of seeing a Marsh Harrier or Bittern. The wader pools or the Reserve hides are not available from this approach. A public observation hide, though, was erected in 1986.

Barton Broad in the upper reaches of the River Ant is pretty inaccessible, except by boat by which means it is only worth looking at. How Hill Estate is easier and best approached on the A1062 from Potter Heigham. Follow this road for 2 miles (3.2 km) to Ludham. A short distance through the village turn off right on a well signposted minor road to How Hill. The public footpath and nature trails are open all year. The splendid Edwardian house and estate is run as a residential Education Centre.

Hoveton Great Broad on the River Bure is also inaccessible except by water, but is well worth a visit. Private hire craft or the organised and escorted tour which starts upriver at Wroxham during the summer season are good ways of viewing Hoveton, Cockshoot and Ranworth Broad further downstream. A whole day would be needed for this trip.

The sleepered nature trail at Hoveton Great Broad crosses extremely dangerous swamps and no one should attempt to step off the trackway provided. Tours start at Wroxham and there is ample car parking.

Ranworth Broad can be seen from the fine floating conservation centre which can be visited between April and October. The centre is open daily, except Mondays, from 10.30 a.m. to 5.30 p.m. and on Saturdays 2.00 p.m. to 5.30 p.m. Entry is free to any conservation trust members; for others there is a small fee. Access is from Norwich via the B1140 to South Walsham, a 10 mile (16 km) journey. Then turn left to Ranworth. Alternatively, take the B1152 for just over 1 mile (1.6 km) south-east of Potter Heigham for about 5 miles (8 km) to Acle and then the B1140 for 3 miles (4.8 km) to South Walsham where a right hand turn just past the church goes to Ranworth, about 1¼ miles (2 km). At Ranworth, park opposite the Granary on the public staithe and walk towards the church keeping this on your left. Take the path on your right, opposite the church, and follow this to the Conservation Centre. On either approach Ranworth can make an interesting port of call on the way to or from the Thurne Valley reserves of Hickling and Horsey.

Upton Broad is well worth a visit and lies off the south side of the River Bure between Ranworth and Acle. Intending visitors should contact the Norfolk Naturalists' Trust before visiting this reserve. From South Walsham on the B1140 take the first road left to Pilsons Green where a road to Upton should be followed for ¼ mile (0.4 km) to a minor crossroads. Take a left hand turn down a very narrow road and about 100 yds (90 m) along look out for a signposted gate entrance to the reserve. The site is an extremely wet one and the logged footpath is only for the nimble footed! This is a good site for Sparrow Hawk, Woodcock, Water Rails and the two black and white woodpeckers.

The RSPB reserve at Stumpshaw Fen can be visited much more easily. From Acle via the A47 it is about 5½ miles (8.80 km); or, from the Norwich outer ring road follow the A47 for about 3 miles (4.8 km) and then take a minor turn off right and then next left to Brundall. Continue through Brundall but after passing under the railway bridge, keep a sharp lookout for another turning on the right marked Low Road (five minor roads almost meet at this point). Follow this road for another ½ mile (0.8 km) and then, where the road takes a sharp right turn, there is a clearly marked car park next to the railway line. Cross the railway line on foot taking great care to make sure no trains are approaching! Here you will find the warden's house and the centre where there are directions for following the various footpaths round the reserve. Strumpshaw Fen is open daily throughout the year and there is a charge to non-RSPB members.

For winter viewing of geese and duck on the Buckenham marshes, minor roads should be followed from the village of Strumpshaw to Buckenham Station, 1½ miles (2.4 km). Park here and go across the railway line (again with great care) to follow a track to the river. Turn left here and walk to a hide by the river bank and not far from an old windmill. The distance from the station to the hide is under 1 mile (1.6 km). Telescopes are useful, if not essential, for goose watching.

Rockland Broad can be reached on foot from a public footpath opposite the New Inn at Rockland St Mary. It passes along the Broad (which is not part of the RSPB reserve) to the River Yare and along its bank. Rockland St Mary is about 5 miles (8.0 km) from Norwich and can only be reached from the A146 Norwich to Loddon road.

For Surlingham Church Marsh there is careful car parking available by Surlingham Church. From here there is a circular route of nearly 2 miles (3.2 km) around the reserve.

Also from the A146 travelling from Norwich, take a left hand turn off to Chedgrave, about 9½ miles (15.2 km) from Norwich. Follow the road through the village past the church to Hardley Street. Turn off right down a minor road past the church (which is some distance from Hardley Street) and over a cross trackway to park where indicated near Hardley Hall. Follow the directions from here to two observation hides. The distance from leaving the A146 is nearly 3 miles (4.8 km). Return by the same route, or head along minor roads at the edge of the marshes to Rockland Broad almost 5½ miles (8.8 km) to the north-west.

Breydon Water and its surrounding marshes is a vast area and could not be explored on a short visit or even in one day. The long distance Weaver's Way footpath from Stalham can be met with from the village of Halvergate about 1 mile (1.6 km) away, off the B1140 halfway between Reedham and Acle. The footpath traverses Halvergate Marshes and is well signposted. It then follows the north bank of Breydon Water to Yarmouth, a distance of about 7 miles (11.2 km). The path often remains boggy as late as May, and adequate footwear should be worn. A winter visit might be worthwhile to watch for Hen Harriers, Short-eared Owls and geese. Alternatively, start at the Yarmouth end of the Weaver's Way (use the British Rail Vauxhall Station) and follow the path along the north bank as far as the two observation hides, the farthest of which is about 1 mile (1.6 km) away. Watch in this north-east corner from about 1½ hours before high tide time. The whole of the wader population on the open mudflats may congregate here which is the last point to be covered by the tide. A telescope is essential when watching over Breydon Water and Marshes. The observation hides are usually kept locked, but the key can be obtained from Great Yarmouth Public Library if you prefer shelter from the elements. Otherwise the viewing is just the same from the banks. To pick up the Weavers Way, drive into the railway station entrance, but bear left towards the river where you can park.

The south bank footpath can be picked up by crossing the South Town bridge in Yarmouth and turning right through a veritable maze of minor roads. It is better to join the footpath at Burgh Castle. Take the A12 south from Yarmouth and turn off right down a minor road at a round-about junction with the A143. Then, just over 3 miles (4.8 km) to Burgh Castle Church where the south bank footpath can be picked up and followed northwards. The Burgh Castle and Fishers Marshes often hold wintering Whooper and Bewick's Swans in addition to Short-eared Owls and Hen Harriers. For the harbour entrance and the power station, follow the seafront southwards for about 2 miles (3.2 km) from the southernmost pier.

There is no road access to Berney Marshes, but the railway from Great Yarmouth stops at Berney Arms Halt. The Weaver's Way footpath crosses the reserve and boat trips with the Warden are available to the reserve from Breydon Marine at Burgh Castle. Bookings only by post (enclose SAE) to the Warden, Mr L. Street, 18 Oaklands Close, Halvergate, Norwich NR13 3PP. Trips depart Sundays 10 a.m. to 2 p.m.

Calendar

Resident Little Grebe, Great-crested Grebe (although largely dispersing from the Broads in autumn to winter on the sea), Bittern, Grey Heron, Grey-lag Goose (feral), Shelduck (largely absent in autumn for moult migration), Gadwall, Shoveler, Pochard, Tufted Duck (restricted to smaller Broads as a rule), Sparrow Hawk, Water Rail, Lapwing, Snipe, Woodcock, Redshank (winter increases in last four species), Stock Dove, Barn Owl, Little Owl, Tawny Owl (scarce), Long-eared Owl, Kingfisher, Green Woodpecker (scarce), Great Spotted Woodpecker, Lesser Spotted Woodpecker, Pied Wagtail, Stonechat (also winter visitor), Cetti's Warbler (fluctuation due to severe winters and good breeding seasons), Goldcrest, Bearded Tits (also subject to fluctuations), Long-tailed Tit, Marsh Tit, Willow Tit, Coal Tit, Nuthatch, Treecreeper, Redpoll (also a winter visitor), and Corn Bunting.

December–February and March Slavonian Grebe, Cormorant, Bewick's Swan, Whooper Swan, Bean Goose, Wigeon, Teal, Pintail, Scaup, Goldeneye, Smew, Red-breasted Merganser (scarce on the Broads), Ruddy Duck (rare, but increase expected), Hen Harrier, Common Buzzard, Rough-legged Buzzard (both latter species uncommon), Merlin, Peregrine (rare), Ringed Plover, Golden Plover, Grey Plover, Knot, Sanderling, Dunlin, Ruff (some birds winter), Jack Snipe, Bar-tailed Godwit, Curlew, Turnstone, Mediterranean Gull, Little Gull, Glaucous Gull, Short-eared Owl, Rock Pipit, Water Pipit, Fieldfare, Redwing (latter two species often very numerous on grazing marshes), Great Grey Shrike, Hooded Crow, Brambling, Siskin, Twite, Lapland Bunting and Snow Bunting (latter two species not usually so common as on the north coast).

March to April–May Spoonbill, Garganey, Ruddy Duck, Red Kite (extremely rare vagrant), Marsh Harrier (has also been known to winter in the area), Montagu's Harrier (not usually before early May), Goshawk, Common Buzzard, Rough-legged Buzzard, Osprey, Hobby (not usually before early May), Avocet, Ringed Plover, Little Stint, Temminck's Stint, Ruff, Black-tailed Godwit, Whimbrel, Greenshank, Common Sandpiper, Green Sandpiper, Wood Sandpiper, Mediterranean Gull, Little Gull, Common Tern, Little Tern, Black Tern, Yellow Wagtail, Black Redstart, Grasshopper Warbler, Savi's Warbler, Garden Warbler, Lesser White-throat and Spotted Flycatcher.

June–July Passage wader less and bird song decreasing.

August–November Cormorant, Spoonbill, Bewick's Swan, Whooper Swan, Brent Goose (the latter three species not before the end of October as a rule), Wigeon, Teal, Pintail, Goldeneye (from November), Ruddy Duck, Marsh Harrier, Hen Harrier (from October), Common Buzzard, Rough-legged Buzzard, Osprey (not after October), Merlin, Peregrine (rare), Spotted Crake, Avocet (not, as a rule, after September), Ringed Plover, Golden Plover, Grey Plover, Knot (not usually before end of August), Sanderling, Little Stint, Temminck's Stint, Pectoral Sandpiper (rare), Curlew Sandpiper (erratic), Dunlin, Ruff (some winter), Jack Snipe (not before September), Black-tailed Godwit, Bar-tailed Godwit, Whimbrel (not after October), Curlew, Spotted Redshank, Greenshank, Green Sandpiper, Wood Sandpiper, Common Sandpiper, Turnstone, Red-necked Phalarope (rare), Mediterranean Gull, Little Gull, Common Tern (not after September), Little Tern (not after August), Black Tern (more usual in spring), Short-eared Owl, Rock Pipit (from October), Water Pipit (rare visitor from late September), Black Redstart, Great Grey Shrike (from October), Hooded Crow, Siskin, Lapland Bunting and Snow Bunting (the latter two species never very common as on the north coast).

Habitat

Although we grumble about the loss of hedgerows to make way for prairie-like fields in Norfolk we have much less to complain about than our colleagues in the other counties of East Anglia! Throughout the interior of Norfolk there are still many very attractive estates – most are private of course, but some are open to the public. The greatest change of land use in Norfolk over the past 50 years has been in the Brecks, although newcomers to the area would not realise the vast extent of the transformation created by farming and forestry interests.

Breckland consists of nearly 250,000 acres (100,000 ha) lying between Swaffham in the north, Bury St Edmunds (Suffolk) in the south, East Harling in the east and Lakenheath in the west. Part of this great area of light sandy soils straddles the Suffolk border. Some 200 and more years ago flocks of Great Bustards used to roam and nest in this treeless plain until the species became extinct with the shooting of the last bird in 1838.

It is believed that Neolithic man devastated the oak forests in order to work the light sandy soils. From Roman times sheep grazed the open sandy heathlands and until the twentieth century it was probably the main sheep rearing district in Britain. However, sheep farming had begun to decline from the seventeenth century and the waste grounds were unprofitable for crops. The rabbit alone was left to keep the stony ground barren with close cropped turf and this it very effectively did, multiplying in vast numbers. When myxomatosis arrived in 1954–5 it decimated the rabbit legions almost overnight, with the remarkable result that, within a year or so, the heathland vegetation had changed out of recognition. This in turn speedily led to the decline of Stone Curlews, Woodlarks and Wheatears, all species dependent on the original barren habitats. From there farming moved in with modern machines, improved fertilisers, modern herbicides and insecticides all helping to speed the process of reclamation. An estimated 54,000 acres (21,600 ha) of heathland survived in 1880 but by 1968 this area had been reduced to a pitifull 6,500 acres (2,600 ha). Most of this area still survives, but only about one-fifth is protected as nature reserves. In

Woodlark

addition afforestation has been taking place since 1922 when the first conifers were established on Lakenheath Warren. There are now 82 square miles (205 sq.km) of mostly conifer plantations in the Norfolk and Suffolk Brecks, and this operation alone has made the most striking changes to the landscape and wildlife.

Birds and plants of open habitats have sadly declined, while large numbers of deer have colonised the forests including roe, red and fallow deer. The small muntjac also occurs. One plant, the creeping ladies' tresses has become established from more northern pine forests. Some of the forest rides and firebreaks still provide suitable habitat for a few Stone Curlews and Woodlarks. One of the largest warrens at Lakenheath survived intact into this century, but in 1942 the Lakenheath air base was built which destroyed the west side of the warren.

In addition 12,600 acres (5,040 ha) of the Brecks were enclosed by the Ministry of Defence as a battle training area during the Second World War. In some respects this has safeguarded an area which might also have completely disappeared. Some of the typical Breckland birds and plants still occur there. Nature conservation stood little chance then against such powerful interests and indeed, it was not the highly organised and influential movement that it is today.

When only twelve years in existence the Norfolk Naturalists' Trust (founded 1926) established East Wretham, 362 acres (144.8 ha), as the first Breckland Reserve. This was followed by the acquisition of Weeting Heath, 343 acres (137.2 ha) and some 250 acres (100 ha) of Thetford Heath which is now a National Nature Reserve managed by the Nature Conservancy Council. They also manage Tuddenham and Cavenham Heaths over the Suffolk border. Some of the management objectives for these reserves include conserving the botanically rich grazed heath-lands, protecting the rare nesting birds and furthering public interest in conservation.

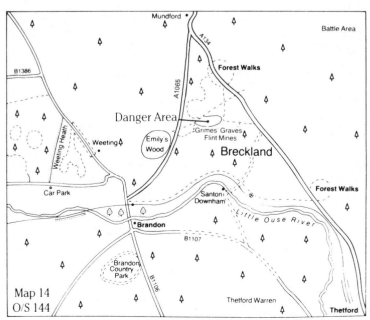

Four small rivers, the Wissey, Little Ouse, Thet and Lark drain the area and all flow eastwards to enter the great Fenland basin with its sea outlet at King's Lynn. The climate of this unique region is quite distinct from the rest of Norfolk. It has a low annual rainfall, warmer summers and colder winters, which are characteristic conditions of a semi-Continental type of climate. There is also a greater variety in temperatures with ground frosts recorded in every month of the year. Warm spring days often start with a white frost transforming the countryside into a picturesque winter wonderland.

The vast conifer plantations of the Forestry Commission offer little of outstanding interest to the birdwatcher except on the edges of the plantations where broad leaved trees have been planted for amenity value; along woodland rides which have been made as firebreaks and on land where trees have been clear felled and newly replanted. The latter sites can be good for Woodlarks, Tree Pipits and Nightjars, but after a few years the increasing height of the trees encourages instead Redpolls, Siskins, Goldcrests, tits, Jays and Wood Pigeons. Several picnic areas near Santon Downham have been provided by the Forestry Commission and these are a favourite resort of birdwatchers, hoping to see some of the Breckland specialities.

Some of the ancient stands of pine with mature deciduous woodlands of beech and hornbeam are a feature of the reserve at East Wretham, which also includes sheep grazed heath and two of the Breckland Meres – Ringmere and Langmere. Toads breed in large numbers, while adders, grass snakes, common lizards, great-crested newts and common newts are present. Butterflies are prolific. Red squirrels occur, but their place is being taken by the invading grey squirrel. Roe deer are resident and there is a good marginal flora round the Meres.

Weeting Heath is one of the few remaining heathlands, and lies on the western edge of the Brecks only about 2 miles (3.2 km) from the Fenland plain. It has a rich flora and fauna with a particularly fine example of chalk grassland. One of the most spectacular of the rare Breckland plants – the spiked speedwell occurs here and is protected from rabbits by wire enclosures. Butterflies include the small heath, common blue, brown argus, small skipper, holly blue and the Essex skipper. This site is also the home of one of Britain's rarest spiders – *Wideria stylifrons*.

Thompson Common is an extensive area of 309 acres (123.6 ha). It has cattle grazed fen, meadow grassland, a large number of small ponds known as 'pingos' and woodlands. Pingos are water filled hollows created by subsidence after the cessation of the permafrost during the Ice Age. There is a remarkable range of vegetation with a number of attractive wetland plants such as greater spearwort, yellow flag, marsh marigold, marsh orchids, water violet and ragged robin. Aquatic plants include amphibious bistort, bog bean, bitter cress and stonewort, while on the nearby drier land, thyme, red bartsia and hairy hawkbit flourish.

Dragonflies and damselflies literally occur in swarms while common butterflies are usually abundant. Roe deer are resident and the bird life is interestgng especially in spring. There is a marked (NNT) pathway and visitors are requested to keep to it as this wetland site is a delicate one.

Leaving aside the attractions of Breckland, there are four areas in the west and three areas in mid-Norfolk which are of great interest to the birdwatcher. The three areas in mid-Norfolk are no more than 13 miles (20.8 km) apart and within the same distance from the city of Norwich. Lenwade Water and Sparham Pools are about 3 miles (4.8 km) apart and

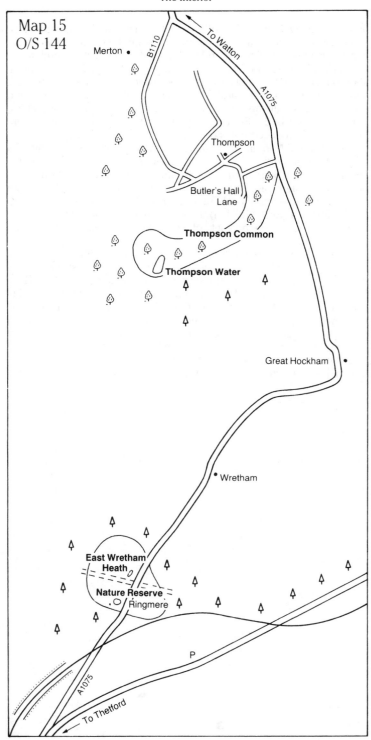

Map 15
O/S 144

Merton

B1110

To Watton

A1075

Thompson

Butler's Hall
Lane

Thompson Common

Thompson Water

Great Hockham

Wretham

**East Wretham
Heath**

Nature Reserve
Ringmere

P

A1075

To Thetford

both are managed by the Norfolk Naturalists' Trust under nature reserve agreements. The attractions of the two sites are the old gravel workings which have become flooded and surrounded by interesting scrublands. Lenwade, 37 acres (14.8 ha), has 5 large ponds and 7 smaller ones. Many butterflies (including speckled wood) and dragonflies are attracted; and the area is rich in birdlife. Sparham Pools consist of deep and shallow ponds with an island, again, the main interest is butterflies, dragonflies and birds. Both reserves lie in the Wensum Valley where there is an extensive complex of gravel workings and pools.

The third mid-Norfolk site is the National Trust-owned Blickling Hall and Park. Well worth a visit it is 13 miles (20.8 km) north of Norwich and 2 miles (3.2 km) north of Aylsham. Non-birding attraction is the perfect example of an English country house, dated about 1620, with magnificent state rooms. There is a beautiful landscaped park with a lake about 1 mile (1.6 km) long which all sounds rather formal. However, there is a good variety of woodland birds and wildfowl on the lake in winter.

In the west of the region three important habitats merit attention and all are owned or managed by the Norfolk Naturalists' Trust. Syderstone lies within 10 miles (16 km) of the north coast at the source of the River Tat, a small tributary of the Wensum. The 62 acres (24.8 ha) of acid heathland have alkaline pools in the valley bottom. The plant life is varied with large areas of broom and gorse and unusually large amounts of petty whin. Gatekeeper, ringlet and green hairstreak butterflies occur, but the major importance of this reserve is the colony of rare natterjack toads. It was the largest inland breeding colony of this amphibian in Britain, but sadly, in the last three years this has been in decline because

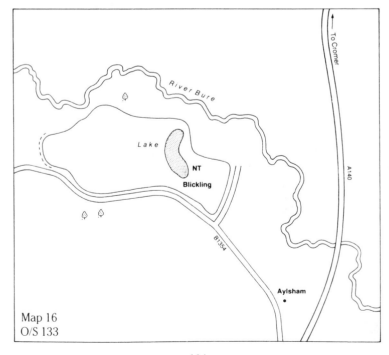

Map 16
O/S 133

114

of scrub encroachment (now halted) and declining water levels.

Roydon Common is within 5 miles (8 km) of the coast and only 4 miles (6.4 km) from King's Lynn. It is one of the most important reserves because the various plant communities associated with the valley mire are regarded as probably the best example of their type in Britain. Much of the reserve consists of heather-dominated heath. The wet heath along the sides of the mire supports cross-leaved heather with abundant patches of purple moor grass, cotton grass and deer grass. Sphagnum mosses are widespread, sundews and bog asphodel can also be found. There is a wide variety of insects including butterflies, dragonflies and one or two rare wasps. Common lizards and adders can be found on the drier heathland. Birdlife is quite good with special emphasis on winter watching.

East Winch Common, 80 acres (32 ha), lies about 4 miles (6.4 km) to the south of Roydon Common. This is another heathland with patches of boggy ground. It is threatened by invading birch trees from the birch and oak woods surrounding the reserve. This attractive site is rich in birdlife, especially in summer.

Last, but by no means least, the Wildfowl and Wetland Trust reserve at Welney occupies 850 acres (340 ha) in the very south-west corner of Norfolk on its border with Cambridgeshire. In the seventeenth century, two great drainage channels were created by the Dutch engineer Vermuyden, to drain the huge Fenland basin over an estimated 1,300 square miles (3,250 sq.km). Between these two channels, known as the Old and New Bedford Rivers, is a strip of land about 21 miles (33.6 km) in length and about ½ mile (0.8 km) wide. This land has become known as the Ouse Washes and it is the largest area of regularly flooded freshwater grazing marshland left in Britain. It is now a habitat of international importance, providing sanctuary to thousands of wildfowl during the winter months and a nesting place for over 60 species in the summer. When The Washes recede in spring ideal pasture land is left for nesting birds. Expert management has encouraged some long lost birds to return and nest on The Washes. Parts of the Ouse washes in Cambridgeshire are owned and managed as reserves by the RSPB and by the Cambridgeshire and Isle of Ely Naturalists' Trust (CWT).

Maps 14, 15, 16, 17, 18, 19 and 20

Species

The main purpose of visiting inland sites in Norfolk is to see some of the breeding specialists or perhaps the winter visitors that are not so frequent on the coast. The odd autumn passerine and a few passage waders (especially at Welney) do occur and probably the interior is understandably neglected during the autumn months. Woodlands and heathlands can be very quiet for birds after June.

However, the vast conifer plantations of the Brecks are well worth a visit in the spring and early summer months, but it is wise to concentrate on woodland rides or areas which have been newly felled. This type of managed habitat may change quickly and a good site one year might be unsuitable the next. Some rides or other areas of the forests may be closed at times for management purposes.

The picnic sites in the area between Thetford, Mundford (both on the A134) and Brandon (A1065) are well known sites. Golden Pheasants may be seen along some of the minor roadside verges while Hawfinches can be found in winter, when occasionally, a Great Grey Shrike occurs. Flocks of Redpolls, Siskins and Bramblings can also be found during the winter months. In spring and summer Woodlarks, Stone Curlews and Nightjars nest, but all are birds which are either declining or at risk. Birdwatchers are especially requested to keep to paths or rides and exercise the greatest care if breeding birds are located. Other summer birds which occur in small numbers are Redstarts, Grasshopper Warblers, Wheatears and Tree Pipits. Resident birds include Crossbills, Long-eared Owls, Sparrow Hawks and all three woodpeckers. Hawfinches obviously breed, but this species is notoriously shy and there is a better chance of seeing birds in winter.

The East Wretham National Nature Reserve is another good spot for Hawfinches which frequent the large hornbeams there. Crossbills and Long-eared Owls can be found while Hen Harriers hunt the area in winter. Ringmere and Langmere attract a few passage waders, but their water levels are unpredictable – greatly fluctuating from empty to full. Other birds which have been seen here from time to time include Red-backed and Great Grey Shrikes and Nightjars.

Stone Curlew. Summer visitor to Breckland

Weeting Heath is a marvellous example of the old stony Breckland heath and, not surprisingly, several pairs of Stone Curlews and Wheatears nest. Pairs of breeding Stone Curlews can usually be seen from one of the two excellent (NNT) observation hides. Several pairs of Common Curlews also breed in the area and this small colonisation of the region has only taken place since 1949.

Apart from its rich flora and abundant insects Thompson Common has a good selection of the commoner breeding birds. Thompson Water at the south-west end of the reserve often attracts waders on passage and Goosanders in hard weather. Large flocks of Gadwall may occur and the Golden Pheasant can also be seen in this area.

The gravel pit complexes at Lenwade and Sparham Pools hold a very good variety of breeding birds including Kingfisher, Great-crested Grebes, Tufted Duck, Gadwall and Egyptian Geese. Common Terns also nest on one of the gravel pits – some 17 miles from the coast!

Blickling Hall and Park are good for woodland birds, with special attractions being Wood Warbler and Hawfinch. Tufted Duck and Great-crested Grebe breed and in hard winter weather Goosanders may visit the lake.

Unless you have botanical or amphibian interests, Syderstone Common might prove rewarding only during the winter months when Hen Harrier and Great Grey Shrikes have been noted.

Roydon Common is also a notable winter watching site, but Nightingale, Woodcock and Curlew breed in the area. In addition, the bog flora makes a summer visit well worthwhile. From late autumn and throughout the winter a few Hen Harriers frequent the common, often coming in to roost during the late afternoon. A Great Grey Shrike too, has often wintered here and Hooded Crows and the odd Merlin are usually to be seen. East Winch Common to the south is rich in birdlife with Nightingales, Garden Warblers, Blackcaps and occasionally Grasshopper Warblers during the summer. It is usually neglected in the winter months, but similar species to those seen on Roydon probably also occur here.

Before leaving the interior a few other species must be mentioned. The Ringed Plover is a common enough breeding species on the north coast, but visitors to the Brecks may well be surprised to encounter this shore bird many miles away from the coast. However, this small plover has been breeding on the Brecks for very many years and has successfully adapted to nesting on arable fields.

Its smaller cousin, the Little Ringed Plover, has colonised the interior in the past 25 years with a dozen or so pairs breeding on gravel pits in the west and mid-Norfolk areas. It usually favours gravel pits which are still being worked and therefore private. Birdwatchers are advised to seek Little Ringed Plovers on coastal passage (and Holme is a favourite spot for them).

Along the river course there are several private water mills and quite often Grey Wagtails can be seen on the fast running stretches of the river. More unusually, one or two Black-bellied Dippers have turned up at these water mills to stay for some weeks in winter. We can only suggest that where one of these birds occurs in an area where watchers can see them without causing annoyance to private property owners this will be the best place to go.

There are two extremely rare breeding species, the Goshawk and the Golden Oriole, which have deliberately been omitted for the sake of security. The Goshawk has nested, or attempted to nest, in the Breckland area; sadly, some have been shot and eggs were taken from another. The Golden Oriole has been well established at one site on the edge of the Brecks for several years and there are indications that this beautiful bird is spreading out to other areas. Again, it would be wrong to pin-point the main nesting area which in any case is mainly in private woodlands.

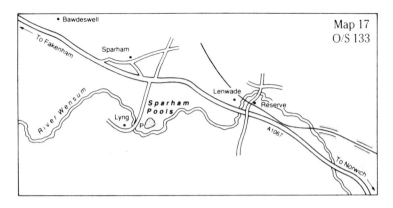

There remains the greatest wildfowl sanctuary in Norfolk tucked away in the south-west corner of the Fens. At Welney, 20 wildfowl species have been recorded, but more impressive are the legions of swans and duck which gather on The Washes during the winter months. Counts have included up to 3,000 Bewick's Swans, 30,000 Wigeon together with thousands of Pochard, Tufted Duck, Teal, Shoveler, and Pintail. Scaup, Gadwall, Smew and Goldeneye are also seen. The facilities provided for watchers are first-class with an excellent observatory overlooking the Bewick's Swan lagoon. Although, all 'laid on' as it were, no one can remain unmoved by the sight of such vast numbers of wild swans content on these desolate Fens until the time comes for them to return to their breeding grounds on the northern Siberian tundra. There are generally a few Whooper Swans on The Washes, while Short-eared Owls and Hen Harriers are regular winter visitors in varying numbers. In spring and summer Welney attracts more than 60 breeding species. Careful management has brought back the Ruff and Black-tailed Godwit to nest on the Ouse Washes. Migrant birds include hundreds of Golden Plover, and large flocks of Lapwings. Black Terns often pass through on spring passage and this species has stayed to nest. In autumn, passage waders may include Common, Wood and Green Sandpipers.

Timing

For the inland wood and heathland sites visit either in spring or early summer or in winter. Early morning is always best for woodland birds

Golden Orioles

118

and usually the best time also for observing Golden Pheasants along minor Breckland roads. Golden Orioles are also notably early singers and it is unlikely that you will hear them after noon. Stone Curlews are rather more active in early morning or late evening. Forestry Commission picnic sites are liable to be more popular in the summer season. Visit East Wretham in the winter months for Hawfinches. Wintry weather may bring more duck to the Breckland Meres. Blickling Hall and Park are best avoided on Bank Holidays if possible. Roydon Common is good at any time of day, but especially so on late winter afternoons when Hen Harriers come in to roost.

Welney Washes are good also at any time of day, while during the winter months the Observatory is open for an hour to view the swans under floodlight, but this visit must be booked in advance through the Wildfowl and Wetland Trust.

Access

The best Forestry Commission sites are in the triangle formed by Thetford, Brandon and Mundford. The town of Thetford can be approached on the A11, A134, A1088 or A1066. From Thetford take the A134 north to Mundford 8 miles (12.8 km) away. After about 3 miles (4.8 km) look out for a picnic site on the right and a forest walk of about 2 miles (3.2 km). Trails are waymarked and there is an information board at the start of all forest trails. Almost opposite this site there is a minor road turn off to the village of Santon Downham 2½ miles (4 km) away.

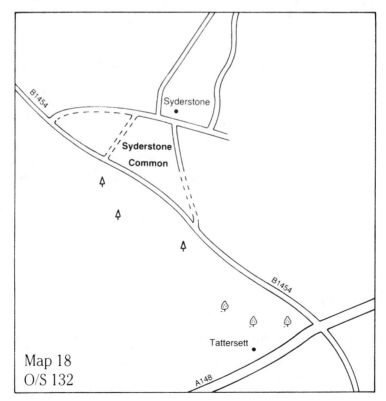

Map 18
O/S 132

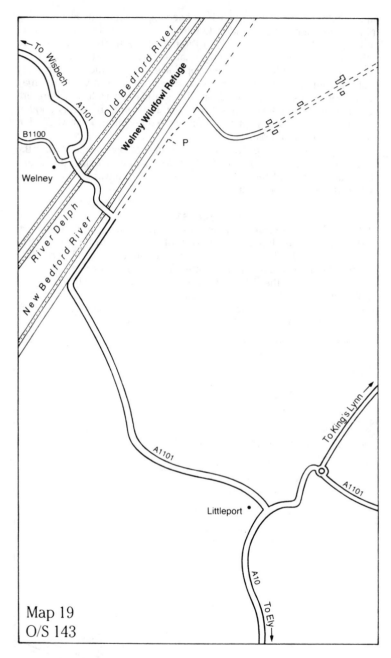

Map 19
O/S 143

Once over the level crossing, turn left to the signposted picnic site (there is no walk at this point, but it is good for woodland birds and Hawfinches may be seen in winter). Kingfishers are sometimes seen along the river and Golden Pheasants along the minor road from Santon Downham, south-east 1 mile (1.6 km) to the B1107 and Thetford. Still on the A134 approach to within 1½ miles (2.4 km) of Mundford to find another picnic site on the right and the start of a 6 mile (9.6 km) forest walk. (There are public conveniences at this site.) This is a good area for butterflies, plants and woodland birds. The walk traverses a heathland site where Curlews breed; and from the walk, there is an entrance to Grimes Graves where there are prehistoric flint mines. Yet another picnic site can be found on the A1065 between Mundford and Brandon which are about 5 miles (8 km) apart. From Brandon going northwards look out for Emilys Wood picnic site on the left after 2 miles (3.2 km).

Wretham Heath lies on the A1075 (off the A11) from Thetford to Great Hockham which are about 9 miles (14.4 km) apart. From Thetford after about 4 miles (6.4 km) look out on the left for the warden's office and obtain the necessary (NNT) permits. Here there is a wide range of habitats and a nature trail. Teaching notes and leaflets are available at the office. Both Langmere and Ringmere are within a short distance of the main road.

The Weeting Heath Reserve lies to the north-west of Brandon which is on the A1065. Head north from Brandon and on the outskirts of the town take a left turn (B1106) to Weeting, nearly 2 miles (3.2 km) away. After about 1½ miles (2.4 km) look out for a minor road on the left to Hockwold. After about 1 mile (1.6 km) along this road stop on the left at the end of a belt of pine trees where a warden's caravan is parked. Obtain permits and directions to the hides. Generally, two observation hides are in situation to view the Stone Curlews on their breeding grounds. The reserve and hides are only open from April to August inclusive, but anyone wishing to visit outside these dates should apply to the Nature Conservancy Council.

Thompson Common can be reached from the A1075 running between Thetford and Watton which are nearly 16 miles (25.6 km) apart. Head for the village of Thompson which is only 2½ miles (4 km) south of Watton. Travelling south from Watton take the third turning right signposted for Thompson. Proceed for ½ mile (0.8 km) and turn left at a 'Y' junction into Butters Hall Lane. The (NNT) car park is immediately on the left; visitors are asked to keep to the marked pathway. The main interest of this reserve is the flora and insects, but Thompson Water may hold wintering wildfowl.

Sparham Pools and Lenwade Water are in the Wensum Valley beside the A1067 Norwich to Fakenham road. Both reserves are north-west of Norwich; Lenwade is 9 miles (14.4 km) from the city and Sparham Pools 12 miles (19.2 km). Take the first turn-off on the right in Lenwade village for Lenwade Water. The turn to Sparham Pools is on the left of the A1067, 1½ miles (2.4 km) farther on, and signposted to Lyng.

The village of Blickling lies about 1½ miles (2.4 km) north-west of the old market town of Aylsham on the A140 to Cromer, 10 miles (16 km) away. For Blickling Hall and Park take the B1354 from Aylsham and look out for the entrance to Blickling Hall on your right. The Park is open throughout the year. The Hall is open from the end of March to the end of October daily, except on Mondays and Thursdays when times are from 12.00 p.m. to 5.00 p.m.

Syderstone Common is midway between Fakenham (on the A1065, A1067 and A148) and Docking (on the B1454). This is also a popular route to the coast, so a brief stay at Syderstone may produce a raptor in winter. Take the A148 west from Fakenham. Turn off right after nearly 4 miles (6.4 km) on to the B1454. After 1 mile (1.6 km) take the minor road on the right to Syderstone and park by the common on your left.

Roydon Common is another favourite pop-in point on the way to or from the coast. A late afternoon call in winter will often bring the reward of a Hen Harrier, Hooded Crow or Merlin. Roydon Common is about 3 miles (4.8 km) east-north-east of King's Lynn. Take the A149 coastal road from Hunstanton along the by-pass to the top of the hill and roundabout. Here make the left hand turn along the A148 for only about 300 yds (270 m) before turning off right down a minor road. Continue for about another ½ mile (0.8 km) and look for a rough track on your right. Follow this track for about 100 yds (90 m) where there is a small parking space from which the return of the roosting harriers can be observed.

For East Winch Common take the A47 from King's Lynn (or retrack from the common to the roundabout and take the A47 from the second roundabout). Follow the A47 for nearly 5 miles (8 km) to East Winch and look out for a by-road into the reserve on the right. A small pull in on the left is situated a short distance along this. Visitors are requested to contact the (NNT) Honorary Warden.

The best approach to Welney Wildfowl Trust Reserve is via the A1101 from Littleport which is on the A10 and some 23 miles (36.8 m) south of King's Lynn. Follow the A1101 from Littleport for nearly 5 miles (8 km) to where the road runs alongside the high bank of the New Bedford River. Where the road bends sharp left across The Washes, proceed straight on along a minor road for about 1 mile (1.6 km). Park on the right and obtain a permit from the Reception Office. This is open throughout the year except on Christmas Eve and Christmas Day. Opening hours are from 10.00 a.m. to 5.00 p.m. daily. During winter evenings swans can be seen under floodlight for about an hour from 6.45 p.m., but these visits *must be booked in advance*. There are special programmes to suit classes of schoolchildren from Primary to 'A' level, guided tours, illustrated talks and worksheets.

Calendar

Resident Little Grebe, Great-crested Grebe (on larger sheets of water), Egyptian Goose, Gadwall, Tufted Duck, Goshawk (very rare), Sparrow Hawk, Golden Pheasant, Woodcock, Barn Owl, Tawny Owl, Long-eared Owl, Kingfishers, Great Spotted Woodpecker, Lesser Spotted Woodpecker, Green Woodpecker, Woodlark, Goldcrest, Marsh Tit, Coal Tit, Nuthatch, Treecreeper, Redpoll (also winter visitor), Crossbill and Hawfinch.

November to December–February Bewick's Swan, Whooper Swan, Shelduck, Wigeon, Teal, Pintail, Shoveler, Pochard, Scaup, Goldeneye, Smew, Goosander (last four species more likely in hard weather), Hen Harrier, Golden Plover, Curlew, Redshank, Short-eared Owl, Great Grey Shrike, Hooded Crow, Brambling and Siskin.

March–May Shelduck, Shoveler, Pochard, Marsh Harrier (mainly in The Ouse Washes), Osprey (always a chance that this large raptor might appear at inland lakes), Stone Curlew, Little Ringed Plover (mostly odd pairs on private gravel pits), Ringed Plover (on Breckland arable), Ruff, Black-tailed Godwit, Curlew, Little Gull, Black Tern, Nightjar, Tree Pipit, Yellow Wagtail, Nightingale, Redstart, Whinchat, Wheatear, Grasshopper Warbler, Garden Warbler, Blackcap, Wood Warbler (rare),

Spotted Flycatcher, Golden Oriole, Red-backed Shrike and Siskin (has bred).

June to September Not the best time to visit the interior, unless you are also keen on botany and entomology.

SUFFOLK

Lowestoft Area
Kessingland to Southwold
Walberswick to Aldeburgh
Aldeburgh to Felixstowe
Wolves Wood
Redgrave and Lopham Fens

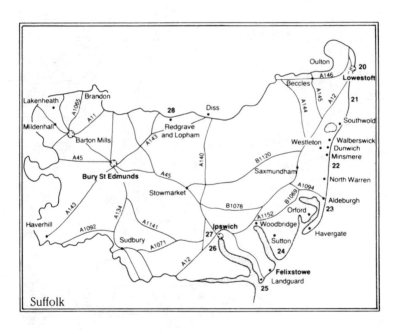

Habitat

The north Suffolk coastal region is largely dominated by the town of Lowestoft which is partly linked to the holiday trade and partly to fishing and other industries. However, the town itself is of great interest to birdwatchers and there are several nearby areas which provide good birdwatching. About 6 miles (9.6 km) north-west of Lowestoft on the border with Norfolk the 2½ mile (4 km) long Fritton Lake lies in well wooded grounds. The lake is believed to have originated by the same

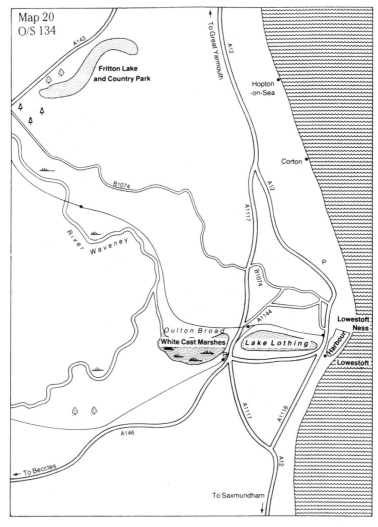

processes which formed the Norfolk Broads, i.e. ancient peat diggings which were naturally flooded at a later date. Fritton Lake is historically famous for the old duck decoy that used to account for hundreds of duck annually. Between 1862 and 1905 over 43,000 duck were killed in the decoy which was used up to 1960. Since 1976 Fritton Lake and estate, 232 acres (92.8 ha), have been open as a private Country Park, with beautifully landscaped grounds. There is a large colony of Great-crested Grebes nesting on the 500 acre (200 ha) lake. Before the last revision of the county boundaries, Fritton Lake and the estate used to be wholly in Suffolk, but now the boundary with Norfolk runs along the centre of the lake. The town of Lowestoft is separated by Lake Lothing. The lake is tidal and, at its western end, Oulton Broad still attracts quite a few birds in spite of increasing holiday pressures and its proximity to a large town. One or two parks in Lowestoft attract migrant birds from time to time; a Collard Flycatcher once stayed in one such park near the sea-front! Most birdwatching visitors will wish to go during the summer months to see the colony of nesting Kittiwakes.

Lowestoft Ness is the most easterly point in Britain. Immediately north of the harbour, a promenade (with numerous groynes) edges the old Lowestoft Denes where a gorse-covered common and marram sand hills were once extensive, with the short turf making a sea barrier. All this had gone, but the area is still very attractive to autumn migrants and winter visitors.

Map 20

Species

Like most east coast towns Lowestoft does not seem a particularly inviting place to go birdwatching, but nevertheless it does provide some very interesting species that cannot be found elsewhere in Suffolk with such regularity. With the usual holiday attractions, a nice beach and within easy reach of Minsmere, the family birdwatcher could do worse!

One of the unique ornithological attractions of Suffolk is the thriving colony of Kittiwakes to be found at Lowestoft nearly 150 miles (241 km) south of their southernmost colony on the east side of Britain at Flamborough Head. Small parties of Kittiwakes began to frequent Lowestoft harbour in the late 1940s with birds staying from late summer to early spring. In 1958 two pairs were found nesting on the South Pier, but the nests and eggs came to grief. Five pairs returned the following year and some were successful. From then onwards the colony steadily increased until the present time when between 70 and 90 pairs breed annually. From their original site on the pier, pairs have colonised many of the buildings near the sea front. (It should be remembered that the South Pier is not the southernmost pier! Claremont Pier lies to the south and no birds nest on it.)

Black Redstarts are the other speciality of the town itself and up to eight pairs nest almost annually. This species also began to colonise the town in the 1940s, first using bombed buildings as nesting sites, and then taking over any new industrial building which proved suitable. Apart from visits to observe these two breeding species the best time to visit Lowestoft would be in the autumn, winter or early spring. The harbour area is the most regular spot on the Suffolk coast for Purple Sandpipers with usually up to 30 birds frequenting the weed-covered concrete of the harbour walls or the groynes between November and

April. Recently some birds have stayed into May while early birds may re-appear from July. Another regular non-breeding visitor from the northern seabird colonies is the Shag, which occurs in single numbers in and around the harbour. It is more usually seen during the winter months, but summer records are increasing; in northern seabird colonies it is a close nesting companion of the Kittiwake, so it may well be induced to start a colony amongst its cogeners. Sanderling are usually pretty scarce on the Suffolk coast, but small parties of up to 30 birds particularly favour the sandy Lowestoft beaches during the winter months, when they can be seen scurrying along the edge of the tide like clockwork toys, pausing every now and then to pick up some morsel from the bubbling sand.

Black Redstart. Breeds in East Anglia coastal towns

Several rare gulls also favour the Lowestoft area. The Glaucous Gull is an annual visitor to the Suffolk coast and usually one or two birds can be found near the Lowestoft harbour or along the beaches. Although this species is strictly marine and rarely seen away from the coastline, some birds have been seen inland from the town where they have been attracted by fish offal or refuse on the fields. All stages of plumages have been noted from the pale brown immatures (more usual) to the ghostly all white adults. The Iceland Gull is much rarer, and in some years completely unrecorded. Lowestoft, again, is favoured with a bias towards records in the first four or five months of the year, which is a similar pattern to Norfolk records. The Mediterranean Gull is a regular annual visitor which has been seen in every month of the year. Individual birds show a great attachment to a particular wintering area returning for a number of successive years. Lowestoft harbour is a

A·R·W·

Glaucous Gull

favoured spot and birds have been seen there regularly. Pairs have been seen displaying here and at Minsmere, so it seems likely that this species will nest in the county before too long.

The coastline on either side of Lowestoft, as far as Corton to the north and Kessingland to the south, is also favoured by small parties of Snow Buntings during the winter months. Flocks totalling two or three score can usually be found, particularly in the Denes area immediately north of the town where they frequent the barren area of a camp site and, more strangely, the lawns of public gardens adjoining the sea-front! The broader beaches just to the south of Kessingland are also a good wintering spot for them.

The Suffolk coast is not noted for its sea watching, but the Ness Point immediately north of Lowestoft town has long been known as a reasonable place for sea watching as well as for watching passerine migration. In recent years it has been discovered that numbers of seabirds do occur off the coast elsewhere, but not usually so close inshore as they are off the Norfolk coast, or in such numbers. Some of the more usual seabirds to be seen include Eiders, Gannets, Fulmars, Little Gulls and Arctic Skuas, but even so, total numbers in the course of a year may be well under three figures. Some 2,000 non-breeding Common Scoters used to gather off Kessingland while winter counts were up to 5,000 off Hopton (now in Norfolk), but these large numbers have greatly declined to a few hundred birds here and there offshore all year.

Divers are usually in very small single numbers off Lowestoft, but all three are seen with the Red-throated being the most frequent. In recent years large numbers of Red-throated Divers have been discovered off the coast, but rather more to the south of Lowestoft. This sudden increase coincides with the recent appearance of sprats off the coast between December and February. Shearwaters are also very scarce with hardly more than 20 sightings of Manx Shearwaters anywhere on the Suffolk coast in one year. One or two Sooty Shearwaters have been noted off Lowestoft. During gales in autumn there has been the odd record of Leach's Petrel, Storm Petrel and a few Little Auks. Arctic Skuas are only in small numbers and Great Skuas in single figures. An adult Sabine's Gull was seen one February and mention must be made of the famous Franklin's Gull from the New World that was found in Lowestoft harbour in November 1977 where it stayed for several weeks.

Just to the north of Ness Point the Lowestoft Denes are uninspiring with a concrete promenade and groynes keeping the sea at bay. Part of the Denes was used for dumping the town's refuse in the 1960s, but this has long since been covered with soil and is now used as a summer camp site. It floods regularly during the winter months to provide a good habitat for waders, gulls, Snow Buntings and finches, while wagtails and pipits use the area on spring and autumn migrations. The low cliffs here are of great importance for studying the falls of autumn passerines and many rarities have been noted amongst the parties of Pied Flycatchers, Redstarts and warblers which may arrive on east or south-east winds. Some of the public gardens in Lowestoft are also well worth watching. Semi-rarities seen fairly often include Icterine Warbler, Barred Warbler and Wryneck while rarer migrants have included Yellow-browed Warbler, Red-breasted Flycatcher and the Collared Flycatcher.

In spite of ever-increasing holiday pursuits Oulton Broad is still attractive to birds with a few pairs of Great-crested Grebes nesting. There are often large numbers of Pochard wintering with small parties of Bearded Tits in the reed beds. Short-eared Owls and Hen Harriers are regular winter visitors to the nearby marshes which are also notable for Jack Snipe in varying numbers from one winter to the next. Up to 30 were seen in the area one winter. Rarities seen in the area include Ferruginous Duck, Rough-legged Buzzard, Hoopoe, White Stork and Red Kite.

Timing

May and June would be the best months for seeing the breeding Kitti-wakes and Black Redstarts. It is difficult to say what time of day might be best in a busy town, but perhaps early morning would be an advantage. For passerine migrants any time from August to November, but falls of migrants depend on east or south-east winds. However, apart from falls, there is a good migration of outgoing and incoming passerines to be seen along the Suffolk coast in spring and autumn. Seabirds may occur offshore in any winds, but autumn on-shore gales might produce the rough-weather birds such as shearwaters or skuas in small numbers. Watch the harbour and shore from October onwards for Purple Sand-pipers, Sanderling, Glaucous Gulls and Snow Buntings. Watching seawards in early morning is difficult when the sun rises in the east.

Access

The coastal town of Lowestoft lies in the north-east corner of Suffolk and is served by the A12 from Saxmundham 21 miles (33.6 km) away, the A146 from Beccles, 8½ miles (13.6 km), and the A12 from Great Yarmouth, 10 miles (16 km).

As with all towns it is difficult to pin-point routes to car parks, but make for the northern half of the town to find a car park at the north end of the Denes. Walk south 1½ miles (2.4 km) to explore the Denes and the harbour. Beaches to the south of the town are best explored from Kessingland which is 3 miles (4.8 km) to the south. Find somewhere to park near the sea-front at the end of the B1437 (from the A12).

Fritton Lake and Country Park are open during the summer season. The Park and Lake lie roughly midway between Lowestoft and Great Yarmouth, but about 3 miles (4.8 km) from the coast. Entrance to the Park is off the left hand side of the A143 from Yarmouth to Beccles. Alternatively, take the B1074 from Lowestoft to St Olaves and turn right at the A143.

Calendar

December–February Red-throated Diver, (occasionally) Black-throated and Great Northern, Little Grebe, Great-crested Grebe, Fulmar, Gannet, Cormorant, Shag, Bewick's Swan, Pochard, Tufted Duck, Eider, Common Scoter, Velvet Scoter, Hen Harrier, Golden Plover, Sanderling, Purple Sandpiper, Mediterranean Gull, Glaucous Gull, Iceland Gull (rare), Kittiwake, Short-eared Owl, Rock Pipit, Bearded Tit and Snow Bunting.

March–May Great-crested Grebe, Cormorant, Shag, Pochard, Tufted Duck, Eider, Common Scoter, Purple Sandpiper, Mediterranean Gull, Glaucous Gull, Iceland Gull, Kittiwake, Short-eared Owl, Black Redstart and Snow Bunting (not after March).

June–July A quiet time, but Kittiwakes and Black Redstarts still in evidence.

August–November Red-throated Diver, Little Grebe, Great-crested Grebe, Fulmar, Manx Shearwater, Sooty Shearwater (rare), Cormorant, Shag, Pochard, Tufted Duck, Eider, Common Scoter, Velvet Scoter, Hen Harrier, Golden Plover, Sanderling, Purple Sandpiper, Arctic Skua, Mediterranean Gull, Little Gull, Glaucous Gull, Kittiwake, Short-eared Owl, Black Redstart, Redstart, Whinchat, Wheatear, Icterine Warbler, Barred Warbler (the latter two are rare), Firecrest, Pied Flycatcher, Bearded Tit and Snow Bunting.

Habitat

The coastal region to the south of Lowestoft is extremely interesting for birdwatchers, although holiday traffic inevitably adds to coastal pressures in season. The coastline between Kessingland and Southwold is mainly unbroken with low cliffs, nowhere more than 70 ft (21 m) high, of clay or sand. The beaches are mainly a mixture of sand and small shingle, but a wide area of foreshore between Kessingland and Benacre comprises sand dunes, grassy tracts and stretches of pebbles where large clumps of the beautiful sea pea can be found. A good variety of plants includes yellow-horned poppies, sea-kale, stonecrop and devil's bit scabious. Erosion is constant and wide stretches of the beach have been 'taken' by the sea over the years. Care should be exercised if following the Suffolk Coast Path which runs along the foreshore here, as it may become impassable at high tide although there are alternative inland routes. Dead trees can be seen along the foreshore, their limbs sculptured by the winds and tides. The 7 miles (11.2 km) stretch of coast between Kessingland and Southwold is very scenic and there are several small broads and old gravel pits which regularly attract a variety of duck, grebes, divers, waders, hawks and passerines. All these broads are within a stone's throw of the beach and in places sea surges have broken through the shingle ridge on several occasions to inundate Benacre Broad (NCC), which is reed-fringed and surrounded by woodlands. The salt water from the sea surges have killed off some of the reed growth to leave muddy edges which are attractive to waders.

Kessingland Levels are low-lying marshes between Kessingland and Benacre which were very attractive to large numbers of wildfowl over 60 years ago, but reclamation and drainage have drastically reduced these numbers. To the south of Benacre, the two smaller broads of Easton and Covehithe are equally attractive to several species during the course of the year. At the southern end of this stretch of coast, and north of the Rivery Blyth estuary, the small holiday town of Southwold is worth visiting during the autumn and winter months. To the south of the town another small area of Denes is attractive to passerine migrants while the headland can be quite good for sea watching.

Map 21

Species

In general the coastline between Kessingland and Southwold should prove more rewarding during the autumn and winter months, although a Hobby or passing Osprey may fly through the area in spring or summer. Little and Common Terns can be seen at Benacre Broad during the summer months and there are generally a few Kittiwakes in evidence. Even at the most unlikely times a rare bird can turn up almost anywhere and who could have predicted the arrival of a Wilson's Phalarope at the Kessingland Wildlife Park in June 1976, or a bird completely new to Britain, the White-crowned Black Wheatear, that also appeared at Kessingland in June 1982!

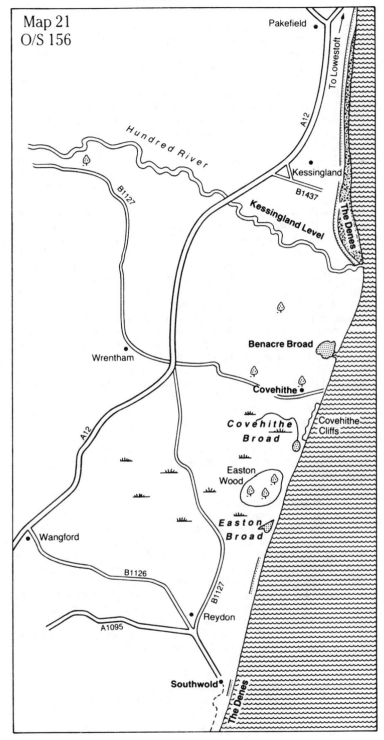

Map 21
O/S 156

Pakefield

To Lowestoft

A12

Hundred River

Kessingland

B1437

B1127

Kessingland Level

The Denes

Benacre Broad

Wrentham

Covehithe

Covehithe Cliffs

A12

Covehithe Broad

Easton Wood

Easton Broad

Wangford

B1126

B1127

Reydon

A1095

Southwold

The Denes

However, from August it may be worth looking out for some of the more usual drift migrants such as Pied Flycatchers, Redstarts and Wheatears while Wrynecks and Barred Warblers have occasionally been seen. At this time, the first waders will be on the move southwards from Scandinavia. Although this stretch of coast does not have so much attractive wader habitat as the region to the south, there are some good records from the coastal broads and, in particular, Benacre Broad where salt water has provided a muddy edge on the south side. More usual waders on passage include Little Stints, Wood, Green and Common Sandpipers, Spotted Redshanks and Ruff. Rarer waders which have been noted from time to time include Kentish Plover, Dotterel, Temminck's Stint and White-rumped Sandpiper. As everywhere Curlew Sandpipers are erratic in their autumn appearances and may be altogether absent in some years.

From autumn onwards raptors might include a Common Buzzard, Merlin or Peregrine. Two extremely rare raptors which are often seen here are the Goshawk and Red Kite. The latter species is probably a wanderer from the Continent as immature birds are known to disperse soon after they have fledged. In the winter of 1985–6 an immature White-tailed Sea Eagle spent some weeks frequenting the Benacre Broad area. From November large numbers of Pochard and Teal frequent Benacre Broad and there are often other rarer duck to be seen here or on Easton or Covehithe Broads. These have included Long-tailed Duck, Goosander and Smew quite frequently (especially in hard weather); Ferruginous Duck, Red-crested Pochard and Ruddy Duck. After storms at sea Scaup, Goldeneye, Red-breasted Mergansers and Velvet Scoter may be driven to seek refuge on the calmer waters.

Nesting duck in summer include Gadwall and Tufted Duck, while the low cliffs attract numbers of nesting Sand Martins. Other seabirds which may seek refuge on the Broads from time to time include all three species of divers and all four species of grebes. Little Gulls are also seen, but more often in the late summer months when non-breeding birds may stay awhile. Single Mediterranean Gulls turn up fairly regularly in any month, but more usually between July and March. Along the shore itself other rare wintering gulls have included Iceland and Glaucous Gulls with the latter species being the most frequent.

The wide beaches to the south of Kessingland are a regular resort of Snow Buntings in winter and small parties of up to a few dozen birds frequent the Denes there. Sometimes there are a few Shorelarks in nearby company, but as in Norfolk this species seems to be going through a phase of 'lean years'. The Kessingland Levels still attract a few Bewick's Swans and Whooper Swans together with varying numbers of White-fronted Geese. These three species are more usually to be found from November and up to March. Finally, the Denes immediately to the south of Southwold may also hold a few wintering passerines, but this is another favoured spot for sea watching in rough autumn weather. Numbers are not likely to be great, but divers, grebes, auks, Gannets, skuas and shearwaters have all been seen at times.

Timing

Peak holiday times are best avoided if possible. Autumn and winter months from August to March are usually the most rewarding period. Spring or early summer could yield some breeding species and a passing Osprey or Hobby. Bear in mind that this coastline faces east, therefore watching seawards in the early morning may prove difficult. Look at coastal Broads after gales at sea or during severe weather. Beware of high tides making the coastal footpath along the foreshore impassable, although it is unlikely that anyone could be trapped. For migrating passerines visit the coast when east or south-east winds are blowing.

Access

Kessingland is served by the A12 from Great Yarmouth or Saxmundham. At Kessingland take the B1437 which ends at the car park by the seafront. Walk south to explore the Denes, gravel-pit pools and Benacre Broad. The Coast Path continues along the foreshore past Covehithe and Easton Broad to Southwold which is a distance of about 7 miles (11 km). Alternatively, take the A12 south from Kessingland to Wrentham, about 3½ miles (5.6 km), and then a minor road at a five road junction to Covehithe. Park and follow the coast to north or south. For Southwold leave the A12 at Wangford (if coming from Great Yarmouth) and turn left along the B1126 or, if approaching from the south on the A12, take the A1095 on the right about ¾ mile (1.2 km) north of Blythburgh. At Southwold follow the minor road south of the town for about ½ mile (0.8 km) to Denes and the mouth of the River Blyth. At Benacre Broad (NCC) there is a large observation hide on the south side.

Calendar

Resident Gadwall, Tufted Duck and Great-crested Grebe.

December–February Red-throated Diver, Black-throated Diver, Great Northern Diver (the latter two species rarest), Red-necked Grebe, Slavonian Grebe, Black-necked Grebe (all rare), Cormorant, Shag, Bewick's Swan, Whooper Swan, White-fronted Goose, Wigeon, Teal, Pochard, Scaup, Long-tailed Duck, Common Scoter, Velvet Scoter, Goldeneye, Smew, Goosander, Ruddy Duck (rare), Red Kite (rare), White-tailed Sea Eagle (extremely rare), Hen Harrier, Goshawk, Merlin, Peregrine, Mediterranean Gull, Glaucous Gull, Iceland Gull, Shorelark, Hooded Crow and Snow Bunting.

March–May Several of the above named winter visitors may stay into March or early April. Marsh Harrier, Osprey, Hobby (from end April), Mediterranean Gull, Little Gull, Common Tern, Little Tern and Sand Martin.

June–July Usually quiet.

August–November Slavonian Grebe, Black-necked Grebe, Cory's Shearwater, Sooty Shearwater, Manx Shearwater (all scarce or rare), Gannet, Cormorant, Shag, Bewick's Swan, Whooper Swan, White-fronted Goose (last three from November), Wigeon, Teal, Pochard, Scaup, Eider, Long-tailed Duck, Common Scoter, Velvet Scoter, Goldeneye, Smew, Red-breasted Merganser, Goosander, Red Kite, White-tailed Sea Eagle (extremely rare), Hen Harrier, Goshawk, Common Buzzard, Merlin, Peregrine, Kentish Plover, Dotterel (the latter two rare), Little Stint, Temminck's Stint, White-rumped Sandpiper (the latter two rare),

Curlew Sandpiper, Ruff, Spotted Redshank, Green, Wood and Common Sandpipers, Pomarine Skua, Great Skua (*all* skuas are rare), Mediterranean Gull, Little Gull, Glaucous Gull, Kittiwake, Wryneck, Shorelark (late October), Redstart, Wheatear, Barred Warbler (rare), Hooded Crow and Snow Bunting.

Habitat

The long sweep of the Suffolk coast for 12 miles (19.2 km) between Walberswick and Aldeburgh encompasses some of the finest country-side in Suffolk and includes the Minsmere Nature Reserve, which is internationally recognised as a model reserve for nature conservation.

This coastline is also an even one without indentations. Mostly it is low lying, but a short range of cliffs between Dunwich and Minsmere gives superb views over Minsmere Level to the south and the Dingle Marshes to the north. The River Blyth enters the North Sea between Walberswick and Southwold, but some 3 miles (4.8 km) upstream a vast area of tidal mudflats has been formed because of serious breaks in the river's embankments during 1921, 1926 and 1943. The surrounding marshes were flooded and now the mudflats below the Blythburgh bridge are one of the finest areas in the county for migrating waders. Saltmarshes (which are not too common on the Suffolk coast) can be found on the edge of this estuary where sea lavender, sea aster and sea purslane are dominant while the invasive cord-grass is colonising the mudflats.

Many years ago the Suffolk Sandlings were a wide tract of sandy heathland which extended almost continuously from Ipswich to Blyth-burgh. Many kinds of 'development' in the past 50 years have occurred, notably housing, farming, afforestation and the construction of airfields and golf-courses, all of which have reduced the unique Sandlings to scattered remnants. These heathlands were used for sheep grazing and of course the type of habitat that was created attracted many Stone Curlews, Nightjars, Wheaters and Woodlarks. With the cessation of sheep farming, reclamation and afforestation accounted for large areas while after the scourge of myxomatosis the heathlands faced a new natural threat in the form of scrub and bracken invasion. Some of the remaining Sandling habitats have come into the conservation fold, notably those at Dunwich Heath and Walberswick Nature Reserve. Management work is carried out to try and halt the invasive spread of bracken and scrub by the introduction of sheep to some areas. An advisory body called the Sandlings Group has been set up to research, plan and carry out conservation work on the heaths.

Walberswick Nature Reserve covers 1,270 acres (508 ha) of extremely diverse and important habitats and lies roughly between the villages of Blythburgh and Walberswick. Not only does the reserve have one of the best remaining areas of the Sandling heathlands, but it also includes the saltings and intertidal mudflats south of the river in the Blyth Estuary. The reserve also includes most of the extensive Westwood Marshes to the south. This marsh was reclaimed in the early eighteenth century by the usual system of embankments, sluices, dykes and wind pumps. This reclaimed land on which horses and cattle were grazed was reckoned to be one of the finest farms in the county. The Second World War changed all that when the marshes were flooded as an emergency defence measure. Since then the marshes have reverted to their original state and in the past 30 years phragmites has spread to such an extent that the

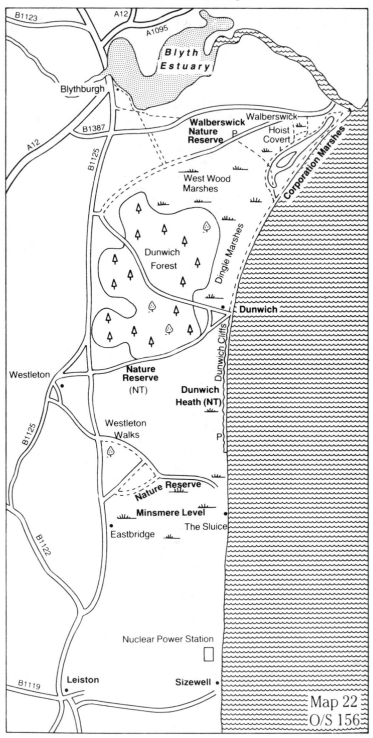

B1123

A12

A1095

*B l y t h
E s t u a r y*

Blythburgh

B1387

A12

B1125

**Walberswick
Nature
Reserve**

Walberswick

P

Hoist
Covert

Corporation Marshes

West Wood
Marshes

Dunwich
Forest

Dingle Marshes

Dunwich

Dunwich Cliffs

Westleton

**Nature
Reserve**
(NT)

**Dunwich
Heath (NT)**

B1125

Westleton
Walks

P

Nature Reserve

Minsmere Level

Eastbridge

The Sluice

B1122

Nuclear Power Station

B1119

Leiston

Sizewell

Map 22
O/S 156

area of continuous reed-beds is reckoned to be the largest in Britain. Not surprisingly, reedland birds have colonised this habitat. The area is also outstanding for rare moths – particularly the wainscots whose caterpillars live on reeds; the rarer species include fenn's and powdered wainscots and the white-mantled wainscot which was thought to be extinct in Britain at one time.

Management work has included the replacement of the old sluice gates to prevent entry of saltwater during sea surges and to retain freshwater in order to encourage reed growth. Dyke dredging and the excavation of new pools is aimed at encouraging aquatic plants and animals, while muddy shallows have been created for wading birds and dabbling ducks. Various footpaths and a minor road from Walberswick make this a very attractive area to explore. The Suffolk Coast Path from Walberswick southwards to Dunwich, about 2½ miles (4 km), skirts the shingle beach on one side and the Corporation and Dingle Marshes on the other. Here and there along the path there are attractive muddy bays where a few waders may be seen. Extensive reed-beds can be overlooked for harriers, Bearded Tits and Short-eared Owls. In summer the shingle beaches are bright with golden cushions of stonecrop and the occasional clump of sea pea. Small heath, small copper and common blue butterflies frequent the path especially along the wider grassy tracts nearer to Dunwich. Beyond the reed-beds the extensive Dunwich Forest covers the higher slopes.

Westleton Heath National Nature Reserve (NCC) is another remnant of the Suffolk Sandlings and adjoins the similar country of Dunwich Heath (NT) and the edge of the Minsmere Reserve (RSPB). From the Minsmere cliffs beside Dunwich Heath there are extensive views over the marshes and woods that comprise the prestigious Minsmere Nature Reserve. Nearly 3 miles (4.8 km) to the south the squat monster of Sizewell – in the form of the Nuclear Power Station – is a landmark that cannot be missed.

The story of Minsmere Reserve is already too well documented to warrant repetition here. Suffice to say that the Minsmere Level was reclaimed land similar to that at the Westwood Marshes until the area was also deliberately flooded in the Second World War as a defence measure. The reserve was at first leased in 1947 and later purchased in 1977 by the RSPB. There can be few watchers who have never visited this reserve of wader lagoons, reed-beds and mature woodlands. Minsmere is the flagship of the RSPB and while there are a few purists who might criticise that everything is 'laid on', the facilities and observation hides provided are excellent. They have to be, for birdwatching is 'big business'. With a reserve like this, on which nearly 300 species have been claimed including regular rarities, there are obviously great pressures from birdwatchers who must be carefully catered for without detriment to the wildlife.

South of Sizewell, where the warmer waters from the nuclear power station often attract various gulls, terns and ducks, are the Walks, another remaining pocket of the old sheep-grazed heaths. The Meare at Thorpeness is an artificial one and rather 'has the air' of tame ducks and boats in the summer season, but to the west of the Meare there is the adjoining North Warren Reserve (RSPB) of 130 acres (52.8 ha). This is an area of scrub, birchwood, bracken, heather, bogs and reed-beds which is very attractive to both resident and passage migrants. Farther south still, the arts-oriented town of Aldeburgh lies on the north side of the

Alde estuary with some interesting marshes between the town and the River Alde. This whole wedge of scenic coast is served by B or minor roads from the A12 which links Blythburgh to Saxmundham, 9 miles (14.4 km), and the A1094 from Farnham to Aldeburgh, 6½ miles (10.4 km).

Map 22

Species

The small town of Walberswick is an extremely good centre at which to stay for birdwatching trips. From the town there are a number of attractive footpaths connecting with the nearby National Nature Reserve and it is within easy reach of Minsmere being about 6 miles (9.6 km) on foot along the coast or, by road, about 10 miles (16 km).

Birdwatching is good all year round, but mid-summer is probably least rewarding unless one has botanical or entomological interest. Some 3 miles (4.8 km) upstream of the River Blyth, the intertidal mudflats and saltings are particularly important for passage waders and wintering wildfowl. A minor road skirting the edge of the Westwood Marshes is a well-known winter rendezvous for watching various raptors and ten species have been claimed for the area not including owls. Harriers delight in this open marshland country; Marsh Harriers are to be seen frequently during the summer months and fairly regularly even during the winter months in small numbers. Hen Harriers are more frequent in winter when several birds may be hunting over the marsh or heathlands. On a late winter's afternoon these beautiful hawks may arrive from all quarters to roost in the extensive reed-beds; perhaps en-route making a sortie on the huge flocks of Starlings that also seek a night refuge here.

This is a good spot too, for Rough-legged Buzzards who are almost annual visitors to the coast in varying numbers. In late October 1974 a total of 45 birds were seen arriving and 13 of these were in the air together which must have been a memorable sight. This magnificent bird of prey is almost certainly increasing in numbers which we can only hope is due to stricter protection on its Continental breeding grounds and to the tolerance of landowners in this country. It is one of the best birdwatching thrills to see this large raptor hunting, pausing every now and then to 'hover' in flight with its long wings lazily beating to maintain its position (never to be confused with the rapid shallower wing beats of the Kestrel which is also diminutive by comparison). The first buzzards may arrive in mid-September, but more usually from mid-October, while most will have departed by late March or early April.

The Common Buzzard, too, seems to be increasing as a visitor between September and May and lone birds are often seen over the more wooded areas of the reserve. This species used to nest commonly in Suffolk over 150 years ago and, with a more enlightened attitude towards conservation today, perhaps some of these Continental immigrants may re-colonise the region in future.

This area is also notable for the infrequent, but increasing, visits of Red Kites. Single birds have been recorded almost annually in the coastal region of Suffolk. One bird stayed in the Walberswick area throughout the winter of 1974–5 and all these birds are probably immigrants from the Continent. The Goshawk must rank as one of Britain's rarest breeding birds, but it too, is on the increase and becoming an almost annual visitor here. Breeding has been suspected elsewhere in the county. Sightings in or near wooded areas are more usual between November and April with a bias towards the end of this period.

The tiny Merlin is a regular visitor to marsh and heath. It can arrive as early as September and stay as late as May, but the winter months are the best times to see this fast flying falcon speeding after some luckless Meadow Pipit or Reed Bunting. Although the Sparrow Hawk is present all the year it has become an extremely rare breeding bird since the great hawk kill of the 1960s, when all birds of prey at the top of the food chain were decimated by farm chemicals. It has not yet recovered, but increasing numbers visit this region in winter. The Peregrine is the other winter raptor that may be seen in the area in any month from September to March, but it is still rather scarce.

The coastal strip is well worth a visit in winter to look for the parties of Greenfinches, Yellow Hammers, Reed Buntings and Twite who frequent the flat grassy tracts beside the shingle beaches. Towards Dunwich the wider flats may hold a few wintering Snow Buntings and Shorelarks as well as giving a chance of seeing some of the region's raptors. The coastal walk in winter might produce Water Rails in the small pools at the edge of the marshlands or you may well see a Bittern flapping over the reed-beds and a Short-eared Owl quartering the marshes. On calm days parties of Bearded Tits may be seen exploring the brown reed fronds. The predatory Great Grey Shrike is another exciting visitor which can regularly be found on the heathlands.

The mudflats of the Blyth Estuary are a good wintering area for Wigeon, Shelduck, Redshank and Dunlin. It has become a regular wintering place for a few Spotted Redshank which used to be practically unheard of outside the migration seasons. Fairly high numbers of Black-tailed Godwits also use the Blyth Estuary in early spring when some birds have assumed the beautiful bronze red breeding plumage. Ospreys have been recorded on spring passage from time to time – no doubt attracted by the variety of fish which can be found here including eels and grey mullet which are sometimes abundant. Small parties of Spoon-bills have been known to visit, also – but more rarely – Little Egret and Black-winged Stilt.

Passage waders in spring include Common Sandpiper, Whimbrel, Bar-tailed Godwits and smart Grey Plover in their black and white summer plumage. Mediterranean Gulls might be seen in any month, but

Stonechat

Black Terns and Little Gulls are more likely on spring passage. A few pairs of Common Terns nest. The late spring or early summer months along the heath and marshlands can be sheer delight. Nightingales still breed along the edge of the oak coverts and there is a wealth of common summer warblers. A few pairs of Redstarts frequent the area while passage migrants such as Pied Flycatchers, Red-backed Shrikes and Wrynecks are regularly seen in small numbers. Over 100 breeding species have been noted on the reserve including Marsh Harriers, Bitterns, Bearded Tits, Water Rails and occasionally Garganey. Such local species as Grasshopper Warblers, Stonechats and Nightjars can be seen and heard on the breeding grounds, but all visitors should keep strictly to the footpaths from which most species can be seen or heard.

One or two pairs of Savi's Warblers have stayed the summer in recent years while the sedentary Cetti's Warbler has been heard annually. Both may increase as breeding species. The Hobby which is often seen between May and September has been suspected of breeding, but the Red-footed Falcon is only an extremely rare visitor from eastern Europe which has been noted in May. Other rarities recorded in the area during the summer have included Black Kite, Honey Buzzard, Crane, White-winged Black Tern and Bee-eater.

Minsmere Nature Reserve is open throughout the year although by no means on every day. Nevertheless, by careful advance planning all the specialities of this model reserve can be seen in the course of a few visits; but the unexpected rarities may not be encountered except with luck and regular visiting. Not a few birdwatchers have retired to live in this area for the year-round attractions it offers. Even if the reserve itself is closed there is a public hide and, moreover, there are many attractive footpaths across the adjoining Dunwich Heath which all yield a good variety of birds.

Seabird buffs though, must never expect to see the numbers and variety that can occur off south-west England or the north Norfolk coast. While the 'bulge' at Lowestoft is the most easterly point in Britain the rest of the Suffolk coastline lacks any clear headland and indeed the coast rather follows a course west of south. Therefore, in a typical year only single numbers of grebes, divers, shearwaters, Gannets and Shags might be expected off the coast between Walberswick and Minsmere. There are exceptions of course, as witness the cyclonic weather systems in November 1982 which brought 15,000 Brent Geese, over 1,700 Wigeon, 350 Pintail, 250 Teal, 2,200 Common Scoter, 100 Red-breasted Mergansers and numbers of waders to within identification range of the Minsmere coast.

In spite of the lack of seabird numbers, more than 200 species are seen in the Minsmere area in most years. There are about 100 species breeding annually on the reserve and this is a greater variety than can be found in any other comparable area elsewhere in Britain. Some species which used to breed no longer do so on a regular basis and 'lost' species sadly include Stone Curlew, Woodlark, Wheatear, Whinchat and Red-backed Shrike.

In the early spring the marsh begins to liven up as some species take up their territories. Avocets return in mid-March and more than 40 pairs usually frequent the scrape. A few pairs of Ringed Plovers begin to indulge in piping courtship displays, while Redshank and Lapwings return from their winter foraging on the marshlands. Flocks of Canada Geese, up to 200 strong during the winter, now split up into honking,

Bittern. Breeds in the reed-beds of Norfolk and Suffolk

courting pairs. Bitterns may begin to make their famous booming call in February, but more frequently from the end of March at any time of day. Between five and twelve 'pairs' probably nest, but as always with polygamous birds it is difficult to determine how many spouses a cock Bittern might be looking after in the dense reed-beds. Short flights low across the reeds are frequently made in the spring and summer, but as always for the watcher it is a case of being in the right spot at the right time.

Other species with nesting in mind are Bearded Tits, of which there are some 80 pairs and Sandwich Terns, which first arrive from Africa at the end of March or early April. Thanks to careful management of the pools and scrapes between 200 and 500 pairs of these beautiful, but raucous-voiced terns nest almost annually. Ever secretive, Water Rails find the dense cover to their liking, and an estimated 40 pairs nest annually. A few pairs of the Grey Heron – which is also a very early breeding bird – nest in the reed-beds and this is an extremely unusual site for them as they more commonly nest in tree-tops. At this time, one or two pairs of Little and Great-crested Grebes may return to take up nesting territories: the former from a winter sojourn in the marshland dykes and the latter from a few months visit to coastal waters.

On suitable days in February and March the outgoing migration of winter visitors may be witnessed. These movements may include members of the crow and thrush family who have spent the winter in western or middle parts of Britain. Flocks of Starlings too, may be seen crossing the coastline on their way back to the Continent. Other wintering species which may pass through include Common Buzzard, Rough-legged Buzzard, Glaucous Gulls and Peregrine. In April the marsh becomes a hub-bub of nesting birds – courting; squabbling and settling down to brood their eggs. The rare Marsh Harrier, a few adults of which may have wintered in a wider area of the region, now establish their territories, causing a daily commotion to their lesser neighbours. Large numbers of beautiful Black-tailed Godwits in their splendid red breeding plumage usually arrive in this month to stay for a short time. One or two pairs of Garganey still drop in, but as everywhere in Britain this attractive duck is on the decline.

Of the rarest smaller migrants one or two Firecrests are usually seen in the coastal bushes during March or April; and occasionally in the pine woods, where this species may well nest before long. A few Ring Ouzels are often seen in the more open habitats.

Commoner migrants began to fill the woodlands, now bursting with delicate greenery and life. Everywhere the fragile song of the Willow Warbler proclaims the arrival of spring, while Blackcaps, Whitethroats, Lesser Whitethroats and Garden Warblers begin to add their notes to the increasing dawn chorus. In mid-April the first Nightingales begin to arrive. This is another species which has declined from 50 pairs about twenty years ago to about 10 pairs, but in recent years their numbers have steadily climbed up again to near their original levels.

In April, and sometimes continuing into May, there is a northward passage of Goldfinches and Linnets along the coast which are probably birds returning from their winter foraging in southern Europe. By the end of April and early May most of the summer birds have returned. The reed-beds are alive with Reed and Sedge Warblers, while Grasshopper Warblers reel from any suitable tussocky marsh. High numbers of Goldfinches and Redpolls have filtered back into the sylvan areas of the reserve and resident woodland birds are prominent. Three species of woodpecker nest and there are very good numbers of all the usual tit species, Nuthatches, Treecreepers and Goldcrests. Several pairs of Tawny Owls breed, but only one or two Long-eared Owls. The Barn Owl has greatly declined in agricultural Suffolk and it is rarely seen at Minsmere.

Hirundines make their presence obvious, especially on colder days when the meres attract swarms of Swallows, House Martins and Sand Martins to feed on the various flies which abound in such an aquatic environment. About 200 pairs of Sand Martins breed on the reserve and, not least, in the hand-constructed sandpit by the reserve centre. Other colonies exist on the face of Dunwich cliffs where the birds can be seen feeding over the heathery cliff-top slopes. Stonechats have also decreased, but a few pairs nest early in the year on the gorse-covered heathlands. Adders are common in this type of habitat, while the harmless slow-worm can be found along the more leafy rides. A few pairs of Tree Pipits can be found where the heathland is sparse or bare from clearance. The very last summer migrants to arrive are a few pairs of Spotted Flycatchers, and Nightjars. The latter species seems to be maintaining about ten breeding pairs despite a decline in the last 15 years. There are usually a dozen or more pairs of Redstarts nesting in the woodland areas of the reserve, but the Wood Warbler is only a rare visitor although sporadic pairs have nested.

Of the other passerines, Cetti's Warbler has been present since 1971 and it is likely that breeding has taken place. The Savi's Warbler reached a peak of six pairs in 1973, but since then it has remained steady at one or two pairs annually. In early May the volume of the dawn chorus is totally inspiring with the combined songs and calls from the feathered inhabitants of woodland and marsh. On the meres and scrapes there is now peak spring activity. Common and Little Terns have returned to nest on the scrapes amongst noisy multitudes of larger Sandwich Terns and Black-headed Gulls. A few dozen pairs of brightly coloured Shelduck enhance the wildfowl scene, while a score or so of soberly plumaged Gadwall make this one of their county breeding strongholds. Nearly as many pairs of the delightful Teal also breed in the area as well as slightly smaller numbers of long-billed Shovelers. This is the best time to watch out for the arrival of non-breeding passage waders and there may be as many as 15 species on the scrape in summer. Small single numbers of such delightful species as Little Ringed Plover (has bred), Kentish Plover, Little Stint and Temminck's Stints are fairly regular. Commoner, but still superb, are black-bellied Dunlin who may stay a few days before moving on to the north. Similarly bound travellers may include a few Spotted Redshank, Greenshank, Common, Wood and Green Sandpipers. Male Ruffs (which may have appeared in March or even wintered elsewhere in the county) now sport their ever-confusing array of multi-toned plumages. One or two dainty Red-necked Phalaropes often turn up in May to stay for a while on the food-abundant meres.

Temminck's Stint and Dunlin

Of other rarities, the Broad-billed Sandpiper has occurred several times in May and there are single records of Lesser Yellowlegs and Terek Sandpiper in this month. Regular Minsmere specialities include the stately Spoonbill which is a frequent visitor and most likely candidate for a new nesting species. Odd birds of this species may occur as early as March and stay as late as November. Several adults usually spend some weeks on the reserve in summer. In 1970 two pairs displayed and indulged in rudimentary nest building. The Purple Heron is another contender for the title of new breeding species for one or two are present in the reed-beds almost annually and a pair of adults were seen displaying in 1968. Usually, it is immature birds who may turn up anytime from late April to July with odd birds sometimes up to November. Single Mediterranean Gulls are recorded in most years between February and August while Little Gulls may occur in any month, but more often between April and September. One or two magnificent Ospreys occur annually on passage between April and October. Some birds have stayed for a week or more, no doubt attracted by the plentiful supplies of eels and rudd in the Island Mere and River Minsmere.

Perhaps because of the good fishing several non-breeding Cormorants are present all year and one (sometimes two) pair of Kingfishers also, no doubt attracted by the abundant sticklebacks. Vagrants which have been recorded in May include Hoopoe, Bee-eater and White-winged Black Tern. In mid-summer there is still great hustle and bustle as youngsters become fully fledged and able to fend more for themselves on the greater expanse of mud created by deliberately lowered water levels. There is also much to see in the way of plants and insects.

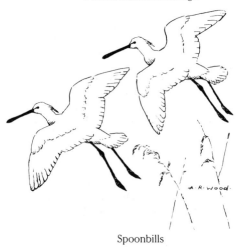

Spoonbills

As early as June waders are on the move with Lapwings and Curlews arriving from the Continent. It seems there is hardly a pause before the last of the late spring passage waders, mainly composed of non-breeding birds, and the return of breeding birds from northern Europe. Perhaps the first comers are birds which have failed to rear a family, but from early July through to late September the wader passage is in full swing. Perhaps the greatest variety of wader species might be found between the end of July and mid-August. By this time a comparatively peaceful armistice has descended upon the marshland scene. The youngsters have grown up, there is no territory to defend and there is food in plenty. Most of the screaming gulls and terns have departed – the gulls to the estuaries and the terns on a leisurely trek back to Africa. Tranquility though, is disrupted whenever a young Marsh Harrier appears, now strong on the wing and hoping to make a kill for itself!

Waders using the reserve in autumn include most of the species that came through in the spring with some in greater numbers. Dunlin and Snipe are two of the commonest waders with a hundred or two of each present throughout the autumn. A score or two of Spotted Redshanks may be present from late August. Black-tailed Godwits do not appear in such large numbers as in the spring and only a few are present in early autumn. Varying small numbers of Ruff, Greenshank and Bar-tailed Godwits occur regularly, but the unreliable Curlew Sandpiper may or may not come. The three smaller sandpipers, Green, Common and Wood all appear regularly in small numbers, while a dozen or more Little Stints can be present from early June. Very small numbers of Jack Snipe may arrive from early September and may be present throughout the winter months.

Extremely rare autumn vagrants have included Stilt Sandpiper, Upland Sandpiper, Lesser Yellowlegs, Baird's Sandpiper, Buff-breasted Sandpiper, Long-billed Dowitcher and Broad-billed Sandpiper. More frequent, but still rare, are Pectoral Sandpiper and White-rumped Sandpipers. The Grey Phalarope has been noted on several occasions between September and November.

With easterly or north-easterly winds at any time from August, falls of passerines may occur in the coastal bushes. Species most commonly seen are Willow Warblers, Pied Flycatchers and Wheatears, while a

Wryneck, Icterine or Barred Warbler may be found amongst them on occasions. Rarer migrants are recorded, but not with such regularity as on the Norfolk coast. There have been a few single records of Radde's Warbler, Yellow-browed Warbler, Pallas's Warbler, Greenish Warbler and Melodious Warblers. The odd Red-backed Shrike and Red-breasted Flycatcher may also turn up in the coastal bushes.

Being more used to these small autumn falls, Suffolk birders look back in wonder at the greatest fall of migrants ever recorded in the British Isles on the 3 September 1965 when thousands of small migrants rained out of the skies in appalling weather conditions. It was estimated that 7,000 Redstarts, 4,000 Wheatears, 500 Willow Warblers, 400 Robins, 300 Spotted Flycatchers, 200 Whitethroats, 25 Wrynecks, 25 Bluethroats and lesser numbers of many other species were in the Minsmere area. Next day a count revealed the staggering estimate of 200,000 small passerines within the reserve area.

Another feature of the autumn is the high numbers of Bearded Tits; they muster an estimated 1,000 birds in the reed-beds. Large irruption flights take place from mid-September and only about 100 birds are left in the reeds throughout the winter months where they are joined by many foraging Blue Tits and Wrens. Water levels are raised for the winter months to provide sanctuary for hundreds of Teal, Wigeon and Shoveler. Single numbers of Goldeneye, Red-breasted Mergansers, Goosanders and Smew may arrive; the latter two species especially in hard weather. Several nice raptors hunt the area apart from the usual Marsh Harriers. One or two Hen Harriers are present, while both Common and Rough-legged Buzzards are occasionally seen. One or two Great Grey Shrikes are regular visitors to the heathland areas. Small numbers of Twite, Shorelarks and Snow Buntings can usually be found frequenting either the scrape or the grassy shingle embankments. Small numbers of Ruff have taken to wintering on the reserve in recent years; and another speciality, which is usually present at this time, is the Water Pipit. Single numbers frequent the muddy edges of meres or drains. On the adjoining private marshlands to the south there may be a few Bewick's and Whooper Swans with the former species staying until early spring.

Bearded Tit (female). Breeds in East Anglia reed-beds

By comparison with Minsmere other sections of the coastal habitat seem less important, but if one can ignore the omnipresent pile of the Sizewell Nuclear Power Station, it is worth a visit, if only to look at the sea area where hot water from the cooling plant is discharged into the sea. Here, the temperature of the sea is significantly raised which has attracted marine life and, of course, seabird predators to the feast; there is usually a cloud of gulls and terns of various species feeding by the outlet. The coastal stretch of sparse dunes and shingle also attracts passerine migrants; and Hoopoe, Wryneck, Tawny Pipit, Great Grey and Woodchat Shrikes have been noted in the area.

Nearby, another remnant of the Sandlings known as The Walks attracts a few heathland birds. To the south, the North Warren was one of the first reserves to be acquired by the RSPB in 1937. The 270 acres (108 ha) are composed of grass heath, wet fen and deciduous woodland which attracts a variety of small birds. Yellow Hammers and Linnets breed freely on the gorse-covered heath while the scrub woodland entices Nightingales, Blackcaps, Lesser Whitethroats, Whitethroats and Garden Warblers. A pair of Stonechats sometimes nests and Kingfishers are often seen along the River Hundred where roach, rudd, eels, sticklebacks, toads and frogs can be found. The commonest breeding birds in the reed and sedge fen are Reed and Sedge Warblers, while the Grasshopper Warbler occurs in lesser numbers. The rare Bittern has been known to nest in the area and sometimes its weird booming can be heard. In autumn, Bearded Tits, which have probably irrupted from the Minsmere reserve, may drop in while a Marsh Harrier might be seen hunting. Flocks of finches and thrushes frequent the nearby fields in winter and alders of the reserve attract Siskins and Redpolls.

Lying at the southern end of this section of the coastline is the town of Aldeburgh with some marshes to the south bordering the estuary of the Alde. Although drained many years ago and now partly under cultivation the area still attracts some wildfowl during the winter. Bewick's Swans can often be seen on these marshes.

Timing

Time of day is not too important although early morning is best for woodlands in spring and early summer. Wind direction is important at migration periods. An easterly or southerly wind in late April or May may bring a Firecrest, Hoopoe or Wryneck. A similar wind in autumn, from August onwards, may bring several drift migrants to the coastal bushes. A gale force north-easterly is best for bringing seabirds nearer to the coastline, but large numbers are rarely seen. On the estuaries it is best to be placed about two hours before high tide time to watch for birds being forced nearer to the shore by the rising waters. Wood and heathland are best in spring and early summer as this is a popular holiday coastline (sailing is one of the main attractions) with peak season in July and August.

WALBERSWICK NATURE RESERVE

Access

There are so many good footpaths that they could not be fully explored unless several days were spent in the area. Walberswick is a good centre from which to start. It lies about 3½ miles (5.6 km) east of Blythburgh which is on the A12. In Blythburgh village take the B1125 for about ½ mile (0.8 km) and then turn left along the B1387 to Walbersick. Alternatively, if coming from the south take the B1387 on the right, about ½ mile (0.8 km) before reaching Blythburgh. A map of the various footpaths is displayed outside the Village Hall at Walberswick.

To explore the Blyth Estuary follow a footpath starting beside the White Hart public house at Blythburgh and follow the disused railway track along the south side of the estuary. An observation hide at the edge of the estuary gives good views, but a telescope would be very useful. After nearly 2 miles (3.2 km) the path connects with the B1387 and an alternative approach can be made from this point if preferred, but at either access point please park with care.

For good winter raptor watching take the first minor road on the left of Walberswick. Follow this for about 1½ miles (2.4 km) to a spot where it is possible to pull off the road on the right – parking carefully. From here, good views can be obtained over the low-lying valley of the Westwood Marshes.

A good coastal walk, 2½ miles (4 km), which can be done on the left out of Walberswick to Dunwich. Start from Beach Car Park (turn sharp right and then bear left at the end of the B1387 in Walberswick) and go past the beach huts to reach the sea wall by the shingle bank. Turn right and walk south along the beach looking at the brackish pools on your right, some of which were created by extraction of shingle to reinforce the sea defences. Extensive reed-beds on your right also are good for Bearded Tits, Bitterns and raptors. Instead of following the path to Dunwich an alternative route back to Walberswick can be taken after about 1¼ miles (2 km). Look out for two low embankment walls on your right. Take the second bank along for about ½ mile (0.8 km) to a derelict wind pump (which should *not* be explored). From the wind pump take the right-hand track at the bottom of the bank. After about ½ mile (0.8 km) a left-hand path goes into the west side of the village while the right-hand path will take you back to your original starting point. Other footpaths can be followed by consulting the Village Hall map sign and other similar signs on the reserve itself.

Dunwich Heath–Minsmere and North Warren Reserves

These can best be explored from the B1125 from Blythburgh (on the A12) to the B1122 (south of Middleton) which terminates at Aldeburgh (A1094). The easiest approach to Minsmere is from Westleton (on the B1125) taking the road signposted Dunwich/Minsmere and follow sign-posts to the reserve.

For Dunwich Heath travel south from Blythburgh on the B1125 and, after passing the crossroads with the B1387, take the first minor road signposted Dunwich on the left. Bear right in Dunwich village past the church as if going back to Westleton and look out for a minor road on the left which will lead to Minsmere cliffs and (NT) car park.

Sizewell is a tiny coastal village 2 miles (3.2 km) east of Leiston and approached by a good minor road from that town. There is plenty of parking space by the seafront when the footpath to the north or south can be followed.

For the North Warren Reserve take the B1122 road from Leiston (which is also served by the B119, from the A12 at Saxmundham, and the B1069) and after crossing the B1353 look out on the left after just over 1½ miles (2.4 km) for the turning into the reserve and car park. There is a numbered nature trail of about 1½ miles (2.4 km) and access is at all times; but nature trail leaflets are obtainable only from the RSPB and the Minsmere Centre.

The A1094 and B1122 serve Aldeburgh. Follow the A1094 to its end at Fort Green, then a minor trackway to Slaughden Quay. From there the Aldeburgh Marshes can be explored by following a footpath along the seawall which runs alongside the River Alde before curving back towards Aldeburgh.

Calendar

Resident Little Grebe, Great-crested Grebe, Cormorant (not breeding, but present all year), Bittern, Grey Heron, Gadwall, Teal, Shoveler, Pochard, Tufted Duck, Marsh Harrier (usually one or two adults staying in winter), Sparrow Hawk (rare, but slightly increasing), Water Rail, Ringed Plover (leaves breeding grounds in winter), Lapwing, Snipe, Woodcock (the last two species also winter immigrants), Redshank (dispersal to estuaries in winter), Barn Owl (rare), Tawny Owl, Long-eared Owl (rare), Kingfisher, Green, Great Spotted and Lessed Spotted Woodpeckers, Woodlark (rare), Cetti's Warbler (rare), Goldcrest, Firecrest (probably in the process of establishing itself as a breeding resident, also passage migrant), Bearded Tit, Stonechat, Marsh Tit, Willow Tit, Coal Tit, Long-tailed Tit, Nuthatch, Treecreeper, Siskin (also winter visitor) and Redpoll.

December–February (Many winter visitors stay into March.) Red-throated Diver, Black-throated Diver, Great Northern Diver (all divers usually single numbers, but Red-throated may reach 100 or more), Red-necked Grebe, Slavonian Grebe (again single numbers of both these grebes), Shag, Wigeon, Pintail, Scaup, Goldeneye, Long-tailed Duck, Velvet Scoter (the last four sea duck are usually in single numbers), Common Scoter, Eider (small numbers), Red-breasted Merganser, Goosander, Smew (all sawbills in single numbers), Shelduck, White-fronted Goose, Brent Goose, Whooper Swan (usually only in single numbers), Bewick's Swan, Common Buzzard (rare), Rough-legged Buzzard, Red Kite (very rare), Hen Harrier, Peregrine (rare), Merlin, Jack Snipe, Dunlin, Ruff, Glaucous Gull, Iceland Gull (the two latter gulls rare), Mediterranean Gull, Little Gull, Razorbill, Guillemot (both these auks rare), Short-eared Owl, Shorelark, Hooded Crow, Water Pipit, Rock Pipit, Great Grey Shrike, Twite, Brambling, Lapland Bunting (rare) and Snow Bunting.

March–May Shag, Purple Heron, Spoonbill, Garganey, Shelduck, Common Buzzard (rare), Rough-legged Buzzard, Goshawk, Osprey, Hobby (from end of April), Peregrine, Spotted Crake (rare), Oyster-catcher, Little Ringed Plover, Kentish Plover, Grey Plover, Golden Plover, Dotterel (rare), Curlew, Whimbrel, Black-tailed Godwit, Bar-tailed Godwit, Green Sandpiper, Wood Sandpiper, Common Sandpiper, Spotted Redshank, Greenshank, Knot, Dunlin, Ruff, Avocet, Stone Curlew (rare and decreasing), Lesser Black-backed Gull, Glaucous Gull, Iceland Gull (the last two gulls rare), Mediterranean Gull, Little Gull, Kittiwake, Black Tern, Common Tern, Little Tern, Sandwich Tern, Nightjar (May), Hoopoe, Wryneck, Ring Ouzel (the last three species rarish), Wheatear, Whinchat, Redstart, Black Redstart, Nightingale, Grasshopper Warbler, Savi's Warbler (rare), Reed Warbler, Sedge Warbler, Blackcap, Garden Warbler, Whitethroat, Lesser Whitethroat, Wood Warbler (rare), Spotted Flycatcher (May), Tree Pipit, Yellow Wagtail, Great Grey Shrike (has stayed to April), and Red-backed Shrike (rare).

June–July Purple Heron (rare, but regular), Spoonbill, Osprey, Hobby, Red-footed Falcon, Spotted Crake (the last two species rare), Temminck's Stint, Red-necked Phalarope, Caspian Tern (very rare) and Nightjar. Plus most of the other April–May species, but woodland birds now quiet and secretive.

August–November Black-throated Diver, Great Northern Diver, Red-throated Diver, Red-necked Grebe, Slavonian Grebe, Black-necked Grebe, Manx Shearwater, Sooty Shearwater (all the previous species are in very low numbers except the Red-throated Diver which is more frequent) Gannet, Shag, Purple Heron, Spoonbill, Wigeon, Teal, Pintail, Goldeneye, Long-tailed Duck, Velvet Scoter (the last three species in single numbers), Common Scoter, Eider, Red-breasted Merganser, Goosander (the last two species in single numbers), Shelduck, White-fronted Goose, Brent Goose, Whooper Swan (rare), Bewick's Swan (two swans not before late October), Common Buzzard (rare), Rough-legged Buzzard, Red Kite (very rare), Hen Harrier (from September), Osprey (not often after September), Hobby (not after October), Peregrine (rare), Merlin, Oyster-catcher, Grey Plover, Golden Plover, Jack Snipe (rare), Curlew, Whimbrel (rare after October), Black-tailed Godwit, Bar-tailed Godwit, Green Sandpiper, Wood Sandpiper, Common Sandpiper (last three rare after September), Spotted Redshank, Greenshank, Knot, Little Stint (rare after October), Temminck's Stint (not after September), White-rumped Sandpiper (rare), Pectoral Sandpiper (rare), Dunlin, Curlew Sandpiper, Avocet (rare after September although the birds winter at Havergate), Grey Phalarope (rare), Red-necked Phalarope (not after October), Great Skua, Pomarine Skua, Arctic Skua, Long-tailed Skua (all skuas are rare, but Arctic most common), Lesser Black-backed Gull, Glaucous Gull, Iceland Gull (both gulls are rare), Little Gull, Kittiwake, Black Tern (not after October), Common Tern, Little Tern, Sandwich Tern (terns usually gone by September), Razorbill, Guillemot, Little Auk, Puffin (all auks are rare), Short-eared Owl, Wryneck (as a drift migrant August–September), Shorelark, Hooded Crow, Ring Ouzel, Wheatear, Whinchat (chats not after October), Redstart, Black Redstart, Bluethroat (rare), most warblers depart by September but drift migrants may be later, Icterine Warbler, Barred Warbler, Yellow-browed Warbler, Pallas's Warbler, Radde's Warbler (last three warblers very rare), Pied Flycatcher, Red-breasted Flycatcher (rare), Richard's Pipit, Tawny Pipit (both pipits rare), Water Pipit, Rock Pipit, Great Grey Shrike, Twite, Brambling, Lapland Bunting (rare), and Snow Bunting.

ALDEBURGH TO FELIXSTOWE

Habitat

The remaining 22 miles (35.2 km) of the Suffolk coastline south from Aldeburgh to Felixstowe (but sharply south-west from Orford Ness) are, for the most part, extremely low-lying well drained marshlands. For 9 miles (14.4 km) of the coast the great shingle cap of Orford Ness helps protect the marshlands from erosion. Formed entirely from sea-deposited shingle, this great natural defence barrier commencing south of Aldeburgh has diverted the mouth of the River Alde which now has to flow southwards behind the entire length of the spit. According to old maps Orford was once a seaport with direct access to the sea, but from the mid-1500s the shingle spit built up southwards past the town. Havergate Island, 267 acres (106.8 ha), may have been formed at this time. Up to the beginning of the Second World War the island had long been used for sheep and cattle grazing and for growing cereals. Nowadays, the island is managed by the RSPB with a series of bank enclosed shallow lagoons, small islands and mudflats for breeding birds and wintering waders and wildfowl. Outside the grassy embankments a saltmarsh zone contains such typical plants as sea purslane and sea lavender. This island was colonised by Avocets at the same time as Minsmere in 1947.

South-west of Orford the Butley River flows into the land locked Alde which still flows southwards for another 2 miles (3.2 km) before escaping into the North Sea as the River Ore. In its higher reaches the River Alde forms a large estuary nearly 3 miles (4.8 km) long and nearly 1 mile (1.6 km) across at one spot, which all proves very attractive to passage waders and winter wildfowl. But it is in the very south of the county that the two great rivers, the Deben and the Orwell, provide the main wintering habitats in Suffolk whilst the River Stour, which divides the county from neighbouring Essex, is equally, if not more important.

The town of Woodbridge lies some 8 miles (12.8 km) upstream from the mouth of the River Deben, while Ipswich is about 9 miles (14.4 km) from the mouth of the River Orwell. The Deben Estuary is the narrowest of the three rivers. The Orwell is almost 1 mile (1.6 km) wide in places and has more extensive mudflats. The Stour has the largest expanse of tidal water on the Suffolk coast, averaging a width of 1 mile (1.6 km) for its length of about 9 miles (14.4 km) to Manningtree.

There are huge mudbanks off both the Suffolk and Essex shores with correspondingly huge concentrations of wildfowl and waders. One of Suffolk's few headlands terminates the county's southern boundary at Landguard Point immediately south of Felixstowe. This whole region is popular yachting country and many pathways to the estuaries are uninvitingly signposted or not at all.

It is nice to record a valuable gain in habitats with the creation of Alton Water reservoir in recent times. This 2 mile (3.2 km) stretch of water lies between the upper reaches of the great Stour and Orwell Estuaries and is increasingly attracting a variety of interesting species.

Turning aside from the immediate coastline the vast area between the estuaries of the Deben and Alde, roughly 10 miles (16 km), is the best woodland habitat in the region although much of the alder woodland has been felled and replanted with conifers; other large woods have also been felled to make way for airfields. However, some mature mixed forest still exists near Butley and on Sutton Common there is still a very attractive remnant of the Suffolk Sandlings despite its proximity to Woodbridge airfield.

HAVERGATE ISLAND
Map 23

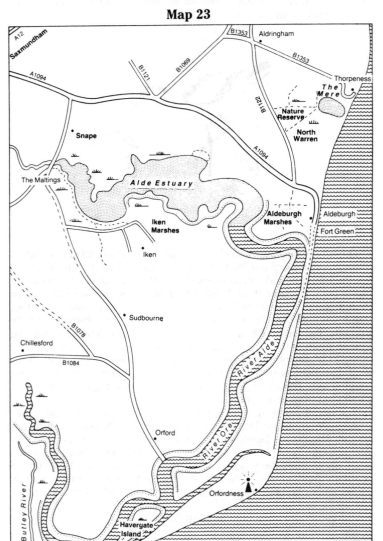

Map 23
O/S 156 and 169

Species

Although Havergate Island is difficult of access it is a notable breeding sanctuary for Avocets and four species of terns. Outside the breeding season there is an impressive list of waders and wildfowl. The Avocet colony has fluctuated greatly since the original four pairs established the colony. It increased to 97 pairs in 1957 but then, in 1964, declined to 49 pairs. In the late 1960s it reached 100 pairs and has remained fairly stable ever since. The Avocets' breeding season extends from April to late August and they used to be only a summer visitor with the first birds arriving in mid-March and all departing by October. However, increasing numbers of them now stay on the island, along the Butley River, or in the Alde Estuary for the winter.

A·R·Wood·

Avocet

Other breeding waders include Redshank, Oyster-catcher and Ringed Plover. A colony of between 150 and 250 pairs of Sandwich Terns nest on the island in addition to thousands of Black-headed Gulls adding to the general clamour at the height of the breeding season in May. A few dozen pairs of Common Terns also nest while Little Terns from their nearby colony on Orford beach can also be seen fishing over the lagoons. Two or three pairs of Arctic Terns also nest most years and this is well south of their normal breeding range. Spring wader passage may bring in scores of Black-tailed Godwits, some Bar-tailed Godwits, a few Ruff, Greenshank or even a Kentish Plover. A wider variety in autumn may include Turnstone, Little Stint and Curlew Sandpiper. Dotterel have been seen from time to time.

The island is well used by wintering duck which may include several hundred Wigeon and Teal with lesser numbers of Shoveler, Gadwall and Pintail. The deeper lagoons might support Goldeneye and Red-breasted Mergansers. White-fronted Geese, Brent Geese and Bewick's Swans regularly fly over the island, while Short-eared Owls and Hen Harriers regularly frequent the saltings and grasslands. Winter waders include Grey Plover, Bar-tailed Godwit, Dunlin, Curlew, Redshank and Knot.

Map 23

Alde Estuary

The main attractions of this wide estuary are wildfowl and waders in winter and waders on passage, but it cannot be compared with the bird-thronged estuaries to the south; Grey Plover, Shelduck, Avocet, Pintail and Wigeon can be seen in winter, while numbers of Curlew may be present after the breeding season.

Map 24

Sutton Common

A few heathland species may still be met with in this area, but increasing pressure from more and more people enjoying the usual countryside pursuits may hasten their end. The occasional pair of Stonechats and Wheatears may nest in the area. This heath used to be frequented by Red-backed Shrikes, Yellow Wagtails and Stone Curlews, but all have

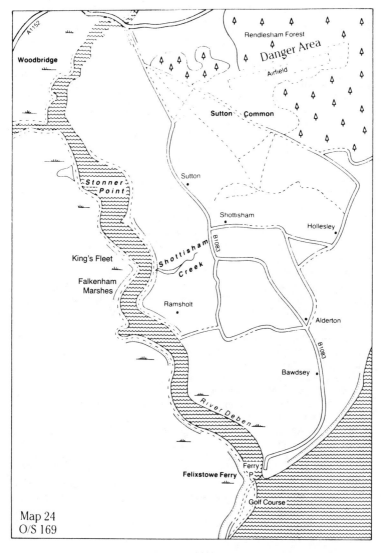

Map 24
O/S 169

gone as regular breeders. Where conifer forests are felled and replanted there are good populations of Willow Warblers, Yellow Hammers, Tree Pipits and Nightjars for a few years, until the advancing density and height of the trees precludes all undergrowth. The mature conifer woodlands attract Siskins, Redpolls, Bramblings and Crossbills. In winter a Goshawk is often seen and a Red Kite has been recorded.

Map 24

Deben Estuary
The mouth of the River Deben at Felixstowe Ferry is worth watching for winter wildfowl, waders and passage migrants. Five hundred or more Brent Geese usually winter. Good numbers of wintering Black-tailed Godwits can usually be found along the mudflats of the river while Dunlin may reach four figures. Several hundred Teal, Shelduck and Pintail may be present especially in the higher reaches. Goldeneye are regularly seen in the lower reaches while hard weather may bring Smew, Red-breasted Mergansers, Red-necked and Slavonian Grebes. The approach from Felixstowe can be good for small open ground passerines where the unfenced road skirts the golf-course. A Little Egret was once seen by a concrete pool at the edge of the fairway! The footpath along the south shore of the River Deben is good in winter for Twite, Rock Pipit, one or two Short-eared Owls and occasional Hen Harrier.

LANDGUARD POINT

Map 25

A more unprepossessing site for a bird observatory is difficult to imagine, yet at the extremity of the peninsula, which juts south from Felixstowe, a bird observatory was officially opened in September 1983. Landguard is a reserve of 40 acres (16 ha) owned by the Suffolk County Council and managed by the Suffolk Wildlife Trust (SWT). It was designated a Local Nature Reserve in 1979. The reserve area was occupied by the Ministry of Defence for over 200 years and the observatory operates from land owned by English Heritage, and is surrounded by a high perimeter fence with padlocked gate! It encloses a wartime fort (over 100 years old), search-light emplacements and look-out towers. Nearby the din of the dockland with its plethora of cranes and ships is somewhat daunting! Yet some-how, despite all this human activity, migrant birds appear and rare species survive on the adjoining beach. The scrub bushes of tamarisk, ilex, bramble and elder manage to attract an amazing variety of passerine migrants. Incredibly, over 43,000 birds of over 120 species have already been trapped and ringed, including such rarities as Wryneck, Bluethroat, Thrush Nightingale, Melodious Warbler, Barred Warbler, Icterine Warbler, Pallas's Warbler, Red-breasted Flycatcher and Great Grey Shrike. Other semi-rarities such as Firecrest and Nightingales have proved to be quite regular visitors. Obviously a bird in transit must break its journey when necessary wherever it happens to be – over a life-sustaining oasis or in a barren habitat such as this busy dockland area. Long-eared Owl, Kingfisher, Nightjar, Wood Warbler and Ortolan Bunting are other surprising records.

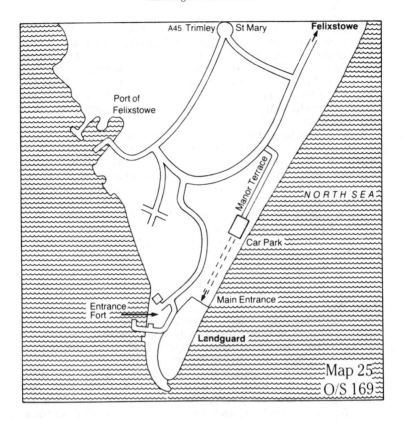

Thrush Nightingale. A rare vagrant, trapped and ringed in Norfolk and Suffolk

157

Black Redstarts – more understandably – actually nest on the reserve as do a few pairs in the nearby town of Felixstowe. There is also a small well guarded colony of Little Terns which is one of Britain's rarest breeding seabirds. The commoner migrants may include numbers of Pied Flycatchers, Willow Warblers, Chiff-chaffs, Redstarts, Robins, Blackcaps, Garden Warblers, Spotted Flycatchers, Whitethroats, Lesser White-throats, Whinchats, Wheatears, Blackbirds, Song Thrushes, Redwings and Goldcrests.

Even sea watching here can be rewarding with waders and wildfowl passing offshore. Thousands of Brent Geese move south in late autumn heading for the Essex Marshes. Hundreds of Teal, Mallard, Wigeon, Shelduck together with lesser numbers of Common Scoter, Eider and Red-breasted Mergansers have been observed. Thousands of hirundines moving south have been noted in September while in October similar numbers of incoming winter thrushes and finches have been noted. There is no doubt that Landguard Point – ringed by pressures as it is – will, in the course of time, contribute very significantly to the study of migration in Suffolk.

Map 26

Alton Water

This comparatively new reservoir goes from strength to strength with a score or so pairs of Great-crested Grebes now breeding annually and passing Osprey calling in quite frequently. However, the autumn and winter months will provide the greatest number and variety of birds. In autumn a few waders on passage include Spotted Redshank, Greenshank, Curlew Sandpiper, Dunlin, Wood, Common and Green Sandpipers. The latter two species have been known to spend the winter here. Temminck's Stint and Jack Snipe have been recorded. In winter hundreds of Shoveler, Tufted Duck, Pochard, Gadwall and Wigeon frequent the reservoir. Often there are a few Little Grebes, Goldeneye and single numbers of Red-breasted Mergansers and Long-tailed Duck present. Single Red-throated and Black-throated Divers and Black-necked Grebes have also been noted. The appearance of a few Ruddy Duck may herald future colonisation. Other rare duck have included Ring-necked and Ferruginous Duck while Garganey have been noted in summer. Other rare spring highlights have included Black Terns and Montagu's Harrier. Rare autumn raptors have included Honey Buzzard and Hobby. Several pairs of Yellow Wagtails breed in the surrounding areas. It is hoped that sporting activities on the reservoir will be controlled, in order that these good bird populations will not diminish.

Map 26

Orwell Estuary

Between the mouth of the River Orwell at Harwich Harbour and the city of Ipswich the sluggish river supports a very important population of waders and wildfowl. The greatest concentrations however, may be in the upper reaches while the south side generally provides better access for viewing. Trimley Reserve is a new 200 acre (81 ha) wetland area currently being created by the SWT. It lies west of the Felixstowe Docks whose company have funded this project to help compensate for wild-life habitat lost during docks expansion.

Winter duck species running into counts of hundreds include Shelduck, Mallard, Wigeon, Pintail, Teal and Pochard. There are lesser numbers of Shoveler, Red-breasted Mergansers and Goldeneye. In severe weather small numbers of Scaup, Eider, Long-tailed Duck, Velvet Scoter, Smew and Goosander may be recorded. Tufted Duck may appear if frozen out from freshwater. A thousand or more Brent Geese may be present and there are usually scores of Cormorants. Great-crested Grebes often winter by the score and one or two of the rarer grebes such as Red-necked, Black-necked and Slavonian have been recorded. Black-throated and Great Northern Divers might also appear in hard weather.

Winter waders such as Dunlin and Redshank can be found in their thousands while hundreds of Curlew, Grey Plover, Ringed Plover and Oyster-catcher make the Orwell a very important winter habitat. It is of note that there is an unusual winter assembly of about 100 Carrion Crows on the strand by Wherstead by the upper reaches of the river.

Map 26

Ipswich Docks
This might also appear to be an uninspiring place for birdwatching, but winter watching can be extremely good with fairly medium range viewing of several uncommon seabirds and wildfowl in small numbers. Anything up to 200 Mute Swans may winter in the harbour and perhaps their tameness may help induce confidence in other birds as, in fact, a wild Whooper Swan has been recorded. Red-throated, Black-throated and Great Northern Divers have all been noted at times. One or two Shags are often present. Single numbers of Long-tailed Ducks are seen while in hard weather Red-necked Grebe or Scaup may turn up. Brent Geese and Goldeneye are other winter visitors. The docks are also another regular place for Turnstones in the spring.

Grey Plover and two Ringed Plovers

Map 29

Stour Estuary
Devotees of winter flock watching agree that the extensive Stour Estuary supports the greatest concentrations of waders and wildfowl in Suffolk. Wide estuaries are not easy places to watch and a telescope is essential. There is also a great interchange by some species flying from this estuary to the Orwell and the sea coast. Although a footpath follows most of the Suffolk shore of the Stour Estuary, road access points are limited.

However, the greatest attraction of the Stour Estuary is the thrill of seeing very large numbers of birds. This is the main wintering area in the county for Black-tailed Godwits with over 1,000 birds present in some winters. Colossal numbers of Dunlin are present, wheeling across the estuary in tight flocks if disturbed by a raptor. In most winters several thousand birds are present, and counts of 14,000 to 17,000 are not unusual. The Stour is also a very important habitat for Redshank with usually between 2,000 and 4,000 birds present. Strangely enough, the Knot is never found in the vast numbers that occur off the north-west Norfolk coasts or off the Essex coasts; but this estuary does muster about one or two thousand birds. Grey Plover usually total between 400 and 1,000 birds throughout the winter months. Curlew flocks in similar numbers help to swell the throngs of waders. Turnstone numbers are always a bit thin on the Suffolk coast, but the Stour regularly provides sanctuary for about 500 birds. Two other waders, the Ringed Plover and Oyster-catcher, usually occur in slightly smaller numbers.

Of the wildfowl the most numerous is the Wigeon with winter counts ranging from 1,000 to 3,000 birds. Shelduck are not far behind with between 1,000 and 2,000 birds regularly using the estuary in late autumn, winter and early spring. Mallard numbers can be well over 2,000 but stocks are raised and released by shooting interests. Several hundred Teal are present, but greatest numbers occur in late autumn. This is also the stronghold of the delightful Pintail with some 200 to 300 birds present annually. The only diving duck to occur regularly in any number is the Goldeneye and a few score birds are usually found there.

Other diving duck such as Smew and Red-breasted Mergansers may turn up in hard weather. Brent Geese numbers fluctuate annually and during a winter season birds may often interchange their feeding areas. Usually there are somewhere between 500 and 2,000 birds present with the highest numbers occurring after a successful breeding season in Siberia.

Timing

Havergate Island
Visit between April and June for breeding birds, autumn for passage waders, and winter months for wildfowl. Timing is fully dependent on tides and the times that the boat goes. All visits to the island are restricted and need (RSPB) permit applications in advance.

Alde Estuary
Best to visit in May and from August throughout the winter months. Try to time visits to about two hours before high tide as this will push birds nearer to the shore.

Sutton Common
Summer Bank Holidays are best avoided. Any time of the day is suitable, but early morning is best in spring. All heathlands are quiet in late summer. Winter months may produce raptors and finches.

Deben Estuary
The Deben is a very popular sailing river so it is best avoided during peak holiday times. Watch the mouth of the river in spring, autumn and winter for migrants and wildfowl.

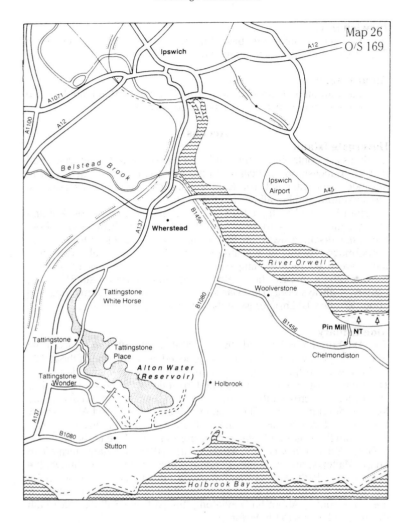

Landguard Point

Go in late April or May for spring migrants and from August to November for sea watching and passerines. Incoming tide time is best, so up to two hours before high tide time is advisable. Easterly winds in autumn are best for falls of passerines and on-shore gales for sea watching.

Alton Water

The best time of year is from late autumn to early spring. Some spring passage up to May does occur. The reservoir is also used for water sports so it is best to avoid holiday times. Although obviously not a tidal water, high tide on the coast may bring birds inland.

Orwell Estuary

From November to March is the best time of year while hard weather may bring more unusual wildfowl. Again, tides are important and it is best to be on site about two hours before high tide.

Ipswich Docks

Again, winter months are best, but in May there are gatherings of Turnstones. Best at or before high tide.

Stour Estuary

The late autumn and winter months from October to March are best. Up to two hours before high tide will be an advantage.

Access

Havergate Island

Landings are controlled by the RSPB and by boat from Orford Quay. Full details of access on application to the RSPB is recommended, well in advance of the intended visit. Numbers are restricted to twelve persons, the maximum number allowed in the boat.

Orford is served by the B1078 from Wickham Market on the A12 and about 9 miles (14.4 km) away; and the B1084 from Bromeswell about the same distance away on the A1152 and 3½ miles (5.6 km) from Woodbridge. Parking is available by Orford Quay. Several observation hides are used for watching over the lagoons. Pack waterproof and warm clothing in case the weather deteriorates during visit. The open estuary is always cool. The island is nearly 2 miles (3.2 km) long and about ½ mile (0.8 km) across at its widest point.

Alde Estuary

The Aldeburgh Marshes and River Alde at Aldeburgh can be explored from a footpath which is reached by proceeding to the end of the A1094 in the town and then continuing along a trackway to Slaughden Quay. The footpath of about 3½ miles (5.6 km) follows the bends of the river and eventually crosses the marshes back to the town (the marshes are likely to flood in winter). The southern shore of the inland Alde Estuary is more easily accessible than the northern side where roads are scarce, apart from the Coast Path which does not run very close to the shores.

From Aldeburgh take the A1094 to the B1069 left-hand turn-off to Snape Maltings, about 6 miles (9.6 km). Once over the river bridge, the Suffolk Coast Path can be picked up along a dead-end minor road on the left. Follow this footpath along for nearly 2 miles (3.2 km) and return by the same route. (About halfway along this path the Suffolk Coast Path diverts southwards to Chillesford.)

Sutton Common

Take the A1152 out of Woodbridge on the A12 and turn off at the roundabout along the B1083. After about 1¾ miles (2.8 km) there is a picnic site on the left at a junction of three trackways. Explore the various footpaths for heathland birds.

Deben Estuary

A very scenic stretch lies to the south of Sutton Common between Sutton and Ramsholt, an area orientated towards sailing so the footpaths are poorly indicated. It is easier to follow the B1083 south from Sutton Common and take the first minor road on the right past Shottisham. Then take a second minor turn on your right after 1½ miles (2.4 km) to Ramsholt Quay. From here it is possible to watch over the estuary. There is also a footpath for miles along the south bank of the Deben from Felixstowe Ferry.

Landguard Point

This peninsula is immediately on the southern outskirts of Felixstowe, which is served by the A45 but which by-passes the town to Felixstowe Port. Just past the end of the road, turn off left along Manor Terrace, which ends at a car park. From here follow the track to the reserve entrance which is signposted. Further details about visiting the observatory area should be obtained from the Secretary, Jane Bourne, c/o The Hand Cottage, 320 High Road, Trimley St Martin, Suffolk IP10 ORL.

Alton Water

Take the A137 south from Ipswich and, after about 3 miles (4.8 km), turn off left to Tattingstone White Horse. Take the road onwards to Tattingstone, but look out for car park and toilets beside the reservoir. Walk east or west on both banks, but do not enter the conservation area (this is clearly signposted) on the north bank of the western end. Proceed on to Tattingstone village and take the footpath out to the reservoir by Tattingstone Place. This is the best spot for waders and wildfowl when conditions are right. For yet another viewing point proceed south from Tattingstone for about ½ mile (0.8 km) to Tattingstone Wonder (a cottage that looks like a church). A car park is opposite and you can walk east along the reservoir. Last, but not least, is the official entrance gate. Continue along minor roads through Sutton on the Holbrook road. Look out on the left-hand side for an entrance and follow this along to the car park and toilets. Walk along to the dam which is the best end for observing divers.

Orwell Estuary

There are several access points. Take the A137 south from Ipswich. After about 1½ miles (2 km) look out for Fox's Boatyard car park at the junction of the B1456 on the left. A footpath can be followed along Wherstead Strand. Continue following the B1456 which turns left to Woolverstone after about 2 miles (3.2 km). Continue to Chelmondiston in just over 1 mile (1.6 km) and then turn off left in the village to the riverside hamlet of Pin Mill. Walk right to Chelmondiston Woods (NT) which clothe the river's edge. Approach Trimley Reserve from High Road, Trimley St Mary (west of Felixstowe) turning down Station Road. Open at all times. Hides available. Further details from SWT.

Ipswich Docks

It is difficult to give a route to the docks at Ipswich as there is a maze of minor roads. Near the Customs House off Key Street there is a wet dock area. Walk right round to Lock Gates. Another point is at end of Bath Street, off the Wherstead Road. Both these access points are on the south side of the town.

Stour Estuary

This large estuary is probably easier watched from the Essex side at Copperas Bay. See Map 29.

Calendar

Havergate Island

Resident Avocet is particularly resident as few birds now stay in winter.

December–February Wigeon, Teal, Shoveler, Gadwall, Pintail, Goldeneye, Red-breasted Merganser, Short-eared Owl, Hen Harrier, Grey Plover, Curlew, Dunlin, Redshank, Knot and Bar-tailed Godwit.

March–July Redshank, Oyster-catcher, Ringed Plover, Sandwich Tern, Common Tern, Little Tern, Arctic Tern, Black-headed Gull, Black-tailed Godwit, Bar-tailed Godwit, Ruff, Greenshank and Kentish Plover (rare).

August–November Turnstone, Little Stint, Curlew Sandpiper and Dotterel (rare).

Alde Estuary
December–February Pintail, Wigeon, Avocets.

July–November Grey Plover, Shelduck, Pintail, Wigeon and Curlew.

Sutton Common
Resident Stonechat, Yellow Hammer, Siskin, Redpoll and Crossbill.

November–March Brambling, Goshawk and Red Kite (last two species rare).

April–June Wheatear, Tree Pipit and Nightjar.

Deben Estuary
November–March Black-tailed Godwit, Dunlin, Shelduck, Teal, Pintail, Goldeneye. In hard weather, Smew, Red-breasted Merganser, Red-necked and Slavonian Grebes are to be seen. Usually Twite, Rock Pipits, one or two Short-eared Owls and occasionally Hen Harrier, Bewick's and Whooper Swans.

Spring and autumn months Open ground migrants such as chats, pipits, wagtails and larks.

Landguard Point
March–June Firecrest, Black Redstart, Little Tern, Wheatear, Whinchat, Wryneck, Pied Flycatcher, Red-backed Shrike, Nightingale, Bluethroat, Ortolan Bunting, Long-eared Owl, Redstart, Ring Ouzel, Thrush Nightingale, Melodious Warbler (the last two species very rare).

August–November Wryneck, Bluethroat, Barred Warbler, Icterine Warbler, Pallas's Warbler, Red-breasted Flycatcher, Great Grey Shrike, Nightingale, Long-eared Owl, Kingfisher, Nightjar, Wood Warbler, Pied Flycatcher, Redstart, Robin, Willow Warbler, Chiff-chaff, Goldcrest (good numbers of the last four species as migrants), Blackcap, Garden Warbler, Spotted Flycatcher, Whitethroat, Lesser Whitethroat, Whinchat, Wheatear, Blackbird, Song Thrush, Redwing (good numbers of the last three species on passage, and many hirundines moving south in September).

Alton Reservoir
April–June Great-crested Grebe, Garganey, Black Tern, Yellow Wagtail, Monatagu's Harrier (rare) and Osprey (occasionally).

July–November Honey Buzzard, Hobby (not after September), Spotted

Redshank, Greenshank, Curlew Sandpiper, Dunlin, Wood Sandpiper, Common Sandpiper, Green Sandpiper, (the latter two species have wintered), Temminck's Stint and Jack Snipe.

September–February Shoveler, Pochard, Tufted Duck, Gadwall, Wigeon, Goldeneye, Little Grebe, Long-tailed Duck, Red-breasted Merganser, Red-throated Diver, Black-throated Diver, Black-necked Grebe, Ruddy Duck and Ferruginous Duck.

Orwell Estuary
October–March Shelduck, Mallard, Wigeon, Pintail, Teal, Pochard, Shoveler, Red-breasted Merganser, Goldeneye, Scaup, Eider, Long-tailed Duck, Velvet Scoter, Smew, Goosander (the last six more likely in hard weather), Brent Geese, Cormorant, Great-crested Grebe, Red-necked Grebe, Black-necked Grebe, Slavonian Grebe (the last three grebes scarce and more likely in hard weather), Black-throated Diver, Great Northern Diver, Dunlin, Redshank, Curlew, Grey Plover, Ringed Plover, Oyster-catcher and Carrion Crow (a gathering of 100 birds).

Ipswich
November–March Mute Swan (a large gathering), Red-throated Diver, Black-throated Diver, Great Northern Diver, Shag, Long-tailed Duck, Red-necked Grebe, Scaup (the last two species in hard weather), Brent Goose, Goldeneye and Turnstone (also up to May).

Stour Estuary
September–March Black-tailed Godwit, Dunlin, Redshank, Knot, Grey Plover, Curlew, Turnstone, Ringed Plover, Oyster-catcher, Wigeon, Shelduck, Mallard, Teal, Pintail, Goldeneye, Smew, Red-breasted Merganser (last two species more in hard weather) and Brent Goose.

WOLVES WOOD

MAP 27
OS map 155

Habitat

Most of East Anglia before Anglo-Saxon times was covered with a broad-leaved primeval forest which was steadily cleared during and after that period. Those isolated pockets which were too wet to clear and plough survived, but came under threat again with the advent of mechanised farming. About 3 miles (4.8 km) east of Hadleigh on the A1071 Wolves Wood (SS1) still survives under the guardianship of the RPSB who purchased the 92 acres (36.8 ha) in 1972 to form a reserve of great importance to nature conservation. Nearby are two other ancient woodlands – Hintlesham and Ramsey Woods – and together they form one of the last strongholds of primeval forests left in East Anglia. It is likely that these woods were coppiced up to the present century. In Wolves Wood there are 27 species of trees and shrubs with some fine hornbeams. The entire wood is very damp being situated on a heavy boulder-clay plateau in a gently undulating landscape. There is a rich flora, insect and bird population. Important archaeological features include a medieval boundary bank, an extensive network of ditches, and a remarkable total of 43 ponds. Of these, only four retain water throughout the year to provide a habitat for frogs, toads, newts and dragonflies. The woodland rides and paths which are kept cut are also an important habitat for butterflies, 22 species have been recorded including the white-letter hairstreak, the purple hairstreak and the Essex skipper, which is in large numbers. Nearly 300 plants have been recorded including dog's mercury, yellow pimpernel, yellow archangel and herb paris (the last two species being typical of ancient woodlands) and several species of orchids.

Map 27

Species

Although some 50 species of birds nest in Wolves Wood, pride of place must go to the Nightingale, whose powerfully rich song on a May evening is completely in accord with the natural auditorium of this relict forest. Up to eight pairs nest annually and they have benefited from management work which includes coppicing and clearing rides.

Other uncommon breeding species include the Hawfinch which is more easily seen in winter when it is attracted to the hornbeam trees. Several pairs of Lesser and Great Spotted Woodpeckers nest, but the Green is very infrequent. Other smaller inhabitants include Willow Warblers in profusion, dozens of Blackaps and Garden Warblers, small numbers of Whitethroats, Lesser Whitethroats, Coal, Marsh and Willow Tits, Long-tailed Tits, Treecreepers and Spotted Flycatchers. Migrants passing through in the spring include Wood Warbler and Firecrest. Winter brings many Fieldfares and Redwings to seek safe roosting places in the wood, while parties of Siskins and Redpolls resort to the silver birches. Woodcock occur and probably breed as 'roding' flights are observed in spring.

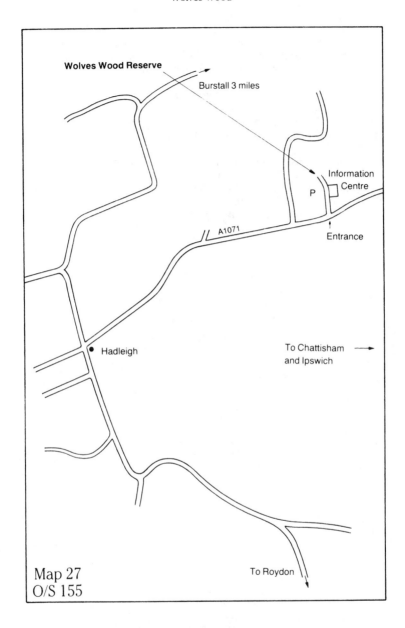

Map 27
O/S 155

Timing
Late April or May is the best time to visit, although some resident species are more easily seen in the bare winter months.

Access
Take the A1071 from Hadleigh to Ipswich and, after about 1½ miles (2.4 km), turn left to the reserve entrance. The reserve is open at any time of year. There is an information centre which is open every week-

end from April to September. Permits are not required, but parties intending to visit must contact the RSPB well in advance. It is also essential that all visitors keep to the Nature Trail marked with blue arrows and do not enter other parts of the woodland.

Calendar

Resident Those resident woodland birds more easily seen in December–March are Hawfinch, Great Spotted and Lesser Spotted Woodpeckers, most tits, Treecreeper, and Woodcock.

Winter months Siskin, Redpoll, Fieldfare and Redwing.

April–June Nightingale, Willow Warbler, Blackcap, Garden Warbler, Whitethroat, Lesser Whitethroat, Spotted Flycatcher, Firecrest and Wood Warbler (the last two species are migrants)

Habitat

Most of the extensive fens of the Waveney and Little Ouse valleys have been reclaimed or destroyed by continuous dredging or lowering of the water tables. The largest remaining example of these fens, Redgrave and Lopham totalling 304 acres (121.6 ha) has been secured by the Suffolk Wildlife Trust, with recognition of the site by the Nature Conservancy Council as a Grade 1 (SSSI)

The useful natural resources of these old fens were exploited for many centuries though peat digging declined after Victorian times. Old peat diggers' paths still exist on the reserve and some have been cleared and brought back into use. On either side of the paths are the old peat diggings with some pools deep enough to support aquatic plants such as insectivorous bladderwort.

These small pools amongst the thick saw sedge fen are a haven for frogs and newts. They are also the only habitat in Britain where the great raft spider (*Dolomedes plantarius*) lives. This unique spider lies in wait on a piece of floating débris with its front legs touching the surface of the water so that it can detect any vibrations created by an insect trapped in the surface film. It then dashes across the water, having first secured a silken line to its base, seizes its prey and gives it a poisoned bite. This spider may also pursue its prey under water and it is able to do this by breathing air trapped in its furry body. It also constructs and guards a nursery tent where its egg sac is deposited after being carried for two to three weeks. The spiderlings spend several days in the tent before dispersing to start their own independent life.

In addition to the plant and insect rich sedge fen there are reed-beds, heath and woodlands to be found. The source of the River Waveney starts as a tiny ditch on this reserve.

Map 28

Species

During the winter, Hen Harriers may hunt the area and flocks of Bearded Tits frequent the reed-beds where in summer Reed, Sedge and Grass-hopper Warblers can be seen and heard. In spring and summer the surrounding woodlands are alive with returning migrants. Nightingales can be heard as well as most of the commoner warblers. Woodpeckers, Nuthatches, Treecreepers, tits, Woodcock, and Sparrow Hawks frequent the more mature woodlands.

Timing

The best time to visit is in the spring and early summer months.

Access

From South Lopham on the A1066 (between Thetford and Diss). Turn off on the south side of the road on the B1113 to Redgrave. Take the first minor road on the left after 1 mile (1.6 km), and then first right after ½ mile (0.8 km). Here is the fen entrance to the reserve car park. Access is available to SWT members at all times.

Calendar

Resident Woodcock, Sparrow Hawk, tits, Nuthatch, Treecreeper.

Winter Bearded Tit and Hen Harrier.

Summer Nightingale, Reed, Sedge and Grasshopper Warblers, plus most of the commoner summer warblers.

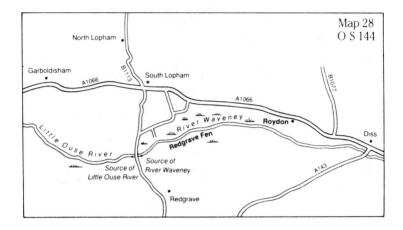

ESSEX

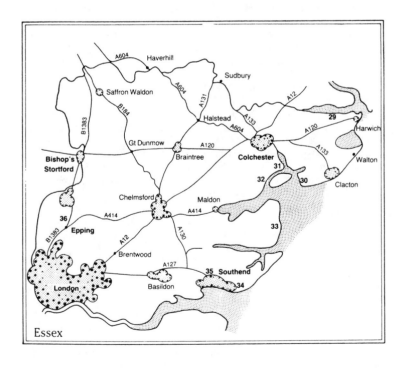

Essex

Habitat

When one digests the staggering statistics relating to Essex it seems an improbable region for birdwatching yet within 50 miles (80 km) of London a total of 339 bird species have been seen within the county. Over 70 per cent of Essex is under cultivation, while another 20 per cent is under bricks and mortar – all habitats which do not support a wide range of species. The advance of building and agriculture, with a considerable growth in population over the past 30 years, has eaten into the Essex countryside. Hedgerows have gone to make way for vast prairie-like fields, woodlands and pastures have been destroyed for all sorts of developments and there seems to be no decline in the pressures that beset this county.

The remaining areas of undeveloped land include a wide range of habitats. There are saltmarshes and creeks along the coast which are of prime importance to birdlife, as are the five major, and many minor, estuaries and over 300 miles (480 km) of seawalls between the Stour Estuary in the north and the Thames Estuary in the south. Then there is a useful spin-off from commercial interests, the creation of reservoirs and gravel pits which have become flooded after being worked out, thereby enhancing wildlife. Woodland is still to be found. Epping Forest is by far the largest woodland complex comprising some 6,000 acres (2.400 ha) which is owned by the Corporation of London. The other principle woodland belts are mainly in the southern half of the county. Many other smaller woodland complexes which have been secured by conservation bodies are typically mixed deciduous, Epping being noted for its fine beeches and pollarded hornbeams. Very few woodlands have been replanted with conifers, but many were neglected in years past resulting in dense overgrown woods colonised only by Jays and Wood Pigeons. However, conservation bodies have now resumed the age old practice of coppicing which greatly benefits a wealth of smaller birds.

Small heaths and commons can be found in many inland regions of Essex, but most of their ornithological specialities have gone.

It is understandable that many birdwatchers nowadays concentrate on the bird rich coastal region between the Stour and Thames estuaries. There are five National Nature Reserves established by the Nature Conservancy Council. Most of the coastline is flat and follows a remarkable winding course. The Essex side of the River Stour, which is the boundary with Suffolk, is attractive 'Constable Country' and is equally attractive to large numbers of wintering wildfowl and waders. Near Wrabness the Stour Wood and Copperas Bay Reserve comprises 134 acres (53.6 ha) of woodland and was set up by the RSPB and the Woodland Trust. There is an adjoining area of 185 acres (74 ha) of intertidal mudflats. Flowers to be found in the wood include moschatel, yellow archangel, bluebells and anemones. The white admiral butterfly, badgers and dormice also occur.

Another vital area for waders and wildfowl is Hamford Water (NNR), a huge tidal complex of islands and creeks. Close by is Naze Point, where the only cliff formations of any note in Essex have been designated a geological SSSI, being a classic example of red crag which contains many fossil shells. These cliffs, which extend only a few miles south to Frinton-on-Sea, are an important landfall for migrant birds in autumn who seek shelter in the extensive areas of gorse and bramble by the large public open space on the cliff-tops. There are tremendous views across the Naze of Hamford Water and, on clear days, Harwich and Felixstowe. The flora includes slender thistle, pepper saxifrage, fenugreek, strawberry-headed clover and sea spurge. The heavy scent of clover attracts many Essex skippers, while the emperor, cream-spot tiger and ground lackey moths fly here. A nature trail has been laid out.

The Colne Estuary south of Clacton-on-Sea is another NNR, but the outstanding plant and animal life is vulnerable to human pressures on the beaches. This estuary provides feeding grounds for a variety of wildfowl in winter. Colne Point is a reserve of 400 acres (160 ha) composed of saltings and shingle spits. It is owned by the Essex Wildlife Trust. There is a rich flora and fauna with sea meadow grass, marram grass, shrubby seablite, sea campion, sea holly, sea bind-weed, sea spurge and yellow-horned poppies to be found. At low tide hundreds of acres of mudflats with shingle pools are exposed and they contain a large range of marine animals and seaweeds.

As well as many small islets in the estuaries, the three large islands of Mersea, Foulness and Canvey have important habitats. Foulness though is controlled by the Ministry of Defence and there is no general public access. At the west end of Mersea Island there is a coastal park which is good in autumn and winter. Cudmore Grove Country Park, 35 acres (14 ha), is a grassland site with mudlflats on the south side and part of the saltmarsh belongs to the Colne Estuary NNR on the eastern side.

Being on the west shore of the River Colne the Fingringhoe Wick Reserve is also part of the Colne Estuary SSSI. The 125 acres (50 ha) of disused gravel workings and adjacent saltings have been developed into a good variety of wildlife habitats and it is now the flagship of the Essex Wildlife Trust who have set up their county headquarters there. They now have a purpose built centre with displays and interpretations of the habitats in the reserve. These include saltmarsh, reed-bed, fresh and brackish ponds, a lake, gorse heath, scrub and secondary woodland.

North of Fingringhoe Wick the Roman River flows into the River Colne. In its upper reaches the Roman flows through a delightful wooded valley. South of the river the Abberton Reservoir of 1,235 acres (494 ha) is an important breeding station for waterfowl, of even greater international importance due to its migrant wintering birds.

Also in this extremely interesting area between the River Colne and River Blackwater are the Old Hall Marshes purchased by the RSPB in 1985. Bounded on either side by tidal channels this reserve of tremendous potential is encompassed by an 8 mile (12.8 km) seawall and footpath. The seawall walk will give terrific views over the desolate marshes and estuaries. Common meadow land butterflies and dragon-flies swarm along the banks in summer.

The wide Blackwater Estuary is deeper than that of the Stour, but attracts great numbers of wildfowl in winter. A footpath topped seawall winds tortuously round the whole estuary, but public access points to this are ill-defined. Minor trackways, like many others in Essex are marked with 'No Entry' signs.

The extensive area of the Dengie Peninsula juts out to the North Sea between the Rivers Blackwater and Crouch. The marshes between

Bradwell-on-Sea and Burnham-on-Crouch encompass one of the most remote coastal regions in England. Behind the 16 miles (25.6 km) long seawall there is a dreary expanse of prairie-like cornfields. This used to be an important region for duck with several decoys in operation on the old grazing marshes. With drainage and the change in cultivation favouring cereals in the last 20 years, the numbers of duck have been much reduced. Walkers along this seawall should be aware that there is no shelter once the seventh century Chapel of St Peter has been left behind at the edge of the saltings north-east of Bradwell-on-Sea. The chapel was built by St Cedd on the site of the third century Roman Fort of Orthona, using the Roman stones and tiles from the old fort. Close by on the edge of the saltings there is a small but very attractive area of trees and bushes where the Bradwell Bird Observatory has been strategically sited. Beside the landward edge of the seawall, borrow-dykes are fringed with reeds which attract several nesting species. These dykes were made by the excavations of soil which was used to build the seawalls and they also serve as drainage channels. On the seaward side of the banks there are very extensive saltmarshes with the receding tide uncovering thousands more acres of mudflats which are the winter home of countless waders and wildfowl. The walker along this bleak wall should be equipped to meet all weathers at any time of year. There are a few trackways diverting inland and some of these make it clear in no uncertain terms that visitors are not welcome to use them.

Immediately south of the Crouch Estuary the large area of Foulness and the adjacent Havengore Island are strictly controlled by the Ministry of Defence and permits to visit may only be given for scientific purposes. Nevertheless, Foulness is thus effectively protected against development to provide a unique winter habitat for thousands of Brent Geese and waders.

Southwards from Foulness a complex of large towns extends west-wards into the City of London – not an inspiring habitat one has to admit! Nevertheless, the marshes to the east of Southend, also subject to the (MOD) Foulness restrictions, are still very attractive to birds and there is limited access here at several points to the shore where vast areas of mudflats are another important habitat for waders and wildfowl. A similar habitat with sand and shingle beaches extends all along the Southend seafront; the Southend Pier, over 1 mile (1.6 km) long, is a well known point from which to watch for passing seabirds!

West of Southend the Leigh NNR comprises Two Tree Island and several hundred acres of mudflats. The saltmarsh is one of the best surviving in the Thames Estuary and its flora includes the lax-flowered sea lavender and golden samphire. The mudflats are of international importance because of the concentrations of thousands of Brent Geese who find a good winter living on the particularly abundant eel grass to be found there.

Immediately across the Benfleet Creek, the Canvey Point Reserve (EWT) consists mainly of a saltmarsh spit about 1 mile (1.6 km) long at low tide. There is a path to it of clay mud and cockle shells which – be warned – is covered by the incoming high tide. From this spit there is a wide view over the estuary which is frequented by waders and wildfowl.

From the low coastal region it becomes something of a surprise to note the hills inland at this point. They rise to over 240 ft (72 m). Despite the environs of a big city there are several oases still to be found in the region. The Hadleigh Castle, Benfleet and Leigh are wooded hills, sloping down to the Hadleigh marshes at their foot. They are still extremely attractive to birdlife and give wide views over the Thames Estuary with the Kent coast in the distance. They have now been included in the well-established Hadleigh Country Park. Nearby the Belfairs Great Wood comprises 90 acres (36 ha) of deciduous woodland which is coppiced in rotation.

One of the more delightful reserves in Essex is between the super-market on the A13 at Pitsea and the oil refinery complex on Canvey Island! Perhaps the position of this reserve amongst such obvious commercialisation enhances its attractiveness. This is the Wat Tyler Country Park and Nature Trail established by Basildon Council. The Park is a memorial to Wat Tyler and the people of Essex who rebelled against the poll tax imposed by King Richard II in 1381. It was at one time all part of the Pitsea Hall Estate until the late 1800s and was composed of pasture, arable, some woodlands and saltings. Later the estate was used for the storage of ammunition and then purchased in 1928 by the, then, War Department. After the Second World War it was used for industry, before being developed as a Country Park by the Basildon Council a few years ago. There are now hedgerows, scrub, meadows, brackish water fleets, reed-beds, saltings and brackish ponds to be found in this small corner of Essex together with a wide variety of flowers, butterflies and other creatures.

Sea watching points in Essex cannot be compared with those in Norfolk or Suffolk, but persistent watching in recent years, particularly by members of the Southend Ornithological Group (SOG) has shown that significant numbers of seabirds *do* enter the Thames Estuary under certain weather conditions. In addition to Southend Pier, the coastline in the vicinity of East Tilbury on a sharp bend of the River Thames, is proving to be a vantage point. The most productive site here has proved to be Coalhouse Fort. In its own right it is worth a visit as it is the best example of a Victorian armoured casement fort in south-east England. Its construction was supervised by Gordon of Khartoum.

**Map 29
Species**

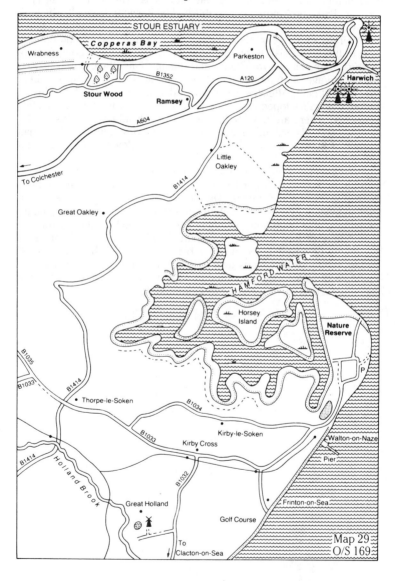

The two large woodlands on the south coast of the Stour Estuary known as Stour Wood and Copperas Wood are extremely good for producing a wide variety of species, especially given the proximity of the adjoining mudflats and reed-beds. The Stour Wood is owned by the Woodland Trust and managed by the RSPB who also protect 185 acres (74 ha) of intertidal mudflats adjoining the wood. Close by, the 34 acres (13.6 ha) of Copperas Wood is owned by the Essex Wildlife Trust.

In both woodlands the practice of coppicing has ceased for some years allowing the canopy of the lush growing sweet chestnut trees to exclude all light and warmth from the woodland floor and, in consequence, vegetation for nesting birds. Management work includes re-introducing coppicing in rotation which allows sunlight to generate a lush undergrowth so beloved by Chiff-chaffs, Blackcaps and Nightingales. The woodland bird populations up to now have proved small, but it is expected that this work will soon bring a good increase. With similar objectives in mind glades and clearings will be opened up which will also benefit the insect populations. Green, Lesser Spotted and Great Spotted Woodpeckers breed in the woods while Lesser Whitethroats, Whitethroats and Blackcaps breed on the less dense outskirts. Wrynecks have been recorded in the past.

On the exposed flats of Copperas Bay there is a wide range of waders and the shallow estuary is internationally important for the large populations that occur. From late summer throughout the winter months and often up to late spring, there is usually plenty of activity on the mudflats with passage waders moving through and winter flocks moving around the estuary. This is one of two of the most important international sites in the county for the Icelandic breeding populations of Black-tailed Godwits with usually up to 700 birds present; and, sometimes, over 1,000 birds. This species is increasing and it is a comparatively new habit for them to over-winter in East Anglia. As with all wintering estuary birds they tend to move over a large territory and may be frequenting Copperas Bay one week and the mudflats off the Suffolk side of the estuary the next week. Impressive concentrations of Dunlin also occur here with an average 9,000 wintering. Other totals include up to 2,500 Redshank, 260 Grey Plover, and 600 Curlews. In lesser numbers are Turnstones, Oyster-catchers and Ringed Plovers. Shelduck also find these mudflats an important winter habitat with around 2,000 birds present in the first month of the year, followed by a dispersal to their breeding grounds in February and March. Some 25 pairs nest on the Essex side of the Stour with most of the adults leaving from late June on a moult migration flight, from which they do not return until the last two or three months of the year. In June and July the ducklings from several pairs often unite in one large crèche guarded by one or two adults who remain behind.

Because of its shallowness the Stour Estuary is not noted for its diving duck, but some Goldeneye can be seen in the deeper channels. The dabbling duck is represented too, this being one of the favourite haunts of the Wigeon; numbers are regularly in excess of 3,000 and in some years over 8,000. By October Wigeon are usually present in strength with the first migrants having arrived from northern Europe in late August or September. Depending on the weather, flocks disperse in March but it is not unusual for a few birds to be seen during the summer and the odd pair has bred in the county. The other important duck species is the Pintail with numbers varying from 200 to 600 with a peak between

December and February. Mallard are usually in large numbers, but only small flocks of Teal like this open habitat. A few hundred Brent Geese usually winter between Copperas Bay and the mouth of the river.

Timing
April and May are best for summer woodland birds with also a chance of waders. The woods and the estuary are very quiet in mid-summer, but there is some improvement from late July and through the winter months, when bare woodlands might reveal woodpeckers. The state of the tide can be very important. At low tide birds may well spread out over a vast area of mudflats. With an incoming tide, feeding is gradually reduced and birds have to move nearer the shore. It is best to be on site about two hours before high tide time.

Access
Both the Stour and Copperas woods are on the south bank of the River Stour. They can be approached from the A137 Colchester to Ipswich road, turning off onto the B1352 though Manningtree. After 5 miles (8 km) turn left to Wrabness Station. Cross the railway bridge, where there is a choice of two footpaths to the shore and woods. Alternatively, there are three other footpaths from B1352 between Wrabness and Ramsey.

There is roadside parking but please do this with care and keep strictly to the public footpaths as indicated on the Ordnance Survey maps. There is no Centre and anyone seeking further information should contact the RSPB and the EWT. About a mile (1.6 km) of the shoreline is worth exploring and the Stour Wood paths are quite extensive. Wellington boots are advised in all but the driest periods in summer as the woodland footpaths are usually damp. A telescope is essential for watching over the estuary.

Calendar
Resident Green, Great and Lesser Spotted Woodpeckers.

April–June Shelduck, Wryneck (rare), Nightingale, Sedge Warbler, Reed Warbler, Lesser Whitethroat, Whitethroat, Blackcap; there are also the passage waders such as sandpiper and stints. Winter waders may linger into April.

August–March Great-crested Grebe, Brent Goose (October), Shelduck (from December), Wigeon, Teal, Pintail, Goldeneye, Black-tailed Godwit, Dunlin, Redshank, Grey Plover, Curlew, Turnstone, Oyster-catcher and Ringed Plover.

WALTON-ON-NAZE AND COLNE POINT

Map 29

Species

The coastal area between Harwich and Clacton-on-Sea (but not including either town) attracts a wide variety of species, but because of the complex of islands and channels it is not an easy region to explore. The coast and marshes to the south of Harwich regularly attract Snow Buntings in scattered parties of anything up to a hundred birds. Only small numbers may be present before November however, and not many are seen after late February. The shingle beaches of the Naze may also hold Snow Buntings in varying numbers while the saltings here are a major wintering area of Twite with usually a scattering of over 1,000 birds, often in nearby company with hundreds of Greenfinches. Small numbers of Shorelarks are often noted in the Naze area, but total numbers for the whole coastline fluctuate considerably. A common winter visitor, the Rock Pipit delights in frequenting the edges of small rills or saltmarshes.

Red-breasted Mergansers

The Hamford Water and Horsey Island complex is the winter home of many waders and sea duck. Red-breasted Mergansers frequent the sea channels between October and March when courtship displays may be seen. Up to 200 or more birds may be here but, as with all sea duck, feeding stations may change according to the food supplies available and the weather conditions. In the same period a few Long-tailed Duck may occur in harder weather when qutie large numbers of Scaup may appear. The gabbling flocks of Brent Geese follow the tides while a few White-fronted Geese regularly winter in the area, either on the coastal fields or on Horsey Island. Some Eider can usually be found in any month of the year while scattered Velvet Scoter are seen off the Naze coast. Shelduck begin to drift back late in the year and about 30 pairs breed in the region.

Of the winter waders this is one of the best areas in Essex for Bar-tailed Godwits who frequent the mudflats. The sandy beaches between Walton-on-Naze and Frinton-on-Sea regularly support a few hundred Sanderling while the seaweed covered groynes and seawalls south of Frinton-on-Sea are a noted spot to see a few Purple Sandpipers in most winters. Inland at this point the grassy pastures adjoining the Holland

Brook attract up to 100 wintering Ruff, but numbers may not build up until the first two months of the year. The Ruff is not known to nest in Essex and it is thought that these birds are moving north from a small European wintering population. Single Spotted Redshank may also winter in the Hamford Water complex; the odd Greenshank may do so as well though numbers of them use the maze of creeks on autumn passage. Of the rarer waders both Marsh Sandpiper and Stilt Sandpiper have been recorded off the Naze.

Winter raptors might include a Merlin dashing after the Twite flocks, or a Short-eared Owl quartering the coastal fields in search of voles. If Rough-legged Buzzards invade the country in late autumn the Naze area is often the haunt of these magnificent birds of prey during the winter months.

The headland and cliffs of the Naze are noted for passerine migration and some seabird passage, though Essex has few such points. The flat coastline, running roughly on a south-westerly course, does not act as a 'catchment' area and large falls of birds are therefore infrequent. The bushes on the Naze cliff-tops, and along the sides of the cliffs northwards from Walton-on-Naze, regularly attract a few of the commoner autumn migrants such as Pied Flycatchers, Redstarts, Willow Warblers and Whitethroats. Good numbers of Wheatears on passage occur here and all along the Essex coast as far as the Thames Estuary. Late autumn movements invariably include many birds of the larger Greenland race of Wheatear. Whinchats too, are a frequent migrant but usually peak numbers occur in August and September. The grassy sward regularly attracts Ring Ouzels in the spring and larger numbers in the autumn when coastal bushes may provide berries.

The Hoopoe has also occurred here and is a fairly regular passage visitor to Essex, liking short grassy meadows or golf-courses. Other open ground migrants have included falls of Meadow Pipits and parties of Yellow Wagtails on passage. The rare Ortolan Bunting has been recorded in May and October and should be looked for on sparse grassy wastelands. Fairly regular rarities in the autumn include the Wryneck which should be looked for on bare patches of grassland near bushes and the tiny Firecrest which may appear in any of the coastal bushes. With calm conditions in late autumn large numbers of Blackbirds and Chaffinches may be on the move. Blackbirds have arrived in thousands on the cliff-tops while similar numbers of Chaffinches may be seen offshore steadily heading north-west. At this time the predatory Great Grey Shrike may arrive, especially if there are any small passerines making a crossing of the North Sea at the same time. Another immigrant at this time may be the beautiful Long-eared Owl.

Icterine and Barred Warblers have been seen here on occasions, but records of the rarer Asiatic warblers remain extremely few and far between. Yellow-browed and Pallas's Warblers have been noted on one to two occasions in October and November. A March record of a Yellow-browed Warbler was extremely unusual. Even more amazingly, the coastal area to the south at Frinton-on-Sea has been the scene for two sightings of extremely rare British vagrants – a cock Collared Flycatcher was seen here in June 1979 while a Desert Warbler, which was only the third record for Britain, was watched in vegetation along the seawall in November 1975. Throw in a Tawny Pipit one September for good measure and Frinton-on-Sea obviously has the potential to attract small migrants under the right conditions.

The Naze has also attracted a few other rarities and these have included one or two Alpine Swifts in September and October, a Red-footed Falcon from southern Europe one July and odd records of Blue-throat, Raven, Little Bunting and Waxwings. There is often some seabird passage off the Naze usually in autumn after gales from a northerly point. A few Arctic Skuas may be passing and rather larger numbers of Gannets in October. One October three Sooty Shearwaters were seen, but in general seabird passage is not notable on the Essex coast.

Proceeding southwards from Walton-on-Naze and leaving the holiday sprawl of Clacton-on-Sea behind, the coastline once again begins to be attractive to the naturalist and birdwatcher. From the heronry at St Osyth Grey Herons resort to the saltings, while clouds of skipper butterflies are attracted by the all-pervading scent of clover flowers.

Snow Buntings and Shorelarks can usually be found on the shingle spits in winter and this is another favourite haunt of Rough-legged Buzzards and Peregrines from time to time. This shingle and grassy headland has also attracted several Tawny Pipits, a rare vagrant from southern Europe in August and September. Colne Point is on a major migration route for finches and chats especially during the autumn months. Wheatears and Whinchats particularly favour this open habitat on passage, while Firecrests and Icterine Warblers have been noted in the sparse coastal bushes.

Wheatear

Nesting species include about 20 pairs of Shelduck, Ringed Plovers, Redshank and Oyster-catchers as well as a fine colony of Little Terns which are closely guarded by the EWT. In winter many waders frequent the mudflats and there are large flocks of Brent Geese. Offshore, Red-breasted Mergansers and Long-tailed Duck can be seen, while Red-throated, Black-throated and Great Northern Divers occur fairly regularly. Immediately inland, the coastal marshes attract large flocks of Lapwings, Golden Plover and Curlew in winter, while a nearby sewage farm is the haunt of Pied and Yellow Wagtails in summer.

Timing

For the chance of coastal migrants an easterly airflow from the Continent is best in spring and autumn. Gales from a northerly point may produce some seabird passage. All fleets and estuaries are best looked at, up to two hours before high water, otherwise birds may be well scattered and far distant on the extensive mudflats. Late June to August, usually a quiet

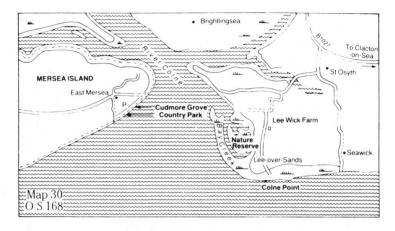

Map 30
O S 168

time for birds, can be very busy with holidaymakers to this attractive area. Winter hard weather may bring increased numbers of Eiders, Scaup and Long-tailed Duck into the area.

Access

The best approach is from the Stour Wood coast on the B1352 from Manningtree. Cross the A120 at Ramsey and then, after 1 mile (1.6 km), turn right on to the B1414 following this through Little Oakley, Great Oakley and Thorpe-le-Soken, make a left hand turn onto the B1033 to Frinton-on-Sea and Walton-on-Naze. Alternatively, after 1 mile (1.6 km), turn left on the B1034 to Walton-on-Naze.

At Walton-on-Naze drive through the town to the north where a minor road ends at a car park. From here, follow a walk along the side of the cliffs where there are clumps of small bushes. The grassy sward of the cliff-top can also be explored and here are extensive patches of gorse, bramble and other short bushes which may harbour migrants. The fenced nature reserve of 9 acres (3.6 ha) on the north edge of the headland is managed by the EWT under an agreement with Tendring District Council. It is only open by prior application to the EWT.

A pleasant seawall overlooks a channel which separates the islets comprising Stone Marsh and Stone Point. There is access across the creeks to these islets but this should not be attempted without first making local enquiries as to the state of the tides; your return from Stone Point could be quickly cut off by the incoming tide. After ¾ mile (1.2 km) the seawall turns sharply left and can then be followed back to the car park, a distance of nearly 2 miles (3.2 km). Trackways across the mudflats exist to Horsey Island and Skipper Island, but these should never be negotiated without expert local advice and obtaining permits beforehand from the EWT.

The seafront from Frinton-on-Sea (next to Walton-on-Naze) is best explored southwards for about 1½ miles (2.4 km). There are several short bushes on the descending cliffs; and the adjoining golf-course can be examined for migrants from the footpath. The seawall here annually attracts a few Purple Sandpipers in winter. About 2 miles (3.2 km) inland the Holland Brook meanders through attractive water meadows where Ruffs winter. The Great Holland Pits Reserve (EWT), 40 acres (16 ha), is on the right-hand side about 1½ miles (2.4 km) west of the village of

Great Holland on the B1032. Further details should be sought from the EWT regarding access.

For Colne Point there is footpath access along a seawall from Seawick, 3 miles (4.8 km) south from Clacton, which is quite a pleasant walk. There is, however, an easier road route from St Osyth which is beside the B1027 from Clacton to Colchester. From St Osyth take the Point Clear road and after crossing St Osyth Creek take the second minor track on the left which leads to Lee-over-Sands via Lee Wick Farm. Use the (EWT) car park though it is liable to be flooded at times of very high tides as indicated and do not drive along the track past the private chalets. During the breeding season all visitors are asked to keep clear of the shingle ridge where birds are breeding. There is a footbridge over Ray Creek to the main part of the Colne Point Reserve. This reserve, 683 acres (273.2 ha), is administered by the EWT as part of the Colne Estuary NNR and can be visited by permit only, which has to be applied for in advance.

Calendar

Resident Grey Heron, Oyster-catcher, Ringed Plover, Lapwing, Redshank (an increase in the last four species in winter) and Pied Wagtail.

April–June Shelduck, Little Tern, Hoopoe (rare), Yellow Wagtail, Whinchat, Wheatear and Ring Ouzel.

August–November Sooty Shearwater (rare), Gannet, Eider, Spotted Redshank, Greenshank, Arctic Skua, Long-eared Owl, Alpine Swift (rare), Wryneck, Tawny Pipit (rare), Meadow Pipit, Waxwing (not before the end of October), Bluethroat (rare), Redstart, Whinchat, Wheatear, Ring Ouzel, Blackbird (large falls), Icterine Warbler, Barred Warbler (the latter two species rare), Whitethroat, Lesser Whitethroat, Pallas's Warbler, Yellow-browed Warbler (the latter two species rare), Willow Warbler, Firecrest, Pied Flycatcher, Great Grey Shrike (not before September), Chaffinch (large passage), Twite (from October), Snow Bunting (not before September) and Ortolan Bunting (rare).

December–March Red-throated Diver, Black-throated Diver, Great Northern Diver, White-fronted Goose, Brent Goose, Shelduck, Scaup, Eider, Long-tailed Duck, Velvet Scoter, Red-breasted Merganser, Rough-legged Buzzard, Merlin, Peregrine, Golden Plover, Grey Plover, Lapwing, Sanderling, Purple Sandpiper, Ruff, Bar-tailed Godwit, Curlew, Short-eared Owl, Shorelark, Rock Pipit, Twite and Snow Bunting.

Map 31

Species

Fingringhoe Wick Reserve is renowned for its birdlife which has been attracted to the disused gravel pits adjacent to the River Colne, only 4 miles (6.4 km) to the south of Colchester. Over 200 species have been seen on this EWT Reserve. A gravel pit reserve rather gives an impression of flooded pools, but it is many years since gravel extraction took place and wildlife has since taken over to produce a richly varied habitat managed expertly by the EWT. The scrub and secondary woodland has clothed many of the countless small hollows and excavations with the result that over 20 pairs of Nightingales can be found, as well as many of the commoner warblers such as Blackcaps, Whitethroats, Lesser White-throats, Willow Warblers and Chiff-chaffs. A freshwater lake on the reserve attracts Little Grebes and Kingfishers, while in summer Sedge Warblers sing from the tangled waterside vegetation. In winter, Water Rails are present and small numbers of Tufted Duck, Pochard, Shoveler and Teal may flight in. Redpolls, Siskins, Goldcrests and Spotted Fly-catchers can all be found on the reserve such is the diversity of the habitat which also includes some heathland and reed-beds. Fieldfares and Redwings favour the tall hawthorn hedges in autumn.

Fingringhoe also has a very important frontage along the River Colne where an old jetty remains as a reminder of this area's commercial history. It now supports an observation hide which overlooks the estuary. At low tide vast expanses of mud are exposed which attract impressive numbers of waders and wildfowl in winter. Goldeneye, Red-breasted Mergansers and Long-tailed Duck are often seen in the estuary. Thousands of Curlew and Dunlin may be present. Up to 1,000 Brent Geese may fly or swim past the strategically placed hides. The adjoining Geedon Marshes, which are also an important habitat for waders and winter passerines, are part of a 'NO ENTRY MOD' firing range! These marshes also provide a good wader roost site with plenty of Grey Plover and Greenshanks on passage. The saltings of the estuary attract Twite, Hen Harriers and Sparrow Hawks.

As with any area there is always a chance of rarities turning up and in the past Fingringhoe has produced Black Kite, Little Bittern, Aquatic Warbler, Sub-alpine Warbler and Common Rosefinch.

Timing

A visit at almost any time of year is well worth while. As is usual, late June and July are quiet for birds, but there are plenty of insects and plants to be seen. With low tide there is the great expanse of mudflats to observe and birds may be distant. Try to get there about two hours before high water. To enjoy the volume of Nightingale song go in late April or early May. The estuary edge of Fingringhoe faces east so morning viewing across the river may be difficult at some points. There are eight hides on the reserve. As with all reserves, weekends are likely to be busier than weekdays.

Access

The best approach is from the B1025 between Colchester and West Mersea, about 8 miles (12.8 km) apart. Turn off at Abberton (which is about midway between the two towns) on a minor road signposted Fingringhoe. After about 1½ miles (2.4 km) look out for a minor turn-off on the right, signposted South Green. Follow this winding narrow road for nearly another 1½ miles (2.4 km) until the entrance to the reserve is signposted. Follow this track for another ½ mile (0.8 km) to the Reserve Centre and Car Park. The EWT have their headquarters in this spacious well-designed building which was built in 1975. The reserve is open to members and visitors from Tuesday to Sunday inclusive and on public holidays except at Christmas. When open on a Bank Holiday Monday the reserve is closed the following Tuesday. Opening hours are from 9.00 a.m. to 4.30 p.m. A Nature Trail encompassing 17 stations is laid out and a leaflet can be obtained from the Centre which has an interpretative display; there is too, an observation tower which gives marvellous views in all directions. There is also a special route for disabled visitors to use. The EWT invites donations from visitors towards the upkeep of the Reserve. Further details from the EWT. Note: the area to the south of the Reserve is a Danger Area as it is used by the army as a firing range!

Calendar

Resident Little Grebe, Kingfisher, Great Spotted Woodpecker and Goldcrest. Also good populations of all the commoner woodland species.

November–March Brent Goose, Shelduck, Teal, Shoveler, Pochard, Tufted Duck, Goldeneye, Red-breasted Merganser, Hen Harrier, Sparrow Hawk, Water Rail, Dunlin, Curlew, Rock Pipit, Fieldfare, Redwing, Siskin, Twite and Redpoll.

April–June Nightingale, Sedge Warbler, Lesser Whitethroat, Whitethroat, Blackcap, Chiff-chaff, Willow Warbler and Spotted Flycatcher.

July–October Grey Plover, Greenshank and several other passage waders such as sandpipers. Whinchat and Wheatear.

ABBERTON

MAP 31

Map 31

Species

The 1,240 acres (496 ha) of this reservoir about 4 miles (6.4 km) south of Colchester might seem a daunting place to watch birds because of its vastness and largely concrete banked walls. Added to this are the strictly controlled and very limited access points. Nevertheless, there is a small corner set aside as a nature reserve and two roads cross the southern-most arm of the reservoir which provide good watching. This huge expanse of water, so near to the Essex coast, attracts phenomenal numbers of wildfowl and ranks as a habitat of prime importance in the county. Not only has Abberton become famous for the variety and abundance of its duck, but it also ranks high with an impressive list of waders, terns and gulls which is hardly overshadowed by north Norfolk coastal records!

Cormorants

First and foremost though, it is the sheer numbers of wildfowl that will impress the casual visitor in late autumn and winter; while in the summer months there is the unique sight of a small colony of about 25 pairs of tree-nesting Cormorants. This is one of the few such sites to be found in Britain in the last 70 years and has been in existence only since 1981 when nine pairs suddenly nested in some marginal willow trees. High winter counts though, are regular with 200 or 300 birds present.

The top seven species using the Abberton Reservoir are Wigeon, Teal, Mallard, Pochard, Tufted Duck, Coot and Black-headed Gulls. Total numbers of these species add up to many thousands. In particular, there are large moulting flocks of several hundred Pochard in July and August with larger numbers present in winter. Some 4,000 to 5,000 Wigeon may spend the winter here or on the adjoining stubble or winter cereal fields. Usually there are 1,000 to 2,000 Teal present and no less than 35,000 have been caught and ringed by the Abberton Ringing Station.

Species whose numbers run into hundreds include the Shoveler, Gadwall and Goldeneye – and usually the Pintail can be included in this category. Autumn gatherings of Great-crested Grebes also run into several hundreds. Rather more unusual visitors include fairly regular numbers of Smew and Goosanders. These 'hard weather' duck may

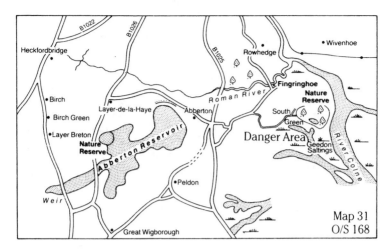

Map 31
O/S 168

increase in numbers during severe winter weather, especially if their Continental habitats are ice-bound. One of the highest counts was just over 100 birds of each species.

The introduced Ruddy Duck has started to colonise Abberton since 1979 and a few pairs are usually present throughout the year. Other rarer duck which have occurred in single numbers from time to time have included Common Scoter, Velvet Scoter, Ferruginous Duck, Ring-necked Duck, Green-winged Teal, Baikal Teal and Red-crested Pochard. Unfortunately the Garganey which has bred (and used to appear in small late summer parties) is declining, in line with the national trend. Up to ten pairs of Great-crested Grebes nest on the reservoir while small numbers of Tufted Duck, Gadwall and Shoveler also breed.

Numbers of Common Terns pass through the area in spring, and usually about 24 birds stay to breed on a floating raft. A few single Black-necked Grebes regularly appear, but the Slavonian Grebe is irregular, preferring the saltwater estuaries. In most winters a few single divers can be found, the Red-throated being more frequent than the Black-throated and Great Northern.

The other regular species include up to 2,000 Golden Plover on the surrounding farmlands, together with small numbers of White-fronted Geese and Bewick's Swans. Yellow Wagtails are regular summer visitors to the area and there are sometimes large gatherings of several hundred birds in August. Even though the edges of the reservoir are largely concrete backed they are still used by several waders who find food washed up along the edge or insects attracted to the wildfowl droppings. There are high counts of Common Sandpipers in July and August when up to a hundred or more birds may be around the reservoir. Odd pairs of Ringed Plovers have nested, while larger flocks appear in autumn. On fairly regular passage, but in small numbers, are Wood Sandpipers, Little Stints, Curlew Sandpipers, Ruff, Black-tailed Godwits, Redshank (also breeds), Spotted Redshank, Temminck's Stint, Green Sandpiper and Little Ringed Plover. Even such coastal waders as Knot, Sanderling and Purple Sandpipers have been noted at times while Dunlin have exceptionally peaked at nearly 3,000 birds. Also very unusual is the annual appearance of a few Snow Buntings, another mainly coastal species.

Of the rarer waders the Grey Phalarope and Kentish Plover have each occurred on a handful of occasions. In lower numbers there has been mostly single numbers of Lesser and Greater Yellow-legs, Long-billed Dowitcher, Buff-breasted Sandpiper, White-rumped Sandpiper, Pectoral Sandpiper, Baird's Sandpiper and Black-winged Pratincole. Singularly, very few of the rare gulls have been noted at Abberton, but a notable record was of an adult Laughing Gull in December 1957. A few Little Gulls appear almost annually, but this species is more often noted by the sea coast. Terns are better represented with the rare White-winged Black Tern showing a decided preference for this reservoir with the majority of records between early August and the third week of September. The commoner Black Tern also favours the large reservoirs on their spring passage, although counts of more than a few dozen are unusual. There are just a couple of records of the extremely rare Caspian Tern and an extraordinary record of a pair of Gull-billed Terns in 1949 and again in 1950 when they made an unsuccessful attempt to breed.

The Osprey is a fairly regular visitor to the reservoir both in late spring and in autumn and these records may involve mainly non-breeding birds. Also fairly regular visitors to the area in small numbers are Rough-legged Buzzards, Hen Harriers, Marsh Harriers and Merlin. Even the declining Montagu's Harrier has been seen on one or two occasions in recent years. The odd Bittern has infrequently appeared and there are single reports of Purple Heron and Night Heron. Even crakes have appeared at this amazing place. The Water Rail is a winter visitor in small numbers while Spotted Crakes have been noted a few times and Baillon's Crake once.

Timing
For the larger gatherings of wildfowl go in autumn or winter. Passage waders are likely in spring and autumn with always a chance of raptors. Even in mid-summer there are plenty of birds on the water and several breeding species. The two roads that cross the southern arm of the reservoir give good viewing in either east or west directions depending on the position of the sun.

Access
Take the B1026 south from Colchester to Maldon and about 1 mile (1.6 km) past the village of Layer-de-la-Haye look out for Nature Reserve Car Park on the left. A new Visitor Centre has been sited by the EWT in addition to the hides for viewing over the Reservoir. Open daily except Mondays, Christmas and Boxing days. Open 9 am to 5 pm.

Continue south for another ½ mile (0.8 km) when the road crosses an arm of the reservoir with viewing on either side of the road. To reach the other road causeway, continue south for just over 1 mile (1.6 km) and then take a minor road on the right which is signposted Layer Breton. After nearly ½ miles (0.8 km) there is good viewing from either side of the road and the Cormorant colony can be seen on the right-hand bank.

The minor roads between the villages of Layer-de-la-Haye and Abberton, about 2½ miles (4 km) apart, are worth exploring as there are footpaths which lead out to the Roman River valley. Thre is no public access to the reservoir banks.

This is a very open area which can be extremely bleak in winter so warm and waterproof clothing is essential. Although many birds are within easy binocular range of the two roads a telescope is desirable for scanning the distant waters.

Calendar

Resident Great-crested Grebe (plus autumn gatherings), Cormorant (also winter increase), Tufted Duck (also winter visitor), Ruddy Duck (a few pairs), Ringed Plover (also passage and winter) and Redshank.

December–March (November) Red-throated Diver, Black-throated Diver, Great Northern Diver (the latter two species scarce), Slavonian Grebe (scarce), Black-necked Grebe, Bittern (scarce), Bewick's Swan, White-fronted Goose, Ferruginous Duck (rare), Wigeon, Gadwall, Teal, Pintail, Shoveler, Pochard, Common Scoter, Velvet Scoter (the latter two species rare), Goldeneye, Smew, Goosander (the latter two species in hard weather). Hen Harrier, Rough-legged Buzzard, Merlin, Water Rail, Spotted Crake, Golden Plover, Knot, Purple Sandpiper (the latter two species rare), Dunlin and Snow Bunting (rare).

April–June Garganey (decreasing), Marsh Harrier, Montagu's Harrier (rare), Osprey, Little Ringed Plover, Temminck's Stint, Black-tailed Godwit, Common Sandpiper, Little Gull, Common Tern, Black Tern and Yellow Wagtail.

July–October Red-crested Pochard, Gadwall, Teal, Pintail, Garganey (decreasing), Shoveler, Pochard, Osprey, Spotted Crake, Little Ringed Plover, Little Stint, Temminck's Stint, Curlew Sandpiper, Ruff, Black-tailed Godwit, Spotted Redshank, Green, Wood and Common Sand-pipers, Grey Phalarope, Little Gull, Common Tern, Black Tern, White-winged Black Tern and Yellow Wagtail.

Map 32

Species

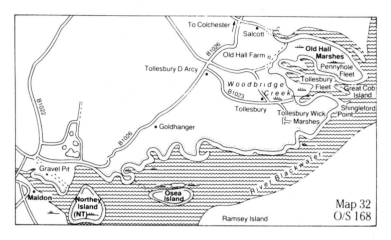

The Tollesbury area has long been renowned for its wildfowl and the Old Hall Marshes were known as a 'jewel amongst duck shoots' by the old wildfowlers. The range of channels, or fleets, along the north shore of the River Blackwater together with the fresh marshes, dykes, mudflats, saltings and seawalls all help to attract large numbers of waders, duck, geese and sea fowl as well as wintering passerines.

Recently ornithological attention has been focused on the area because 1,134 acres (453.6 ha) of the Old Hall Marshes north of Tollesbury were purchased by the RSPB in 1985. This is, in fact, the largest remnant of reclaimed coastal pasture left in Essex, as most of these old grasslands have been drained and ploughed for cereal crops. The seawalls in the Tollesbury area have been well known to birders for many years and the public footpaths on top of the walls circumvent the Old Hall Marshes. Also, around the private Tollesbury Wick marshes which skirt the Blackwater Estuary, there is a good selection of waders and wildfowl to be seen from the paths.

A short distance away, the east end of Mersea Island is another noted coastal point which is often neglected by birders. Some passerine migration occurs and winter wildfowl can be seen offshore or moving into the Colne Estuary. Although there is something of interest all year round in the Tollesbury area the busiest period commences with the arrival of passage waders in the early autumn. On small marshland pools, Ruff, Little Stints, Greenshanks and Dunlin may be found together with Green, Wood and Common Sandpipers and occasionally a Temminck's Stint. Large parties of Curlews may frequent the grassy marshes. Wader roosts on the highest tides may be composed of hundreds of Dunlin, Grey Plover and Ringed Plovers.

Rarities at Old Hall Marshes have included Terek Sandpiper, Long-billed Dowitcher and an Oriental Pratincole. Late autumn will see the Brent Geese returning to the estuaries where scattered Bar-tailed Godwits probe the mud. The Brent Geese will stay all through the winter months following the tides in or out of the estuaries or flighting in to the grasslands when food on the shore becomes scarce.

The first flocks of Twite return to the saltings now red with fleshy salicornia; and flocks may soon total several hundreds. Charms of Goldfinches gather seeds from the marshland thistles, ever on the alert for the sudden appearance of a hunting Merlin, which species also winter in this area. Reed Buntings, too, frequent the seawalls or isolated reed-beds where Bearded Tits have been increasingly noted in recent years. Also moving in for the winter hunting are Hen Harriers and Short-eared Owls who are not averse to either bird or mouse.

Short-eared Owl

With the first 'touch' of winter in the north, Wigeon and Teal will flight on to the grazing marshes or stubble fields in their hundreds. In hard weather the Tollesbury and East Mersea areas are favoured by wary gaggles of White-fronted Geese who may number no more than a few dozen birds in mild winters, but several hundred in hard ones. It is the commonest of the grey geese to frequent Essex. Several score of Bewick's Swans usually frequent the Old Hall Marshes. In winter, on the fleets, or offshore, there are small numbers of Eider, Red-breasted Mergansers, Great-crested Grebes, Slavonian Grebes, Long-tailed Duck and Cormorants. Many of these winter species can be found up to early spring when the first Wheatears on marshland fields may herald the end of winter.

Yellow Wagtails are still to be found nesting fairly commonly on the old grazing marshes. Redshank also return to the marshes to nest and several pairs of Shelduck can be seen. Parties of Whimbrel continue to pass or stay a short while on the marshes up to May. Marsh Harriers too, may pass through the area and this large raptor is being seen increasingly in all seasons, probably because of a population increase in the Netherlands. The marshes in the Tollesbury area have long been noted as a breeding area for a few pairs of Shoveler and Pochard. In summer Common Terns can be seen off Shingle Head Point. It seems that summer is barely through before the first waders begin to return from the north.

Rarities on the Old Hall Marshes have included Whiskered Tern, Red-footed Falcon and Honey Buzzard; while at East Mersea a Desert Wheatear stayed in January and February one year and a Melodious

Warbler was noted one September. At the latter place Bluethroat, Wryneck, Mediterranean Gull, Bittern, Smew, Red-breasted Goose and two Glossy Ibis have been recorded. The Glaucous Gull has been recorded annually. The coastal footpath on the southern shore of Mersea Island is quite good in autumn for small numbers of the commoner passerine migrants who seek cover amongst the stunted trees and bushes along the short cliffs. In winter Hen Harriers and Short-eared Owls are usually present.

Timing

The waterways of this area are popular with yachtsmen so summer and fine weekends are likely to be busy. East Mersea is also a very popular weekend area with a sandy beach. The time of day is not really important, but it is best to be in a place about two hours before high tide time when watching estuaries and the coast. Hard winter weather may increase the numbers of wildfowl.

Access

Tollesbury is a good centre to head for. From Kelvedon by-pass (A12) turn off to Kelvedon on the B1024, then take the B1023 to Tiptree, Tolleshunt D'Arcy and Tollesbury. It is about 9 miles (14.4 km) from Kelvedon to Tollesbury.

From the east side of Tollesbury there are two footpaths out to the seawall skirting the marshes and estuary. The seawall can be followed for miles in either direction. Access to Old Hall Marshes is to take the Salcott road out of Tollesbury and, after 1 mile (1.6 km), look out for a track on the right which is a public footpath leading on to seawall path after about ½ mile (0.8 km). The seawall path round the Old Hall Marshes is about 8 miles (12.8 km) and should not be attempted without adequate protective clothing against the elements as there is no shelter. Those wishing to visit the RSPB's Old Hall Marshes must at present obtain a permit in advance from the Warden, Mr M. Stott, at 5 Old Hall Lane, Tolleshunt D'Arcy, Nr Maldon, Essex, enclosing a SAE. Access daily except Tuesdays.

Mersea Island lies about 8 miles (12.8 km) south of Colchester and is served by the B1025. When over the main bridge and on to the island turn left on a minor road to reach East Mersea in just over 3 miles (4.8 km) where Cudmore Grove Country Park is owned and managed by the Essex County Council. The Park is signposted on the right and has an extensive car park which is freely open at all times with access points to the sandy beach. Though likely to be extremely busy on holiday weekends Mersea Island is well worth exploring in autumn and winter months, when the footpath along the southern shore of the island can be followed for several miles.

Calendar

Resident (Few species are truly resident on the marshes).

November–March Great-crested Grebe, Slavonian Grebe, Cormorant, Bittern, Bewick's Swan, White-fronted Goose, Brent Goose, Shelduck, Wigeon, Teal, Eider, Long-tailed Duck, Red-breasted Merganser, Hen Harrier, Merlin, Grey Plover, Dunlin, Bar-tailed Godwit, Curlew, Redshank, Short-eared Owl, Bearded Tit, Goldfinch, Twite and Reed Bunting.

April–June Shelduck, Shoveler, Pochard, Marsh Harrier, Ringed Plover, Whimbrel, Redshank, Common Tern, Yellow Wagtail and Wheatear.

July–October Marsh Harrier, Ringed Plover, Little Stint, Temminck's Stint, Dunlin, Ruff, Bar-tailed Godwit, Curlew, Redshank, Greenshank, Green Sandpiper, Wood Sandpiper and Common Sandpiper.

Map 33
Species

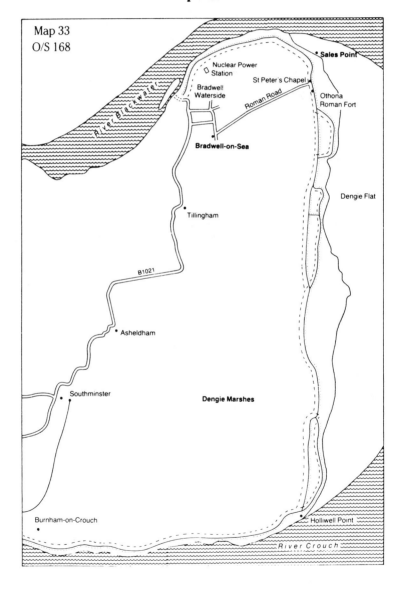

Map 33
O/S 168

Nuclear Power Station

St Peter's Chapel

Sales Point

Bradwell Waterside

Roman Road

Othona Roman Fort

Bradwell-on-Sea

Dengie Flat

Tillingham

B1021

Asheldham

Southminster

Dengie Marshes

Burnham-on-Crouch

Holliwell Point

River Crouch

River Blackwater

From Bradwell-on-Sea a Roman road leads north-eastwards to St Peter's Chapel at the remote headland on the southern shore of the River Blackwater. With the high seawalls dividing the saltmarshes and vast Dengie flats from the 8 miles (12.8 km) of prairie-like farmland on the Dengie marshes, there can hardly be a more bleakly daunting habitat in the whole of Essex. There is no doubt that since drainage and cultivation of the rough marshes, the numbers of duck using the fields have greatly declined. However, the saltings and mudflats are still a vitally important habitat for vast numbers of wintering waders including Knot and Grey Plover, while there are good autumn movements of finches and a fair selection of drift migrants in the right weather conditions.

In spring and summer the shell banks and saltings southwards for a short distance from Sales Point attract fair numbers of nesting Redshank, Ringed Plover and Oyster-catchers with occasionally a few pairs of Little Terns. Access to this area is not permitted at any time and especially during the summer because it is a reserve controlled jointly by the Essex Wildlife Trust and the Essex Birdwatching and Preservation Society (EBWPS). However, much can be seen from the seawalls, where here and there may be a Corn Bunting grinding out its not unpleasant jingle. In autumn and winter, flocks of several hundred of these birds have been noted.

A.R.W.

Corn Bunting

Other breeding passerines include good numbers of Yellow Wagtails who nest freely in the cereal or pea crops. Along the borrow-dykes, which can be found alongside the seawall, invading reeds have attracted good numbers of Reed and Sedge Warblers and quite often a few pairs of Bearded Tits are seen. A dozen or more pairs of Shelduck nest on the Dengie Peninsula, while Stock Doves breed in some of the old wartime artefacts.

From September onwards the wintering wildfowl increase and passage waders stop off on the saltings. Large numbers of Sanderling may be seen on the shell banks and the borrow-dykes may hold Green and Common Sandpipers if the water levels are low enough to provide muddy edges. The saltings and mudflats are one of the most important habitats for Grey Plover and Knot, with the former in hundreds and the latter in thousands.

October is the peak month to see large coastal movements of finches travelling southwards along the coast. The weather has an important bearing on these movements which usually take place when winds are light to moderate from a westerly quarter. All movements usually stop after noon, but in the first hours of the day totals between 1,000 and 2,000 are not unusual being composed of Linnets, Goldfinches and Greenfinches. A return passage to the north takes place from March to May.

Bradwell Bird Observatory (EBWPS), which was established at this point during the 1950s has monitored these passage movements and recorded details of drift migration which *does* occur, given the right winds. Virtually the only cover on this coastal region is in the Observatory's garden which is a thicket of small elms, blackthorn and other bushes. All the commoner migrant species such as Pied Flycatchers, Redstarts, Whitethroats, Lesser Whitethroats, Garden Warblers, Willow Warblers, Chiff-chaffs, Spotted Flycatchers, Blackcaps and Robins have occurred in varying numbers from year to year. Winter arrivals of Redwings and Blackbirds may run into several thousand birds flighting in from Scandinavia. The Firecrest is a regular visitor in spring and autumn while odd Ring Ouzels are more often seen in autumn. Rarities have included Little, Rustic and Ortolan Buntings, Red-breasted Flycatchers, Icterine and Aquatic Warblers.

The Bradwell saltings are noted for wintering Twite with over 1,000 birds in some years. Together with large numbers of Greenfinches, Corn and Reed Buntings, Linnets, Chaffinches and Goldfinches they roam the saltings in search of seeds from the summer saltmarsh plants. A few Snow Buntings are usually present. Occasionally Shorelarks turn up and Lapland Buntings have been recorded. The whole area still remains good for various birds of prey. Both Short-eared Owls and Hen Harriers are annual winter visitors in varying numbers and are likely to be seen on a day visit. Merlins are always present at this time, sometimes glimpsed in high powered flight after a Twite or Bunting. Although it is still a scarce bird (but increasing) the Peregrine Falcon is more likely to be seen hunting over the Dengie Marshes than anywhere else in the county and no doubt it is attracted by the large numbers of Knot and other waders. Montagu's Harriers, too, are very occasionally seen beating across the prairie-like fields in the summer months. Other raptors, rarely recorded, include Rough-legged Buzzard, Honey Buzzard, Red-footed Falcon (in October) and a Black Kite one May.

The southern part of the Dengie Peninsula often holds large numbers of wintering Golden Plovers on the cultivated fields. On the highest tides there are often good mixed wader roosts off Holliwell Point and the Bradwell shingle bank. There are less extensive saltings along the seawall westwards past Sales Point, and the River Blackwater runs fairly close to the banks. There is likely to be a fair selection of estuarine species here, especially Eider, Red-throated Diver, Red-breasted Merganser, Great-crested Grebe, Goldeneye and possibly Slavonian Grebes.

Timing

It is essential to time your visit so that you arrive with the incoming tide otherwise you will see very little in the way of waders and wildfowl. It is best to be there about two hours before high tide time. At low tide birds are hardly likely to be even within telescope range, so vast are the mudflats.

Access

Although there are several minor road routes to Bradwell-on-Sea it is probably best to go via Maldon on the A414 at the head of the Blackwater Estuary. From here go southwards on the B1018, then take the left-hand B1020 to Southminster and then the B1021 northwards to Bradwell-on-Sea. The distance from Maldon is about 20 miles (32 km). At Bradwell-on-Sea (don't confuse it with Bradwell Waterside nearby) take the right-hand fork by the village and park at the end. Then walk ¼ mile (0.4 km) to St Peter's Chapel and the seawall. It is worth exploring the seawall northwards for 2 miles (3.2 km) to look over the Blackwater Estuary. Southwards, the seawall runs for 15 miles (24 km) to Burnham-on-Crouch, via Holliwell Point. This walk should not be undertaken without being well equipped with waterproof and warm clothing, boots and provisions. Holliwell Point, which also has a shell bank, is about 9 miles (14.4 km) south along the seawall at the mouth of the River Crouch. Alternatively, Holliwell Point can be approached from Burnham-on-Crouch by walking about 5 miles (8.0 km) eastwards along the seawalls. It is not advisable to use minor trackways on the Dengie Peninsula unless there is a signposted public right of way. The Bradwell shell bank and saltings are supervised by the Essex Bird Watching and Preservation Society on behalf of the EWT. A telescope is useful at all times.

Calendar

Resident Oyster-catcher, Ringed Plover, Redshank (the last three species are present all year with an increase in winter), Stock Dove, Reed Bunting (also a winter visitor) and Corn Bunting.

November–March Red-throated Diver, Great-crested Grebe, Slavonian Grebe, Shelduck, Eider, Goldeneye, Red-breasted Merganser, Hen Harrier, Merlin, Peregrine, Golden Plover, Grey Plover, Knot, Sanderling, Short-eared Owl, Shorelark, Greenfinch, Goldfinch, Linnet, Twite, Lapland Bunting, Snow Bunting and Reed Bunting.

April–July Shelduck, Eider, Montagu's Harrier, Little Tern, Yellow Wagtail, Sedge Warbler and Reed Warbler.

August–October Eider, Golden Plover, Sanderling, Green Sandpiper, Common Sandpiper. The following either come in as passage migrants, drift migrants or winter visitors: Robin, Redstart, Whinchat, Wheatear, Ring Ouzel, Blackbird, Redwing, Lesser Whitethroat, Whitethroat, Garden Warbler, Blackcap, Chiff-chaff, Willow Warbler, Firecrest, Spotted Flycatcher, Pied Flycatcher, Bearded Tit, Chaffinch, Greenfinch, Goldfinch and Linnet.

FOULNESS AND THE THAMES ESTUARY

Maps 34 and 35

Species

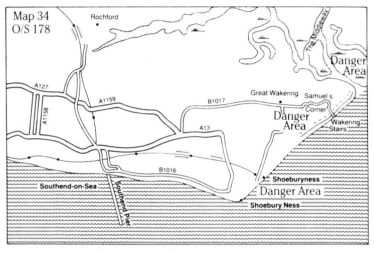

Although the complex of Foulness and Havengore Island are a danger zone with no access permitted to the general public, we feel that some brief mention must be made of this important ornithological region which is effectively protected against anti-conservation development by the Ministry of Defence, who also control the offshore Maplin Sands. This is a major wintering habitat for the Brent Goose and counts in the region of 20,000 have been made. The largest flocks of Oyster-catchers occur here and numbers have reached over 4,000 birds. Knot flocks average 9,000 birds although counts of over 33,000 have been made. Dunlin too, number several thousand with Curlews mustering between 1,000 and 2,000 birds. Redshank and Bar-tailed Godwits are present in their hundreds throughout the winter, but there is an increase on autumn passage when several thousand of each species may be present. Other waders present in their hundreds include Turnstones, Grey Plover and Ringed Plovers.

In general the dabbling and diving duck prefer the estuaries or reservoirs, but 30 pairs of Shelduck nest in the region and off the Maplin Sands there are immense gatherings of Common Scoters with some consorting Velvet Scoters. Hen Harriers, Short-eared Owls and Rough-legged Buzzards regularly hunt over Foulness Island to add to the importance of this 'forbidden land'. Moreover, an experimental hydro-logical bank was constructed offshore at the time of the Maplin airport project and this has been taken over by breeding Little Terns so success-fully that it is one of the largest colonies in Britain!

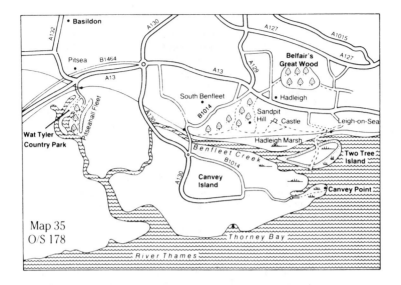

THE SOUTHEND AREA

One of the attractions of birdwatching is that it can be done almost anywhere that you happen to be: for example, õn a Scottish moorland, in the middle of a city or while travelling between the two. It is a question of making the best of what you have; and the best that the Southend area can offer is very good indeed, with an important nature reserve at Leigh-on-Sea. The ornithological riches of the area have been highlighted by members of the small but keen Southend Ornithological Group. On the north-east outskirts of Southend it is possible at certain times to drive past the (MOD) control points to Samuel's Corner and then to a point on the coast at Wakering Stairs where there is a coastal footpath for a short distance in both directions. This is a good spot in winter for seeing Hen Harriers and Short-eared Owls hunting over the adjoining fields. Little Owls are sometimes seen and Marsh Harriers come through on passage. Offshore, there are countless waders on the mudflats and plenty of Brent Geese. Sanderling regularly occur on passage while Black Terns and Arctic Skuas are seen occasionally. The Southend area usually attracts one or two Mediterranean Gulls and these have been seen at Wakering Stairs. Great Grey Shrikes and Black Redstarts have also occurred from time to time.

Brent Geese

199

The shore between Shoeburyness – Southend – Canvey Island is a winter habitat par excellence for large numbers of waders. Thousands of Knot, Dunlin, Redshank, and Oyster-catchers frequent the shore, while Brent Goose numbers may reach five figures. Also, Ringed Plovers, Grey Plovers, Turnstones, Bar-tailed Godwits and Curlew are usually present in their hundreds. East of Shoeburyness there is a regular winter flock of Sanderlings, but most of the other waders can be seen in the vicinity of the pier. At low tide over 1 mile (1.6 km) of mudflats are exposed with the result that birds can be scattered over a very wide area. There is a good high tide roost off the east end of Canvey Island and off the east side of Two Tree Island. Both these well known points are under the jurisdiction of the EWT and the latter site is part of the Leigh NNR which includes 464 acres (185.6 ha) of intertidal mudflats. The saltmarshes are one of the best surviving in the Thames Estuary and the rough grass and scrub which covers part of the island (part of which was a former rubbish tip and sewage works) regularly attracts passerines including Nightingales. An Ortolan Bunting, Little and Spotted Crakes are amongst the rarities noted here. Kingfishers and Twite are recorded annually. Nearby, the Leigh cockle sheds and an active refuse tip regularly attract some of the rarer gulls to the area. These have included Mediterranean Gull, Glaucous Gull, Iceland Gull and the rare American Ring-billed Gull.

Canvey Point though is principally a feeding and roosting sanctuary for the waders of the estuary and is particularly noted for its high tide roosts of waders and some terns. Some sea duck seen from this point include Velvet Scoter, Eiders and Red-breasted Mergansers. Beware of the high tides, which cover the path out to the shingle point, liable to cut off one's retreat.

Essex cannot claim any superlative sea watching points, but it has been discovered in recent years that in certain weather conditions many seabirds enter the Thames Estuary. The Southend pier, jutting out into the estuary for over 1 mile (1.6 k) then becomes an excellent sea watching station. Regular watching has produced small single numbers of all three divers close to the pier. Red-necked, Slavonian and Great-crested Grebes have been seen in similar numbers. Small numbers of Great, Arctic and Pomarine Skuas may be seen after gales from the north or north-east in late autumn. Winter sea duck recorded in small numbers include Red-breasted Mergansers, Common Scoters, Velvet Scoters and Long-tailed Ducks. Gannets and Kittiwakes too, may appear after storms, in which selfsame conditions both Little Auk and Leach's Petrel have been noted. Rarities include a Sooty Shearwater and a Ring-billed Gull.

It comes almost as a relief to leave the flat Essex marshlands and climb the comparatively giddy heights of the South Benfleet and Hadleigh Downs which aspire to over 250 ft (75 m). There are some public footpaths across the Downs and along the edge of Hadleigh Marshes where winter raptors might include Hen Harrier, Sparrow Hawk, Merlin and even a Peregrine. The wooded Downs are a good area for Woodcock; a Goshawk has also been seen here.

Not very far away the 90 acre (36 ha) Belfairs Wood is a local nature reserve long established by the Southend Borough Council. Obviously, being so near such a large residential district, the area is very popular with dog walkers but, nevertheless, the woods do support a few pairs of Nuthatches, Treecreepers, Great and Lesser Spotted Woodpeckers.

Redpolls and Siskins in winter parties of 100 or 200 also occur sometimes.

Pitsea Marsh west of Canvey Island and south of Basildon really does offer a wide range of species. The Wat Tyler Country Park because of its good wildlife habitat has been designated an SSSI by the NCC. There are extensive beds of common reeds along the silted edge of brackish Pitseahall Creek where Reed and Sedge Warblers are in abundance. Cuckoos – which can be heard in the Park – often use the Reed Warblers as foster parents. The reed-beds in late summer often shelter large roosts of Swallows several thousand strong and considerable numbers of Yellow Wagtails occur on passage. Good numbers of Wheatears also pass through the area. Little Grebes, Herons and Tufted Duck can be found throughout the year and sometimes Water Rails and Bearded Tits are present. In the dark entanglement of thorn bushes, Long-eared Owls have been found roosting in the winter months. The hawthorn berries attract flocks of hungry Redwings and Fieldfares in late autumn when Woodcock are often flushed from the scrubland. Corn Buntings are often numerous in winter and a modest number of Twite frequent the saltings. Other winter visitors have included Glaucous Gulls and Hen Harriers. A viewing platform offers good watching over the mudflats where Dunlin, Redshank and Shelduck may be present. Rarities have included Cetti's Warbler, Rose-coloured Starling and Yellow-browed Warbler. There is now a large scrape in the Park and it is hoped to provide a raised hide.

Timing

For watching the Thames Estuary it is best to be in place an hour or two before high water, otherwise birds may be strewn over a vast area of mudflats. High tide roosts at Canvey Point and Two Tree Island are also best on a rising tide, but beware of being cut off on Canvey Point; seawater drains can fill quickly across the return path.

Southend Pier is best after gales at sea preferably from the north or north-east. For the Downs, any time of day, but the early morning should be less populous and best for bird song. Visit the Wat Tyler Country Park at any time of year. High tide is not so important, but a flooded creek may bring the odd sea fowl in and push waders nearer to your observation point.

Access

For Wakering Stairs follow the minor road northwards from Shoeburyness British Rail station for just over 3 miles (4.8 km). Take a right-hand turn before the church at Great Wakering to Samuel's Corner and Wakering Stairs. A footpath can be followed both to the north and south for about ½ mile (0.8 km). This is within the (MOD) Danger Area and any control in force must be strictly observed.

There are many access points to the Southend shore and a promenade extends all the way from Shoeburyness to Leigh-on-Sea. The pier is open throughout the year and there is an admittance fee. Belfairs Wood lies north of Hadleigh on the A13 and between the A13 and A127. For South Benfleet Downs take the B1014, from the British Rail Station, to Hadleigh. After about 1¼ miles (2 km), pull off along a minor road on the left and park. Recross the B1014 on foot and follow a trackway downhill to a footpath over the Downs and alongside Hadleigh Marsh.

For Two Tree Island, locate the British Rail station through a maze of roads at Leigh-on-Sea. Cross the line to the south and drive along a track on to Two Tree Island where there is a car park. There is also a nature trail and a leaflet available in summer. Also on the west end of Two Tree Island there is a public hide overlooking a scrape.

Two roads serve Canvey Island, the A130 and the B1014. Either will do, but once on Canvey get on to the B1014 and follow this to its end on the east side of the island. Park nearby and proceed on foot for a few yards to the seawall and a muddy track to Canvey Point. Walking distance is about ¾ mile (1.2 km). Beware of the incoming tide cutting off your retreat – very easy to forget when engrossed in watching waders, gulls and terns!

The Wat Tyler Country Park lies south of the A13 at Basildon. Turn off south opposite a supermarket on a minor road to Pitsea Britsh Rail station and continue over the level crossing. After nearly ¾ mile (1.2 km) park on the right as indicated. Leaflets can be obtained from the Information Centre which also has an interpretative display.

Calendar

Resident Little Grebe, Grey Heron, Shelduck (absent July–October), Tufted Duck, Little Owl, Kingfisher, Great Spotted and Lesser Spotted Woodpeckers, Nuthatch, Treecreeper and Corn Bunting.

November–March Red-throated Diver, Black-throated Diver, Great Northern Diver, Great-crested Grebe, Red-necked Grebe, Slavonian Grebe, Gannet, Brent Goose, Eider, Long-tailed Duck, Common Scoter, Velvet Scoter, Red-breasted Merganser, Hen Harrier, Sparrow Hawk, Rough-legged Buzzard, Merlin, Peregrine, Water Rail, Spotted Crake (rare), Ringed Plover, Oyster-catcher, Grey Plover, Knot, Sanderling, Dunlin, Woodcock, Bar-tailed Godwit, Curlew, Redshank, Turnstone, Pomarine Skua, Arctic Skua, Great Skua (skuas more usually October–December), Mediterranean Gull, Glaucous Gull, Iceland Gull, Kittiwake, Little Auk (rare), Short-eared Owl, Bearded Tit, Great Grey Shrike, Siskin, Redpoll and Twite.

April–July Eider, Marsh Harrier, Little Tern, Black Tern, Cuckoo, roosts of Swallows, Yellow Wagtails, Nightingale, Black Redstart, Sedge Warbler and Reed Warbler.

August–October Eider, Sanderling, Black Tern, Long-eared Owl (October–November), Fieldfare, Redwing, Bearded Tit and Ortolan Bunting (rare).

EPPING FOREST

MAP 36
OS map 177 (and Part 167)

The ornithological interest in the importance of Epping Forest has declined in the past 20 years partly because improved road systems have opened up the farthest flung regions of East Anglia, all of which are now within a day's drive of London; and partly because Epping Forest has seen a tremendous increase in the number of people using the area for recreational pursuits. It has become a very popular place at weekends in summer with the result that quiet birdwatching spots are increasingly difficult to locate. However, it still remains an attractive birding area, especially for those of us who have to rely solely upon public transport. We can only advise intending birders to go in the early morning and try to avoid weekends, Bank holidays and school holidays.

Habitat

Epping Forest is a crescent-shaped area of woodland of approximately 6,000 acres (2.400 ha) which extends from Forest Gate in the south to Thornwood in the north. It is 12 miles (19.2 km) long, though nowhere is it more than 2 miles (3.2 km) wide. Two thirds of the region is pure woodland while the remaining one third is made up to pastureland and its attendant waterways. These waterways comprise many natural springs, and upwards of 150 ponds. The latter are very diverse as regards size, depth and floral surrounds; some lay half concealed in areas of deep shade, while others are in full sunshine.

The southerly aspect of the forest is gentle, seldom rising more than 46 ft (13.8 m) above sea level; while in the north, some land rises above sea level to 330 ft (99 m). The highest point is 385 ft (115.5 m) close to Ambresbury Banks. Geologically, Epping Forest is made up largely of London Clay, overlaid in places by Claygate Beds, Bagshot Beds and Pebble Gravel. To describe it in another way, we could say that this forest area is a long gravel ridge, separating the agricultural valleys of the Lea and the Roding; its numerous springs occurring at or above the 300 ft (90 m) contour. The many old gravel pits along the ridge are often waterlogged in wet seasons.

Woodland, like every other 'natural' habitat, is ever-changing. Forestry practices over the last 300 years have effected notable changes in this vast landscape. For instance regular pollarding prior to 1878 obviously let in more light, thus encouraging the appearance of primroses, cowslips, bluebells, sorrel, and anemone. Nowadays, these flowers are more difficult to locate, owing to a more dense tree growth. Much open heathland has also been taken over by fast maturing birches. Mature trees are frequently felled by the conservators in an effort to try and maintain a balance between wooded and open areas; yet, in spite of these measures, much of the mature beechwood is too densely canopied, and too compacted underfoot – due partly to the discontinuance of pannage, (putting out pigs to feed on acorns and beechmast) – so that the present-day managers of the forest have been forced to disc-plough certain areas, so that the looser soil encourages the germination of seeds.

Dense woodland lies mostly to the north of a line between Chingford and Loughton. Typical trees are hornbeam, oak, beech and birch, with lesser numbers of holly, crab apple, maple and prunus. Oak is confined to the heavier areas to the west; beech prefers the gravelly slopes; while the hornbeam loves the damper slopes. Birch was previously rare, but has been introduced on the gorse dotted heaths, in an attempt to break up the monotony of these open areas. It has been predicted that, in the immediate future, thorn thicket will predominate over the regeneration of trees, due to their reduction by grazing cattle.

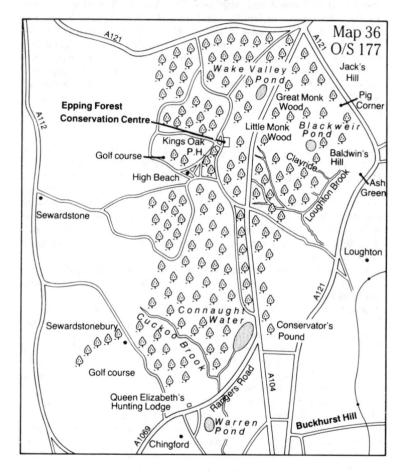

Individual Habitats

Epping Long Green

Detached from the main forest area it is untimbered, but thicketed and has a heavy, waterlogged clay soil.

Galley Hill and Ames Green

This area comprises several long green lanes, radiating from Ames Green. Galley Hills northwards towards Bumbles Green contains unpollarded oaks and shrubs, which attract Nightingales.

Jacks Hill
Beechwoods south of the road and west of Ditches Ride. No under-
growth, but in autumn there is dense leaf-fall and silvergreen moss.
Several clearings were created in 1951.

Honey Lane Quarters
Contains many beeches and hornbeams. Honey Lane Plain is itself open
grassland with dense blackthorn and blackberry thickets.

**Copley Plains, Dusmead Hollow, Fox Burrows, The Furze
Ground, and Hangboy Slade**
These areas comprise large southern-most beechwoods, with some
birch and oak in varied stages of growth. The Furze Ground is noted for
its crab apple trees.

Pillow Mounds
To the south-east of Honey Lane Quarters, these mounds were once
thought to be early Iron Age mounds; but are now considered to be
merely 200-year-old rabbit warrens!

Great and Little Monk Wood
Large pollarded beeches on steep undulations. Waterlogged land
towards the north, where the beeches stand on almost pure gravel.

Baldwins Hill
Renowned for its view across Baldwins Pond and Monks Wood. The
watercourses from Monks Wood and Broadstrood converge at Pig
Corner, from whence they flow in one stream to form Baldwins Pond
and Loughton Brook.

Clay Ride
Runs west-east between the A11 and Ash Green and was constructed in
the mid-nineteenth century. Where it crosses Green Ride in the north-
east is Backweir Pond, which was once a gravel pit.

High Beach
A scattered village on the eastern boundary of Epping, surrounded by
beech trees. A prominent land mark is the church spire, which is visible
from many parts of the forest to the south and east.

Paul's Nursery
Acquired as late as 1920. Once a famous garden, which explains the
presence still of many rhododendrons and other exotica.

Debden Slade
Famous for the rare wild service trees which grow there. And remaining
areas include Broom Hill, Shelley's Hill, Kate's Cellar, Loughton Camp,
and the mixed woodland area of Staples Hill.

Species
One cannot hope to see all the woodland species in this vast area on just
one visit; but often the main reason for a day spent birding in Epping
Forest is to catch a glimpse of the, not rare, but very elusive Hawfinch.
The latter species collects in large flocks in the winter months, when it is

more easily observed. Obviously – as with all woodland birdwatching – one can never predict just what lies beyond the next tree or clearing. Luck and early rising both play a large part in deciding which species one is likely to see. However, one has a fair chance of seeing all the usual forest species – i.e. Nuthatches, all three species of woodpeckers, Treecreepers, all the tit family, and good number of Chaffinches and Greenfinches.

With regard to the less common breeding birds, it must be said that the Common Redstart has declined as a once numerous bird in this area, whereas the Redpoll has increased considerably – due undoubtedly to the introduction of the birch and young conifers, on what was once more open heathland.

Hawfinch

In the summer months one may find established in suitable habitats, Blackcaps, Willow Warblers, Chiff-chaffs, Garden Warblers, White-throats and a few Nightingales; while a few Tree Pipits occur on the more open heaths and commons. Turtle Doves and Yellow Hammers are noticeably fond of the blackthorn hedges at the sides of the roads.

In the winter months, finches flock noisily and a search of the woodland floor will reveal sliced hornbeam seeds, left behind by Chaffinches and Greenfinches; with luck, too, one may come across a mixed party of Siskins and Redpolls in the birches.

Impressive numbers of Fieldfares and Redwings often gather in November and December on the golf-course north of Chingford Plain; while Red-legged Partridges are to be found on open farmland adjoining Yardley Hill. Connaught Water – near Magpie Hill – is a favourite haunt of Canada Geese, Mallard and Moorhens. And it is undoubtedly worth keeping a watch in the open areas near grazing cattle in the summer months for wagtails and warblers.

Timing

Due to the nearness of Epping Forest to London and also to considerable human disturbance in the more popular recreational areas of the forest, it is best to visit very early in the morning between May and early June. Avoid fine summer weekends and Bank Holiday periods. (Although, barring human activity, this area is possibly under-observed?) But, for those who wish to become involved in active conservation – and are young*ish* and fit! – we suggest they write to the Epping Forest Conservation Volunteers, c/o Steve Corney, 13 Oakley Close, Chingford, Essex E4 6XW. These volunteers work hard to maintain the diversity of the various habitats, especially the ponds, bogs and open heaths.

Access

It is probably wise before undertaking a tour of this area to obtain advice from the Epping Forest Conservation Centre which was opened in 1971 and is owned by the Corporation of London. It is situated at High Beach in the very heart of the forest and is easily accessible from both Chingford and Loughton. The Centre has three teaching laboratories, a library, and a lecture hall with a wide range of audio visual aids. There is a permanent Conservation Display in the main entrance. More advanced research work is also encouraged; the staff includes four highly qualified biologists and geographers.

The Centre is within easy reach of Greater London, Essex and Hertfordshire; and its nearness to the M11 and M25 motorways and the Blackwall Tunnel, means that a daily visit from South Buckinghamshire, Cambridgeshire, Suffolk and North Kent is feasible. The London Transport tube (Central Line) to Loughton is a short distance from High Beach, and the travelling time from Liverpool Street is only 30 minutes. It is open from Easter until 31 October (but from 1 November till Easter, Sats. and Sundays only). Closed over Christmas and New Year. Open from 10 a.m.–12.30 p.m.; 2 p.m.–5 p.m. on weekdays and Sats; and from 11 a.m. Sundays and public holidays.

Another important centre is the Queen Elizabeth Hunting Lodge at Chingford. Chingford Bus Station and the British Rail Station are less than 1 mile (1.6 km) away. It can be reached on the A1069 about 1 mile (1.6 km) south-west of its junction with the A104. This three storey Tudor building, which houses a museum, has much information relating to the forest and man's relationship with its development over the centuries.

A suggested walk from the lodge starts at the car park. Take the path on the east side of the lodge, leading across cattle-grazed Chingford Plain and then past Connaught Water. After 1 mile (1.6 km), you arrive at Grimstone's oak. Take the first green ride on the left and walk to the north-west, and then due north for 1 km to Almshouse Plain (the first clearing in the wood). Now take the left-hand path for 1 mile (1.6 km) to Day's Farm, where follow the footpath at the top of the hill to Sewardstone Green. After ¼ mile (0.4 km), bear left on to a path which goes across the West Essex Golf Course to the main road, where take a left turn and walk for 150 yards along the edge of the reservoir. At Gilwell Park's entrance, take the bridle path on the left and make for Yardley Hill. After about 450 yds (405 m) watch out for a path on the left (indicated by a post on the main path) and follow the said path for 1 mile (1.6 km) to the obelisk. Turn left and follow the path that runs between the edge of the golf-course and the housing estate. Cross the road and take the path leading to the lodge again.

This interesting circular tour will give you a fair chance of seeing many different species of birds on a warm spring or summer day.

Calendar

Resident Heron, Mandarin (scarce), Woodcock, Red-legged Partridge, Tawny Owl, Green, Great and Lesser Spotted Woodpeckers, Treecreeper, Nuthatch, Marsh, Coal and Long-tailed Tits, Hawfinch and Yellow Hammer.

Winter Redwing, Fieldfare, Grey Wagtail, Redpoll, and Siskin.

Summer Blackcap, Willow Warbler, Chiff-chaff, Tree Pipit, Garden Warbler, Nightingale (a few, but is still decreasing), Spotted Flycatcher, Redstart (much decreased), Wood Warbler (scarce) and Yellow Wagtail.

CAMBRIDGESHIRE

FOWLMERE
FERRY MEADOWS
WICKEN FEN
OUSE WASHES
GRAFHAM WATER

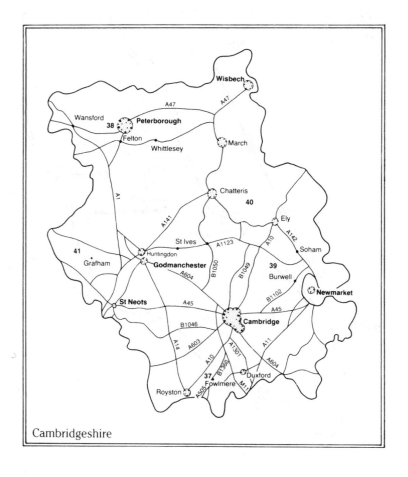

Cambridgeshire

Habitat

Not far from Royston the 66 acres (26.4 ha) of the Fowlmere reserve are at the very southern edge of the great Fenland basin which lies between Newmarket and Peterborough and northwards to within 10 miles (16 km) of King's Lynn. Between Royston and Newmarket a low chalk ridge sweeps up from the North Downs to continue into Norfolk where the overlying sands and gravels of the Brecks changes its appearance. This ridge once continued into the Lincolnshire Wolds, before it was worn away by the tides and rivers that were responsible for forming the Wash.

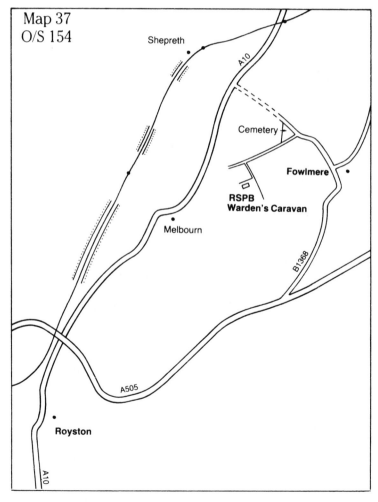

Map 37
O/S 154

Shepreth

A10

Cemetery

Fowlmere

RSPB
Warden's Caravan

Melbourn

B1368

A505

Royston

A10

In prehistoric times this vast area underwent traumatic changes with comparatively quick transitions from fen to forest and back to fen again when unhindered seas devastated woodlands and the rivers swept the accumulated silt into the Wash. Man, ever greedy for land, started to reclaim the fens and tame the great rivers in the seventeenth century. Once drainage was effective most of the fen shrunk considerably. In order to record the expected shrinkage an iron post was driven into the clay beneath the peat in 1848 at Holme Fen with its top level with the ground. Today it is nearly 12 ft (3.6 m) above ground level showing dramatically how land surface levels have changed with the drainage of the fens. With such widespread shrinkage, river banks had to be strengthened and pumps and sluice gates constructed to prevent the newly won land from being flooded. This is still a continuous battle with serious flooding occuring periodically.

Most of Fenland is under intensive cultivation, but some pockets of the old fens have been saved by nature conservation bodies who also face a continuous struggle to prevent these reserves from drying out, because the surrounding reclaimed fen is generally lower and well drained. At Fowlmere, which was originally part of the great Fen Mere, there is a pure spring welling up from the chalk rock which was used to develop a watercress farm at the end of the last century. When this became disused, a large reed-bed sprung up on the site and this is now the RSPB reserve which was purchased in 1977 from funds raised by the Young Ornithologists' Club (YOC) in order to save this oasis for wildlife in an otherwise intensive arable landscape. Apart from the reed swamp there are small meres, hawthorn scrub and an alder wood beside a small river. The plant life is varied with bee-orchids and cowslips to be found on the outcrops of chalk which occur on the reserve. Water shrews, toads, frogs and grass snakes may also be found here.

Species

In winter, roving bands of tits frequent the trees while Siskins and Redpolls are often attracted by their favourite seeds in the woody 'cones' of the alder trees. Winter thrushes such as Redwings and Fieldfares arrive early in the winter to devour the berry crops and may continue to roost on the reserve after foraging in the surrounding fields during the day. Other species to use the reserve for roosting may include large parties of Corn Buntings, sometimes as many as 400 or 500 birds, also drawn in after foraging on the open fields. Parties of Pied Wagtails composed of 200 or 300 birds have roosted in the reed-beds, often in company with large flocks of not so welcome Starlings. The Green Sandpiper has become almost an annual winter visitor to the ditches or open waterways. This black-and-white sandpiper winters sparingly in Britain as its more usual winter home is in the Mediterranean basin. Wintering birds are usually single adults and when flushed greatly resemble a large House Martin. Sparrow Hawks and Hen Harriers have been recorded hunting over the fen.

Of the resident species, Little Grebes are to be seen on the open water, but their floating nests of aquatic vegetation are tucked away amongst the concealing reeds and sedges. In the breeding season their sudden whinnying call is suggestive of a wader rather than an aquatic diving bird. The Water Rail is another resident marshland species which also makes a variety of odd calls usually of a grunting or squealing nature. It is much more likely to be heard than seen, as it only rarely leaves the shelter of the reed and sedge jungle. Kingfishers are occasionally seen, but as with all creatures depending upon the life in our streams and rivers its populations have been reduced to a low level because of pesticides and pollution.

From early spring many other species return to breed in this splendid oasis. The Sedge Warbler's explosive chatter can be heard from sedge-entangled corners while the Reed Warbler arrives later to set up territory with its more leisurely song emanating from the reed-beds. The sudden reeling of a Grasshopper Warbler may be heard from the drier grassy land, the source of the song being difficult to pin-point owing to the bird's habit of turning its head from side to side while singing. Other summer visitors arriving include the cooing Turtle Dove and many pairs of Willow Warblers. Several pairs of Blackcap, Whitethroat and Lesser Whitethroats usually take up territories in the scrubby areas, while the last summer visitors to arrive are the Spotted Flycatchers (they have nested on the reserve).

Other more unusual species recorded have included Great Grey Shrike, Little Ringed Plover, Quail and Wood Warbler.

Timing
Any time of the day or month, but July is usually fairly quiet after spring bird song has ceased and broods have been reared to maturity.

Access
Open at all times. There is a marked trail, from which good views can be obtained and there is also a hide overlooking the open water and reed-beds. Fowlmere is off the A10 Cambridge to Royston road. About 7 miles (11.2 km) south of Cambridge turn off on the left at Shepreth crossroads; or, going north from Royston, it is about 5 miles (8 km) before reaching the crossroads and after going through Melbourn. Follow a minor road and turn sharp right at the cemetery corner before the village of Fowlmere and the reserve entrance track is less than ½ mile (0.8 km) along on the left. There is a hide supported on stilts giving panoramic views over the reserve while a second hide overlooks a natural spring. It is advisable to wear rubber boots in winter and stout shoes at other times. There is a boarded walk suitable for wheelchairs.

Calendar
Resident Little Grebe and Water Rail.

November–March Green Sandpiper, Hen Harrier, Sparrow Hawk, Kingfisher, Pied Wagtail, Redwing, Fieldfare, Siskin, Redpoll and Corn Bunting.

April–June Turtle Dove, Sedge Warbler, Reed Warbler, Grasshopper Warbler, Willow Warbler, Blackcap, Lesser Whitethroat, Whitethroat and Spotted Flycatcher.

Habitat

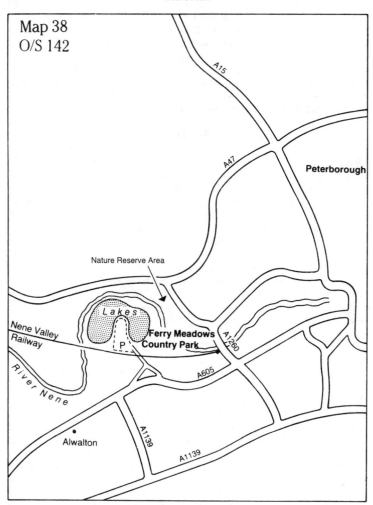

Map 38
O/S 142

A15

A47

Peterborough

Nature Reserve Area

L a k e s

Nene Valley
Railway

**Ferry Meadows
Country Park**

P

A1260

A605

River Nene

Alwalton

A1139

A1139

The 500 acres (200 ha) of Ferry Meadows are part of a new Country Park of over 2,300 acres (920 ha) being created as part of the Peterborough expansion scheme. Although a small area has been set aside as a nature reserve within the country park, the habitat which is composed of flooded gravel pit with islands and wader scrapes regularly attracts a wide variety of birds with nearly 200 species recorded. The value of such wildlife attractions readily available to a large populace is tremendous, providing relaxation and the opportunity to promote understanding and sympathy for wildlife conservation. The Peterborough Development Corporation seems to have achieved the difficult objective of striking a delicate balance between conservation and other recreational interests such as fishing, sailing and golfing.

In 1978 the areas outside Ferry Meadows were still predominantly agricultural. Gravel extraction which commenced in 1972 at Ferry Meadows was carefully planned to leave a series of lakes within a bend of the River Nene. Overton Lake was flooded in 1973 and the larger Gunwade Lake by 1978. Now the 120 acres (48 ha) of lakes which were once gravel pits are fed by connecting links to the adjacent River Nene.

A mature woodland nearby was once part of the Milton Park – the estate of Earl Fitzwilliam. It contains many unusual trees, osier beds and carpets of bluebells. Much of the Park is grassland and efforts are being made to improve the quality of this so that there is a greater range of wild flowers. Heron Meadow, between the lakes and the River Nene, is still subject to periodic flooding which makes it very attractive to waders.

Species

Duck and waders hold the limelight during the winter months at Ferry Meadows. The Pochard and Tufted Duck are the most numerous of the diving duck species and they are able to exist without competition on the same lakes because of their differing diets. The Pochard lives mainly on vegetable matter while the Tufted Duck takes more animal matter including molluscs. Teal are the most numerous of the surface feeders living at this season mainly on the seeds of aquatic plants. Numbers may reach a peak in early autumn before winter numbers level out. Wigeon numbers are usually much smaller and this shyer duck is easily disturbed from grazing on the wet meadows.

Flood waters may bring increased numbers and variety with a few Gadwall, Pintail and Shoveler present. Rarer diving duck such as Goldeneye and a few Goosanders may occur, especially in harder weather. A potential colonist, the Ruddy Duck, has been noted a few times while rarities have included Long-tailed Duck, Scaup, Scoter, Velvet Scoter, Smew, Little Egret, Night Heron and Red-breasted Mergansers.

The breeding duck include Teal, Shoveler, Tufted Duck and Mandarin while a few non-breeding Shelduck are seen almost throughout the year. Great-crested Grebes have bred, but they are more regular as winter visitors. Their smaller relative, the Little Grebe, also visits at this time and probably breeds in the region. Red-necked, Slavonian and Black-necked Grebes have all been recorded. Small numbers of Water Rails winter and are often sighted from the nature reserve hides.

Lapwing and Snipe are amongst the commonest winter waders frequenting the water-logged meadows, and Golden Plover appear in varying numbers on the grassy fields. Small numbers of Redshank are present and this wader has nested. The Green Sandpiper winters and is also a passage migrant in small numbers. Ruff and Jack Snipe are scarce winter visitors, but the latter has also been noted in the early spring months. Short-eared Owls are regular visitors in fluctuating numbers.

Of the passerines one or two Grey Wagtails are often present and mixed parties of Siskins and Redpolls may roam through the woodlands. The Fieldfare is a common winter visitor to the grassy fields, but the Redwing is usually only in small numbers. Bearded Tits have been seen in the reeds by the wader scrape, but it is a rarity. Large numbers of

Canada Geese and Greylags are always present, but both reach their highest peaks in early winter.

In spring the first summer migrants to arrive are Chiff-chaffs, which breed in the woodland, and the Wheatear which is a passage migrant to the bare fields. Breeding summer visitors include many pairs of Reed and Sedge Warblers, good numbers of Willow Warblers in the Park and wooded areas where Spotted Flycatchers are also fairly common from early May. Good numbers of other scrub or woodland warblers include Whitethroat, Lesser Whitethroat, Blackcaps and Garden Warblers. The beautiful Yellow Wagtail is a regular passage migrant and several pairs breed in the area. The Hobby is a scarce summer migrant to Ferry Meadows, but it is increasing in the county and has bred.

Hobby chasing Sand Martin

It always seems surprising that a bird more usually associated with the sea coast should breed in a Country Park, but the Common Tern arrives here in mid-April to nest – over 26 miles (41.6 km) away from the seashore. Even Arctic Terns have been sighted on passage but, less surprisingly, a few Black Terns on spring passage come through. The Little Ringed Plover is a well known coloniser of gravel pits, but usually disappears as the vegetation covers the exposed shingle. A few pairs have remained faithful to Ferry Meadows and can usually be seen in summer on the wader scrape. The odd pair or two of Ringed Plover have also nested.

Passage migrant waders in small numbers in spring and autumn include Temminck's Stint, Dunlin, Ruff, Greenshank, Green and Common Sandpipers. One May, when the habitat was exactly right with shallow water and exposed mud, no less than 14 species of waders were seen in a two-week period, which is an impressive record for the outskirts of a large city. In autumn, larger numbers of waders may drop in and infrequent visitors such as Wood Sandpipers, Little Stints, and Curlew Sandpipers may be seen. Large numbers of Swallows, House Martins, Swifts and Sand Martins may congregate over the lakes in late summer-autumn to exploit the rich food supplies. Resident species include Kingfishers which probably breed along the nearby river and may flash past at any time of the year. Little and Tawny Owls are present all year. Woodland residents include all three woodpeckers, Goldcrests, Hawfinch, Coal Tit, Nuthatch and Treecreeper.

Timing

Birds are to be seen all the year round, but June and July are the best months to avoid. The Park is busier at weekends and Bank Holidays.

Access

Ferry Meadows and the Nene Park are on the south-west outskirts of Peterborough. From Peterborough take the A605 Oundle road and watch for the Ferry Meadows sign on the right. The Park is open all year and there is a visitors centre. Car parking is free except at weekends and Bank Holidays from Easter to October.

Calendar

Resident Greylag Goose, Canada Goose, Redshank (and winter visitor), Little Owl, Tawny Owl, Kingfisher, Green, Great and Lesser Spotted Woodpeckers, Goldcrest, Marsh Tit, Coal Tit, Nuthatch, Treecreeper and Redpoll (also winter visitor).

November–March Little Grebe, Great-crested Grebe (has bred), Shelduck, Wigeon, Teal, Pintail, Shoveler, Pochard, Tufted Duck, Goldeneye, Goosander, Ruddy Duck, Water Rail, Golden Plover, Lapwing, Jack Snipe (rare), Snipe, Green Sandpiper, Short-eared Owl, Grey Wagtail, Fieldfare, Redwing, Bearded Tit, Siskin, Redpoll.

April–June/July Shelduck, Mandarin, Shoveler, Tufted Duck, Ruddy Duck (rare), Little Ringed Plover, Ringed Plover, Temminck's Stint, Jack Snipe (rare), Common Tern, Arctic Tern, Black Tern, Hobby, Yellow Wagtail, Wheatear, Sedge Warbler, Reed Warbler, Lesser Whitethroat, Whitethroat, Garden Warbler, Blackcap, Chiff-chaff, Willow Warbler and Spotted Flycatcher.

August–October Mandarin, Gadwall, Teal, Shoveler, Tufted Duck, Little Stint, Curlew Sandpiper, Dunlin, Ruff, Greenshank, Green, Wood and Common Sandpipers.

WICKEN FEN

MAP 39
OS map 154

Habitat

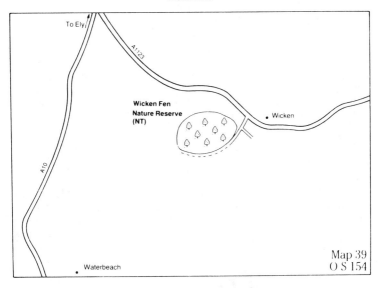

Wicken Fen lies almost in the centre of the great Fenland basin of some 2,500 square miles (6250 s. km). On the seaward side of this basin, silts and clay were laid down in the brackish water while peat formed under predominantly freshwater conditions on the landward side. The land became water-logged partly by the large river systems draining the uplands and partly by land submergence relative to the sea level. Peat formation was restricted to the deeper valleys in Fenland in the period after the last Ice Age but, by Neolithic times, peat formation was more general. It is likely that in this period the great forests of giant oaks, rooted in the boulder clay, flourished in the Wicken area. These forests were killed first by the water-logging around their trunks and then perhaps felled by horrific storm driven tidal surges. Accumulating peat then preserved these enormous trees which were to be revealed 5,000 years later by the deep drainage of the fens. On the Wicken Fen reserve some of these bog oak tree trunks, which were removed from an arable field adjacent to the reserve, can be seen. Some of these forest giants reached a height of 90 ft (27 m) from butt to first fork, with a girth of up to 12 ft (3.6 m).

Wicken Fen, which is owned and managed by the National Trust, is the oldest nature reserve in Britain. Its 605 acres (242 ha) can be divided into three major sections: Wicken Sedge Fen, Adventurer's Fen and St Edmunds Fen. But it is Wicken Fen which is readily accessible to the public and this is one of the few areas in the great levels of East Anglia in which drainage has had little effect. If it were not for the clayed banks of its bordering lodes, which hold the water table at the same height as that in the lodes themselves, the fen would long ago have become completely dry. The striking difference in land levels can easily be seen with the adjacent arable fields some 8 ft (2.4 m) lower which is the result of drainage and cultivation having made the peat shrink, decompose and waste away.

The major threat to the reserve is the lowering of the water table because of improved drainage on the surrounding fields, but attempts are being made to raise the levels. For many centuries Wicken Fen was exploited for its valuable products which included peat and sedge for fuel, litter for hay and animal bedding, sedge and reeds for thatching. Since harvesting of these products ceased in the latter half of the last century, a mosaic of different habitats, each with its own characteristic flora and fauna has been created. These habitats range from open water, through sedge fields to fen carr (scrub) and woodland. Management of this unique reserve seeks to maintain these diverse communities by continuing the traditional harvesting of natural crops.

Many rare and interesting plants can be seen at Wicken Fen. These include the aquatic bladderwort and there are ideal habitats for brooklime, marsh marigold and yellow-flag. In the early stages of the fen carr, alder buckthorn is invasive, but it is later dominated by the common buckthorn to be followed by hawthorn, sallow, guelder rose and privet. Clumps or patches of comfrey, ragged robin, yellow rattle, yellow loosestrife, meadow rue, marsh thistle and marsh orchids all delight the eye in this Fenland sanctuary. The brimstone butterfly abounds, as well it might, for its larvae feed upon both kinds of buck-thorns that grow so well here.

Hen Harrier

Map 39

Species

Although Wicken is a true naturalist's fen, with its rich flora and insect life, its varied bird community is also extremely good. The winter season is notable for Hen Harriers who often come in to roost in the sedge fen in the closing minutes of a short winter's day, after spending the daylight hours hunting over the reserve or adjoining farmlands. In recent years up to eleven or more birds have been observed in the winter months.

Another beautiful bird which occurs fairly regularly is the Great Grey Shrike with its black, white and grey plumage in stark contrast against the various soft brown hues of the winter fen, as it perches on the topmost point of an alder tree. This visitor from northern Europe may arrive as early as October and stay until April or even May; and there again, in some winters, it may not turn up at all.

Other winter specialities which are regular include small parties of Bearded Tits roaming through the reed-beds; and it is nice to record that a pair which bred at Wicken in 1980 was the first breeding record for the county. Every winter one or two Short-eared Owls hunt over this reserve, their long pale brown wings well camouflaged against the sedge fen. Bitterns are fairly regular, but much rarer than they used to be. Unfortunately, the particular fen best suited to their nesting needs had to be drained in order to grow crops in the Second World War; but, who knows, with present day management the Bittern may return as a regular breeding bird.

Early in the year there are sometimes roosts of Corn Buntings and Pied Wagtails while Bramblings may drop in on their way back to their northern homelands. Redpolls and Siskins are sometimes found amongst the birch trees. Merlins, too, are fairly often seen in winter; and Sparrow Hawks may occur at any time from late autumn to early spring. A beautifully constructed and well sited tower hide gives panoramic views over the reserve. It was erected to overlook the nearby 10 acre (4 ha) mere which was excavated in 1955–6, which has since proved very attractive to wintering wildfowl.

Water Rails are present all year round and have bred. Woodcock may be seen and heard roding along the droves on a quiet spring evening and several pairs often breed on the reserve. Other resident breeding birds include Long-eared Owls, Tawny Owls, Great and Lesser Spotted Woodpeckers, Willow Tits, Marsh Tits and Long-tailed Tits. A newcomer to Britain, the Cetti's Warbler has been recorded several times and, given a few reasonable winters, it may establish a colony here. In the spring large numbers of Reed and Sedge Warblers return and there may be up to ten reeling Grasshopper Warblers amongst the sedge fen. The Savi's Warbler, which is another long lost Fenland breeding species, has stayed the summer and probably bred.

Other breeding summer visitors include Nightingale, Spotted Fly-catcher, Whitethroat, Lesser Whitethroat, Blackcap and Garden Warbler. Marsh Harriers not infrequently put in an appearance and a Golden Oriole was heard in song one June. Other rarities have included a White-spotted Bluethroat in March, a Night Heron in May and a Barred Warbler in September. That most secretive of marsh birds, the Spotted Crake, has occurred several times in summer and may even have bred. One bird calling in April could be heard over 1 mile (1.6 km) away!

Spring and autumn wader passage may include small numbers of Black-tailed Godwits, Whimbrel, Curlews, Greenshank, Spotted Redshank, Wood Sandpiper and Ruff. In late summer there can be spectacular roosts of Swallows and Sand Martins in the reeds fringing the mere.

Timing

A good all-year-round reserve especially for all-round naturalists.

Access

Take the A10 northwards from Cambridge. After about 17 miles (27.2 km) turn right on to the A1123 towards Wicken. As you enter the village a large sign, 'Wicken Fen', indicates a right turn along Lode Lane. The reserve car park is on the left. The William Thorpe Centre was completed in 1970 as a laboratory/lecture hall. It also houses the warden's office and a comprehensive display about the development, history and management of Wicken Fen. There are leaflets and guide books available. Permits are required at this point. The trail which can be followed is just over 2 miles (3.2 km) long and rubber boots are advised, especially during the winter to spring period.

Calendar

Resident Water Rail, Woodcock, Tawny Owl, Long-eared Owl, Great and Lesser Spotted Woodpeckers, Cetti's Warbler, Bearded Tit, Long-tailed Tit, Marsh Tit and Willow Tit.

October–March Bittern, Hen Harrier, Sparrow Hawk, Merlin, Short-eared Owl, Pied Wagtail, Great Grey Shrike, Brambling, Siskin, Redpoll and Corn Bunting.

April–September Marsh Harrier, Spotted Crake, Ruff, Black-tailed Godwit, Whimbrel, Curlew, Spotted Redshank, Greenshank, Wood Sandpiper, Sand Martin, Swallow (large roosts of latter two species), Nightingale, Grasshopper Warbler, Sedge Warbler, Reed Warbler, Lesser Whitethroat, Whitethroat, Garden Warbler, Blackcap and Spotted Flycatcher.

OUSE WASHES

MAP 40
OS map 143

Habitat

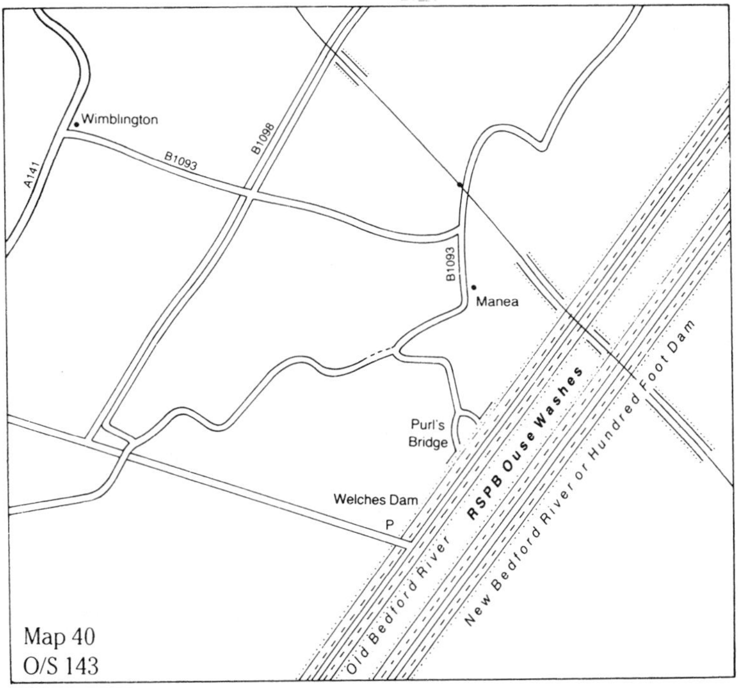

Map 40
O/S 143

The Ouse Washes were not, of course, originally created for birds, but as a flood reservoir when the main drainage system could not cope with the flood waters. In Roman times, and again during the Middle Ages, several abortive attempts were made to drain part of the Fens. For many centuries the area was a huge fen of grass, sedge and reed overlooked by widely spread small towns and villages on higher ground and these are still known as 'isles'. Summer grazing by sheep and cattle provided local people with their livelihood in addition to the exploitation of reed, sedge, osiers, wildfowl and fish. Thus, the Fens were partly accessible during the summer months, but were a water filled marshland during winter, when the rivers overflowed.

In the seventeenth century an ambitious drainage scheme was promoted by a wealthy landowner, the Earl of Bedford, who owned some 20,000 acres (8,000 ha) near Whittlesey. He engaged a Dutch engineer to by-pass the winding of the Great Ouse by making a straight 20 mile (32 km) cut between Earith and Denver to allow the water to flow more smoothly to the sea. This cut – the old Bedford River – was completed in 1637 and succeeded in improving summer grazing, although winter flooding still occurred. Twenty years later another cut was made about ½ mile (0.8 km) parallel to the original one. High barrier banks were raised beside these rivers with the strip of land in between taking the surplus water in times of flood. Thus the Ouse Washes came into being and still remain as one of the few pieces of the vast fens which are managed in much the same way as during the Middle Ages. In summer the Washes are grazed or cut for hay while the ditches which divide the area into fields (washes) contain the cattle and provide watering places for them. In winter the Washes generally become flooded as they have done for centuries.

Black-tailed Godwit with young

Although the birdlife of the Washes was well known, it was not until 1952 that the discovery of breeding Black-tailed Godwits focused attention on this region. Now it is recognised as an internationally important wetland for wildfowl and it is designated as such by the government. The first section of the Washes was purchased by the RSPB in 1964 and now over 2,760 acres (1,104 ha) have been acquired by the RSPB and CWT; and in the Norfolk section, by the Wildfowl and Wetlands Trust. This is more than half the total area of the Washes and further land is still being acquired whenever possible.

Subsequent studies have shown that the area was far more important than had originally been appreciated, both for its birdlife and botanical interests. In the ditches there are nine species of floating aquatic plants which are particularly noteworthy. Other plants include water dropwort, brooklime, starwort, milfoil, and three species of duckweed. The fringed water lily can be seen on the old Bedford River from the bridge to the hides. There is a profusion of comfrey, yellow bur-marigold, purple loosestrife and flowering rush. Marsh yellow cress is sometimes abundant and its starchy roots are much liked by Bewick's Swans. The commonest grasses are reed canary-grass, reed sweet-grass and foxtail. Many rushes, sedges and dock occur along with meadow rue, creeping jenny, creeping thistle and marsh ragwort. Mousetail – a nationally rare plantain – occurs in the field gateways. In all 280 species of flowering plants have been recorded on these open fenlands.

The Old Bedford River and the River Delph hold many fresh water fish and the former is famous for its golden flanked rudd. Eels abound in both these rivers as well as in the New Bedford River which is tidal and can boast of a small run of migrating trout and smelt. Grassland butterflies such as wall, gatekeeper, small copper and common blues are well represented. Several species of damsel and dragon-flies include the azure damselfly, blue-tailed damselfly, broad-bodied libellula and the brown aeshna.

Map 40

Species

With over 30,000 wintering Wigeon, the Ouse Washes Reserves are the most important stronghold for this species in Britain. Added to this, there are six other species of duck, each of which runs into thousands and usually over 3,000 Bewick's Swans. These huge totals emphasise the importance and attractions of these reserves during the winter months. Sheer numbers of birds are always impressive and the flat fen country provides an ideal setting for these winter hordes. With Wigeon 'topping the bill', Teal are generally the second most plentiful duck with counts of over 7,000 being made. Mallard are in similar numbers, while in the 3,000 to 5,000 league are Pintail and Pochard. Not far behind are Shoveler and Tufted Duck still on or above the 1,000 mark. As everywhere the Gadwall is increasing annually and there are generally several hundred present.

Numbers of duck fluctuate from year to year and even from month to month. The Washes are always subject to flood surges after high rainfalls with the result that deeper waters favour the diving duck such as the Pochard and the Tufted. In drier seasons, with shallow water on the meadows, dabbling duck are foremost. With heavy flooding especially after a spell of harder winter weather, rarities such as Smew and Goosanders may turn up and even such marine species as Red-breasted Mergansers and Goldeneye have appeared.

These Washes are not particularly attractive to wild geese, but some White-fronts occur from time to time. There is no doubt though about the liking that Bewick's Swans have for these flooded grazing pastures, to return year after year with their offspring. Apart from the wildfowl though, the Washes are a regular haunt of Hen Harrier and Short-eared Owls. Numbers of these species also vary from year to year, but it is not uncommon to see several Hen Harriers going into roost amongst the sedge fen, causing commotion amongst the dabbling duck and waders. In some winters when vole populations are high, a score or more of Short-eared Owls may be silently quartering the surrounding fields, their round faces intently scanning the ground below. Hundreds of Snipe and Lapwings find a rich living on these soggy meadows while up to 2,000 or more Golden Plover prefer the drier arable fields surrounding the reserve. Kingfishers are more likely to be seen in the winter months, as there is nowhere really suitable for them to nest in the river embankments. Huge numbers of gulls exploit the Washes with counts running into tens of thousands. Even such strictly sea coast rarities as Glaucous and Iceland Gulls have been recorded.

There are isolated records of Bitterns, but the reed-beds are not sufficiently extensive enough to hold them. One or two Jack Snipe have been seen in some winters and usually a few Ruff also stay on. Of the smaller birds, the more notable are a few Stonechats, Bearded Tits and gatherings of Corn Buntings on the arable fields. Curiously, a few Twite also appear on the arable fields and they too are more usually associated with the coastal marshes.

Several Great-crested Grebes linger into early spring before pairing and moving out to the surrounding pits. The marshland dawn chorus has a charm totally different from that of woodlands. In the Ouse Washes the plaintive cry of Lapwings tumbling over their territories, mingle with the drumming of many Snipe in aerial display in the early

Jack Snipe. Winter visitor and passage migrant

spring. It is estimated that over 800 pairs of Snipe nest in the Ouse Washes in addition to many pairs of breeding Redshank and Lapwings.

With the draining of the Fens several species of birds ceased to breed and these included Black-tailed Godwits and Black Terns. The former returned to nest in 1952 and their numbers have now built up to about 50 pairs nesting in favourable years when water levels are 'correct' for them. Black Terns too have attempted to make a comeback and have bred sporadically. The Ruff was another vanquished species, but it returned to breed in small numbers from the mid-1960s. For brief periods in late April, Ruff may be seen on their lek, which is often a slightly drier, bare mound amongst the marshy pools. Here, the males gather and engage in courtship display for the favours of the drab females, and to quarrel amongst themselves. It has been said, with some truth, that no two breeding Ruff are alike. There is a great variety of colour in their loose ruffs and long ear-coverts which are unique in the wader family. The colours of the ruff may be buff, chestnut, purple, white, brown or black with various barring or mottling, while their striking ear-tufts are usually a different colour to the ruffs. There is no pair bond and once mating has taken place the secretive female quietly goes off to lay, brood her eggs and raise her young without any help from the male who, with his fellows, has dispersed elsewhere. The other confusing point about Ruff is that the males soon lose their breeding dress and resemble the smaller females, while in autumn young birds can be much smaller than the adults.

No less than nine species of duck breed, Mallard, Shoveler, Gadwall, Tufted Duck, Shelduck, Teal, Pochard, Pintail and Garganey. This is probably one of the best places to see the delightful Garganey in the early spring although its numbers are on a downward trend. Spotted Crakes are quite rare visitors, but they have favoured this site and breeding has been confirmed; they are more likely to be heard than seen in the breeding season, when their explosive 'whiplash' call is distinctive. Other scarce breeders have included Quail, once seen with young; and

Garganey

the Savi's Warbler which has been suspected of breeding, as birds have stayed to 'sing in summer'.

Resident breeding birds include Little Owls and Stock Doves who nest in the old hollow willow trees. Even Herons will nest in the tops of the taller willows while Goldfinches and Redpolls colonise the lower branches. A few pairs of Little Grebes nest on the shallow weed-strewn meres. Summer breeding passerines include many pairs of Yellow Wagtails spread over the fen and dozens of Reed and Sedge Warblers along the waterways.

Some passage waders such as Spotted Redshank, Greenshank and Wood Sandpipers occur in spring, but generally there is greater variety and numbers in the autumn. Good numbers of Ruff can be found together with Dunlin, Snipe, stints and sandpipers. Marsh Harriers can be seen more frequently at this time and there may be larger numbers of Garganey now in their eclipse plumage. The Welche's Dam area of the reserve has had several rarities over the years and these have included, Collared Pratincole, Crane, Night Heron, Great Reed Warbler and Red-footed Falcon in the spring; and Wilson's Phalarope (which probably summered from May) and Red-necked Phalarope in the autumn.

Timing
Any time of the year. The hides are open at all times free of charge. Wildfowling takes place near the reserve and in consequence some disturbance may occur between September and January.

Access
The Ouse Washes reserves are signposted from Manea Village which can be reached via the B1093 from Wimblington or the B1098 from Chatteris. Both Manea and Chatteris are on the A141 road to March. Follow signposts from Manea to Welche's Dam where there is a car park, toilets and a visitor centre.

Calendar
Resident Little Grebe, Grey Heron, Gadwall, Mallard, Teal, Pintail, Shoveler, Pochard, Tufted Duck (all these duck species increase in winter), Lapwing, Snipe, Redshank, Stock Dove, Little Owl, Goldfinch, Redpoll and Corn Bunting (winter dispersal of latter three species).

October–March Great-crested Grebe, Bittern (scarce), Bewick's Swan, White-fronted Goose (infrequent), Wigeon, Goldeneye, Smew, Red-breasted Merganser, Goosander (the latter four species especially when deep flood waters occur or in hard weather), Hen Harrier, Golden Plover, Dunlin, Ruff, Jack Snipe, Iceland Gull, Glaucous Gull (both gulls rare), Short-eared Owl, Kingfisher, Stonechat, Bearded Tit (occasionally) and Twite.

March/April–September Garganey, Marsh Harrier, Quail, Spotted Crake (rare), Little Stint, Temminck's Stint, Curlew Sandpiper, Dunlin, Ruff, Black-tailed Godwit, Spotted Redshank, Greenshank, Green Sandpiper, Wood Sandpiper, Common Sandpiper, Red-necked Phalarope (rare), Black Tern, Yellow Wagtail, Savi's Warbler (rare), Sedge Warbler and Reed Warbler.

Habitat

Work began in 1962 to construct a vast reservoir in the shallow agricultural valley of Diddington Brook in Huntingdonshire (now part of Cambridgeshire), but it was not completed until late 1964 when the reservoir started to fill. Some of the statistics may give an idea of the vastness of this valuable wildfowl and wader habitat. The surface area at top water level is 1,570 acres (628 ha) and there are nearly 10 miles (16 km) of shoreline! The reservoir is about 3 miles (4.8 km) long and nearly 1½ miles (2.4 km) across at its widest point. It is one of the largest in England and has been developed by the Anglian Water

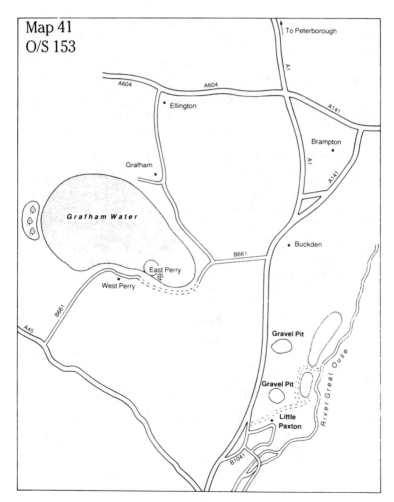

Map 41
O/S 153

Authority (now National River Authority) for multi-purpose use in addition, of course, to its primary function of supplying water. Facilities for recreation, fishing and sailing have been created and, more importantly, a large area has been set aside for wildlife conservation with the Bedfordshire and Huntingdon Naturalists' Trust (BHWT) being appointed in 1967 to manage 370 acres (148 ha) as a nature reserve.

This reserve covers the whole of the Anglian Water Authority's land from the south-east corner of the reservoir, along the western side to the northern shore. Although set in predominantly agricultural country, there are some wooded areas within the reserve and many of the old hedgerows have been retained. There are some rough grassy fields which have not been farmed since the area was taken over and there is 75 acres (30 ha) of new afforestation containing a wide variety of hardwoods and conifers. Two old mature spinneys by the northern edge of the reservoir are carpeted with bluebells and dog's mercury, confirmation that the woodland is well established. The teasel is commonly found while several species of thistles all provide food for winter flocks of finches. Cowslips used to be in abundance and can still be found on some of the grassland. Less common plants which occur on the reserve are wood spurge, musk mallow, nettle-leaved bellflower and the great burnet.

On the reserve 20 species of butterflies have been recorded. They include the grass feeding 'browns' and skippers. There are a few mammals and foxes do occur as well as grey squirrels and the small muntjac deer. At least six species of water snails and bivalves occur in submerged vegetation and in the bottom mud of the reservoir in very large numbers; and these, together with the chironomid larvae, provide food supplies for fish and birds.

In discussing Grafham mention must be made of a series of active gravel pit workings less than 3 miles (4.8 km) to the east and along the Great Ouse River valley. Little Paxton and Stirtloe gravel pits have long been known as traditional bird haunts and it was feared at one time that the creation of Grafham Water would attract birds away from the smaller waters. In fact, the reverse has happened; the addition has proved mutually beneficial for the duck and other species which results in a great deal of interchange between the two sites.

The Huntingdonshire District Council (HDC) have established a new network of footpaths which link up with existing paths. These have created circular paths of varying lengths which are signposted and waymarked.

Map 41

Species

Grafham Water is not an easy reservoir to watch on a casual basis and the winter months provide the most interesting time with the largest numbers of wildfowl occurring between October and December. Mallard, Coot and Tufted Duck are usually well into the 1,000 mark at this time and there are hundreds of Great-crested Grebes, Teal, Wigeon, Pochard and Goldeneye. The latter species particularly favours this reservoir and assembling rafts can be seen on a late winter's afternoon when there might well be a few Smew joining them. Smaller numbers of Little Grebes, Pintail, Shoveler and Goosanders winter. A few Gadwall are present, but this duck prefers the smaller complex of the nearby gravel pits.

Rare winter species such as the marine divers, grebes, Scoter and Scaup, may appear at any time, but especially after gales off the distant sea coast of Norfolk. Around the reservoir, the odd Hooded Crow, Sparrow Hawk and Hen Harrier may be seen from time to time. Occasionally a Great Grey Shrike appears to stay for several weeks. A few Siskins and Bramblings are sometimes seen in the woodlands.

In spring there is some wader passage, although it is never as prominent as in the autumn months. The reserve is noted for several breeding waders which includes a nice colony of Little Ringed Plovers, Ringed Plovers, Lapwing and Redshank. Single numbers of waders which might drop in at this time include Wood Sandpiper, Spotted Redshank and Greenshank, while Kentish Plover and Avocet have been recorded. With such a well stocked fishing water, the Osprey was bound to be attracted and it is now a fairly regular visitor.

The Black Tern too, is a regular visitor both on spring and autumn passage. More remarkable has been an overland passage of Arctic Terns which have appeared at the reservoir in recent springs, with up to 200 birds being noted. A few Little Gulls are usually seen, but these are rather more frequent in the autumn months. Yellow Wagtails are common summer migrants and nest in the surrounding arable fields while Nightingales occasionally breed in the reserve spinney. Other summer passerines which nest include: Blackcap, Garden Warbler, Whitethroat, Lesser Whitethroat and Spotted Flycatcher. Passing Golden Orioles have been noted in spring.

In autumn good numbers of Spotted Redshank, Ruff, Little Stints and Greenshank may occur especially if the water levels are low enough to provide areas of mud. Green, Wood, Common Sandpipers and Knot are fairly regular in small numbers. Either of the two godwits may drop in and a few Curlew and Whimbrel may be passing. In their 'good years' Curlew Sandpipers will almost certainly be seen. The rare waders have included Grey and Red-necked Phalaropes, Temminck's Stint and even New World species such as Pectoral and Buff-breasted Sandpipers. Waders commonly present in winter include Dunlin and Golden Plover, while a Jack Snipe or two may be present.

A surprising list of rarities includes Marsh Sandpiper, Black-winged Stilt, King Eider, Whiskered Tern, Ring-necked Duck and Ferruginous Duck. Other rarities, more typical of the Norfolk coast, have included

Two Lapwings and one Golden Plover

Glaucous and Iceland Gulls, Wryneck, Shorelarks, Bearded Tit, Richard's Pipit, Snow Bunting and Lapland Bunting which have all been recorded once or twice. Even a party of Brent Geese, usually confined to the coastal regions, once stayed for a few days one March, and this is a remarkable record for a land-locked county such as Cambridgeshire.

Timing

With the A1 only 2 miles (3.2 km) away it is worth calling in at any time. Fine summer weekends though should be avoided as the public car parks and access points are pretty crowded. Peak numbers of wildfowl occur between October and December, but reduced numbers remain until March or April. The best time for wader passage is between July and October. On sunny days watching from the north shore can be difficult.

Access

Leave the A1 at Buckden turning left (if going north) on the B661 to East Perry, 2 miles (3.2 km), and West Perry, 3 miles (4.8 km), where there are two public car parks on the south shore of the reservoir. From the Mander car park at West Perry there is a short and a long nature trail, ¾ mile (1.2 k) and 1½ miles (2.4 km) respectively, starting from the display booth on the car park.

There is another public car park on the east shore which can be reached by turning right off the B661 about 1 mile (1.6 km) from the A1. In order to reach the start of the Savage's Spinney nature trail, proceed past the public car park on the left then through the village of Grafham bearing left to Hill Farm car park where the 3½ mile (5.6 km) trail begins. For a short visit try the Plummer car park just before reaching East Perry.

The Little Paxton-Stirtloe gravel pits complex lies on the east side of the A1 between St Neots and Huntingdon. A network of paths have been made by the HDC. These are of varying lengths, signposted and waymarked along the Great River Ouse and around the gravel pits. An eight-page folder can be obtained from the HDC which gives a brief account of the nearby villages and habitats. A telescope is essential for watching Grafham Water. With such a vast expanse of water there are often small waves whipped up by a strong wind and this makes watching difficult. Even in summer this spot can be cool and draughty so go well equipped at all times.

Calendar

Resident Mallard, Tufted Duck, Coot, Lapwing (and winter visitor) and Redshank.

October–March Red-throated Diver, Black-throated Diver, Great Northern Diver, Little Grebe, Great-crested Grebe (has bred), Red-necked Grebe, Slavonian Grebe, Black-necked Grebe, Wigeon, Gadwall, Teal, Pintail, Shoveler, Pochard, Scaup, Common Scoter, Goldeneye, Smew, Goosander, Hen Harrier, Golden Plover, Dunlin, Jack Snipe, Great Grey Shrike, Brambling and Siskin.

April–June Osprey, Avocet (rare), Little Ringed Plover, Ringed Plover, Kentish Plover (rare), Little Gull, Arctic Tern, Common Tern, Yellow

Wagtail, Nightingale, Lesser Whitethroat, Whitethroat, Garden Warbler, Blackcap and Spotted Flycatcher.

July–September Little Ringed Plover, Ringed Plover, Knot, Little Stint (has wintered), Curlew Sandpiper, Dunlin, Ruff, Black-tailed Godwit, Bar-tailed Godwit, Whimbrel, Curlew, Spotted Redshank, Greenshank, Green, Wood and Common Sandpipers, Little Gull, Common Tern and Black Tern

APPENDICES

Glossary
List of Organisations
List of Reserves
List of Additional Sites
Code of Conduct for Birdwatchers
Further Reading List
County Check Lists

GLOSSARY

Ornithological Terms

Auk	A seabird of the auk family – Guillemot, Razorbill, Puffin, etc.
Coasting	Diurnal movement along the coast on spring or autumn passage
Control	Ringing term. A bird ringed at one point and caught again later at a point more than three miles away
Crepuscular	Active at dawn or dusk
Dabbling duck	Duck, such as Mallard and Teal, which feed by dabbling on the surface of the water or by up-ending
Diving duck	Duck, such as Tufted and Pochard, which feed by diving
Diurnal	Mainly active during the day
Drift migrant	A migrating bird drifted off-course by adverse winds and/or bad weather
Fall	A mass arrival of small birds suddenly grounded by weather conditions
Feral	Species escaped or released from captivity and living in a wild state
Hirundine	A member of the swallow or martin family
Irruption	A mass arrival or departure often associated with high populations and/or short food supplies and happening at irregular intervals
Leaf warbler	A member of the *Phylloscopus* family – Willow Warbler, Chiff-chaff, etc.
Nocturnal	Mainly active during the night
Overshooting	A migrant bird flying northwards beyond its normal breeding range
Passage migrant	A bird passing through a region or county in which it does not normally stay to breed
Passerine	A perching bird
Raptor	Generally a diurnal bird of prey – Kestrel, Buzzard. Sometimes including nocturnal birds of prey such as owls
Roding	Territorial flight of male Woodcock which utters a series of croaks with a deliberate wing action
Ringtail	When not possible to distinguish between the young of white-rumped Montagu's and Hen Harriers, or immatures of either species
Redhead	Female Goldeneye and Smew
Sawbill	A fish-eating duck such as Merganser, Goosander and Smew
Sea Duck	Duck mostly confined to the sea
Scrape	A shallow excavation made to attract water birds; *also* Nest Scrape: A small hollow excavated by nesting bird in soil, sand or shingle
Vagrant	A rare accidental visitor hundreds of miles off-course
Wader	Mud or marsh feeding sandpipers, plover, curlews, etc.
Wreck	An arrival of storm blown seabirds on to the coast or miles inland

Other Terms

AONB	Area of Outstanding Natural Beauty
Borrow-dyke	Ditches or dykes formed by the removal of spoil to consolidate adjacent seawalls – as in Essex
Breck	A sandy heathland
Broad	A shallow lake. In Norfolk a water-filled depression formed by medieval peat digging
Carr	Woodland growing in water-logged conditions. Usually willow or alder
Coppiced	Small trees which are periodically cut
Denes	A sandy tract of land along the seashore
Drain	A watercourse
Dyke	A watercourse
Fleet	A creek, inlet or small stream
Inter-tidal mudflats	An area of saltwater mud regularly covered and uncovered by the tide
Meals	A wild tract of sandhills between the shore and arable land
NNR	National Nature Reserve
Pollarded	A tree on which a close head of young branches has been made by lopping off the top
Phragmites	Reeds
Saltings or Salt-marsh	Intertidal mudflats colonised by salt adapted plants
Sandlings	Sandy wastelands in Suffolk covered with heather or gorse
Scalp	A mussel bed
SSSI	A site of special scientific interest
Seawall or bank	A bank made to protect land from the sea

LIST OF ORGANISATIONS

National

NCC	Nature Conservancy Council, Northminster House, Peterborough PE1 1VA
NT	National Trust, 36 Queen Anne's Gate, London SW1H 9AS
RSPB	Royal Society for the Protection of Birds, The Lodge, Sandy, Bedfordshire SG19 2DL
WWT	Wildfowl and Wetlands Trust, Slimbridge, Gloucester GL2 7BT
WWF	World Wide Fund for Nature, Panda House, Weyside Park, Godalming, Surrey GU7 1XR
RSNC	Royal Society for Nature Conservation, The Green, Nettleham, Lincolnshire LN2 2NR
FOE	Friends of the Earth, 377 City Road, London EC1V 1NA
	Greenpeace, 30–31 Islington Green, London N1 8XE
YOC	Young Ornithologists' Club, The Lodge, Sandy, Bedfordshire SG19 2DL
WT	Woodland Trust, Autumn Park, Dysart Road, Grantham, Lincolnshire NG31 6LL

Norfolk

NNT	Norfolk Naturalists' Trust, 72 Cathedral Close, Norwich NR1 4DF
KL and WNBC	King's Lynn and West Norfolk Borough Council, King's Court, Chapel Street, King's Lynn, Norfolk PE36 1EX
NOA	Norfolk Ornithologists Association, Aslack Way, Holme-next-Sea, Hunstanton, Norfolk PE36 6LP
NCC	Nature Conservancy Council, East Anglia Regional Office, 60 Bracondale, Norwich, Norfolk NR1 2BE
NT	National Trust, Eastern Area Office, Blickling, Norwich, Norfolk NR11 6NS
NNDC	North Norfolk District Council, Holt Road, Cromer, Norfolk NR27 9DZ
Norfolk CC	Norfolk County Council, Martineau Lane, Norwich, Norfolk NR1 2DH
	How Hill Trust, How Hill, Ludham, Great Yarmouth, Norfolk NR29 5PG
WWT	Wildfowl and Wetlands Trust, Pintail House, Hundred Foot Bank, Welney, Nr Wisbech, Cambridgeshire PE14 9TN

Suffolk

Suffolk CC	Suffolk County Council, St Edmund's House, Rope Walk, Ipswich, Suffolk IP4 1LZ
SWT	Suffolk Wildlife Trust, Park Cottage, 32 South Entrance, Saxmundham, Suffolk IP17 1DQ
LPBO	Landguard Point Bird Observatory, Secretary: Jane Bourne, c/o The Hand Cottage, 320 High Road, Trimley St Martin, Suffolk IP10 0RL

Essex

EFCC	Epping Forest Conservation Centre, High Beach, Loughton, Essex
EWT	Essex Wildlife Trust, Fingringhoe Wick Nature Reserve, South Green Road, Fingringhoe, Colchester, Essex CO5 7DN

Tendring DC	Tendring District Council, Council Offices, Weeley, Essex
Essex CC	Essex County Council, Clarendon House, Parkway, Chelmsford, Essex CM2 0NT
EBWPS	Essex Bird Watching and Preservation Society, Gregg Bond, 11 Hearsall Avenue, Broomfield, Chelmsford CM1 5DD
Southend BC	Southend Borough Council, Southend, Essex
Basildon BC	Basildon Borough Council, Basildon, Essex

Cambridgeshire (and Huntingdonshire)

Peterborough DC	Peterborough Development Corporation
CWT	Cambridge Wildlife Trust, 5 Fulbourne Manor, Fulbourne, Cambridgeshire CB1 5BN
BHWT	Bedfordshire and Huntingdonshire Wildlife Trust, Wendy Hook, Priory Country Park, Barkers Lane, Bedford MK41 9SH
NCC	Nature Conservancy Council, East Midlands Region, Northminster House, Peterborough PE1 1UA
HDC	Huntingdonshire District Council, Huntingdon

Many other worthy Societies who have made notable contributions to ornithology and conservation include: Norfolk and Norwich Naturalists' Society, Suffolk Ornithologists' Group, Suffolk Naturalists' Society, Southend Ornithologists' Group, Cambridge Bird Club, RSPB Members' Groups, and various ringing groups to name but a few. It is not the purpose of this book to list all the many county societies and we are sure that readers will be able to glean this information from several other books, including John Pemberton's annual *The Birdwatcher's Year Book*.

LIST OF RESERVES

All the reserves listed here are mentioned in the text. For further information apply to the relevant management body shown (see List of Organisations for county and national offices). The reserves are listed by county.

Norfolk

Ringstead Downs	NNT
Snettisham Gravel Pits Reserve	RSPB
Snettisham Coastal Park	KL & WNBC
Holme Bird Observatory	NOA
Holme Dunes Nature Reserve	NNT
Redwell Marsh	NOA
Holme Marsh Bird Reserve	NOA
Titchwell Marsh Reserve	RSPB
Scolt Head Island	NCC
Holkham National Nature Reserve	NCC
Stiffkey and Morston Marshes	NT
Blakeney Point	NT
Cley Marshes Nature Reserve	NNT
Walsey Hills Watch Point	NOA
Arnold's Marsh	NNT
Holt Lowes (Country Park)	NNDC
Beeston Regis Common	Norfolk CC
Winterton Dunes National Nature Reserve	NCC
Horsey Mere	NT
Martham Broad	NNT
Breydon Water	Norfolk CC
Berney Marshes	RSPB
Hickling National Nature Reserve	NNT
Barton Broad	NNT
How Hill Estate	How Hill Trust
Hoveton Great Broad	NCC
Ranworth Broad	NNT
Surlingham Church Marsh	RSPB
Upton Fen	NNT
Strumpshaw Fen	RSPB
Hardley Flood	NNT
Coastal Path, Weaver's Way and Peddar's Way footpaths	Norfolk CC
East Wretham Heath	NNT
Weeting Heath	NNT
Thompson Common	NNT
Lenwade and Sparham Pools	NNT
Blickling Hall Estate	NT
Syderstone Common	NNT
Roydon Common	NNT
East Winch Common	NNT
Welney Wildfowl Reserve	WWT

Suffolk

Benacre Broad	NCC
Coastal Path	Suffolk CC
Minsmere Nature Reserve	RSPB
Walberswick National Nature Reserve	NCC
Dunwich Heath	NT
Westleton Heath National Nature Reserve	NCC
North Warren	RSPB
Havergate Island	RSPB
Languard Point Nature Reserve	SWT
Redgrave and Lopham Fen	SWT
Landguard Point Bird Observatory	LPBO
Trimley Nature Reserve	SWT

Essex

Epping Forest	EFCC
Stour Wood and Copperas Bay	RSPB
Copperas Wood	EWT
Hamford Water National Nature Reserve	NCC
The Naze & Public Open Space	EWT and Tendring DC
Colne Point	EWT
Cudmore Grove Country Park	Essex CC
Fingringhoe Wick	EWT
Old Hall Marsh	RSPB
Bradwell Bird Observatory	EBWPS
Bradwell Shell Bank	EWT
Two Tree Island	EWT
Canvey Point	EWT
Belfairs Great Wood	Southend BC
Wat Tyler Country Park	Basildon C

Cambridgeshire (and Huntingdonshire)

Fowlmere	RSPB
Ferry Meadows	Peterborough DC
Wicken Fen	NT
Ouse Washes	RSPB and CWT
Grafham Water (and Little Paxton Gravel Pits)	BHWT and HDC

LIST OF ADDITIONAL SITES

These additional sites have not been included in the main text for various reasons: restricted access; only a few notable species in one season; accent on botanical or rambling interests; and because other similar areas which have been included have a greater range of species and are easier of access.

Norfolk

Site	Habitat	Birds	Peak	Location
Barnham Cross Common	Grass heath, scrub	Sparrow Hawk, Short-eared Owl, Little Ringed Plover, Kingfisher	summer	Local nature reserve, south of Thetford. Norfolk CC
Litcham Common	Grass heath, scrub	Nightingale	summer	Local nature reserve, north-west of East Dereham. Norfolk CC
Tottenhill Gravel Pits	Water-filled pits	Smew, grebes and other rare duck	winter	Roadside watching, south of King's Lynn
Coast Path (Peddar's Way and Weaver's Way)	Various	Traverses many good bird sites and reserves. Public observation hide at Heigham Corner which overlooks Hickling Broad	any	King's Lynn to Great Yarmouth. Norfolk CC

Suffolk

Site	Habitat	Birds	Peak	Location
Cavenham Heath	Heathland	Wheatear, Nightjar	summer	NNC site, south-east of Mildenhall
Bradfield Woods	Old woodland	Nightingale, Bramblings, Redpolls	all year	SWT site, south-east of Bury St Edmunds
Ickworth Park	Wooded park, lake	Hawfinch, Stock Doves, Kingfishers, woodpeckers, Fieldfares, Redwings, Spotted Flycatchers, tits and Nuthatches	all year	NT site, south-west of Bury St Edmunds
West Stowe	Country Park	Little Grebe, Great-crested Grebe, Ruddy Duck, Little Ringed Plover, Kingfisher and Nightingales	all year	Within the Borough of St Edmundsbury, north-west of Bury St Edmunds
Coast Path	Various	Traverses good birding country and reserves	all year	Lowestoft to Felixstowe. Suffolk County Council managed, some 50 miles (80 km) in all

Essex

Site	Habitat	Birds	Peak	Location
Weald Country Park	Old parkland, lakes, woods	Tree Pipits, Siskins and Hawfinches	all year	Essex County Council site west of Brentwood
Thorndon Country Park	Old parkland, lakes, woods	Woodcock, Nightingales, Tree Sparrows, Siskins, Bramblings, Redpolls, Crossbills and Hawfinches	all year	Essex County Council site, south of Brentwood
Langdon Nature Reserve	Former farmland, woods	Nuthatch, woodpeckers, Siskins and Redpolls	all year	Essex Wildlife Trust, near Basildon
Belhus Woods	Woodland and lakes	Nuthatches, woodpeckers, Kingfishers, Great-crested Grebes. Observation hide	all year	Essex County Council site, near Aveley

240

Site	Habitat	Birds	Peak	Location
Danbury Country Park	Old park, woodland, ornamental gardens	Woodpeckers, Nuthatches, Siskins, Redpolls, Nightingales nearby	all year	Essex County Council site, east of Chelmsford
Marsh Farm Country Park	Farmland by River Crouch. Saltmarsh, brackish pools	Brent Geese, Wigeon, Twite, Hen Harriers, Short-eared Owls and waders	all year	Essex County Council site, south of Woodham Ferrers
Chalkney Wood	Ancient woodland	Hawfinch, Nightingales, Nuthatches, woodpeckers, tits, Woodcock, Siskins, Bramblings, Fieldfares and Redwings	all year	Essex County Council site, near Earls Colne
Hanningfield Reservoir	Water	Waders, ducks and rarities	all year	Roadside watching near West Hanningfield

Cambridgeshire

Site	Habitat	Birds	Peak	Location
Holme Fen National Nature Reserve	Birch woodland, mere	Nightingales	summer	Permits in advance only but minor road intersects fen. NCC site, near Peterborough
Monks Wood National Nature Reserve	Ash-oak woodlands	Woodland birds		Permits in advance only. NCC site, near Peterborough
Wood Walton Fen	Fen, carr, scrub, woodlands	Woodland birds		Permits in advance only. NCC site. Peterborough
Nene Washes Reserve	Flood plain, low-lying meadows	Short-eared Owls, Hen Harriers, Garganey, Yellow Wagtails and Bewick's Swans		RSPB site, east of Peterborough, access by arrangement
Aversley Wood	Old woodland	Woodcock, Grasshopper Warbler, Firecrest, Nuthatches, Lesser Spotted Woodpecker		South of Peterborough. Woodland Trust
Ely Nature Trail	Deep pools, wet meadows	Little Grebes, Great-crested Grebes, Kingfishers and waders	all year	CWT site, near Ely, 3 miles (4.8 km) circular walk

FURTHER READING LIST

The authors would like to acknowledge the following sources of information.

Books

Allard, P.R. *The Birds of Great Yarmouth* (Norfolk and Norwich Naturalists' Society and D. Farrow, Antiquarian Bookseller, 1990)

Axell, H. and Hosking, E. *Minsmere Portrait of a Bird Reserve* (Hutchinson, 1977)

Clarke, W.G. *In Breckland Wilds* (Robert Scott, 1925)

Cox, S. *New Guide to the Birds of Essex* (Essex Bird Watching and Preservation Society, 1984)

Ellis, E.A. *The Broads* (Collins, 1965)

Gooders, J. *Where to Watch Birds* (Deutsch, 1967)

Gooders, J. *New Where to Watch Birds* (Deutsch, 1986)

Hammond, N. (ed.) *RSPB Nature Reserves* (RSPB, 1984)

Manning, S.A. *Nature in East Anglia* (World's Work, 1976)

Norman, D. and Tucker, V. *Where to Watch Birds in Devon & Cornwall* (Croom Helm, 1984)

Parslow, J. (ed.) *Bird Watcher's Britain* (Pan/Ordnance Survey, 1983)

Payn, W.H. *Birds of Suffolk* (Ancient House Publishing, 1978)

Pemberton, J.E. (ed.) *The Bird Watcher's Year Book* (Buckingham Press, 1986–9)

Riviere, B.B. *A History of the Birds of Norfolk* (Witherby, 1930)

Seago, M.J. *Birds of Norfolk* (Jarrold, 1977)

Stevenson, H. *The Birds of Norfolk* (Van Voorst, 1866)

Taylor, M. *Birds of Sheringham* (Poppyland Publishing, 1987)

Turner, E.L. *Broadland Birds* (Country Life, 1924)

Turner, E.L. *Bird Watching on Scolt Head* (Country Life, 1928)

Waugh, M. *Shell Book of Country Parks* (David & Charles, 1981)

Norwich and its Region (British Association for the Advancement of Science, 1961)

Nature in Norfolk: A Heritage in Trust (Jarrold, 1976)

Annual Reports

Cambridgeshire Bird Report (Cambridge Bird Club)

Huntingdon and Peterborough Bird Report (Huntingdon and Peterborough Bird Report Committee and Huntingdonshire Fauna and Flora Society)

Norfolk Bird and Mammal Report (Norfolk and Norwich Naturalists' Society and Norfolk Ornithologists' Association)

Norfolk Ornithologists' Association Report (Norfolk Ornithologists' Association)

Suffolk Birds (Suffolk Naturalists' Society)

The Essex Bird Report (Essex Bird Watching and Preservation Society)

COUNTY CHECK LISTS

A County Check List includes all the species officially accepted by the County Bird Recorder. Some vagrant species may have only occurred once, while other records (such as Pallas's Sandgrouse) may have been made many years ago. Therefore, not all the birds included in these lists are actually mentioned in the text.

We have included five county lists as records for Cambridgeshire and the Huntingdonshire–Peterborough areas are still being kept separately, although under the recent revision of county boundaries this large region is now all included in Cambridgeshire.

Another anomaly occurs in the Norfolk and Suffolk lists. The single records of Allen's Gallinule and White-throated Sparrow were recorded in a part of Suffolk which has now been ceded to Norfolk. Thus, we have included these two extremely rare vagrants in both the Norfolk and Suffolk lists so as to avoid ruffling any feathers!

With regard to the 'Albatross Species' in the Norfolk list this means that the record has been accepted as an Albatross, but the exact species could not be determined.

All lists have been made up to include additions up to the end of 1989.

Birds of Norfolk

Red-throated Diver
Black-throated Diver
Great Northern Diver
White-billed Diver
Pied-billed Grebe
Little Grebe
Great-crested Grebe
Red-necked Grebe
Slavonian Grebe
Black-necked Grebe
Albatross species
Fulmar
Capped Petrel
Cory's Shearwater
Great Shearwater
Sooty Shearwater
Manx Shearwater
Little Shearwater
Storm Petrel
Leach's Petrel
Gannet
Cormorant
Shag
Bittern
Little Bittern
Night Heron
Squacco Heron
Cattle Egret
Little Egret
Great White Egret
Grey Heron
Purple Heron
Black Stork
White Stork
Glossy Ibis
Spoonbill
Mute Swan
Bewick's Swan
Whooper Swan
Bean Goose
Pink-footed Goose
Snow Goose
Greylag Goose
White-fronted Goose

Lesser White-fronted Goose
Canada Goose
Barnacle Goose
Brent Goose
Red-breasted Goose
Egyptian Goose
Ruddy Shelduck
Shelduck
Mandarin
Wigeon
American Wigeon
Gadwall
Teal
Mallard
Pintail
Garganey
Blue-winged Teal
Baikal Teal
Shoveler
Red-crested Pochard
Pochard
Ring-necked Duck
Ferruginous Duck
Tufted Duck
Scaup
Eider
King Eider
Steller's Eider
Harlequin Duck
Long-tailed Duck
Common Scoter
Surf Scoter
Velvet Scoter
Bufflehead
Goldeneye
Smew
Red-breasted Merganser
Goosander
Ruddy Duck
Honey Buzzard
Black Kite
Red Kite
White-tailed Eagle
Marsh Harrier

Hen Harrier
Montagu's Harrier
Goshawk
Sparrow Hawk
Buzzard
Rough-legged Buzzard
Golden Eagle
Osprey
Kestrel
Red-footed Falcon
Merlin
Hobby
Gyrfalcon
Peregrine
Red-legged Partridge
Grey Partridge
Quail
Pheasant
Golden Pheasant
Lady Amherst's Pheasant
Water Rail
Spotted Crake
Little Crake
Baillon's Crake
Corncrake
Moorhen
Allen's Gallinule
Coot
Crane
Little Bustard
Great Bustard
Oyster-catcher
Black-winged Stilt
Avocet
Stone Curlew
Cream-coloured Courser
Collared Pratincole
Black-winged Pratincole
Little Ringed Plover
Ringed Plover
Kentish Plover
Greater Sand Plover
Caspian Plover
Dotterel

Pacific Golden Plover
American Golden Plover
Golden Plover
Grey Plover
Sociable Plover
Lapwing
Knot
Sanderling
Semipalmated Sandpiper
Little Stint
Temminck's Stint
White-rumped Sandpiper
Baird's Sandpiper
Pectoral Sandpiper
Sharp-tailed Sandpiper
Curlew Sandpiper
Purple Sandpiper
Dunlin
Broad-billed Sandpiper
Stilt Sandpiper
Buff-breasted Sandpiper
Ruff
Jack Snipe
Snipe
Great Snipe
Short-billed Dowitcher
Long-billed Dowitcher
Woodcock
Black-tailed Godwit
Bar-tailed Godwit
Little Whimbrel
Whimbrel
Curlew
Spotted Redshank
Redshank
Marsh Sandpiper
Greenshank
Greater Yellowlegs
Lesser Yellowlegs
Solitary Sandpiper
Green Sandpiper
Wood Sandpiper
Terek Sandpiper
Common Sandpiper
Spotted Sandpiper
Turnstone
Wilson's Phalarope
Red-necked Phalarope
Grey Phalarope
Pomarine Skua
Arctic Skua
Long-tailed Skua
Great Skua
Great Black-headed Gull
Mediterranean Gull
Little Gull
Sabine's Gull
Bonaparte's Gull
Black-headed Gull
Slender-billed Gull
Common Gull
Lesser Black-backed Gull
Herring Gull
Iceland Gull
Glaucous Gull
Great Black-backed Gull
Ross's Gull

Kittiwake
Ivory Gull
Gull-billed Tern
Caspian Tern
Lesser-crested Tern
Sandwich Tern
Roseate Tern
Common Tern
Arctic Tern
Sooty Tern
Little Tern
Black Tern
Whiskered Tern
White-winged Black Tern
Guillemot
Razorbill
Black Guillemot
Little Auk
Puffin
Pallas's Sandgrouse
Rock Dove
Stock Dove
Wood Pigeon
Collared Dove
Turtle Dove
Rufous Turtle Dove
Ring-necked Parakeet
Great Spotted Cuckoo
Cuckoo
Barn Owl
Scops Owl
Snowy Owl
Little Owl
Tawny Owl
Long-eared Owl
Short-eared Owl
Tengmalm's Owl
Nightjar
Swift
Alpine Swift
Pacific Swift
Kingfisher
Bee-eater
Roller
Hoopoe
Wryneck
Green Woodpecker
Great Spotted Woodpecker
Lesser Spotted Woodpecker
White-winged Lark
Short-toed Lark
Woodlark
Skylark
Shore Lark
Sand Martin
Swallow
Red-rumped Swallow
House Martin
Tawny Pipit
Richard's Pipit
Olive-backed Pipit
Tree Pipit
Meadow Pipit
Red-throated Pipit
Rock Pipit
Water Pipit
Yellow Wagtail

Citrine Wagtail
Grey Wagtail
Pied Wagtail
Waxwing
Dipper
Wren
Dunnock
Alpine Accentor
Robin
Thrush Nightingale
Nightingale
Bluethroat
Redstart
Black Redstart
Whinchat
Stonechat
Wheatear
Pied Wheatear
Black-eared Wheatear
Desert Wheatear
Isabelline Wheatear
Rock Thrush
White's Thrush
Siberian Thrush
Ring Ouzel
Blackbird
Black-throated Thrush
Fieldfare
Song Thrush
Redwing
Mistle Thrush
Cetti's Warbler
Fan-tailed Warbler
Grasshopper Warbler
Pallas's Grasshopper
  Warbler
River Warbler
Savi's Warbler
Aquatic Warbler
Sedge Warbler
Blyth's Reed Warbler
Marsh Warbler
Reed Warbler
Great Reed Warbler
Booted Warbler
Icterine Warbler
Melodious Warbler
Dartford Warbler
Subalpine Warbler
Sardinian Warbler
Barred Warbler
Lesser Whitethroat
Whitethroat
Garden Warbler
Blackcap
Greenish Warbler
Arctic Warbler
Pallas's Warbler
Yellow-browed Warbler
Radde's Warbler
Dusky Warbler
Bonelli's Warbler
Wood Warbler
Chiff-chaff
Willow Warbler
Goldcrest
Firecrest

Spotted Flycatcher
Red-breasted Flycatcher
Collared Flycatcher
Pied Flycatcher
Bearded Tit
Long-tailed Tit
Marsh Tit
Willow Tit
Coal Tit
Blue Tit
Great Tit
Nuthatch
Red-breasted Nuthatch
Wallcreeper
Treecreeper
Penduline Tit
Golden Oriole
Isabelline Shrike
Red-backed Shrike
Lesser Grey Shrike
Great Grey Shrike
Woodchat Shrike

Jay
Magpie
Nutcracker
Jackdaw
Rook
Carrion Crow
Raven
Starling
Rose-coloured Starling
House Sparrow
Tree Sparrow
Rock Sparrow
Chaffinch
Brambling
Serin
Citril Finch
Greenfinch
Goldfinch
Siskin
Linnet
Twite
Redpoll

Arctic Redpoll
Two-barred Crossbill
Crossbill
Parrot Crossbill
Scarlet Rosefinch
Bullfinch
Hawfinch
Black & White Warbler
White-throated Sparrow
Lapland Bunting
Snow Bunting
Yellowhammer
Cirl Bunting
Ortolan Bunting
Yellow-browed Bunting
Rustic Bunting
Little Bunting
Yellow-breasted Bunting
Reed Bunting
Black-headed Bunting
Corn Bunting
Indigo Bunting

Birds of Cambridgeshire

Red-throated Diver
Black-throated Diver
Great Northern Diver
Little Grebe
Great-crested Grebe
Red-necked Grebe
Slavonian Grebe
Black-necked Grebe
Black-browed Albatross
Fulmar
Manx Shearwater
Cory's Shearwater
Storm Petrel
Leach's Petrel
Gannet
Cormorant
Shag
Bittern
Little Bittern
Night Heron
Squacco Heron
Little Egret
Great White Egret
Grey Heron
Purple Heron
Black Stork
Glossy Ibis
Spoonbill
Mute Swan
Bewick's Swan
Whooper Swan
Bean Goose
Pink-footed Goose
Greylag Goose
White-fronted Goose
Canada Goose
Barnacle Goose
Brent Goose
Egyptian Goose
Ruddy Shelduck
Shelduck
Mandarin

Wigeon
American Wigeon
Gadwall
Teal
Mallard
Pintail
Garganey
Blue-winged Teal
Shoveler
Red-crested Pochard
Pochard
Ring-necked Duck
Ferruginous Duck
Tufted Duck
Scaup
Eider
Long-tailed Duck
Common Scoter
Velvet Scoter
Surf Scoter
Goldeneye
Smew
Red-breasted Merganser
Goosander
Ruddy Duck
Honey Buzzard
Red Kite
White-tailed Eagle
Marsh Harrier
Hen Harrier
Montagu's Harrier
Goshawk
Sparrow Hawk
Buzzard
Rough-legged Buzzard
Osprey
Kestrel
Red-footed Falcon
Merlin
Hobby
Gyrfalcon
Peregrine

Red-legged Partridge
Grey Partridge
Quail
Pheasant
Water Rail
Spotted Crake
Little Crake
Baillon's Crake
Corncrake
Moorhen
Coot
Crane
Little Bustard
Great Bustard
Oyster-catcher
Black-winged Stilt
Avocet
Stone Curlew
Collared Pratincole
Black-winged Pratincole
Little Ringed Plover
Ringed Plover
Kentish Plover
Dotterel
Golden Plover
Grey Plover
Sociable Plover
Lapwing
Knot
Sanderling
Little Stint
Temminck's Stint
Least Sandpiper
White-rumped Sandpiper
Baird's Sandpiper
Pectoral Sandpiper
Curlew Sandpiper
Purple Sandpiper
Dunlin
Stilt Sandpiper
Ruff
Jack Snipe

Snipe
Great Snipe
Woodcock
Black-tailed Godwit
Bar-tailed Godwit
Whimbrel
Curlew
Upland Sandpiper
Spotted Redshank
Redshank
Marsh Sandpiper
Greenshank
Lesser Yellowlegs
Green Sandpiper
Wood Sandpiper
Common Sandpiper
Spotted Sandpiper
Turnstone
Wilson's Phalarope
Red-necked Phalarope
Grey Phalarope
Pomarine Skua
Arctic Skua
Great Skua
Mediterranean Gull
Little Gull
Sabine's Gull
Black-headed Gull
Common Gull
Lesser Black-backed Gull
Herring Gull
Iceland Gull
Glaucous Gull
Great Black-backed Gull
Kittiwake
Ivory Gull
Gull-billed Tern
Caspian Tern
Sandwich Tern
Roseate Tern
Common Tern
Arctic Tern
Little Tern
Black Tern
White-winged Black Tern
Guillemot
Razorbill
Little Auk
Puffin
Pallas's Sandgrouse
Stock Dove
Wood Pigeon
Collared Dove
Turtle Dove
Ring-necked Parakeet
Cuckoo
Barn Owl
Little Owl
Tawny Owl

Long-eared Owl
Short-eared Owl
Nightjar
Swift
Alpine Swift
Kingfisher
Roller
Hoopoe
Green Woodpecker
Great Spotted Woodpecker
Lesser Spotted Woodpecker
Wryneck
Shorelark
Short-toed Lark
Woodlark
Skylark
Sand Martin
Swallow
Red-rumped Swallow
House Martin
Tawny Pipit
Richard's Pipit
Tree Pipit
Meadow Pipit
Red-throated Pipit
Rock Pipit
Water Pipit
Yellow Wagtail
Grey Wagtail
Pied Wagtail
Waxwing
Dipper
Wren
Dunnock
Alpine Accentor
Robin
Thrush Nightingale
Nightingale
Bluethroat
Redstart
Black Redstart
Whinchat
Stonechat
Wheatear
Ring Ouzel
Blackbird
Fieldfare
Song Thrush
Redwing
Mistle Thrush
Cetti's Warbler
Grasshopper Warbler
Aquatic Warbler
Moustached Warbler
Sedge Warbler
Marsh Warbler
Reed Warbler
Great Reed Warbler
Icterine Warbler

Dartford Warbler
Barred Warbler
Lesser Whitethroat
Whitethroat
Garden Warbler
Blackcap
Wood Warbler
Chiff-chaff
Willow Warbler
Goldcrest
Firecrest
Spotted Flycatcher
Pied Flycatcher
Bearded Tit
Long-tailed Tit
Marsh Tit
Willow Tit
Coal Tit
Blue Tit
Great Tit
Nuthatch
Treecreeper
Penduline Tit
Golden Oriole
Red-backed Shrike
Great Grey Shrike
Woodchat Shrike
Jay
Magpie
Nutcracker
Jackdaw
Rook
Carrion Crow
Raven
Starling
Rose-coloured Starling
House Sparrow
Tree Sparrow
Chaffinch
Brambling
Serin
Greenfinch
Goldfinch
Siskin
Linnet
Twite
Redpoll
Crossbill
Pine Grosbeak
Bullfinch
Hawfinch
Lapland Bunting
Snow Bunting
Yellowhammer
Cirl Bunting
Reed Bunting
Corn Bunting

Birds of Suffolk

Red-throated Diver
Black-throated Diver
Great Northern Diver
White-billed Diver
Little Grebe
Great-crested Grebe
Red-necked Grebe
Slavonian Grebe
Black-necked Grebe
Fulmar
Cory's Shearwater
Great Shearwater
Sooty Shearwater
Manx Shearwater
Storm Petrel
Leach's Petrel
Gannet
Cormorant
Shag
Bittern
Little Bittern
Night Heron
Squacco Heron
Cattle Egret
Little Egret
Great White Egret
Grey Heron
Purple Heron
Black Stork
White Stork
Glossy Ibis
Spoonbill
Mute Swan
Bewick's Swan
Whooper Swan
Bean Goose
Pink-footed Goose
Greylag Goose
White-fronted Goose
Lesser White-fronted Goose
Snow Goose
Canada Goose
Barnacle Goose
Brent Goose
Red-breasted Goose
Egyptian Goose
Ruddy Shelduck
Shelduck
Mandarin
Wigeon
American Wigeon
Gadwall
Baikal Teal
Teal
Mallard
Pintail
Garganey
Blue-winged Teal
Shoveler
Red-crested Pochard
Pochard
Ring-necked Duck
Ferruginous Duck
Tufted Duck
Scaup
Eider

Long-tailed Duck
Common Scoter
Velvet Scoter
Goldeneye
Smew
Red-breasted Merganser
Goosander
Ruddy Duck
Honey Buzzard
Black Kite
Red Kite
White-tailed Eagle
Marsh Harrier
Hen Harrier
Montagu's Harrier
Goshawk
Sparrow Hawk
Buzzard
Rough-legged Buzzard
Spotted Eagle
Osprey
Kestrel
Red-footed Falcon
Merlin
Hobby
Gyrfalcon
Peregrine
Red-legged Partridge
Red Grouse
Black Grouse
Grey Partridge
Quail
Pheasant
Golden Pheasant
Lady Amherst's Pheasant
Water Rail
Spotted Crake
Little Crake
Baillon's Crake
Corncrake
Moorhen
Allen's Gallinule
Coot
Crane
Little Bustard
Houbara Bustard
Great Bustard
Oyster-catcher
Black-winged Stilt
Avocet
Stone Curlew
Cream-coloured Courser
Collared Pratincole
Oriental Pratincole
Black-winged Pratincole
Little Ringed Plover
Ringed Plover
Kentish Plover
Great Sand Plover
Dotterel
Golden Plover
Grey Plover
Sociable Plover
Lapwing
Knot
Sanderling

Semi-palmated Sandpiper
Little Stint
Temminck's Stint
White-rumped Sandpiper
Baird's Sandpiper
Pectoral Sandpiper
Curlew Sandpiper
Purple Sandpiper
Dunlin
Broad-billed Sandpiper
Stilt Sandpiper
Buff-breasted Sandpiper
Ruff
Jack Snipe
Snipe
Great Snipe
Long-billed Dowitcher
Woodcock
Black-tailed Godwit
Bar-tailed Godwit
Eskimo Curlew
Whimbrel
Curlew
Upland Sandpiper
Spotted Redshank
Redshank
Marsh Sandpiper
Greenshank
Greater Yellowlegs
Lesser Yellowlegs
Green Sandpiper
Wood Sandpiper
Terek Sandpiper
Common Sandpiper
Spotted Sandpiper
Turnstone
Wilson's Phalarope
Red-necked Phalarope
Grey Phalarope
Pomarine Skua
Arctic Skua
Long-tailed Skua
Great Skua
Mediterranean Gull
Laughing Gull
Franklin's Gull
Little Gull
Sabine's Gull
Black-headed Gull
Slender-billed Gull
Ring-billed Gull
Common Gull
Lesser Black-backed Gull
Herring Gull
Iceland Gull
Glaucous Gull
Great Black-backed Gull
Kittiwake
Ivory Gull
Gull-billed Tern
Caspian Tern
Sandwich Tern
Roseate Tern
Common Tern
Arctic Tern
Sooty Tern

Little Tern
Black Tern
Whiskered Tern
White-winged Black Tern
Guillemot
Razorbill
Black Guillemot
Little Auk
Puffin
Pallas's Sandgrouse
Feral Pigeon
Stock Dove
Wood Pigeon
Collared Dove
Turtle Dove
Ring-necked Parakeet
Cuckoo
Yellow-billed Cuckoo
Barn Owl
Scops Owl
Snowy Owl
Little Owl
Tawny Owl
Long-eared Owl
Short-eared Owl
Tengmalms Owl
Nightjar
Swift
Pacific (Fork-tailed) Swift
Alpine Swift
Kingfisher
Bee-eater
Roller
Hoopoe
Wryneck
Green Woodpecker
Great Spotted Woodpecker
Lesser Spotted Woodpecker
Short-toed Lark
Woodlark
Skylark
Shore Lark
Sand Martin
Swallow
Red-rumped Swallow
House Martin
Tawny Pipit
Richard's Pipit
Tree Pipit
Pechora Pipit
Meadow Pipit
Red-throated Pipit
Rock Pipit
Water Pipit
Yellow Wagtail
Citrine Wagtail
Grey Wagtail
Pied Wagtail

Waxwing
Dipper
Wren
Dunnock
Alpine Accentor
Robin
Thrush Nightingale
Nightingale
Bluethroat
Redstart
Black Redstart
Whinchat
Stonechat
Wheatear
Desert Wheatear
White-crowned Black
    Wheatear
White's Thrush
Ring Ouzel
Blackbird
Fieldfare
Song Thrush
Redwing
Mistle Thrush
Cetti's Warbler
Grasshopper Warbler
River Warbler
Savi's Warbler
Aquatic Warbler
Sedge Warbler
Paddyfield Warbler
Marsh Warbler
Reed Warbler
Great Reed Warbler
Booted Warbler
Icterine Warbler
Melodious Warbler
Dartford Warbler
Sub-alpine Warbler
Barred Warbler
Lesser Whitethroat
Whitethroat
Garden Warbler
Blackcap
Greenish Warbler
Pallas's Warbler
Yellow-browed Warbler
Radde's Warbler
Dusky Warbler
Bonelli's Warbler
Wood Warbler
Chiff-chaff
Willow Warbler
Goldcrest
Firecrest
Spotted Flycatcher
Red-breasted Flycatcher
Collared Flycatcher

Pied Flycatcher
Bearded Tit
Long-tailed Tit
Marsh Tit
Willow Tit
Crested Tit
Coal Tit
Blue Tit
Great Tit
Nuthatch
Treecreeper
Penduline Tit
Golden Oriole
Isabelline Shrike
Red-backed Shrike
Lesser Grey Shrike
Great Grey Shrike
Woodchat Shrike
Jay
Magpie
Nutcracker
Jackdaw
Rook
Carrion Crow
Raven
Starling
Rose-coloured Starling
House Sparrow
Tree Sparrow
Red-eyed Vireo
Chaffinch
Brambling
Serin
Greenfinch
Goldfinch
Siskin
Linnet
Twite
Redpoll
Arctic Redpoll
Two-barred Crossbill
Crossbill
Parrot Crossbill
Trumpeter Finch
Scarlet Rosefinch
Bullfinch
Hawfinch
White-throated Sparrow
Lapland Bunting
Snow Bunting
Yellowhammer
Cirl Bunting
Ortolan Bunting
Rustic Bunting
Little Bunting
Reed Bunting
Corn Bunting

Birds of Huntingdonshire and Peterborough

Red-throated Diver
Black-throated Diver
Great Northern Diver
Little Grebe
Great-crested Grebe
Red-necked Grebe
Slavonian Grebe
Black-necked Grebe
Fulmar
Manx Shearwater
Sooty Shearwater
Storm Petrel
Leach's Petrel
Gannet
Cormorant
Shag
Bittern
Little Bittern
Night Heron
Little Egret
Great White Egret
Grey Heron
Glossy Ibis
Spoonbill
Mute Swan
Bewick's Swan
Whooper Swan
Bean Goose
Pink-footed Goose
Greylag Goose
White-fronted Goose
Canada Goose
Barnacle Goose
Brent Goose
Egyptian Goose
Shelduck
Mandarin
Wigeon
Gadwall
Teal
Mallard
Pintail
Garganey
Blue-winged Teal
Shoveler
Red-crested Pochard
Pochard
Ring-necked Duck
Ferruginous Duck
Tufted Duck
Scaup
Eider
Long-tailed Duck
Common Scoter
Surf Scoter
Velvet Scoter
Goldeneye
Smew
Red-breasted Merganser
Goosander
Ruddy Duck
Honey Buzzard
Red Kite
White-tailed Eagle
Marsh Harrier
Hen Harrier

Montagu's Harrier
Goshawk
Sparrow Hawk
Buzzard
Rough-legged Buzzard
Golden Eagle
Osprey
Kestrel
Merlin
Hobby
Red-footed Falcon
Peregrine
Black Grouse
Red-legged Partridge
Grey Partridge
Quail
Pheasant
Golden Pheasant
Water Rail
Spotted Crake
Corncrake
Moorhen
Coot
Crane
Great Bustard
Oyster-catcher
Black-winged Stilt
Avocet
Stone Curlew
Collared Pratincole
Black-winged Pratincole
Little Ringed Plover
Ringed Plover
Killdeer
Kentish Plover
Dotterel
Golden Plover
Grey Plover
Lapwing
Knot
Sanderling
Semipalmated Sandpiper
Little Stint
Temminck's Stint
Pectoral Sandpiper
Curlew Sandpiper
Purple Sandpiper
Dunlin
Buff-breasted Sandpiper
Ruff
Jack Snipe
Snipe
Great Snipe
Woodcock
Black-tailed Godwit
Bar-tailed Godwit
Whimbrel
Curlew
Spotted Redshank
Redshank
Marsh Sandpiper
Greenshank
Lesser Yellowlegs
Green Sandpiper
Wood Sandpiper
Common Sandpiper

Turnstone
Wilson's Phalarope
Red-necked Phalarope
Grey Phalarope
Pomarine Skua
Arctic Skua
Long-tailed Skua
Great Skua
Mediterranean Gull
Little Gull
Sabine's Gull
Black-headed Gull
Common Gull
Lesser Black-backed Gull
Herring Gull
Iceland Gull
Glaucous Gull
Great Black-backed Gull
Kittiwake
Gull-billed Tern
Caspian Tern
Sandwich Tern
Roseate Tern
Common Tern
Arctic Tern
Little Tern
Black Tern
Whiskered Tern
White-winged Black Tern
Guillemot
Razorbill
Little Auk
Puffin
Pallas's Sandgrouse
Stock Dove
Wood Pigeon
Collared Dove
Turtle Dove
Ring-necked Parakeet
Cuckoo
Barn Owl
Scops Owl
Little Owl
Tawny Owl
Long-eared Owl
Short-eared Owl
Tengmalm's Owl
Nightjar
Swift
Alpine Swift
Kingfisher
Bee-eater
Blue-cheeked Bee-eater
Hoopoe
Wryneck
Green Woodpecker
Great Spotted Woodpecker
Lesser Spotted Woodpecker
Woodlark
Skylark
Shore Lark
Sand Martin
Swallow
Red-rumped Swallow
House Martin
Richard's Pipit

Tree Pipit
Meadow Pipit
Rock Pipit
Water Pipit
Yellow Wagtail
Grey Wagtail
Pied Wagtail
Waxwing
Wren
Dunnock
Robin
Nightingale
Bluethroat
Redstart
Black Redstart
Whinchat
Stonechat
Wheatear
Ring Ouzel
Blackbird
Fieldfare
Song Thrush
Redwing
Mistle Thrush
Cetti's Warbler
Grasshopper Warbler
Savi's Warbler
Sedge Warbler

Marsh Warbler
Reed Warbler
Lesser Whitethroat
Whitethroat
Garden Warbler
Blackcap
Wood Warbler
Chiff-chaff
Willow Warbler
Goldcrest
Firecrest
Spotted Flycatcher
Pied Flycatcher
Bearded Tit
Long-tailed Tit
Marsh Tit
Willow Tit
Coal Tit
Blue Tit
Great Tit
Nuthatch
Treecreeper
Golden Oriole
Isabelline Shrike
Red-backed Shrike
Great Grey Shrike
Jay
Magpie

Nutcracker
Jackdaw
Rook
Carrion Crow
Raven
Starling
Rose-coloured Starling
House Sparrow
Tree Sparrow
Chaffinch
Brambling
Greenfinch
Goldfinch
Siskin
Linnet
Twite
Redpoll
Crossbill
Bullfinch
Hawfinch
Lapland Bunting
Snow Bunting
Yellowhammer
Cirl Bunting
Reed Bunting
Corn Bunting

Birds of Essex

Red-throated Diver
Black-throated Diver
Great Northern Diver
Little Grebe
Great-crested Grebe
Red-necked Grebe
Slavonian Grebe
Black-necked Grebe
Fulmar
Cory's Shearwater
Sooty Shearwater
Manx Shearwater
Storm Petrel
Leach's Petrel
Gannet
Cormorant
Shag
Bittern
Little Bittern
Night Heron
Little Egret
Grey Heron
Purple Heron
Black Stork
White Stork
Glossy Ibis
Spoonbill
Mute Swan
Bewick's Swan
Whooper Swan
Bean Goose
Pink-footed Goose
Snow Goose
Greylag Goose
White-fronted Goose
Lesser White-fronted Goose

Canada Goose
Barnacle Goose
Brent Goose
Red-breasted Goose
Egyptian Goose
Ruddy Shelduck
Shelduck
Mandarin
Wigeon
American Wigeon
Gadwall
Baikal Teal
Teal
Mallard
Pintail
Garganey
Blue-winged Teal
Shoveler
Red-crested Pochard
Pochard
Ring-necked Duck
Ferruginous Duck
Tufted Duck
Scaup
Eider
King Eider
Long-tailed Duck
Common Scoter
Velvet Scoter
Goldeneye
Smew
Red-breasted Merganser
Goosander
Ruddy Duck
Honey Buzzard
Black Kite

Red Kite
White-tailed Eagle
Egyptian Vulture
Marsh Harrier
Hen Harrier
Montagu's Harrier
Goshawk
Sparrow Hawk
Buzzard
Rough-legged Buzzard
Spotted Eagle
Osprey
Lesser Kestrel
Kestrel
Red-footed Falcon
Merlin
Hobby
Peregrine
Red-legged Partridge
Grey Partridge
Quail
Pheasant
Water Rail
Spotted Crake
Little Crake
Baillon's Crake
Corncrake
Moorhen
Coot
Crane
Little Bustard
Great Bustard
Oyster-catcher
Black-winged Stilt
Avocet
Stone Curlew

Cream-coloured Courser
Oriental Pratincole
Collared Pratincole
Black-winged Pratincole
Little Ringed Plover
Ringed Plover
Kentish Plover
Dotterel
Lesser Golden Plover
Golden Plover
Grey Plover
Sociable Plover
Lapwing
Knot
Sanderling
Western Sandpiper
Little Stint
Temminck's Stint
White-rumped Sandpiper
Baird's Sandpiper
Pectoral Sandpiper
Broad-billed Sandpiper
Curlew Sandpiper
Purple Sandpiper
Dunlin
Stilt Sandpiper
Buff-breasted Sandpiper
Ruff
Jack Snipe
Snipe
Great Snipe
Long-billed Dowitcher
Woodcock
Black-tailed Godwit
Bar-tailed Godwit
Whimbrel
Curlew
Spotted Redshank
Redshank
Marsh Sandpiper
Greenshank
Greater Yellowlegs
Lesser Yellowlegs
Solitary Sandpiper
Green Sandpiper
Wood Sandpiper
Terek Sandpiper
Common Sandpiper
Spotted Sandpiper
Turnstone
Wilson's Phalarope
Red-necked Phalarope
Grey Phalarope
Pomarine Skua
Arctic Skua
Long-tailed Skua
Great Skua
Mediterranean Gull
Laughing Gull
Little Gull
Sabine's Gull
Black-headed Gull
Ring-billed Gull
Common Gull
Lesser Black-backed Gull
Herring Gull
Iceland Gull

Glaucous Gull
Great Black-backed Gull
Kittiwake
Gull-billed Tern
Caspian Tern
Sandwich Tern
Roseate Tern
Common Tern
Arctic Tern
Little Tern
Black Tern
Whiskered Tern
White-winged Black Tern
Guillemot
Razorbill
Black Guillemot
Little Auk
Puffin
Pallas's Sandgrouse
Stock Dove
Wood Pigeon
Collared Dove
Turtle Dove
Ring-necked Parakeet
Cuckoo
Barn Owl
Scops Owl
Snowy Owl
Little Owl
Tawny Owl
Long-eared Owl
Short-eared Owl
Tengmalm's Owl
Nightjar
Needle-tailed Swift
Swift
Alpine Swift
Kingfisher
Bee-eater
Roller
Hoopoe
Wryneck
Green Woodpecker
Great Spotted Woodpecker
Lesser Spotted Woodpecker
Short-toed Lark
Woodlark
Skylark
Shore Lark
Sand Martin
Swallow
Red-rumped Swallow
House Martin
Tawny Pipit
Richard's Pipit
Tree Pipit
Meadow Pipit
Red-throated Pipit
Rock Pipit
Water Pipit
Yellow Wagtail
Citrine Wagtail
Grey Wagtail
Pied Wagtail
Waxwing
Dipper
Wren

Dunnock
Alpine Accentor
Robin
Nightingale
Bluethroat
Redstart
Black Redstart
Whinchat
Stonechat
Wheatear
Desert Wheatear
Black-eared Wheatear
White's Thrush
Ring Ouzel
Blackbird
Fieldfare
Song Thrush
Redwing
Mistle Thrush
Cetti's Warbler
Grasshopper Warbler
Savi's Warbler
Aquatic Warbler
Sedge Warbler
Marsh Warbler
Reed Warbler
Great Reed Warbler
Icterine Warbler
Melodious Warbler
Dartford Warbler
Sub-alpine Warbler
Desert Warbler
Barred Warbler
Lesser Whitethroat
Whitethroat
Garden Warbler
Blackcap
Greenish Warbler
Pallas's Warbler
Yellow-browed Warbler
Wood Warbler
Bonelli's Warbler
Chiff-chaff
Willow Warbler
Dusky Warbler
Goldcrest
Firecrest
Spotted Flycatcher
Red-breasted Flycatcher
Collared Flycatcher
Pied Flycatcher
Bearded Tit
Long-tailed Tit
Marsh Tit
Willow Tit
Coal Tit
Blue Tit
Great Tit
Nuthatch
Short-toed Treecreeper
Treecreeper
Penduline Tit
Golden Oriole
Red-backed Shrike
Isabelline Shrike
Lesser Grey Shrike
Great Grey Shrike

Woodchat Shrike
Jay
Magpie
Nutcracker
Jackdaw
Rook
Carrion Crow
Raven
Starling
Rose-coloured Starling
House Sparrow
Tree Sparrow
Chaffinch
Brambling

Serin
Greenfinch
Goldfinch
Siskin
Linnet
Twite
Redpoll
Arctic Redpoll
Two-barred Crossbill
Crossbill
Parrot Crossbill
Scarlet Rosefinch
Bullfinch
Hawfinch

Trumpeter Finch
Lapland Bunting
Snow Bunting
Yellowhammer
Cirl Bunting
Ortolan Bunting
Rustic Bunting
Little Bunting
Reed Bunting
Black-headed Bunting
Corn Bunting
Rose-breasted Grosbeak
Northern Mocking Bird

CODE OF CONDUCT FOR BIRDWATCHERS

Today's birdwatchers are a powerful force for nature conservation. The number of those of us interested in birds rises continually and it is vital that we take seriously our responsibility to avoid any harm to birds.

We must also present a responsible image to non-birdwatchers who may be affected by our activities and particularly those on whose sympathy and support the future of birds may rest.

There are 10 points to bear in mind:
1. The welfare of birds must come first.
2. Habitat must be protected.
3. Keep disturbance to birds and their habitat to a minimum.
4. When you find a rare bird think carefully about whom you should tell.
5. Do not harass rare migrants.
6. Abide by the bird protection laws at all times.
7. Respect the rights of landowners.
8. Respect the rights of other people in the countryside.
9. Make your records available to the local bird recorder.
10. Behave abroad as you would when birdwatching at home.

Welfare of birds must come first
Whether your particular interest is photography, ringing, sound recording, scientific study or just birdwatching, remember that the welfare of the bird must always come first.

Habitat protection
Its habitat is vital to a bird and therefore we must ensure that our activities do not cause damage.

Keep disturbance to a minimum
Birds' tolerance of disturbance varies between species and seasons. Therefore, it is safer to keep all disturbance to a minimum. No birds should be disturbed from the nest in case opportunities for predators to take eggs or young are increased. In very cold weather disturbance to birds may cause them to use vital energy at a time when food is difficult to find. Wildfowlers already impose bans during cold weather: birdwatchers should exercise similar discretion.

Rare breeding birds
If you discover a rare bird breeding and feel that protection is necessary, inform the appropriate RSPB Regional Office, or the Species Protection Department at the Lodge. Otherwise it is best in almost all circumstances to keep the record strictly secret in order to avoid disturbance by other birdwatchers and attacks by egg-collectors. Never visit known sites of rare breeding birds unless they are adequately protected. Even your presence may give away the site to others and cause so many other

visitors that the birds may fail to breed successfully.

Disturbance at or near the nest of species listed on the First Schedule of the Wildlife and Countryside Act 1981 is a criminal offence.

Copies of *Wild Birds and the Law* are obtainable from the RSPB, The Lodge, Sandy, Beds. SG19 2DL (send two 2nd class stamps).

Rare migrants

Rare migrants or vagrants must not be harassed. If you discover one, consider the circumstances carefully before telling anyone. Will an influx of birdwatchers disturb the bird or others in the area? Will the habitat be damaged? Will problems be caused with the landowner?

The Law

The bird protection laws (now embodied in the Wildlife and Countryside Act 1981) are the result of hard campaigning by previous generations of birdwatchers. As birdwatchers we must abide by them at all times and not allow them to fall into disrepute.

Respect the rights of landowners

The wishes of landowners and occupiers of land must be respected. Do not enter land without permission. Comply with permit schemes. If you are leading a group, do give advance notice of the visit, even if a formal permit scheme is not in operation. Always obey the Country Code.

Respect the rights of other people

Have proper consideration for other birdwatchers. Try not to disrupt their activities or scare the birds they are watching. There are many other people who also use the countryside. Do not interfere with their activities and, if it seems that what they are doing is causing unnecessary disturbance to birds, do try to take a balanced view. Flushing gulls when walking a dog on a beach may do little harm, while the same dog might be a serious disturbance at a tern colony. When pointing this out to a non-birdwatcher be courteous, but firm. The non-birdwatchers' goodwill towards birds must not be destroyed by the attitudes of birdwatchers.

Keeping records

Much of today's knowledge about birds is the result of meticulous record keeping by our predecessors. Make sure you help to add to tomorrow's knowledge by sending records to your county bird recorder.

Birdwatching abroad

Behave abroad as you would at home. This code should be firmly adhered to when abroad (whatever the local laws). Well behaved birdwatchers can be important ambassadors for bird protection.

This code has been drafted after consultation between the British Ornithologists' Union, British Trust for Ornithology, the Royal Society for the Protection of Birds, the Scottish Ornithologists' Club, the Wildfowl Trust and the Editors of British Birds.

Further copies may be obtained from The Royal Society for the Protection of Birds, The Lodge, Sandy, Beds. SG19 2DL.

INDEX

Index

Index

Index